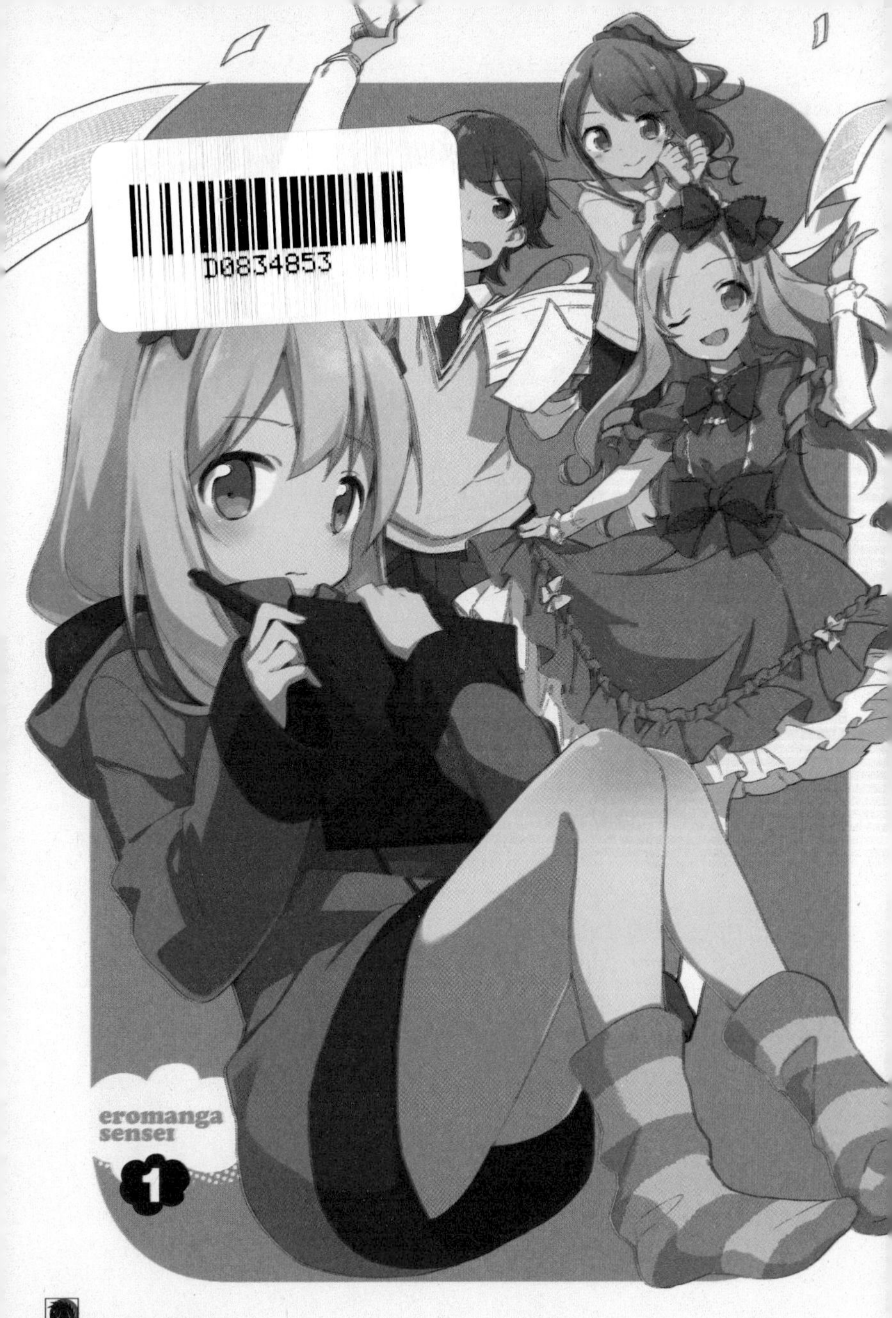
eromanga
sensei
1

DARK HORSE MANGA

Story by
TSUKASA FUSHIMI

Art by
rin

Character Design by
KANZAKIHIRO

Based on the light novel series by
TSUKASA FUSHIMI

Translation
DINKY SPATZ

Assistant Editor
JEMIAH JEFFERSON

Lettering and touch-up
SUSAN DAIGLE-LEACH

Special thanks to
CARL GUSTAV HORN and **MICHAEL GOMBOS**

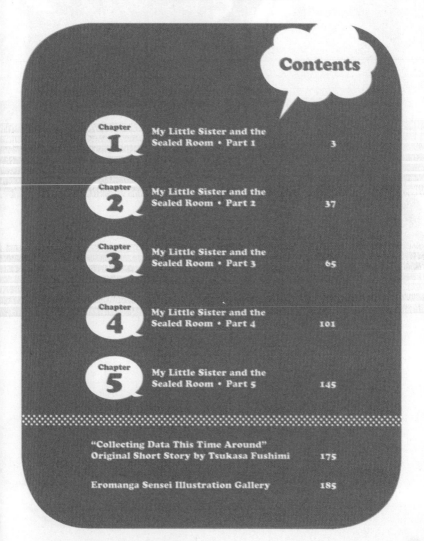

Contents

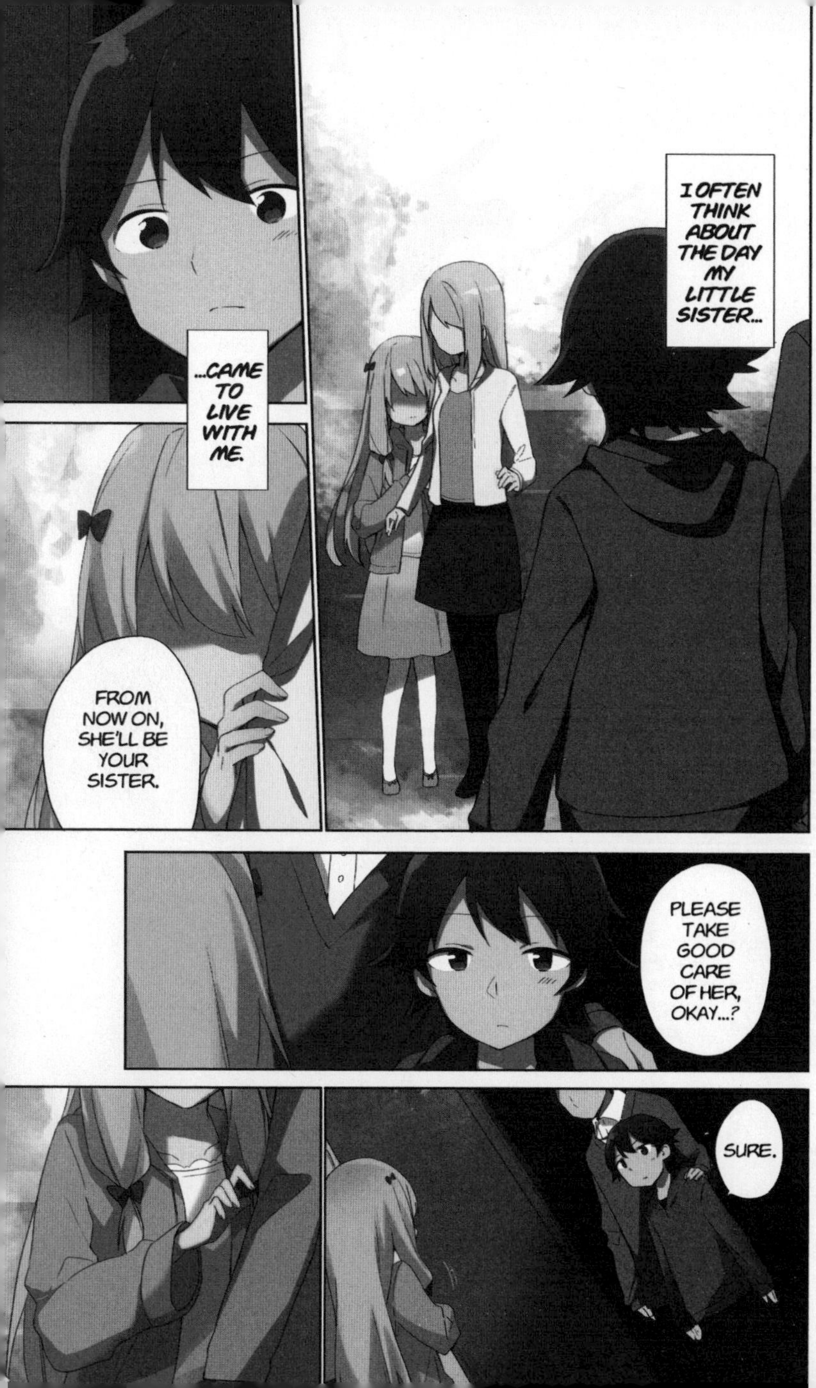
I OFTEN THINK ABOUT THE DAY MY LITTLE SISTER...
...CAME TO LIVE WITH ME.
FROM NOW ON, SHE'LL BE YOUR SISTER.
PLEASE TAKE GOOD CARE OF HER, OKAY...?
SURE.

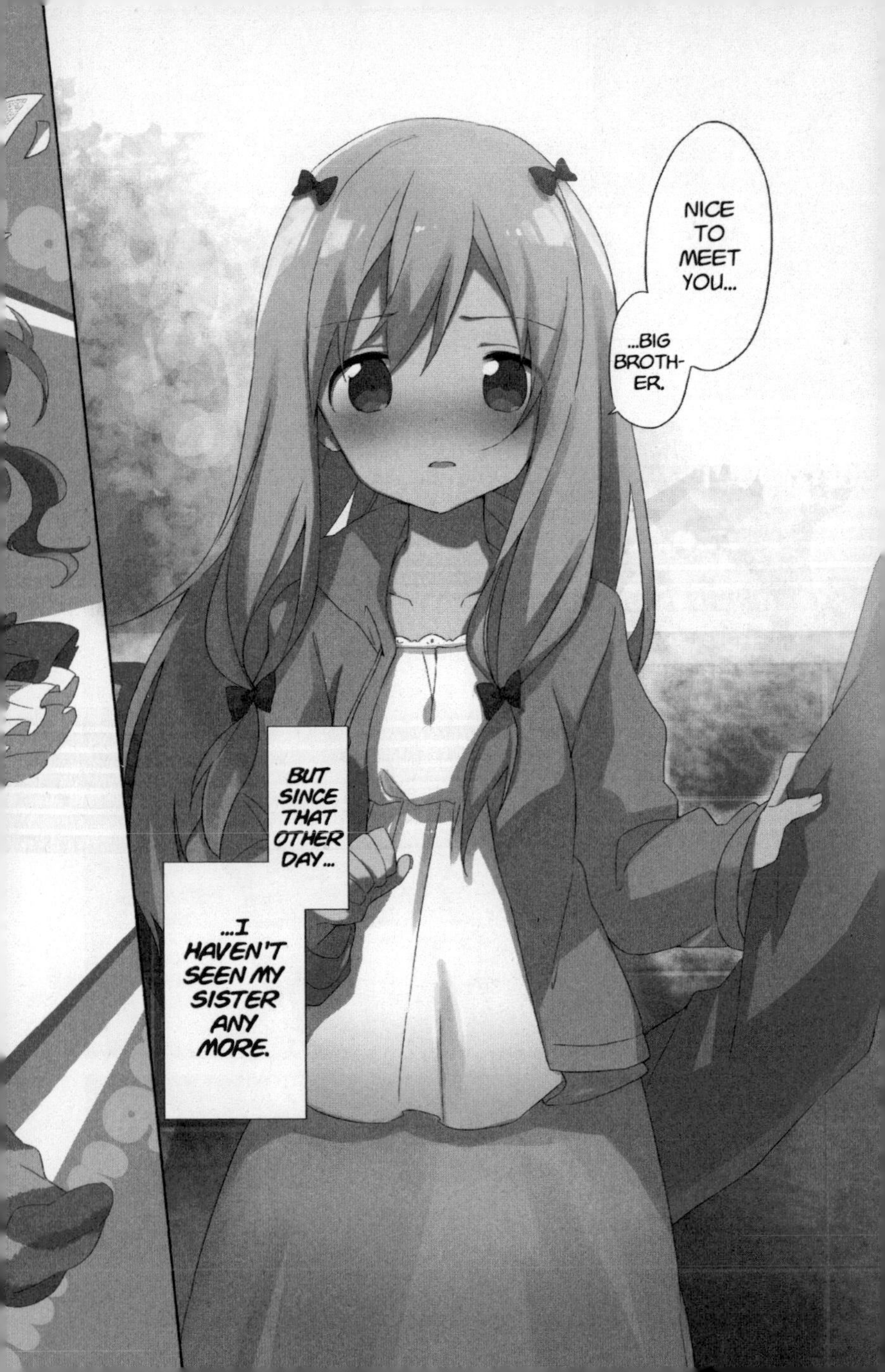
NICE TO MEET YOU...
...BIG BROTHER.
BUT SINCE THAT OTHER DAY...
...I HAVEN'T SEEN MY SISTER ANY MORE.

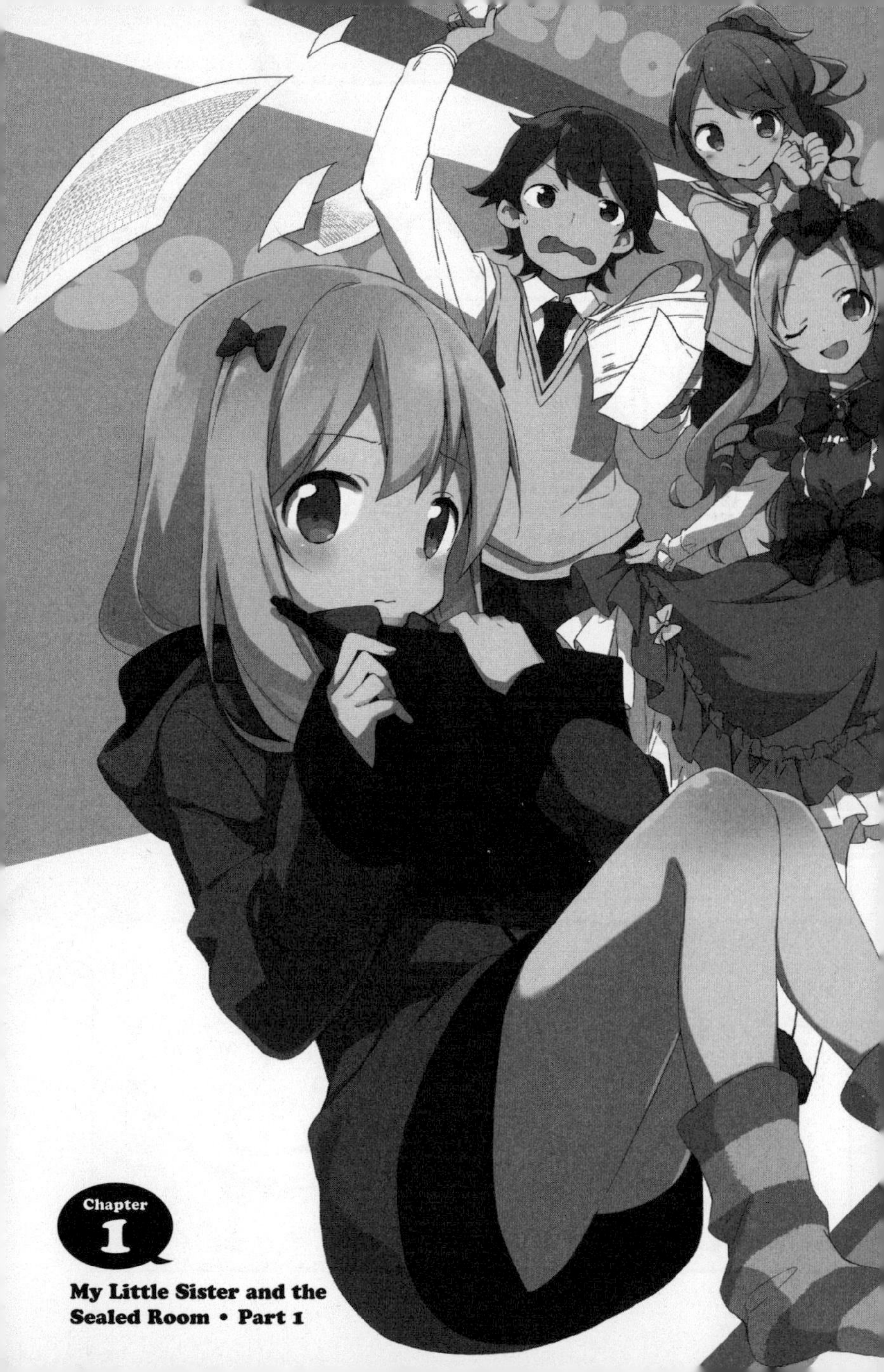

Chapter 1

My Little Sister and the Sealed Room • Part 1

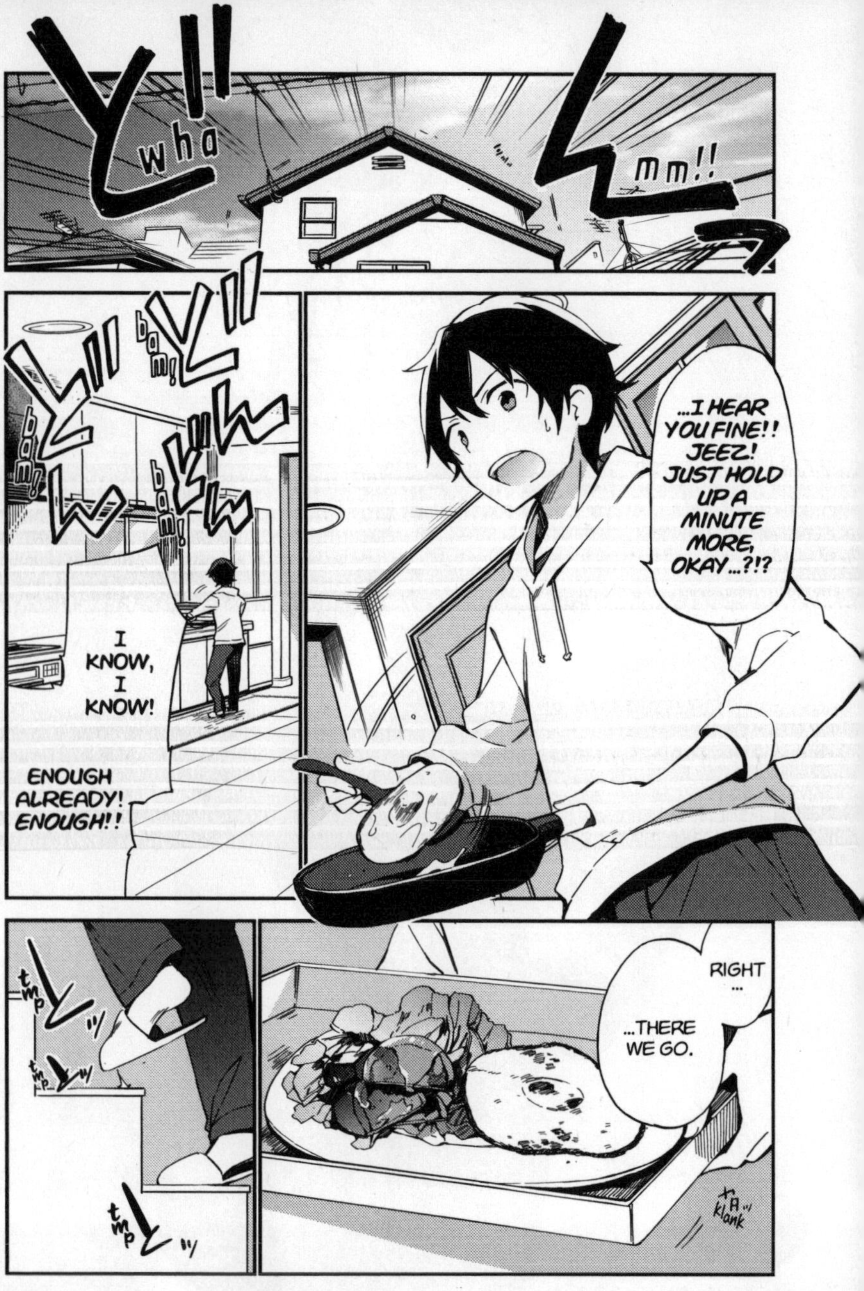
wha
mm!!
...I HEAR YOU FINE!! JEEZ! JUST HOLD UP A MINUTE MORE, OKAY...?!?
bam!
bam!
bam!
I KNOW, I KNOW!
ENOUGH ALREADY! ENOUGH!!
RIGHT...
...THERE WE GO.
klank
tmp
tmp
tmp

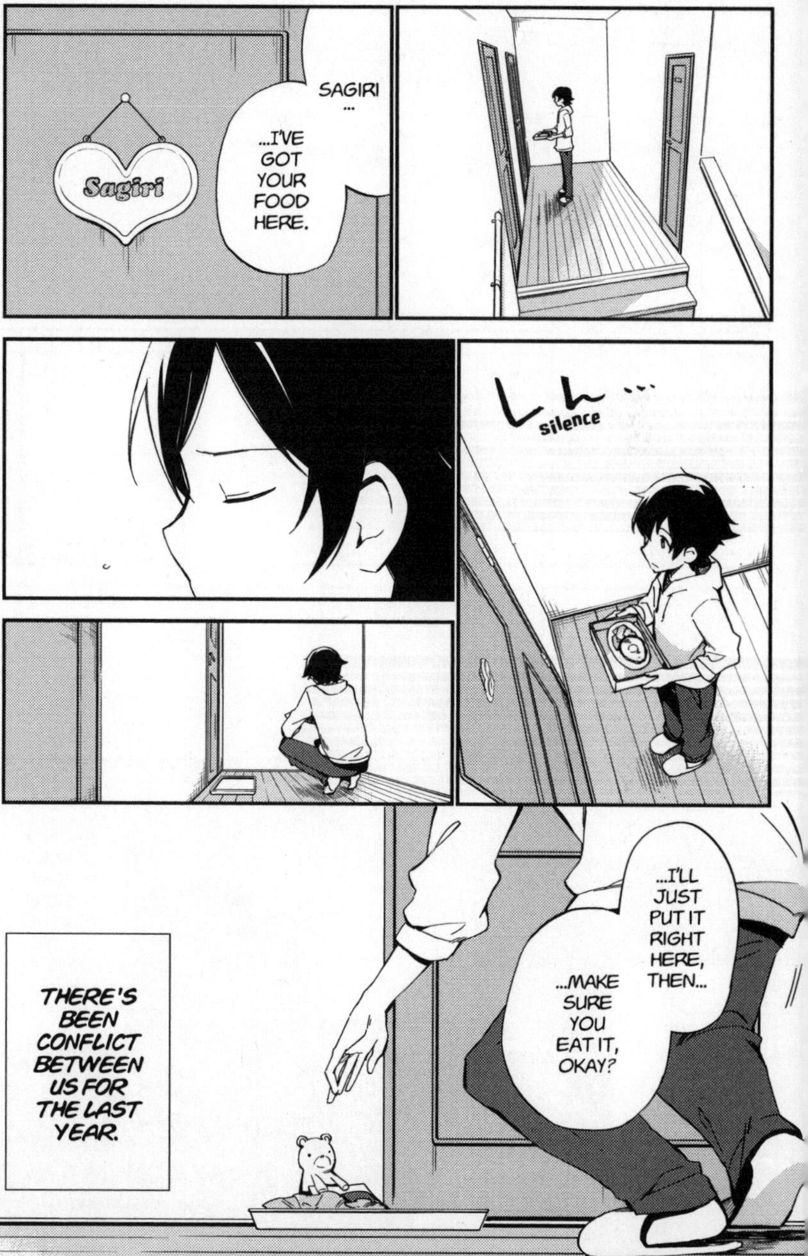

SAGIRI ... ...I'VE GOT YOUR FOOD HERE.
Sagiri
しん…
silence
...I'LL JUST PUT IT RIGHT HERE, THEN...
...MAKE SURE YOU EAT IT, OKAY?
THERE'S BEEN CONFLICT BETWEEN US FOR THE LAST YEAR.

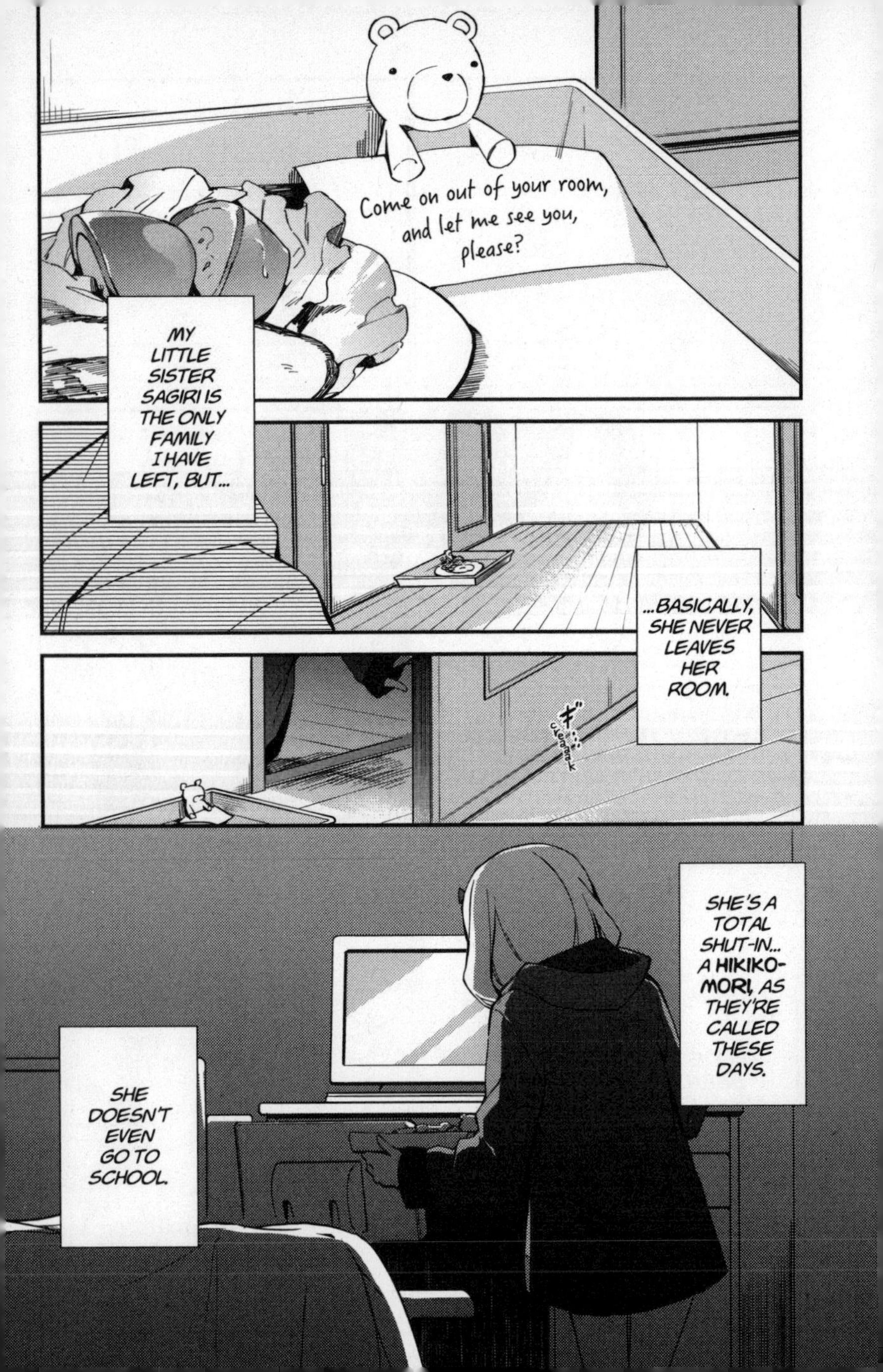
Come on out of your room, and let me see you, please?
MY LITTLE SISTER SAGIRI IS THE ONLY FAMILY I HAVE LEFT, BUT...
...BASICALLY, SHE NEVER LEAVES HER ROOM.
ギ…
creaaak
SHE'S A TOTAL SHUT-IN... A **HIKIKOMORI**, AS THEY'RE CALLED THESE DAYS.
SHE DOESN'T EVEN GO TO SCHOOL.

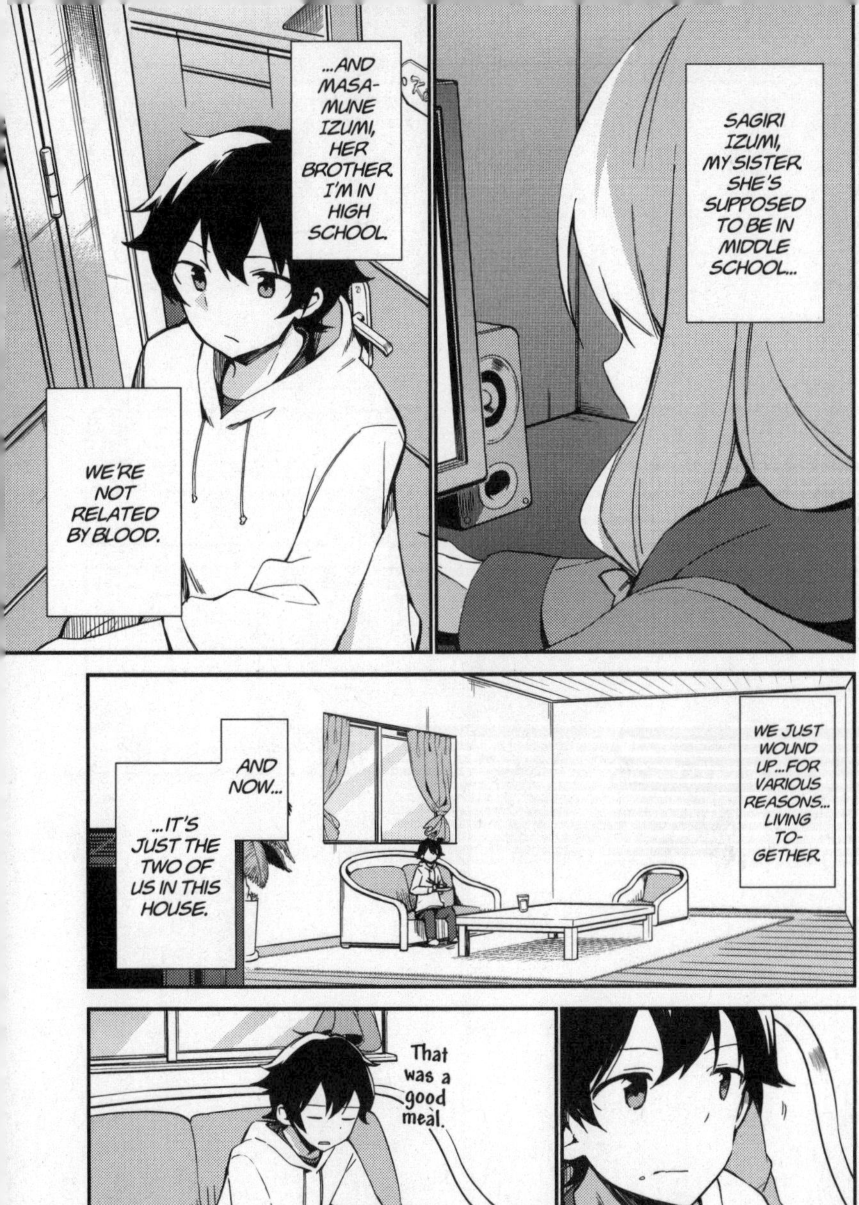
SAGIRI IZUMI, MY SISTER. SHE'S SUPPOSED TO BE IN MIDDLE SCHOOL...
...AND MASAMUNE IZUMI, HER BROTHER. I'M IN HIGH SCHOOL.
WE'RE NOT RELATED BY BLOOD.
WE JUST WOUND UP...FOR VARIOUS REASONS... LIVING TOGETHER.
AND NOW...
...IT'S JUST THE TWO OF US IN THIS HOUSE.
That was a good meal.

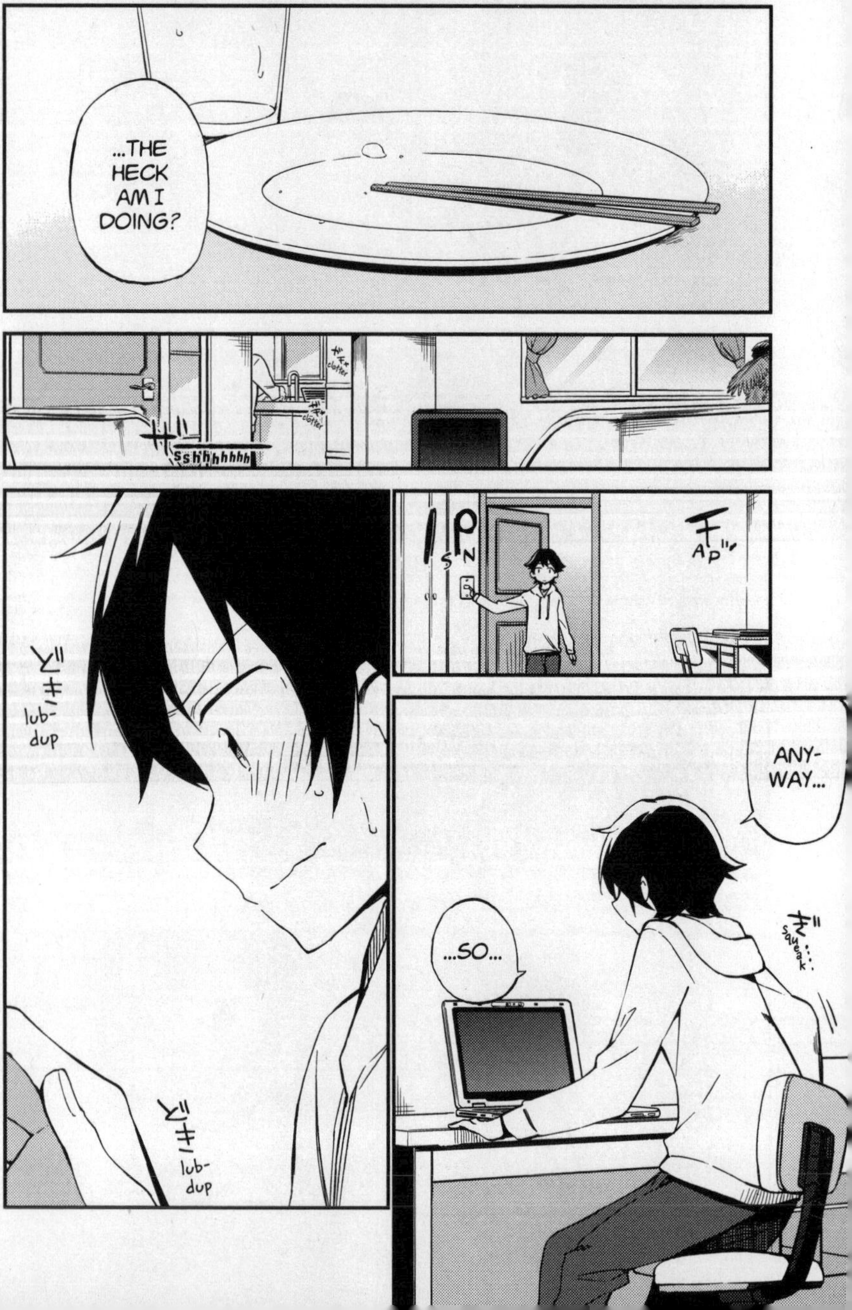
...THE HECK AM I DOING?
clatter
clatter
sshhhhhhh
SNAP
ANY-WAY...
squeak...
...SO...
lub-dup
lub-dup

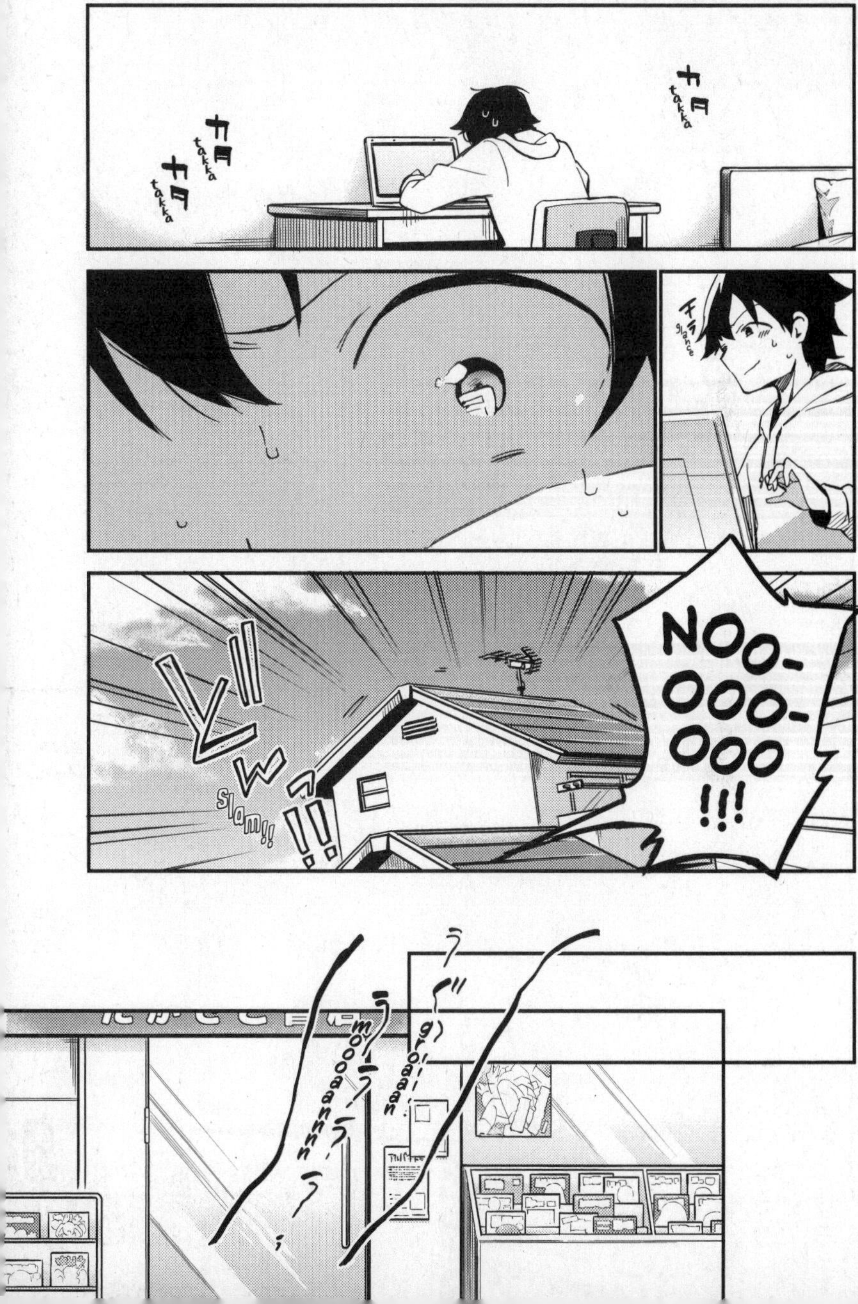

カタ takka
カタ takka
カタ takka
チラ glance
NOO-OOO-OOO!!!
slam!!
groaaan
moooaannnn

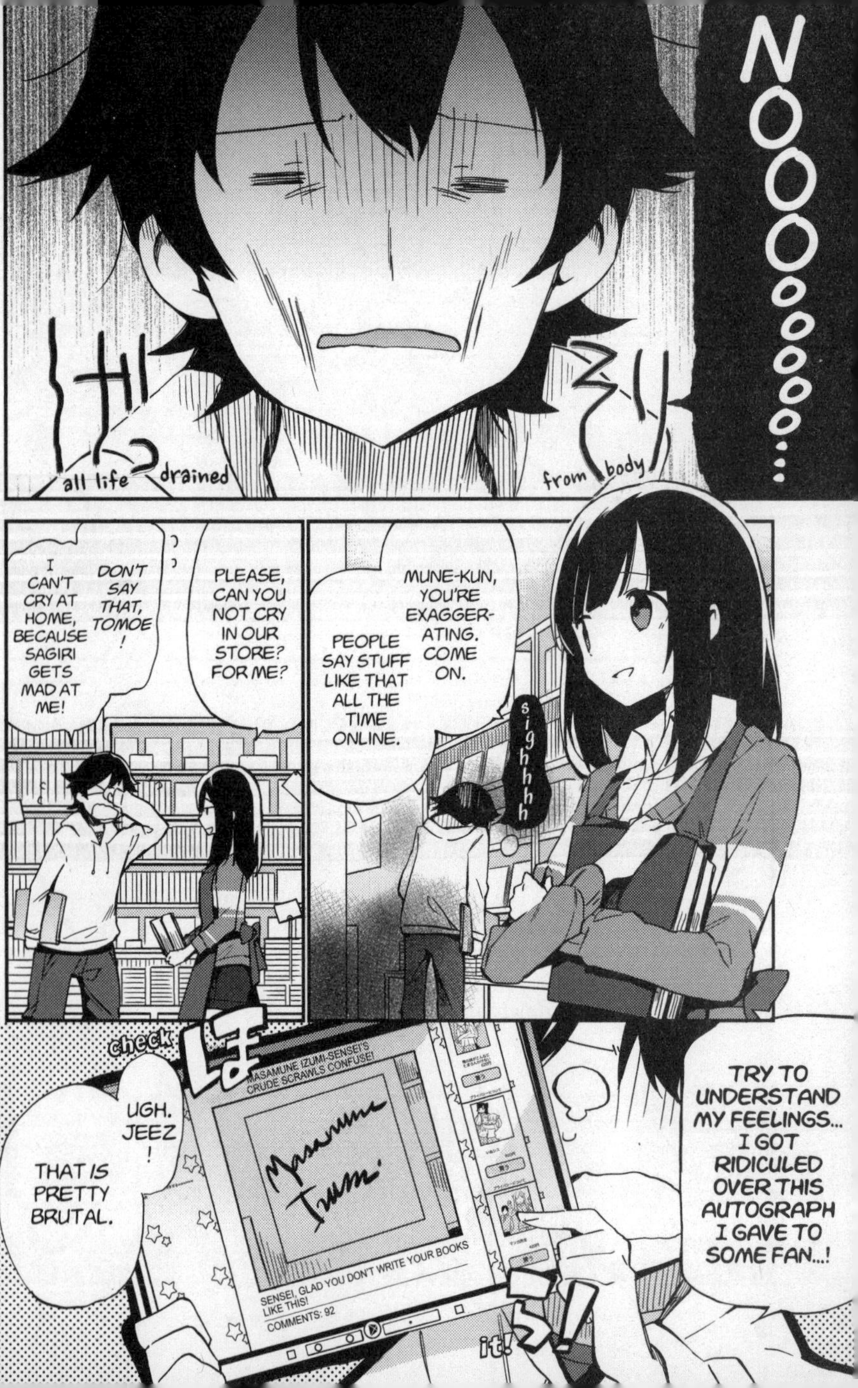
NOOOoooooo...
all life drained from body
MUNE-KUN, YOU'RE EXAGGER-ATING. COME ON.
PEOPLE SAY STUFF LIKE THAT ALL THE TIME ONLINE.
sighhhh
PLEASE, CAN YOU NOT CRY IN OUR STORE? FOR ME?
DON'T SAY THAT, TOMOE!
I CAN'T CRY AT HOME, BECAUSE SAGIRI GETS MAD AT ME!
TRY TO UNDERSTAND MY FEELINGS... I GOT RIDICULED OVER THIS AUTOGRAPH I GAVE TO SOME FAN...!
check it!
MASAMUNE IZUMI-SENSEI'S CRUDE SCRAWLS CONFUSE!
Masamune Izumi
SENSEI, GLAD YOU DON'T WRITE YOUR BOOKS LIKE THIS!
COMMENTS: 92
UGH. JEEZ!
THAT IS PRETTY BRUTAL.

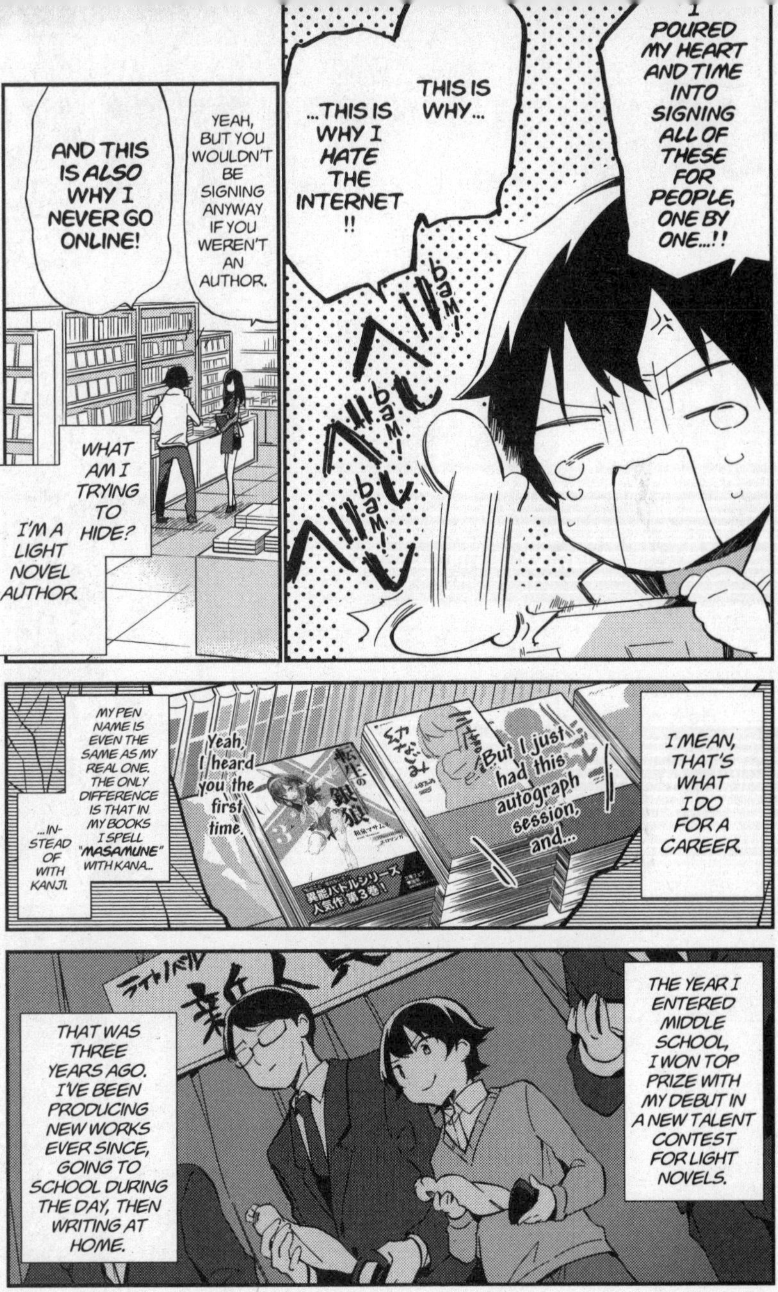
I POURED MY HEART AND TIME INTO SIGNING ALL OF THESE FOR PEOPLE, ONE BY ONE...!!
THIS IS WHY...
...THIS IS WHY I HATE THE INTERNET !!
bam!
bam!
bam!
YEAH, BUT YOU WOULDN'T BE SIGNING ANYWAY IF YOU WEREN'T AN AUTHOR.
AND THIS IS ALSO WHY I NEVER GO ONLINE!
WHAT AM I TRYING TO HIDE?
I'M A LIGHT NOVEL AUTHOR.
I MEAN, THAT'S WHAT I DO FOR A CAREER.
But I just had this autograph session, and...
Yeah, I heard you the first time.
転生の銀狼
異能バトルシリーズ 人気作 第3巻!
MY PEN NAME IS EVEN THE SAME AS MY REAL ONE. THE ONLY DIFFERENCE IS THAT IN MY BOOKS I SPELL "MASAMUNE" WITH KANA...
...INSTEAD OF WITH KANJI.
THE YEAR I ENTERED MIDDLE SCHOOL, I WON TOP PRIZE WITH MY DEBUT IN A NEW TALENT CONTEST FOR LIGHT NOVELS.
THAT WAS THREE YEARS AGO. I'VE BEEN PRODUCING NEW WORKS EVER SINCE, GOING TO SCHOOL DURING THE DAY, THEN WRITING AT HOME.

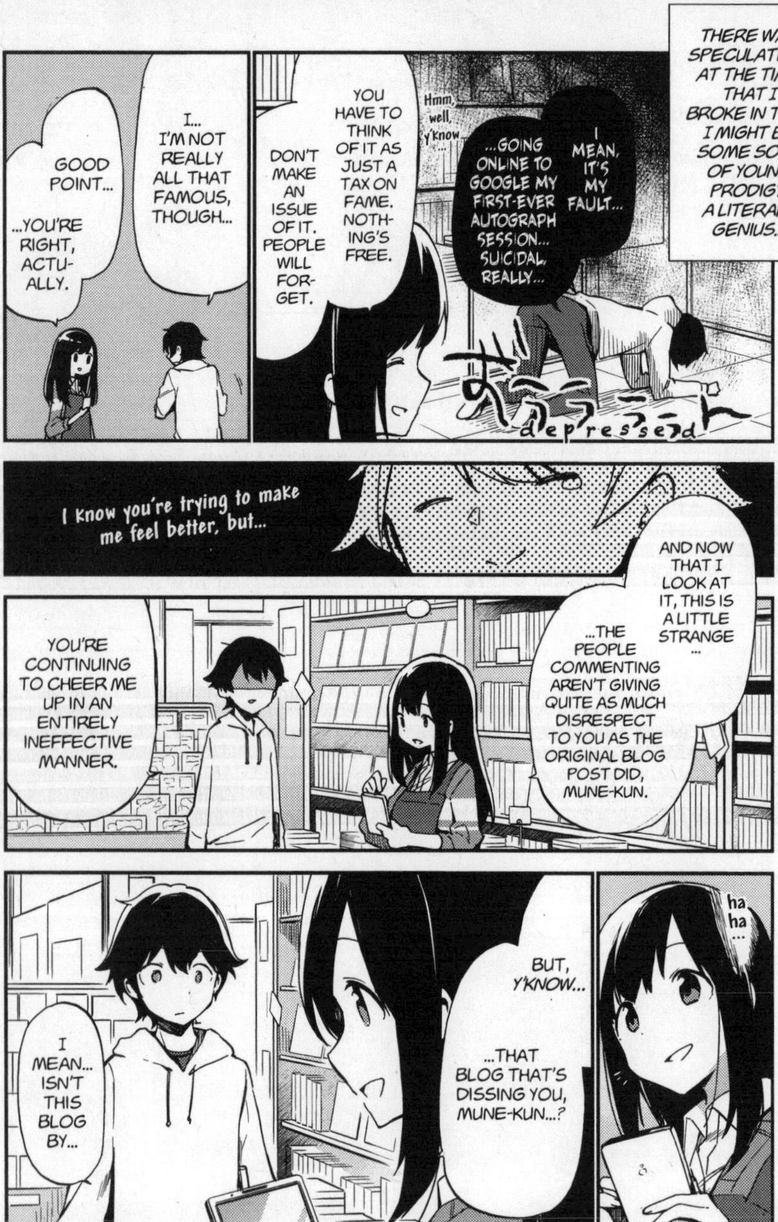
THERE WAS SPECULATION, AT THE TIME THAT I BROKE IN THAT I MIGHT BE SOME SORT OF YOUNG PRODIGY, A LITERARY GENIUS...
I MEAN, IT'S MY FAULT...
...GOING ONLINE TO GOOGLE MY FIRST-EVER AUTOGRAPH SESSION... SUICIDAL, REALLY...
Hmm, well, y'know...
YOU HAVE TO THINK OF IT AS JUST A TAX ON FAME. NOTHING'S FREE.
DON'T MAKE AN ISSUE OF IT. PEOPLE WILL FORGET.
depressed
I... I'M NOT REALLY ALL THAT FAMOUS, THOUGH...
GOOD POINT...
...YOU'RE RIGHT, ACTUALLY.
I know you're trying to make me feel better, but...
AND NOW THAT I LOOK AT IT, THIS IS A LITTLE STRANGE...
...THE PEOPLE COMMENTING AREN'T GIVING QUITE AS MUCH DISRESPECT TO YOU AS THE ORIGINAL BLOG POST DID, MUNE-KUN.
YOU'RE CONTINUING TO CHEER ME UP IN AN ENTIRELY INEFFECTIVE MANNER.
ha ha...
BUT, Y'KNOW...
...THAT BLOG THAT'S DISSING YOU, MUNE-KUN...?
I MEAN... ISN'T THIS BLOG BY...

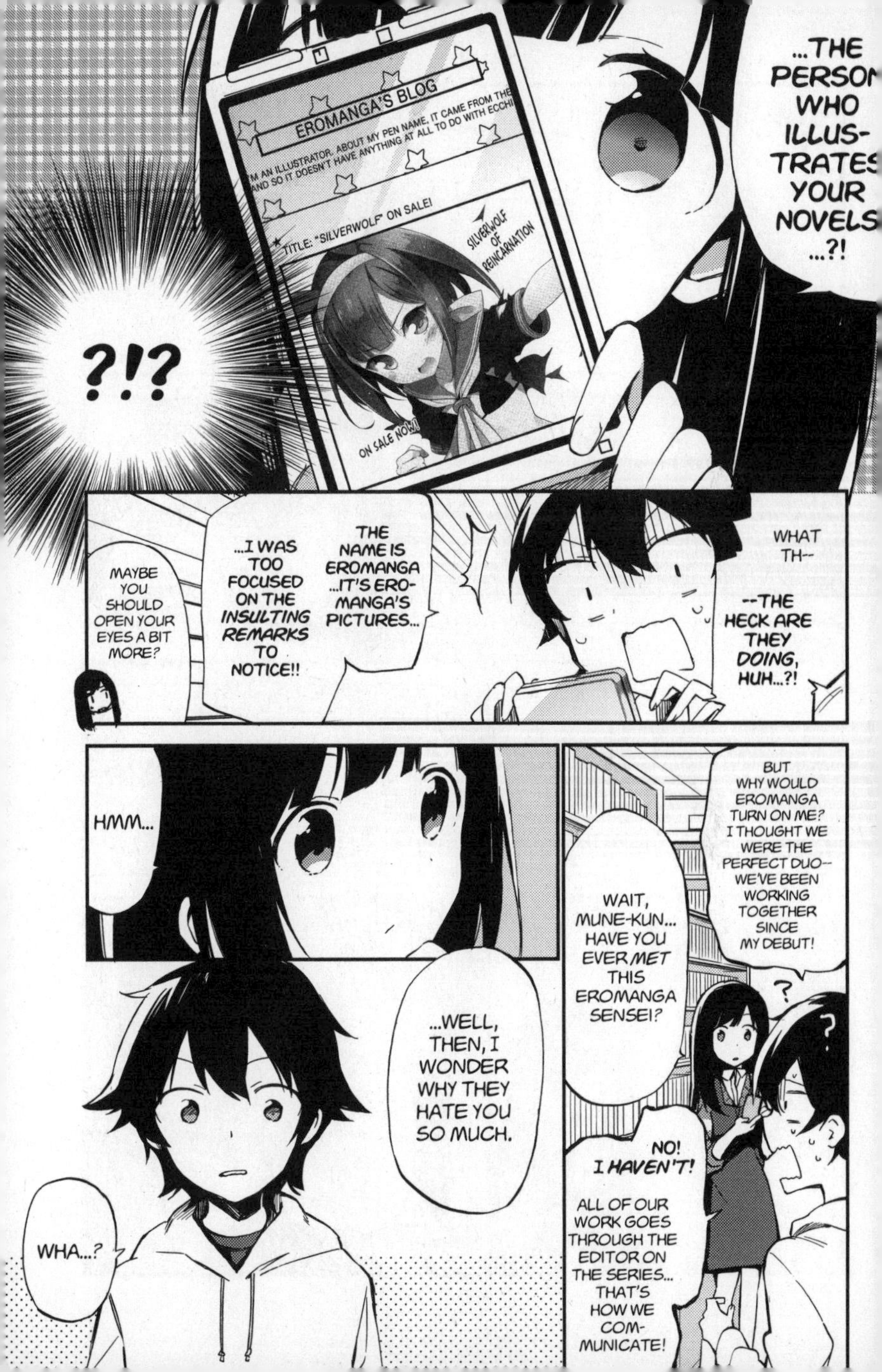
...THE PERSON WHO ILLUS-TRATES YOUR NOVELS ...?!
EROMANGA'S BLOG
I'M AN ILLUSTRATOR. ABOUT MY PEN NAME, IT CAME FROM THE
AND SO IT DOESN'T HAVE ANYTHING AT ALL TO DO WITH ECCHI
TITLE: "SILVERWOLF" ON SALE!
SILVERWOLF OF REINCARNATION
ON SALE NOW!
?!?
WHAT TH--
--THE HECK ARE THEY *DOING*, HUH...?!
THE NAME IS EROMANGA ...IT'S ERO-MANGA'S PICTURES...
...I WAS TOO FOCUSED ON THE *INSULTING REMARKS* TO NOTICE!!
MAYBE YOU SHOULD OPEN YOUR EYES A BIT MORE?
BUT WHY WOULD EROMANGA TURN ON ME? I THOUGHT WE WERE THE PERFECT DUO-- WE'VE BEEN WORKING TOGETHER SINCE MY DEBUT!
WAIT, MUNE-KUN... HAVE YOU EVER *MET* THIS EROMANGA SENSEI?
?
?
NO! I *HAVEN'T*!
ALL OF OUR WORK GOES THROUGH THE EDITOR ON THE SERIES... THAT'S HOW WE COM-MUNICATE!
HMM...
...WELL, THEN, I WONDER WHY THEY HATE YOU SO MUCH.
WHA...?

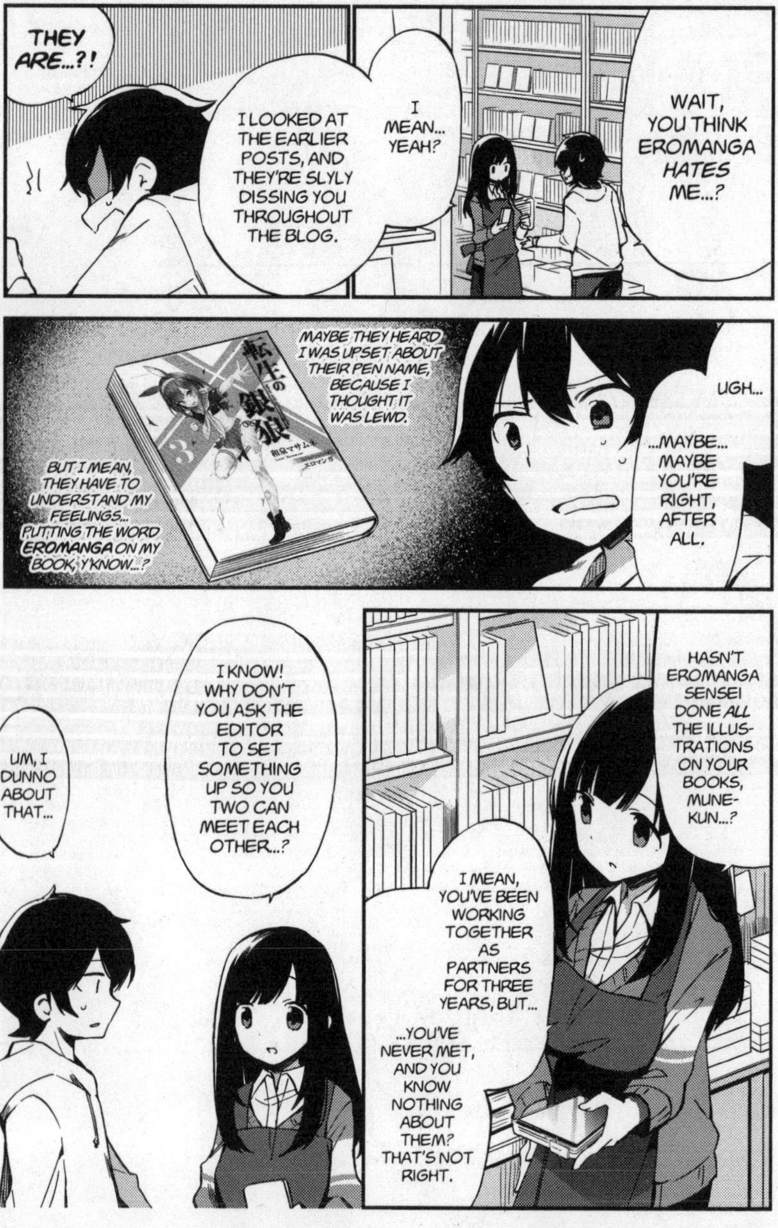
WAIT, YOU THINK EROMANGA HATES ME...?
I MEAN... YEAH?
I LOOKED AT THE EARLIER POSTS, AND THEY'RE SLYLY DISSING YOU THROUGHOUT THE BLOG.
THEY ARE...?!
UGH...
...MAYBE... MAYBE YOU'RE RIGHT, AFTER ALL.
転生の銀狼
3
和泉マサムネ
エロマンガ
MAYBE THEY HEARD I WAS UPSET ABOUT THEIR PEN NAME, BECAUSE I THOUGHT IT WAS LEWD.
BUT I MEAN, THEY HAVE TO UNDERSTAND MY FEELINGS... PUTTING THE WORD EROMANGA ON MY BOOK, Y'KNOW...?
HASN'T EROMANGA SENSEI DONE ALL THE ILLUS-TRATIONS ON YOUR BOOKS, MUNE-KUN...?
I MEAN, YOU'VE BEEN WORKING TOGETHER AS PARTNERS FOR THREE YEARS, BUT...
...YOU'VE NEVER MET, AND YOU KNOW NOTHING ABOUT THEM? THAT'S NOT RIGHT.
I KNOW! WHY DON'T YOU ASK THE EDITOR TO SET SOMETHING UP SO YOU TWO CAN MEET EACH OTHER...?
UM, I DUNNO ABOUT THAT...

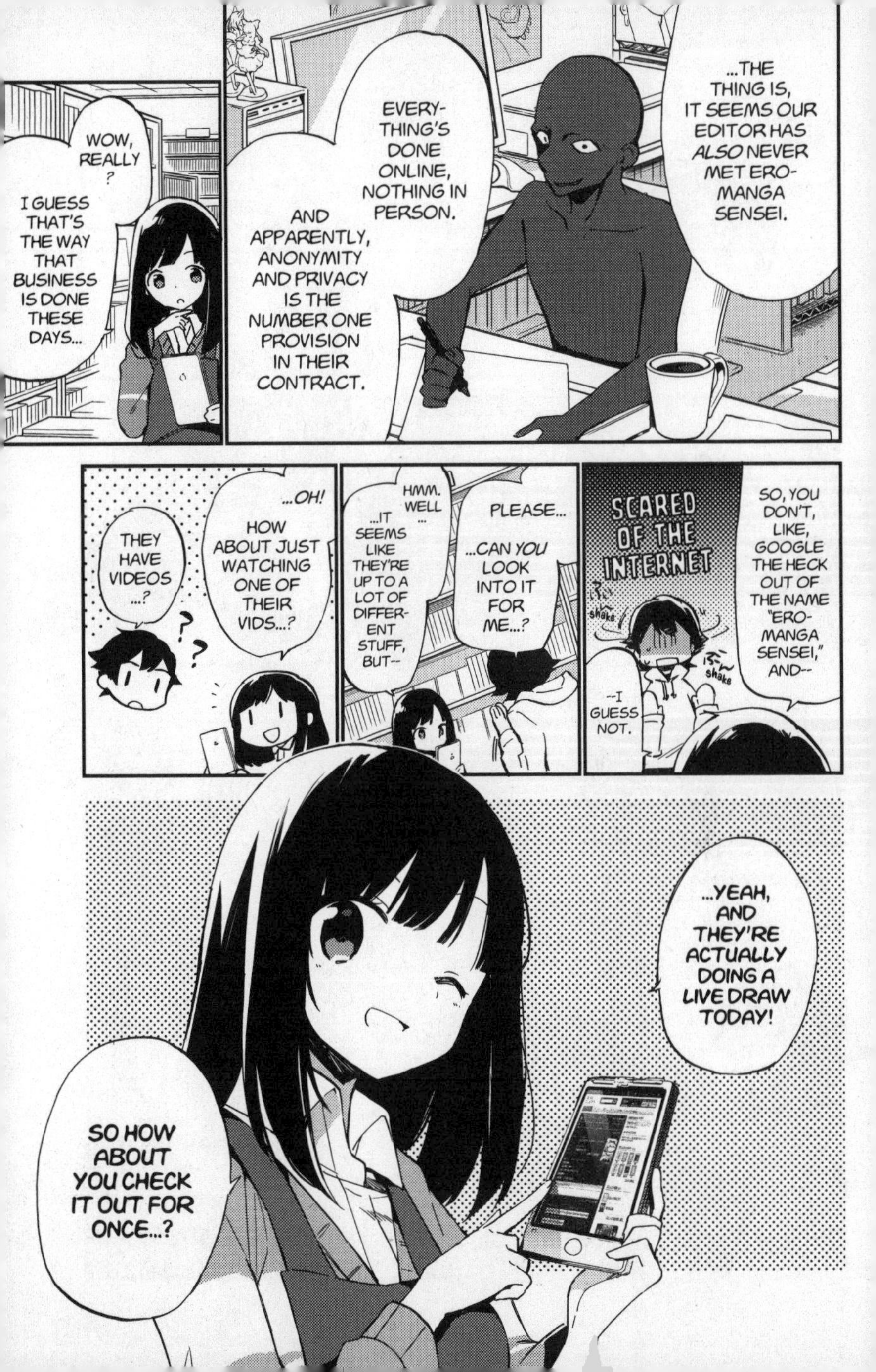
...THE THING IS, IT SEEMS OUR EDITOR HAS ALSO NEVER MET ERO-MANGA SENSEI.
EVERYTHING'S DONE ONLINE, NOTHING IN PERSON.
AND APPARENTLY, ANONYMITY AND PRIVACY IS THE NUMBER ONE PROVISION IN THEIR CONTRACT.
WOW, REALLY?
I GUESS THAT'S THE WAY THAT BUSINESS IS DONE THESE DAYS...
SO, YOU DON'T, LIKE, GOOGLE THE HECK OUT OF THE NAME "ERO-MANGA SENSEI," AND--
SCARED OF THE INTERNET
shake
shake
--I GUESS NOT.
PLEASE... ...CAN YOU LOOK INTO IT FOR ME...?
HMM. WELL... ...IT SEEMS LIKE THEY'RE UP TO A LOT OF DIFFERENT STUFF, BUT--
...OH! HOW ABOUT JUST WATCHING ONE OF THEIR VIDS...?
THEY HAVE VIDEOS...?
...YEAH, AND THEY'RE ACTUALLY DOING A LIVE DRAW TODAY!
SO HOW ABOUT YOU CHECK IT OUT FOR ONCE...?

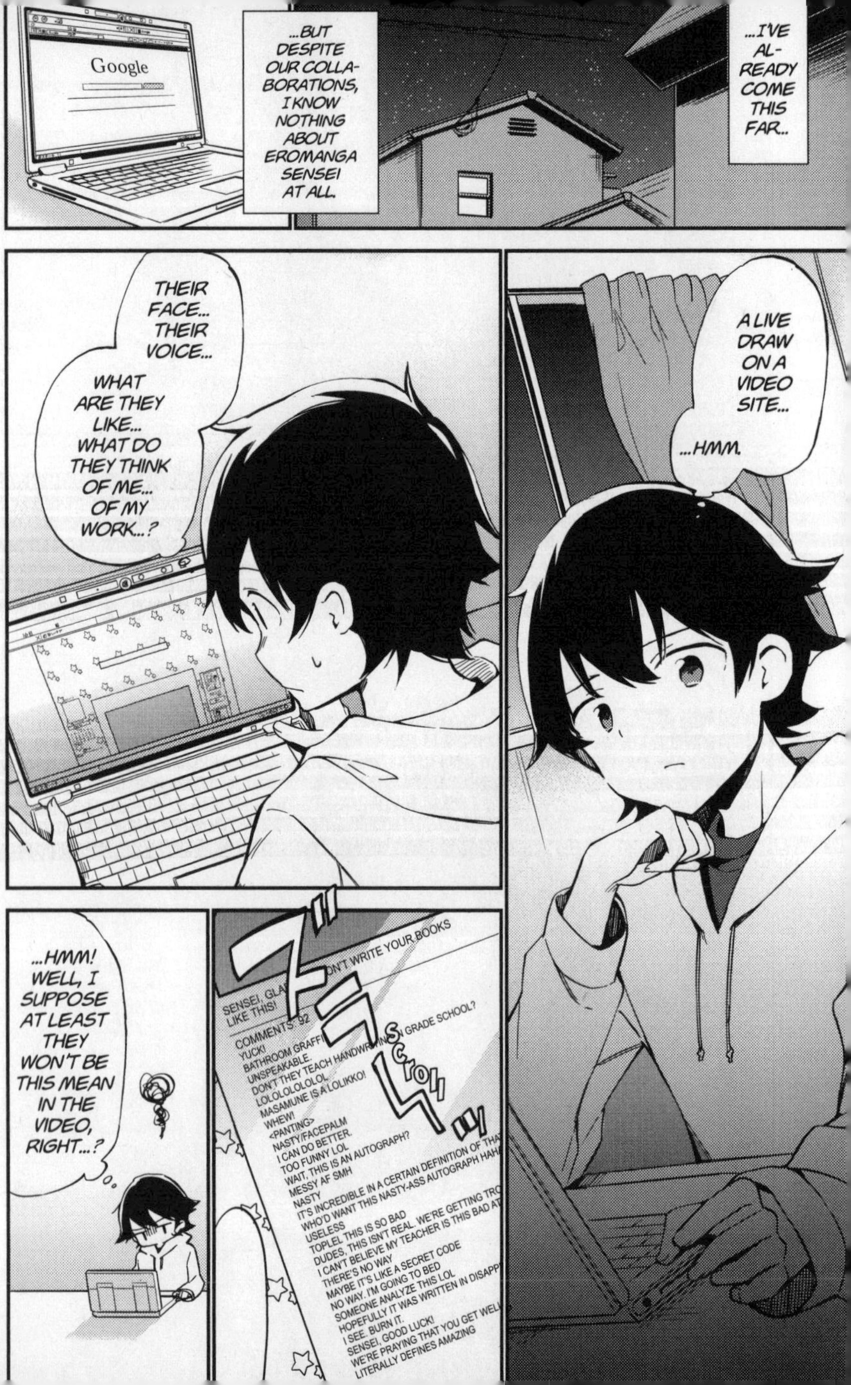
...I'VE ALREADY COME THIS FAR...
...BUT DESPITE OUR COLLABORATIONS, I KNOW NOTHING ABOUT EROMANGA SENSEI AT ALL.
Google
A LIVE DRAW ON A VIDEO SITE...
...HMM.
THEIR FACE... THEIR VOICE...
WHAT ARE THEY LIKE... WHAT DO THEY THINK OF ME... OF MY WORK...?
ON'T WRITE YOUR BOOKS
SENSEI, GLA
LIKE THIS!
COMMENTS: 92
YUCK!
BATHROOM GRAFFI
UNSPEAKABLE.
DON'T THEY TEACH HANDWR
GRADE SCHOOL?
LOLOLOLOLOLOL
MASAMUNE IS A LOLIKKO!
WHEW!
<PANTING>
NASTY/FACEPALM
I CAN DO BETTER.
TOO FUNNY LOL
WAIT, THIS IS AN AUTOGRAPH?
MESSY AF SMH
NASTY
IT'S INCREDIBLE IN A CERTAIN DEFINITION OF THA
WHO'D WANT THIS NASTY-ASS AUTOGRAPH HAH
USELESS
TOPLEL THIS IS SO BAD
DUDES, THIS ISN'T REAL. WE'RE GETTING TRO
I CAN'T BELIEVE MY TEACHER IS THIS BAD AT
THERE'S NO WAY
MAYBE IT'S LIKE A SECRET CODE
NO WAY. I'M GOING TO BED
SOMEONE ANALYZE THIS LOL
HOPEFULLY IT WAS WRITTEN IN DISAPP
I SEE. BURN IT.
SENSEI, GOOD LUCK!
WE'RE PRAYING THAT YOU GET WEL
LITERALLY DEFINES AMAZING
scroll
...HMM! WELL, I SUPPOSE AT LEAST THEY WON'T BE THIS MEAN IN THE VIDEO, RIGHT...?

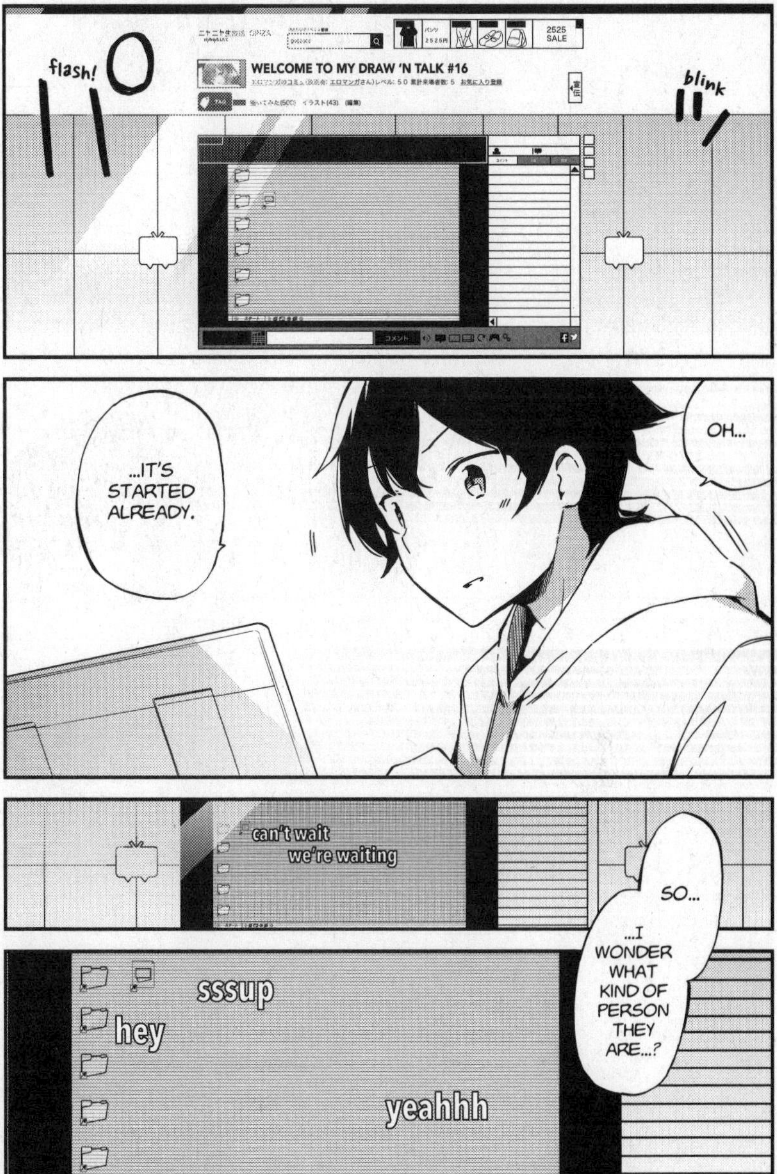
blink
flash!
2525 SALE
WELCOME TO MY DRAW 'N TALK #16
OH...
...IT'S STARTED ALREADY.
can't wait
we're waiting
SO...
...I WONDER WHAT KIND OF PERSON THEY ARE...?
sssup
hey
yeahhh

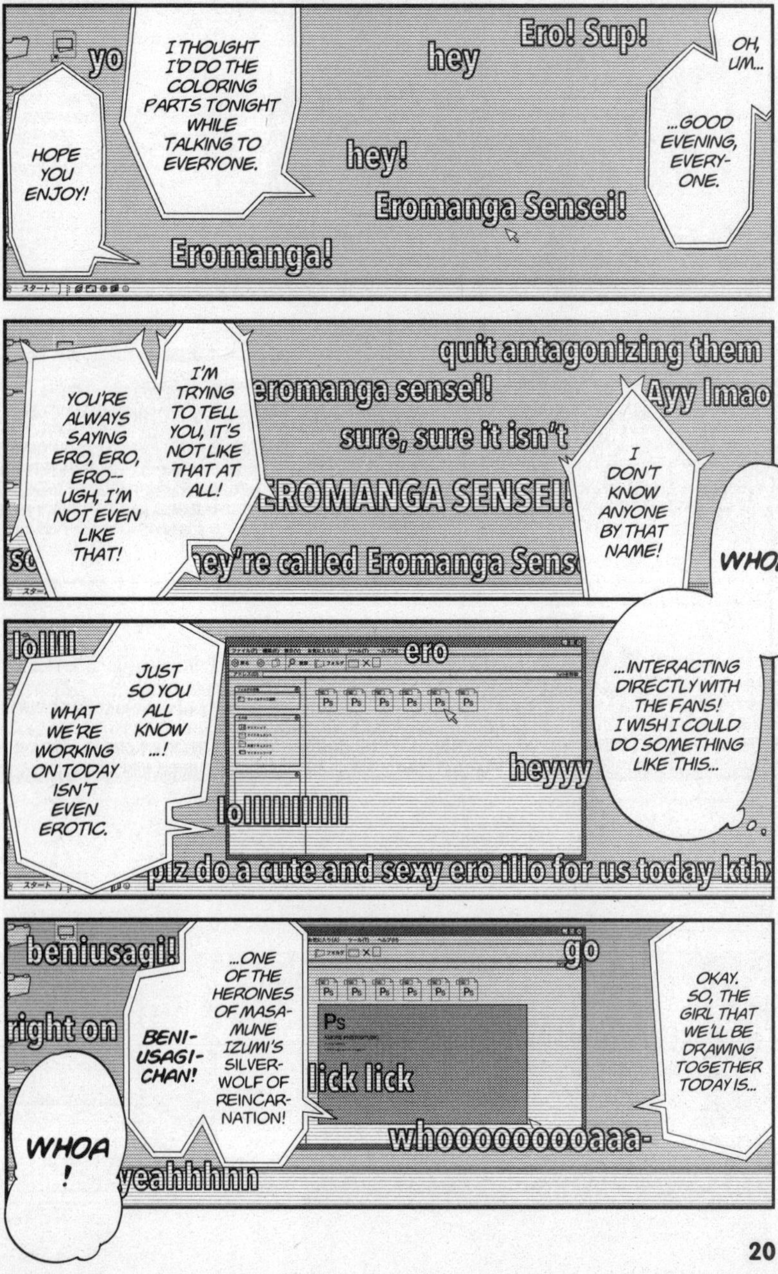

OH, UM...
...GOOD EVENING, EVERYONE.
Ero! Sup!
hey
hey!
Eromanga Sensei!
Eromanga!
I THOUGHT I'D DO THE COLORING PARTS TONIGHT WHILE TALKING TO EVERYONE.
yo
HOPE YOU ENJOY!
quit antagonizing them
Ayy lmao
I DON'T KNOW ANYONE BY THAT NAME!
eromanga sensei!
sure, sure it isn't
EROMANGA SENSEI!
I'M TRYING TO TELL YOU, IT'S NOT LIKE THAT AT ALL!
YOU'RE ALWAYS SAYING ERO, ERO, ERO-- UGH, I'M NOT EVEN LIKE THAT!
WHOA...!
...INTERACTING DIRECTLY WITH THE FANS! I WISH I COULD DO SOMETHING LIKE THIS...
ero
heyyy
JUST SO YOU ALL KNOW...!
lollll
WHAT WE'RE WORKING ON TODAY ISN'T EVEN EROTIC.
lollllllllllll
plz do a cute and sexy ero illo for us today kthx
OKAY. SO, THE GIRL THAT WE'LL BE DRAWING TOGETHER TODAY IS...
go
...ONE OF THE HEROINES OF MASAMUNE IZUMI'S SILVERWOLF OF REINCARNATION!
lick lick
whooooooooaaa-
BENI-USAGI-CHAN!
beniusagi!
right on
yeahhhhn
WHOA!

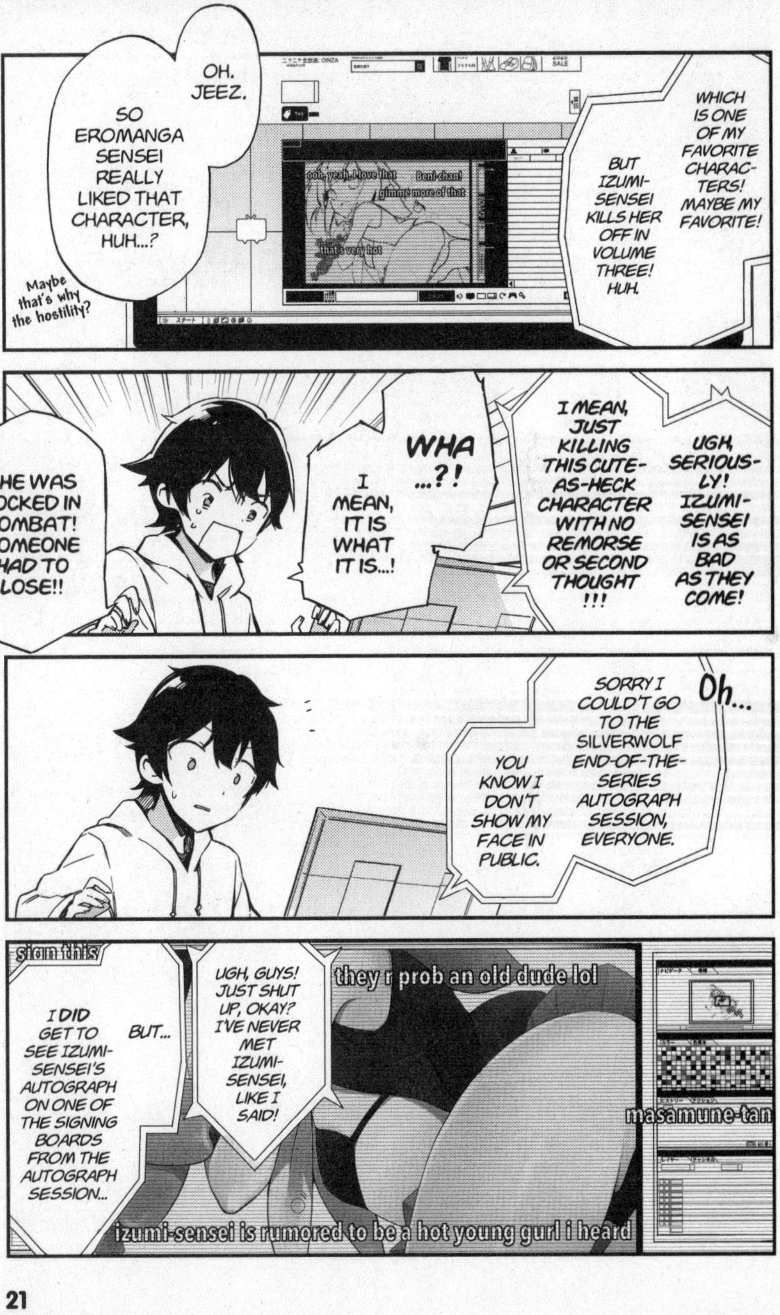
WHICH IS ONE OF MY FAVORITE CHARACTERS! MAYBE MY FAVORITE!
BUT IZUMI-SENSEI KILLS HER OFF IN VOLUME THREE! HUH.
Beni-chan!
gimme more of that
ooh, yeah, I love that
that's very hot
OH. JEEZ.
SO EROMANGA SENSEI REALLY LIKED THAT CHARACTER, HUH...?
Maybe that's why the hostility?
UGH, SERIOUSLY! IZUMI-SENSEI IS AS BAD AS THEY COME!
I MEAN, JUST KILLING THIS CUTE-AS-HECK CHARACTER WITH NO REMORSE OR SECOND THOUGHT!!!
WHA...?!
I MEAN, IT IS WHAT IT IS...!
SHE WAS LOCKED IN COMBAT! SOMEONE HAD TO LOSE!!
Oh...
SORRY I COULDN'T GO TO THE SILVERWOLF END-OF-THE-SERIES AUTOGRAPH SESSION, EVERYONE.
YOU KNOW I DON'T SHOW MY FACE IN PUBLIC.
masamune-tan
they r prob an old dude lol
UGH, GUYS! JUST SHUT UP, OKAY? I'VE NEVER MET IZUMI-SENSEI, LIKE I SAID!
BUT...
I DID GET TO SEE IZUMI-SENSEI'S AUTOGRAPH ON ONE OF THE SIGNING BOARDS FROM THE AUTOGRAPH SESSION...
sign this
izumi-sensei is rumored to be a hot young gurl i heard

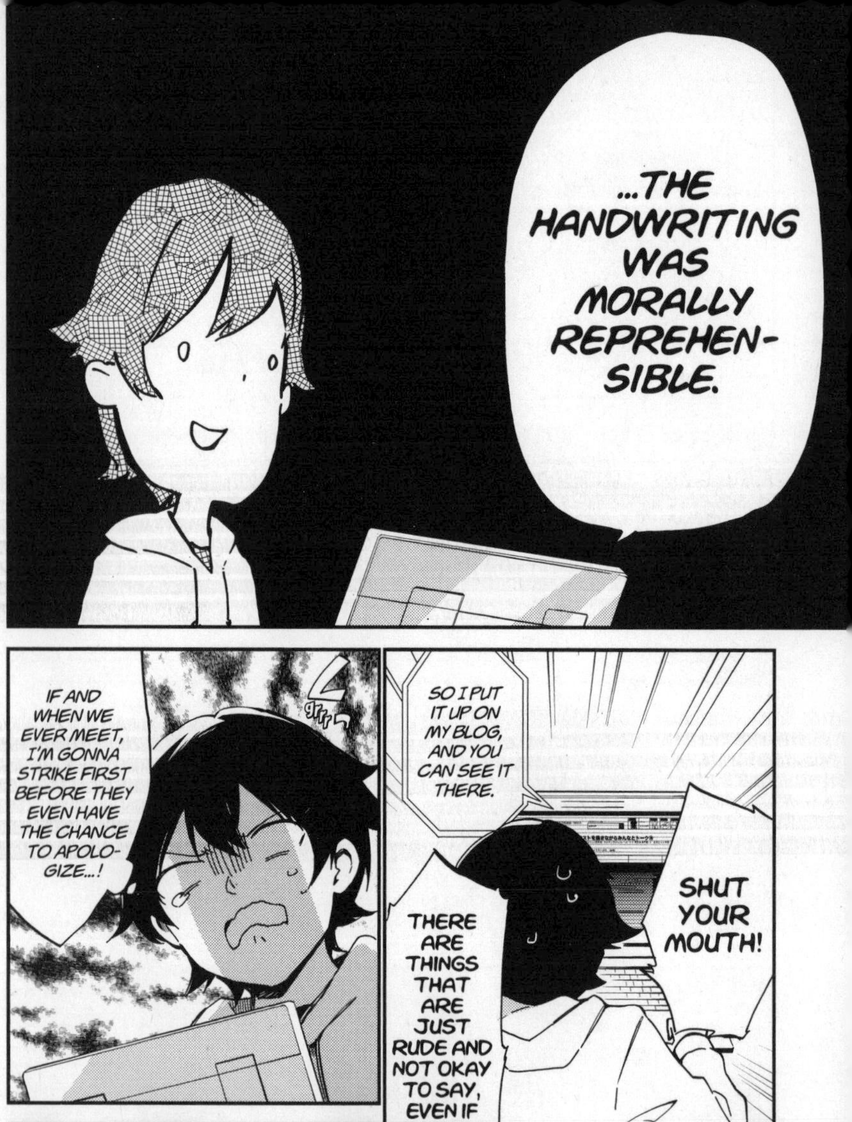
...THE HANDWRITING WAS MORALLY REPREHEN-SIBLE.
SO I PUT IT UP ON MY BLOG, AND YOU CAN SEE IT THERE.
SHUT YOUR MOUTH!
THERE ARE THINGS THAT ARE JUST RUDE AND NOT OKAY TO SAY, EVEN IF THEY'RE THE BITTER UNVAR-NISHED TRUTH!
grrr
IF AND WHEN WE EVER MEET, I'M GONNA STRIKE FIRST BEFORE THEY EVEN HAVE THE CHANCE TO APOLO-GIZE...!

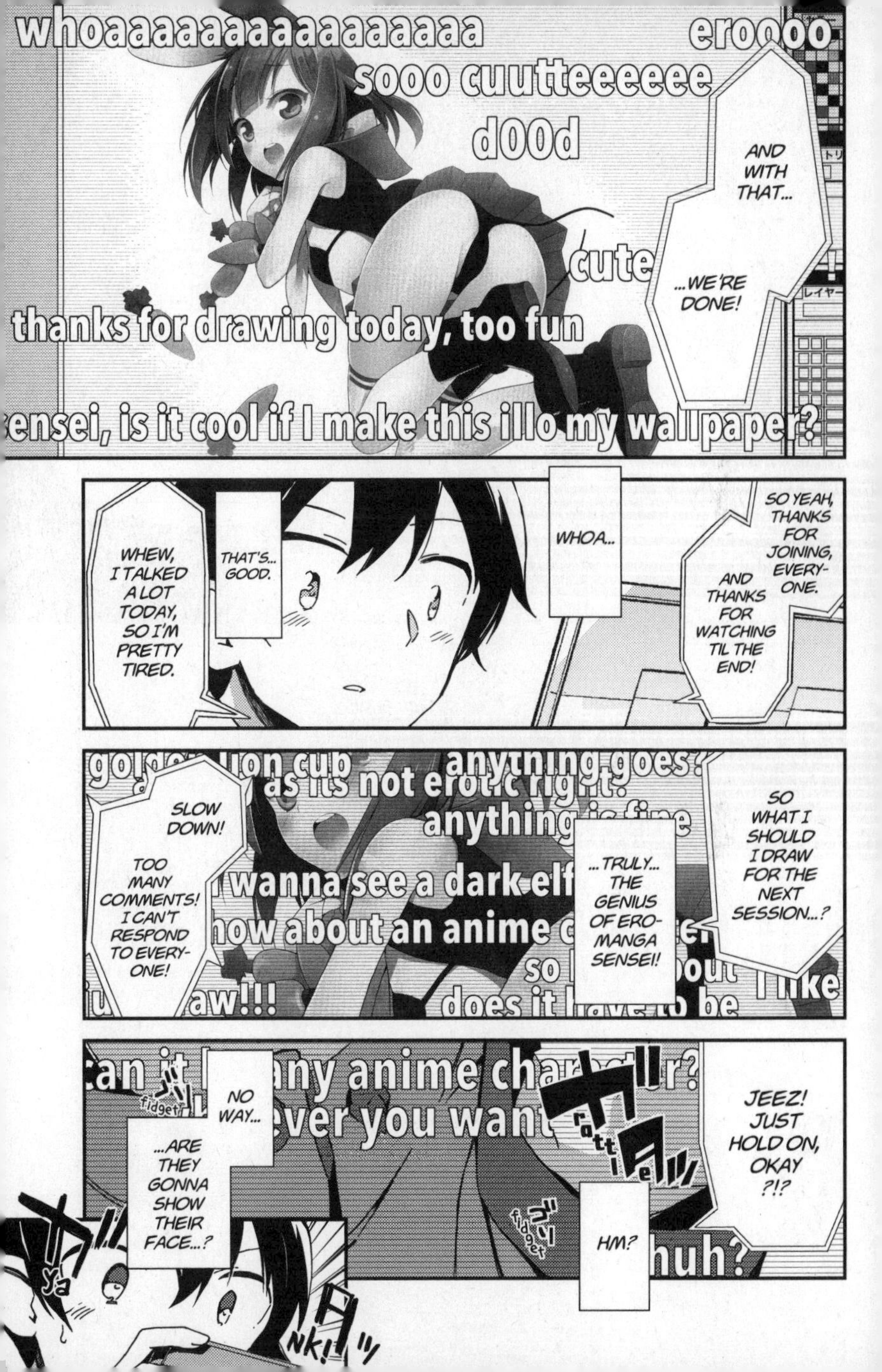
AND WITH THAT...
...WE'RE DONE!
eroooo
whoaaaaaaaaaaaaaaa
sooo cuutteeeeeee
d00d
cute
thanks for drawing today, too fun
ensei, is it cool if I make this illo my wallpaper?
SO YEAH, THANKS FOR JOINING, EVERYONE.
AND THANKS FOR WATCHING TIL THE END!
WHOA...
THAT'S... GOOD.
WHEW, I TALKED A LOT TODAY, SO I'M PRETTY TIRED.
SO WHAT I SHOULD I DRAW FOR THE NEXT SESSION...?
...TRULY... THE GENIUS OF ERO-MANGA SENSEI!
SLOW DOWN!
TOO MANY COMMENTS! I CAN'T RESPOND TO EVERYONE!
as its not erotic right?
wanna see a dark elf
JEEZ! JUST HOLD ON, OKAY?!?
HM?
huh?
rattle
fidget
NO WAY...
...ARE THEY GONNA SHOW THEIR FACE...?
fidget

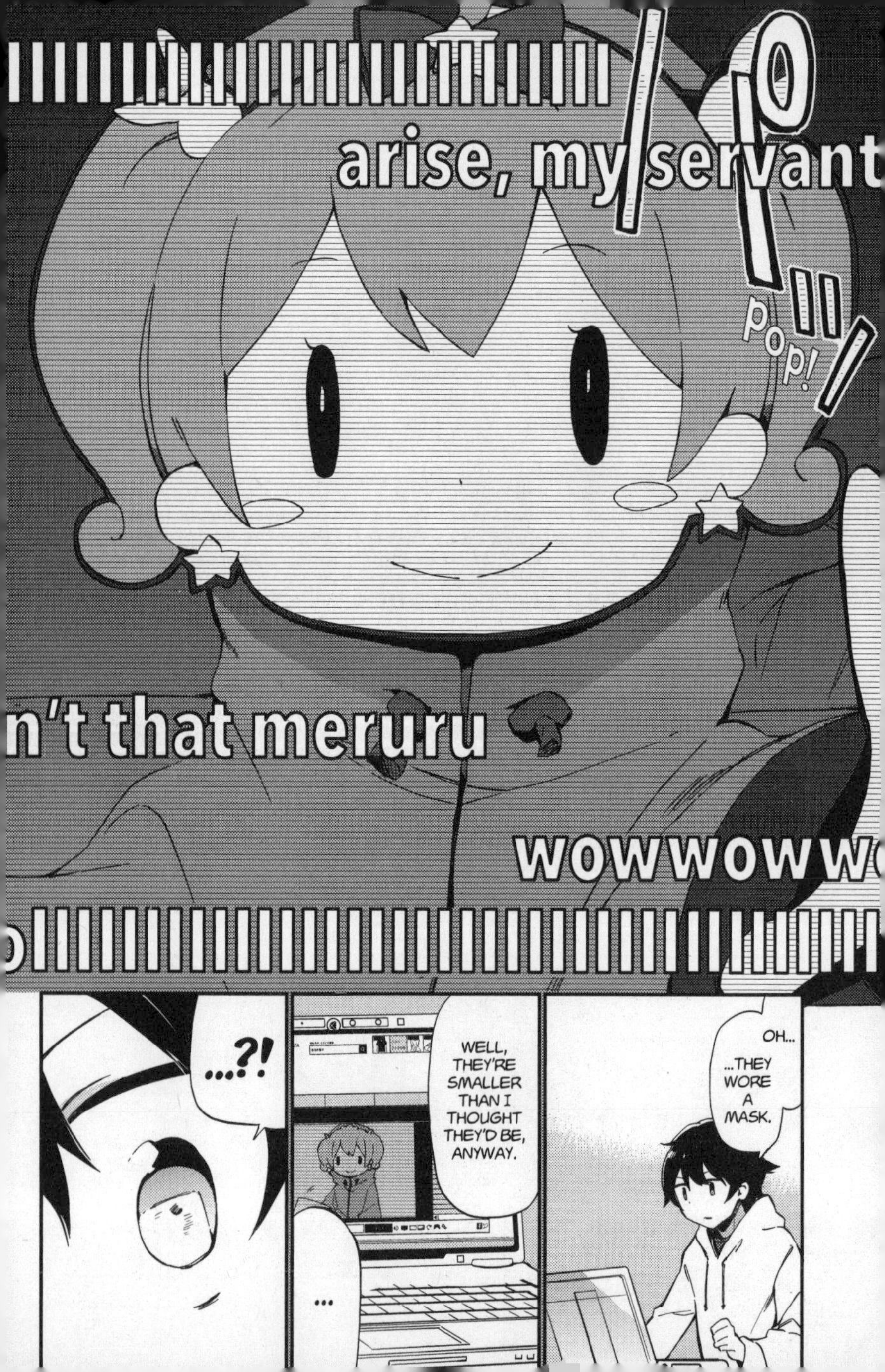
arise, my servant
pop!
wowwowwo
n't that meruru
OH...
...THEY WORE A MASK.
WELL, THEY'RE SMALLER THAN I THOUGHT THEY'D BE, ANYWAY.
...?!
...

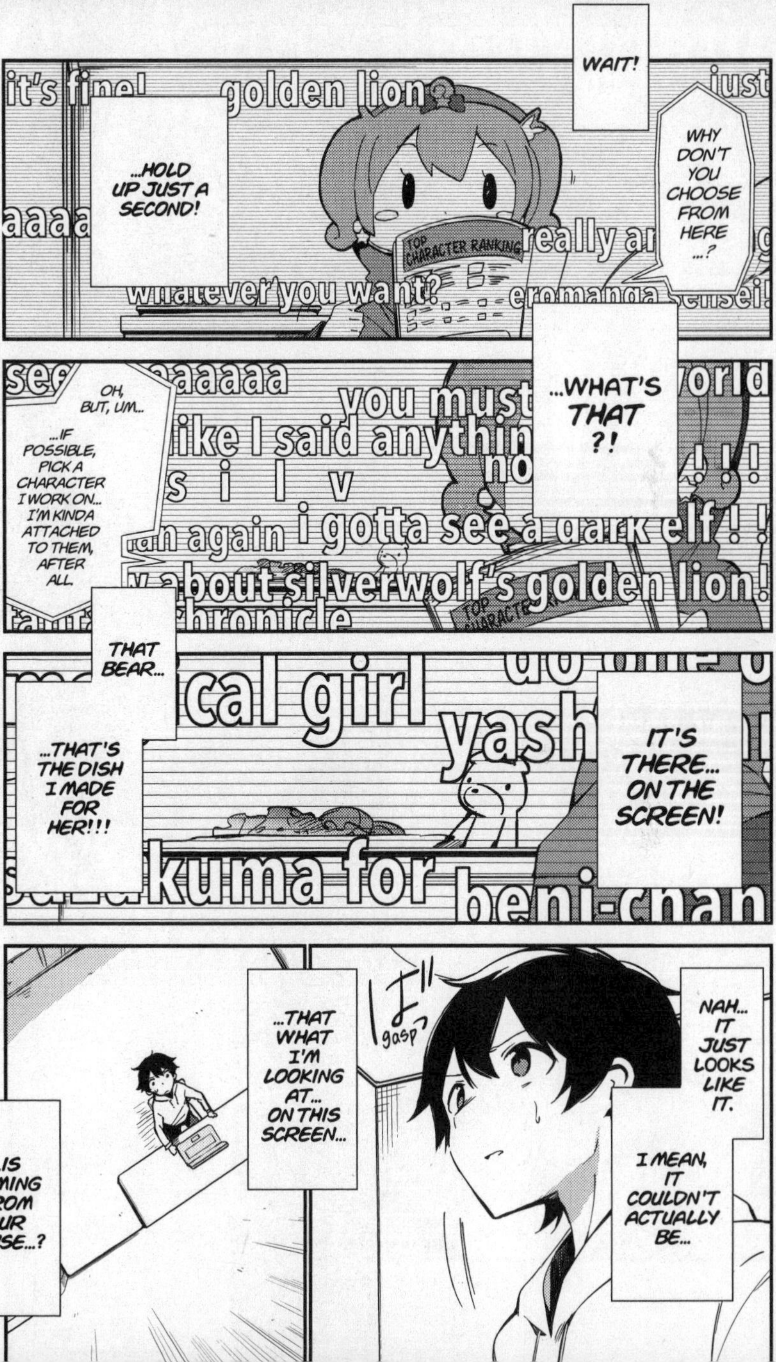
WAIT!
WHY DON'T YOU CHOOSE FROM HERE ...?
...HOLD UP JUST A SECOND!
it's fine!
golden lion
whatever you want?
TOP CHARACTER RANKING
...WHAT'S THAT ?!
OH, BUT, UM...
...IF POSSIBLE, PICK A CHARACTER I WORK ON... I'M KINDA ATTACHED TO THEM, AFTER ALL.
you must
like I said anythin
i gotta see a dark elf!!
about silverwolf's golden lion!
chronicle
IT'S THERE... ON THE SCREEN!
THAT BEAR...
...THAT'S THE DISH I MADE FOR HER!!!
cal girl
kuma for
NAH... IT JUST LOOKS LIKE IT.
gasp
...THAT WHAT I'M LOOKING AT... ON THIS SCREEN...
I MEAN, IT COULDN'T ACTUALLY BE...
...IS COMING FROM OUR HOUSE...?

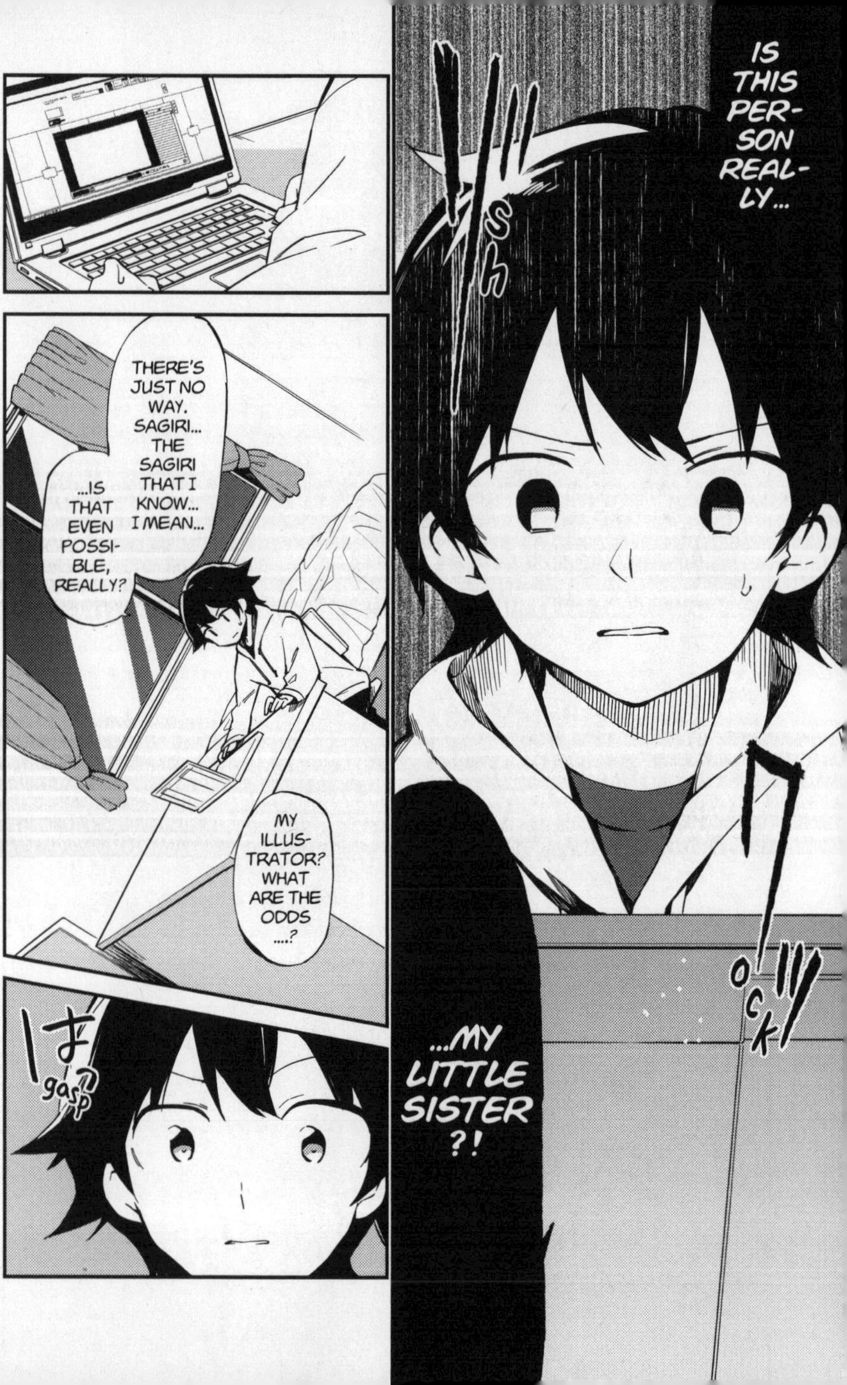
IS THIS PERSON REALLY...
...MY LITTLE SISTER ?!
THERE'S JUST NO WAY. SAGIRI... THE SAGIRI THAT I KNOW... I MEAN...
...IS THAT EVEN POSSIBLE, REALLY?
MY ILLUSTRATOR? WHAT ARE THE ODDS ...?
gasp

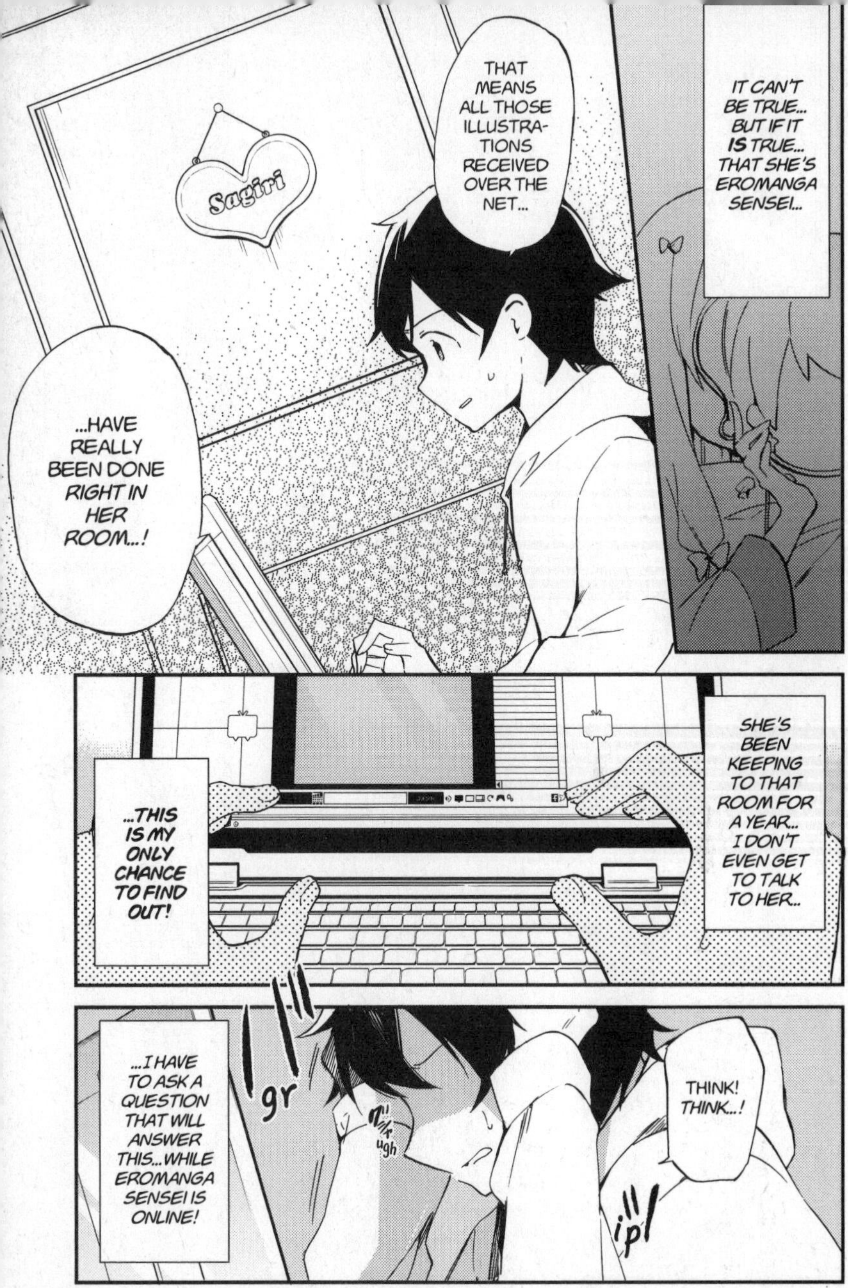
IT CAN'T BE TRUE... BUT IF IT IS TRUE... THAT SHE'S EROMANGA SENSEI...
THAT MEANS ALL THOSE ILLUSTRATIONS RECEIVED OVER THE NET...
...HAVE REALLY BEEN DONE RIGHT IN HER ROOM...!
SHE'S BEEN KEEPING TO THAT ROOM FOR A YEAR... I DON'T EVEN GET TO TALK TO HER..
...THIS IS MY ONLY CHANCE TO FIND OUT!
THINK! THINK...!
ip
ugh
gr
...I HAVE TO ASK A QUESTION THAT WILL ANSWER THIS...WHILE EROMANGA SENSEI IS ONLINE!

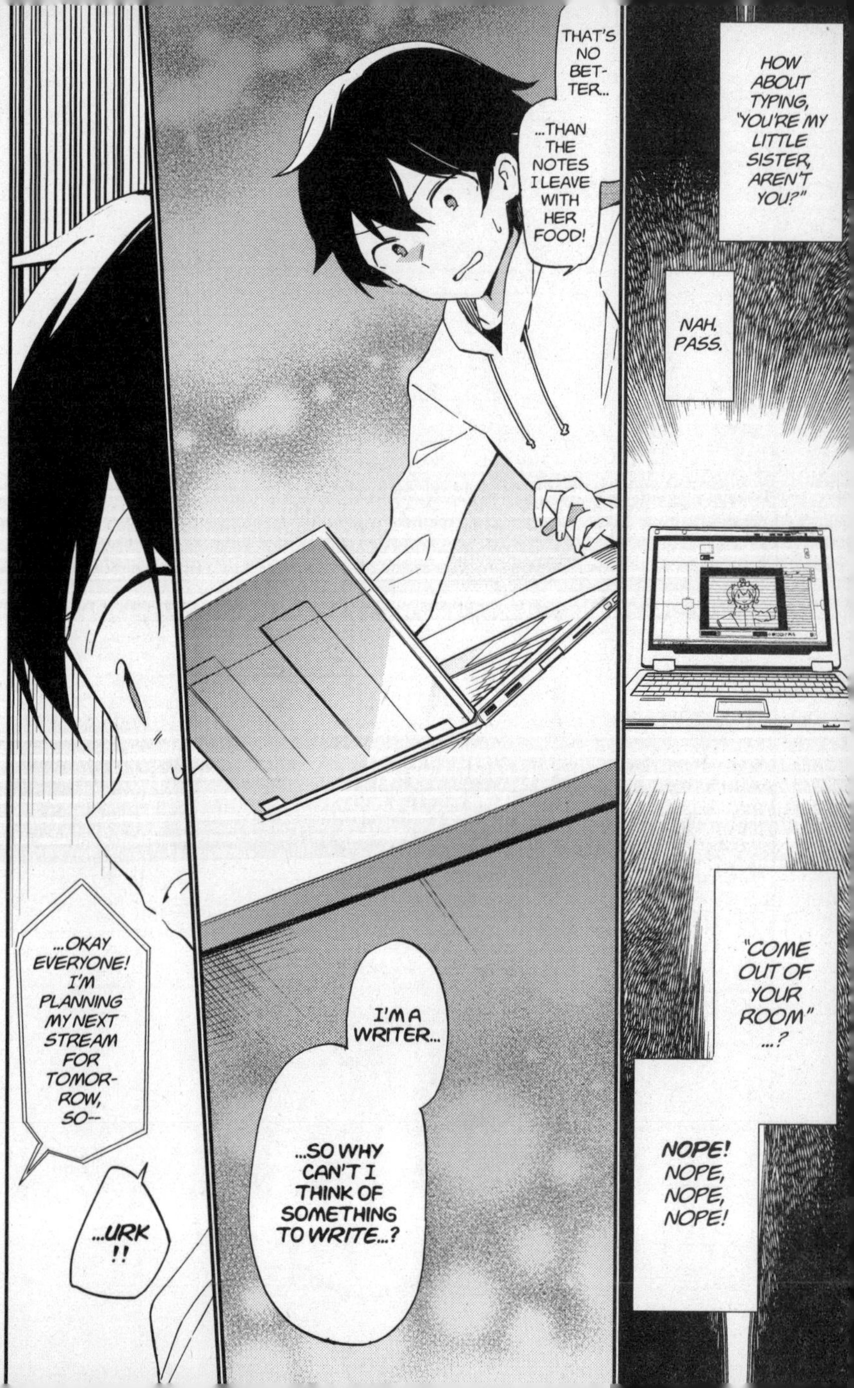
HOW ABOUT TYPING, "YOU'RE MY LITTLE SISTER, AREN'T YOU?"
NAH. PASS.
"COME OUT OF YOUR ROOM" ...?
NOPE! NOPE, NOPE, NOPE!
THAT'S NO BET-TER...
...THAN THE NOTES I LEAVE WITH HER FOOD!
I'M A WRITER...
...SO WHY CAN'T I THINK OF SOMETHING TO WRITE...?
...OKAY EVERYONE! I'M PLANNING MY NEXT STREAM FOR TOMOR-ROW, SO--
...URK !!

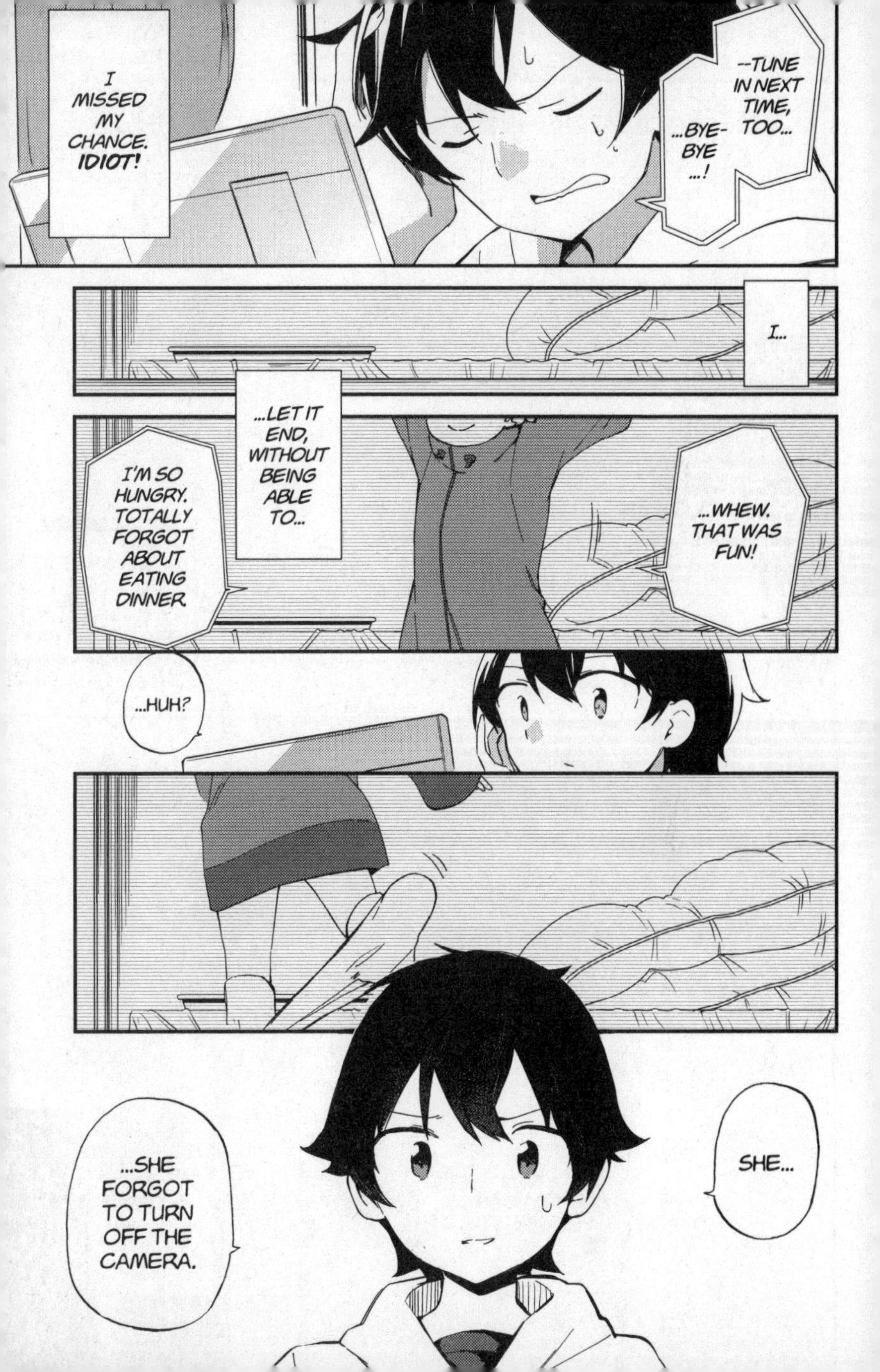
--TUNE IN NEXT TIME, TOO...
...BYE-BYE ...!
I MISSED MY CHANCE. **IDIOT!**
I...
...LET IT END, WITHOUT BEING ABLE TO...
...WHEW. THAT WAS FUN!
I'M SO HUNGRY. TOTALLY FORGOT ABOUT EATING DINNER.
...HUH?
SHE...
...SHE FORGOT TO TURN OFF THE CAMERA.

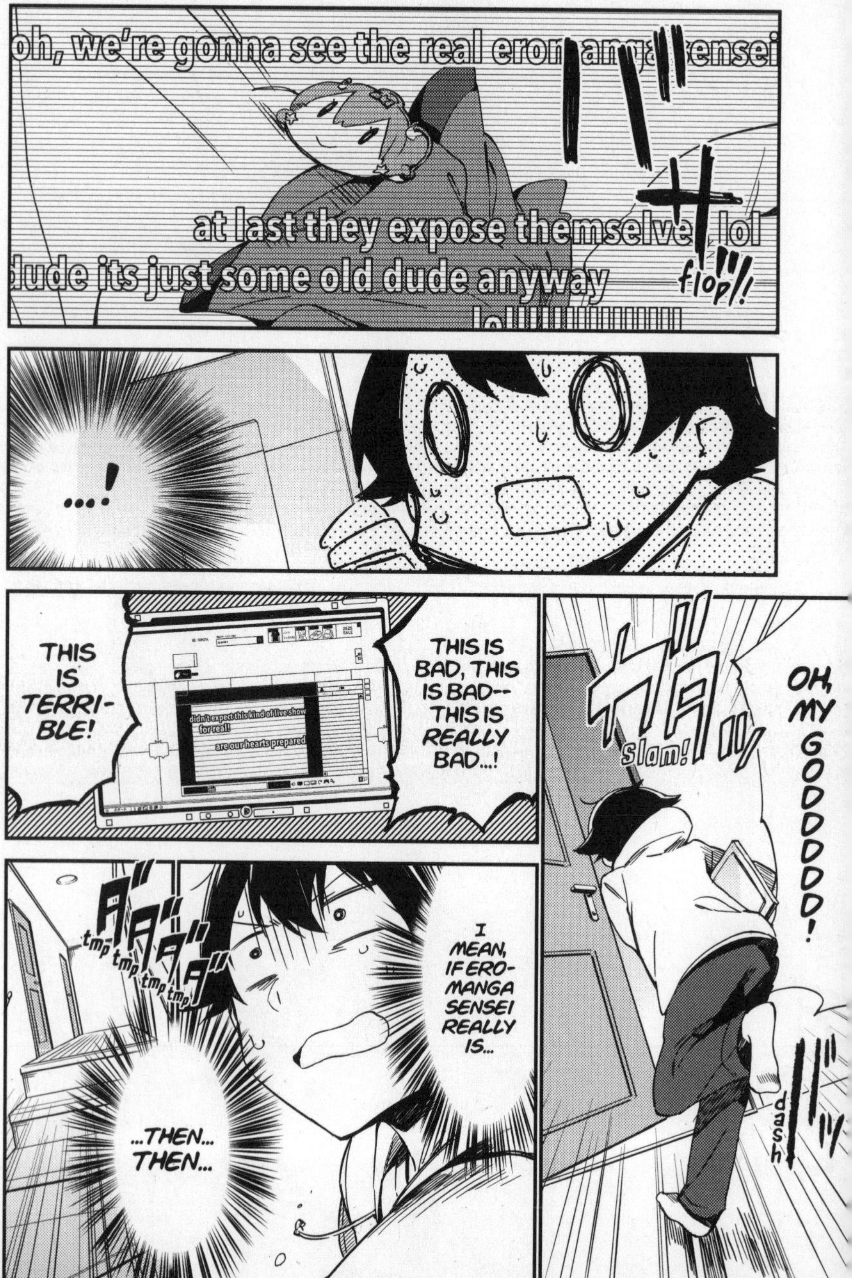
oh, we're gonna see the real eromanga sensei
at last they expose themselve lol
dude its just some old dude anyway
flop!!
...!
slam!
OH, MY GODDDDDDD!
dash
THIS IS BAD, THIS IS BAD-- THIS IS REALLY BAD...!
THIS IS TERRIBLE!
didn't expect this kind of live show for real!
are our hearts prepared
tmp tmp tmp tmp
I MEAN, IF EROMANGA SENSEI REALLY IS...
...THEN... THEN...

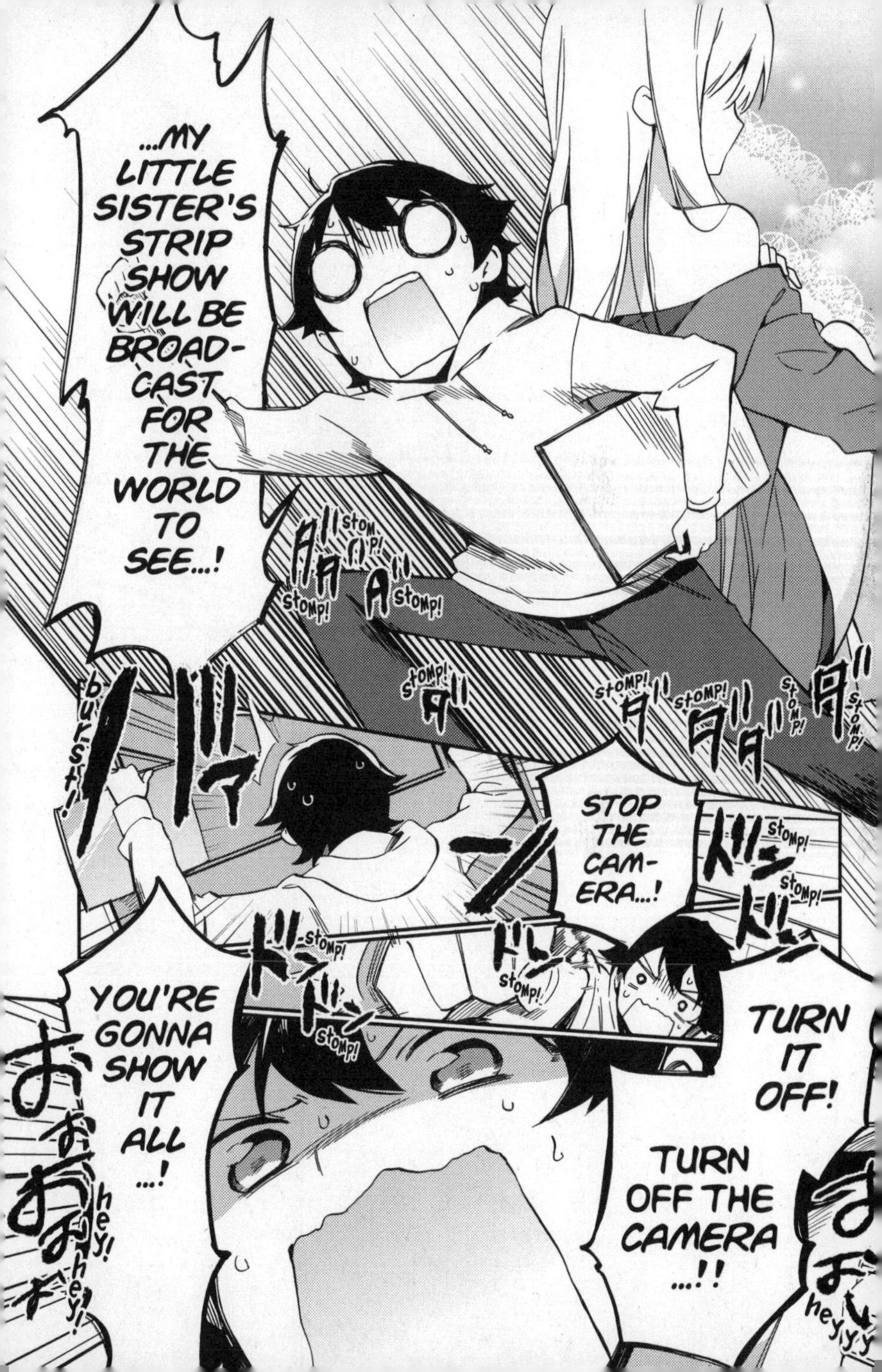
...MY LITTLE SISTER'S STRIP SHOW WILL BE BROAD-CAST FOR THE WORLD TO SEE...!
stomp! stomp! stomp!
stomp! stomp! stomp! stomp! stomp!
burst!
stomp! stomp!
STOP THE CAM-ERA...!
stomp! stomp! stomp!
TURN IT OFF!
TURN OFF THE CAMERA ...!!
heyyy
YOU'RE GONNA SHOW IT ALL ...!
hey! hey! hey!

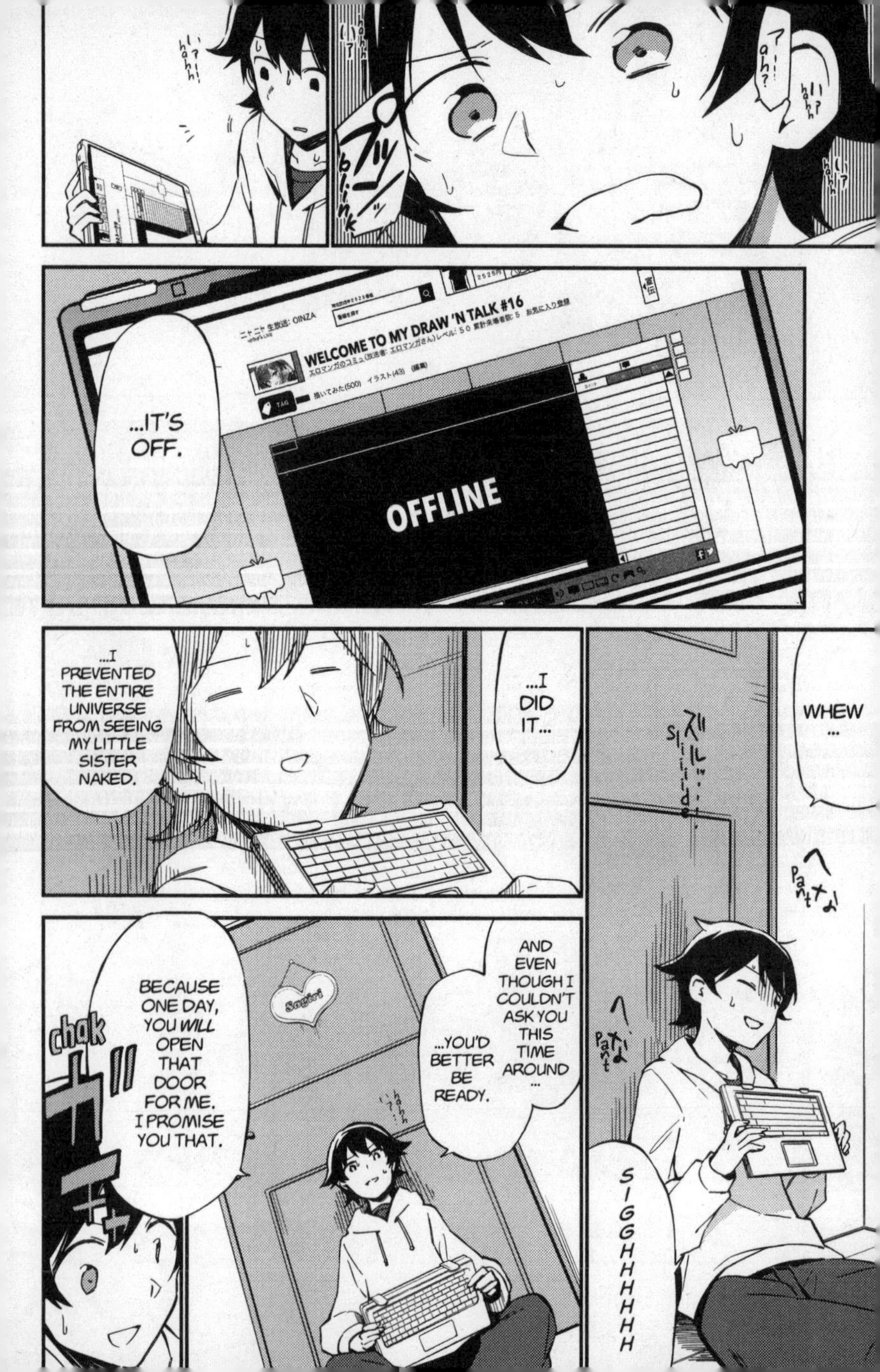
ah?
hah hah
blink
hah hah
WELCOME TO MY DRAW 'N TALK #16
OFFLINE
...IT'S OFF.
WHEW ...
sliiide
pant
SIGGHHHHHH
...I DID IT...
...I PREVENTED THE ENTIRE UNIVERSE FROM SEEING MY LITTLE SISTER NAKED.
AND EVEN THOUGH I COULDN'T ASK YOU THIS TIME AROUND ...
...YOU'D BETTER BE READY.
Sagiri
BECAUSE ONE DAY, YOU WILL OPEN THAT DOOR FOR ME. I PROMISE YOU THAT.
chak

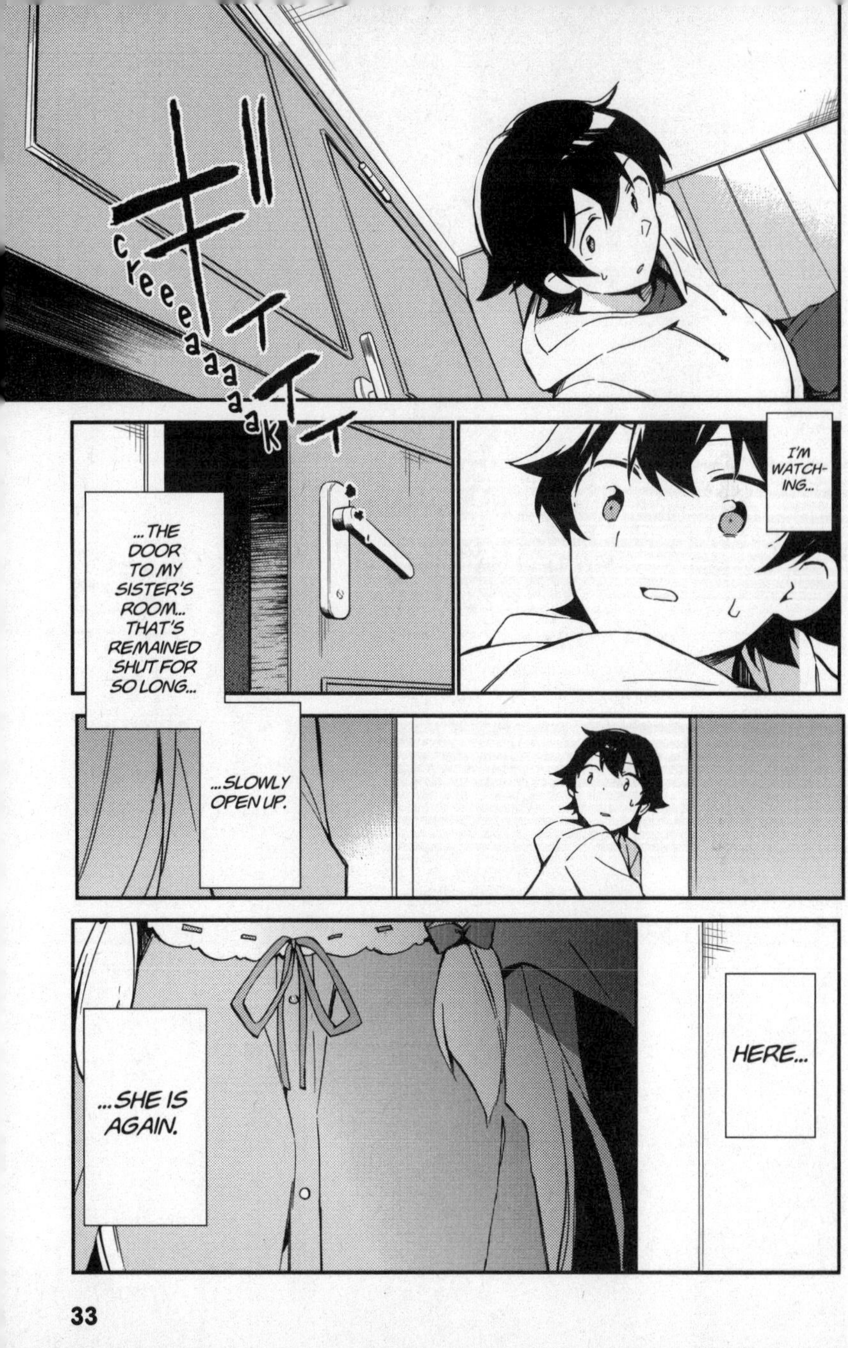
キィィ
creeeaaaaak
I'M WATCHING...
...THE DOOR TO MY SISTER'S ROOM... THAT'S REMAINED SHUT FOR SO LONG...
...SLOWLY OPEN UP.
HERE...
...SHE IS AGAIN.

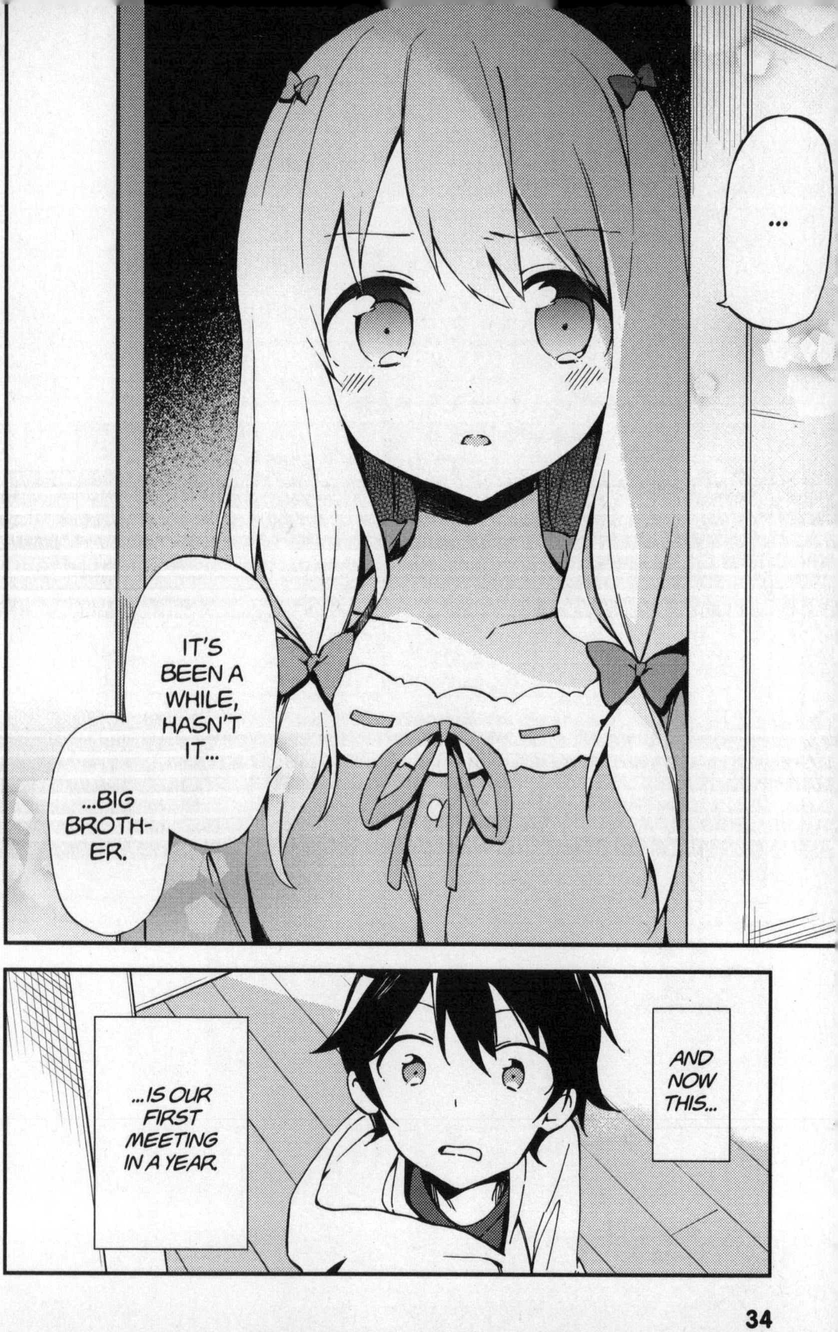
...
IT'S BEEN A WHILE, HASN'T IT...
...BIG BROTHER.
AND NOW THIS...
...IS OUR FIRST MEETING IN A YEAR.

eromanga sensei

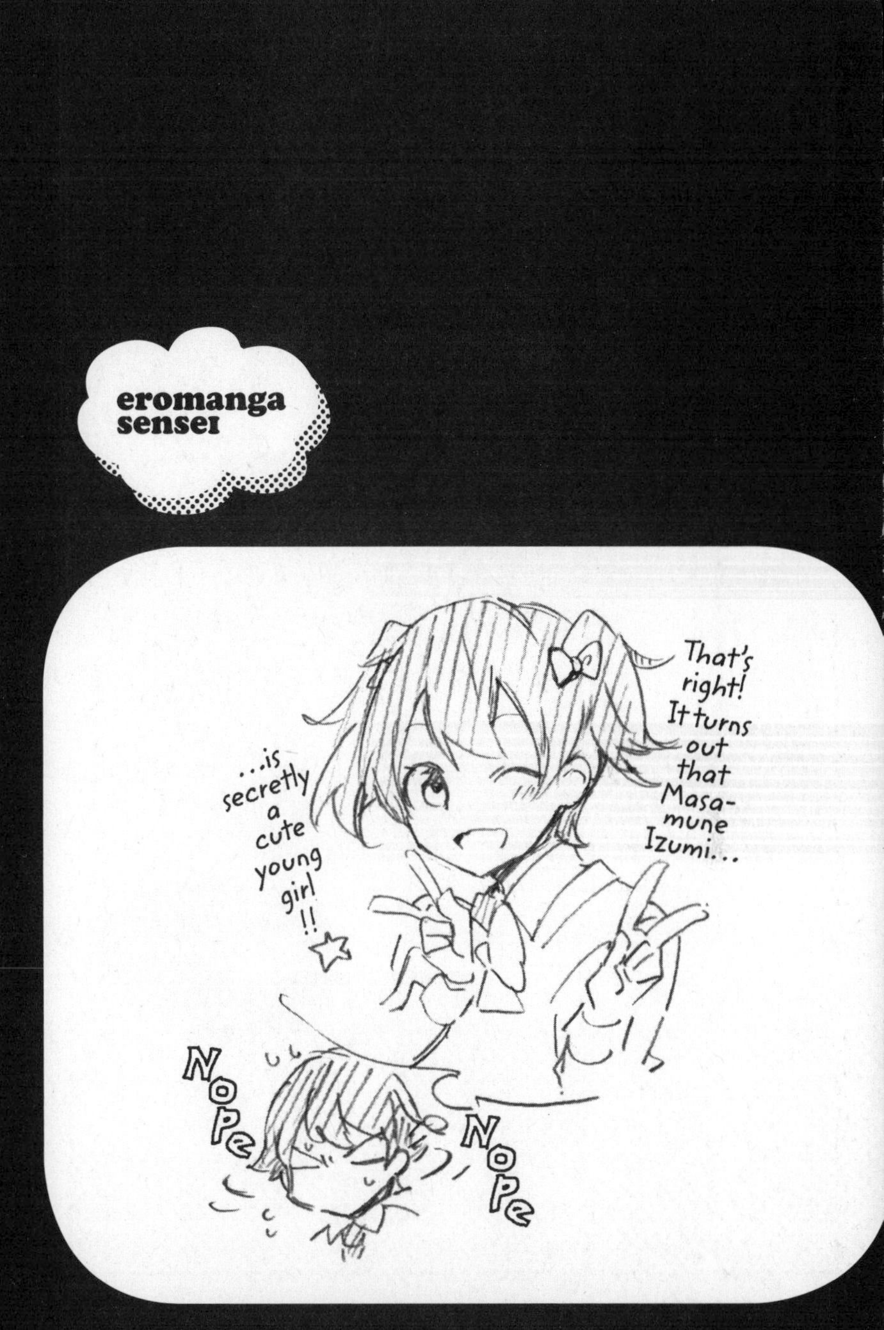
That's right! It turns out that Masa-mune Izumi...
...is secretly a cute young girl!!
Nope
Nope

eromanga
sensei

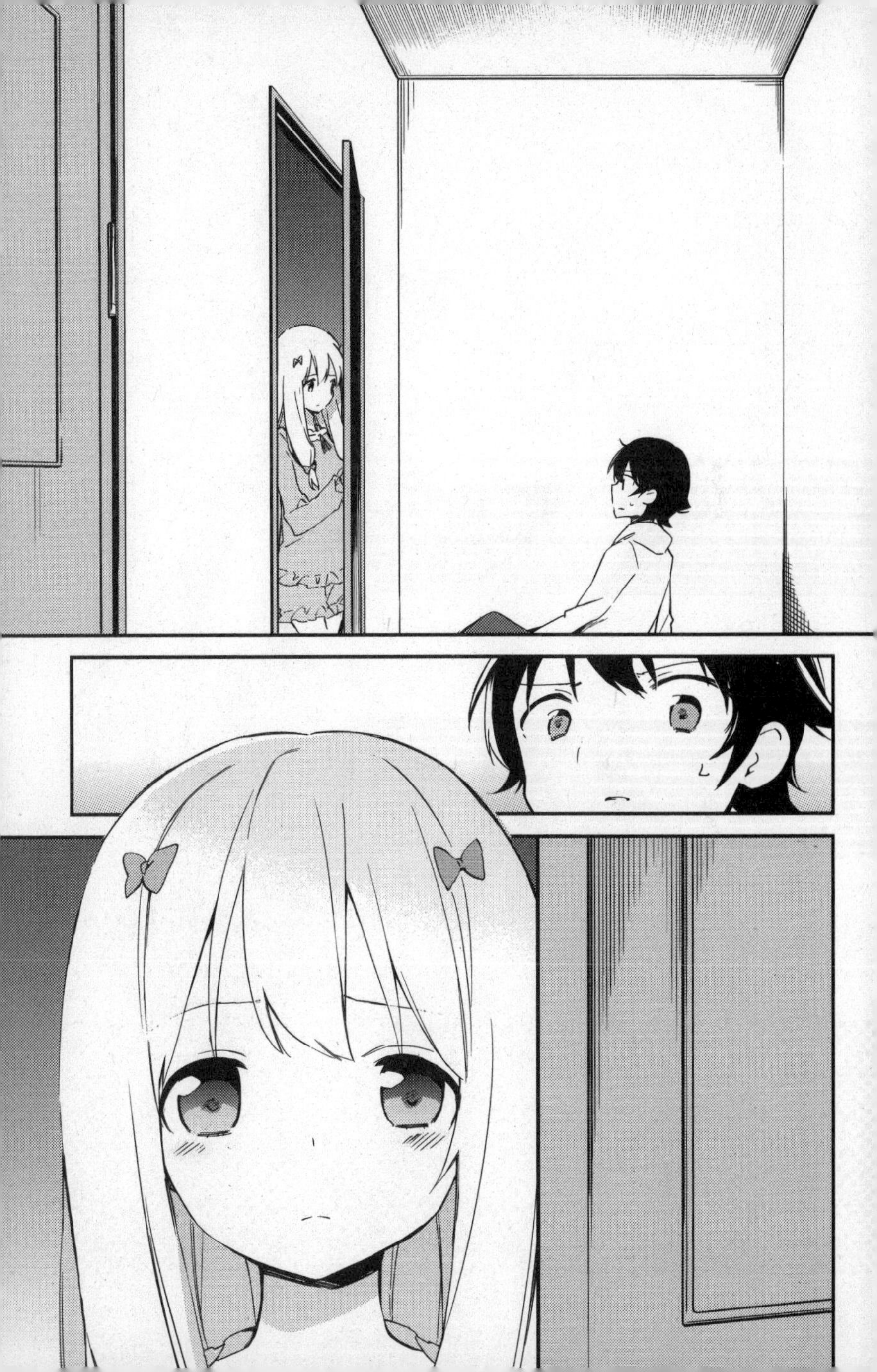

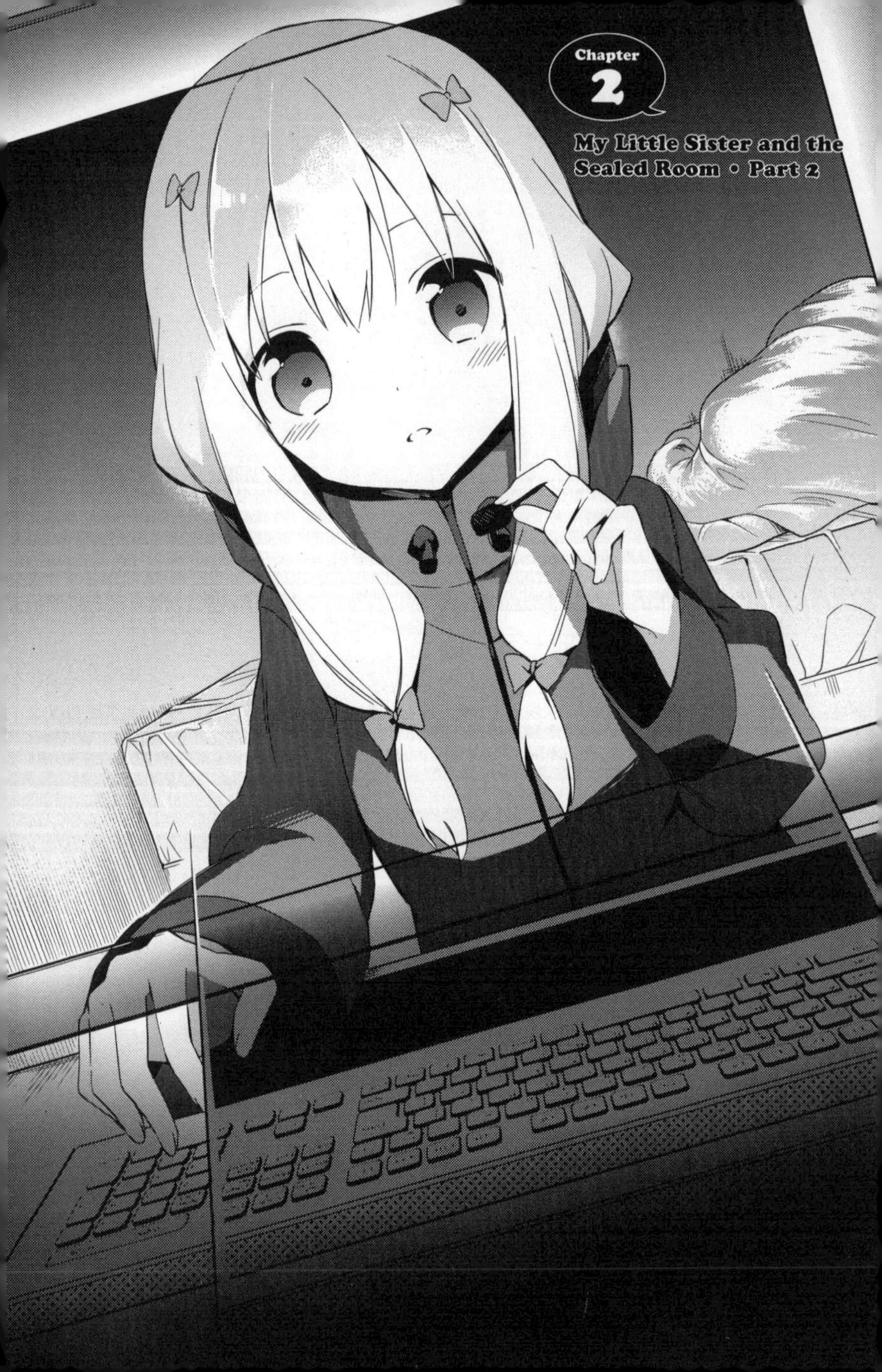
Chapter 2
My Little Sister and the Sealed Room • Part 2

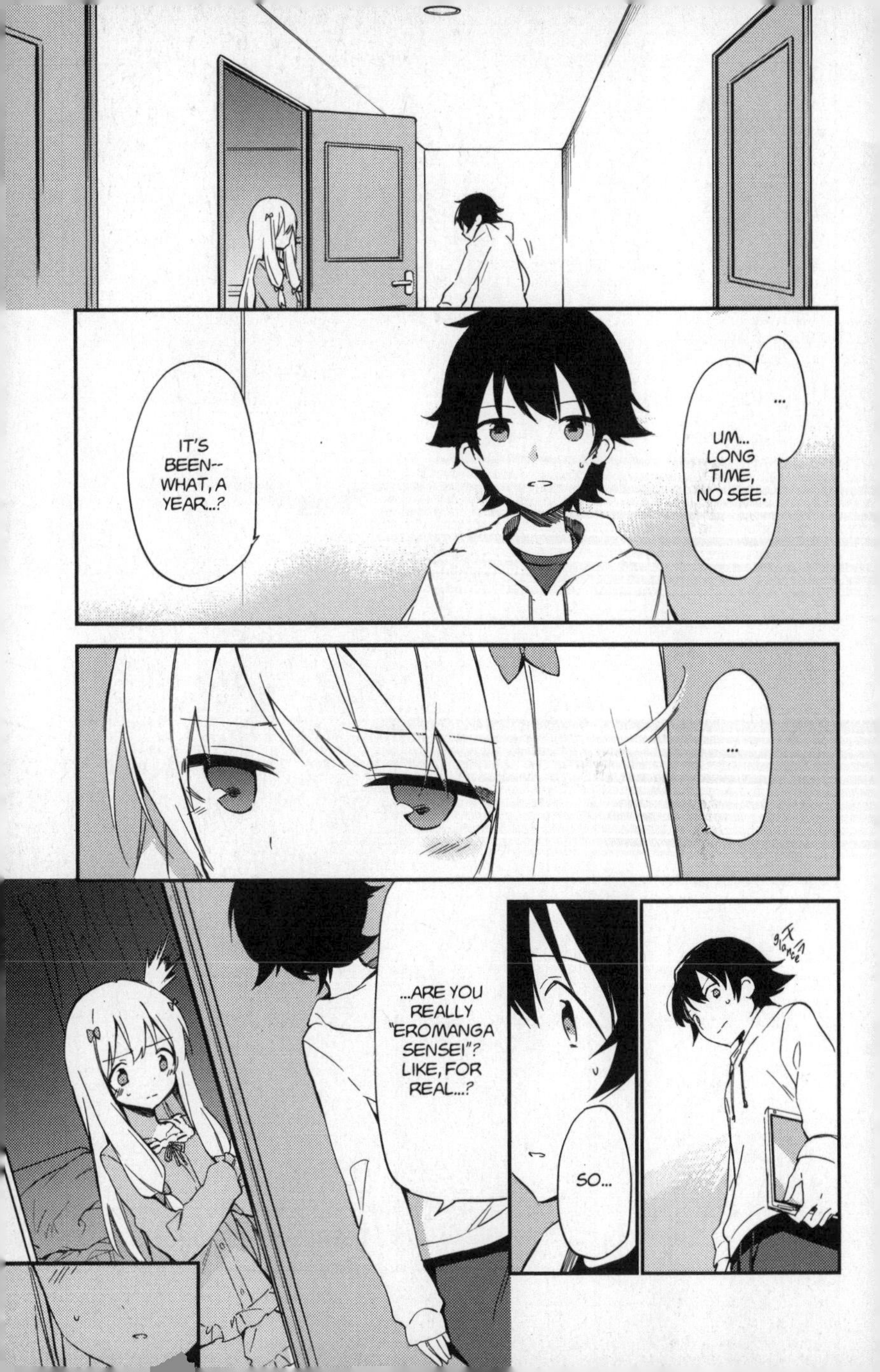
...
UM... LONG TIME, NO SEE.
IT'S BEEN-- WHAT, A YEAR...?
...
glance
SO...
...ARE YOU REALLY "EROMANGA SENSEI"? LIKE, FOR REAL...?

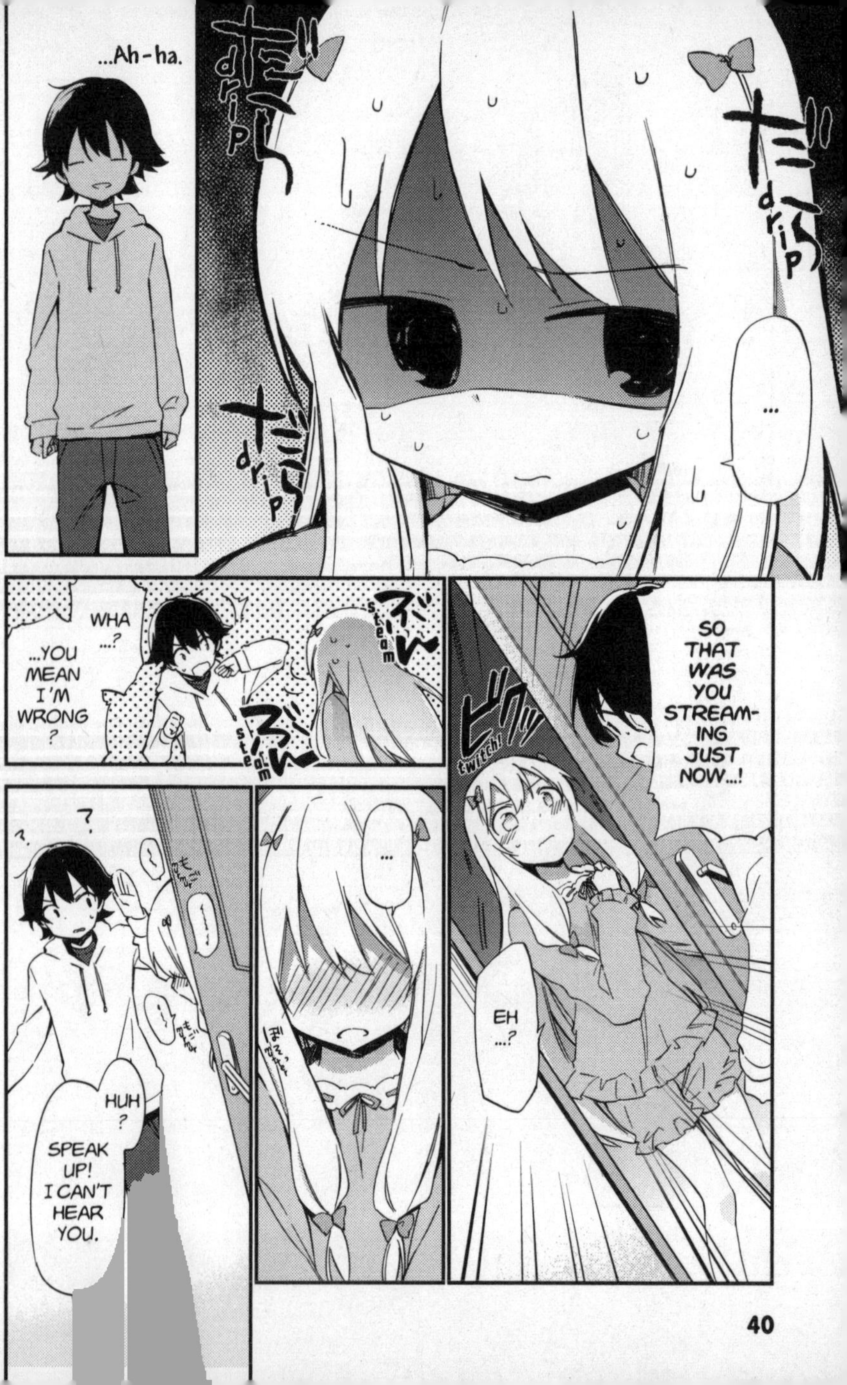
drip
drip
drip
...
...Ah-ha.
SO THAT WAS YOU STREAMING JUST NOW...!
twitch!
EH ...?
steam
steam
WHA ...?
...YOU MEAN I'M WRONG?
...
HUH?
SPEAK UP! I CAN'T HEAR YOU.

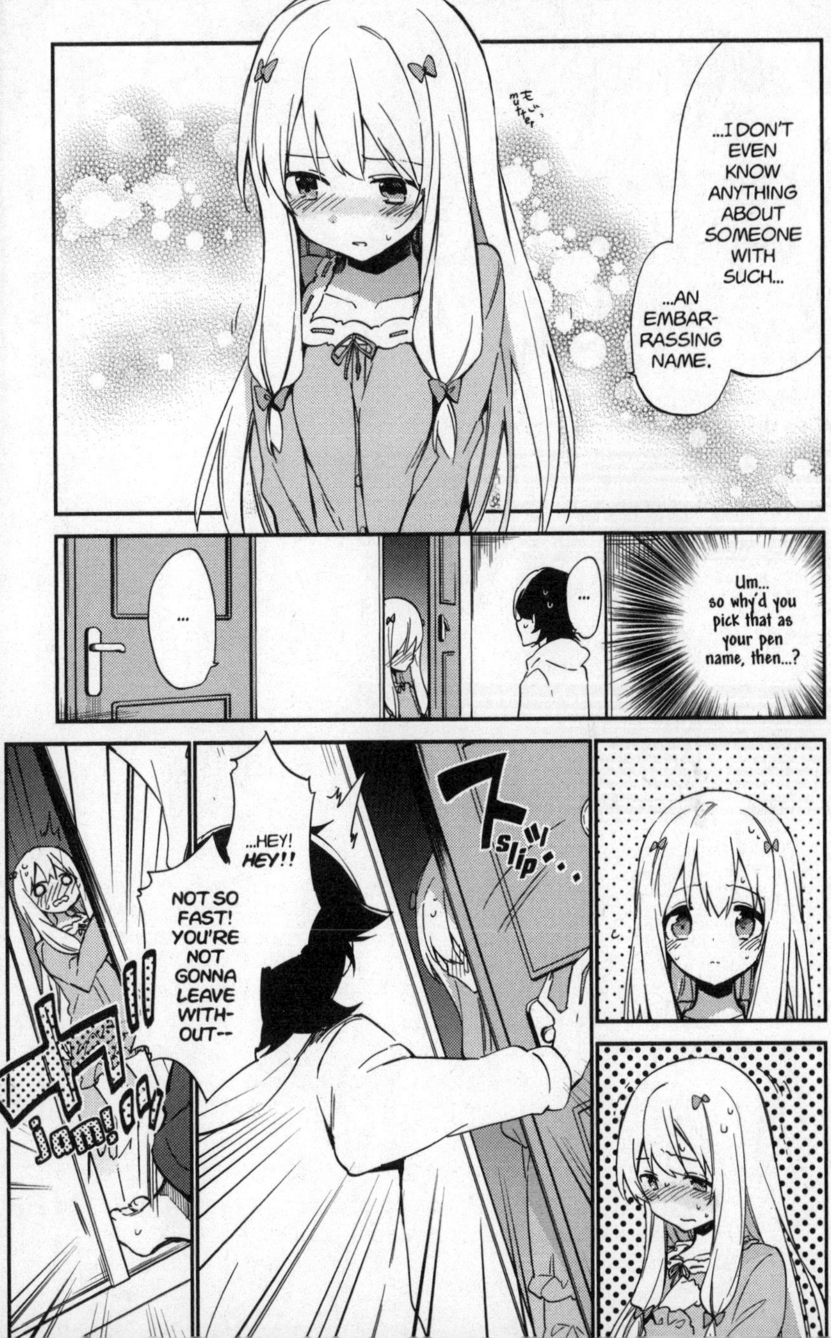
mutter
...I DON'T EVEN KNOW ANYTHING ABOUT SOMEONE WITH SUCH...
...AN EMBARRASSING NAME.
Um... so why'd you pick that as your pen name, then...?
...
...
slip...
...HEY! HEY!!
NOT SO FAST! YOU'RE NOT GONNA LEAVE WITHOUT--
jam!!

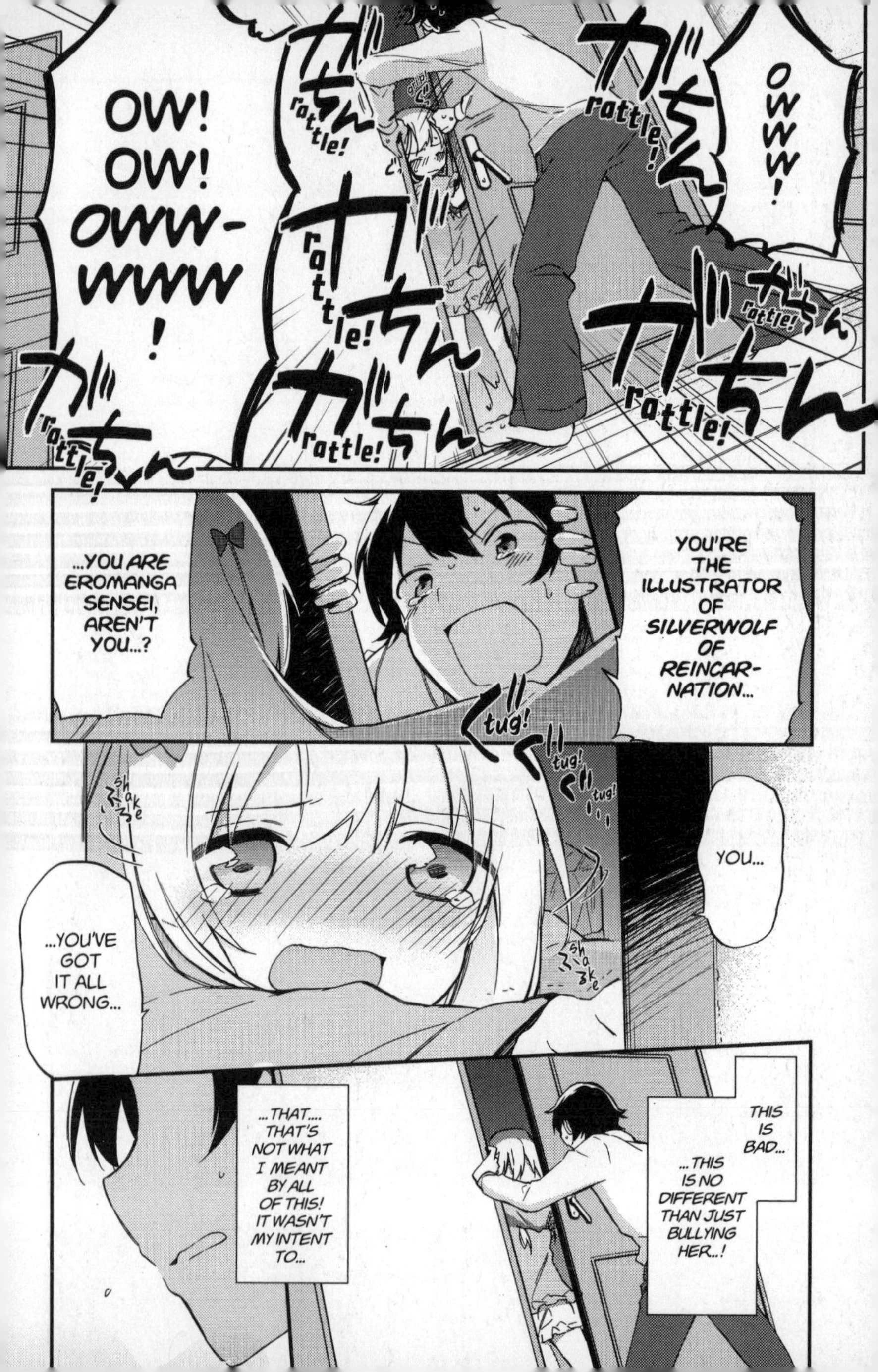
OWWW!
がちん rattle!
がちん rattle!
がちん rattle!
がちん rattle!
がちん rattle!
grip
OW! OW! OWW-WWW!
がちん rattle!
YOU'RE THE ILLUSTRATOR OF SILVERWOLF OF REINCARNATION...
くい tug!
...YOU ARE EROMANGA SENSEI, AREN'T YOU...?
くい tug!
くい tug!
YOU...
shake
shake
...YOU'VE GOT IT ALL WRONG...
THIS IS BAD...
...THIS IS NO DIFFERENT THAN JUST BULLYING HER...!
...THAT.... THAT'S NOT WHAT I MEANT BY ALL OF THIS! IT WASN'T MY INTENT TO...

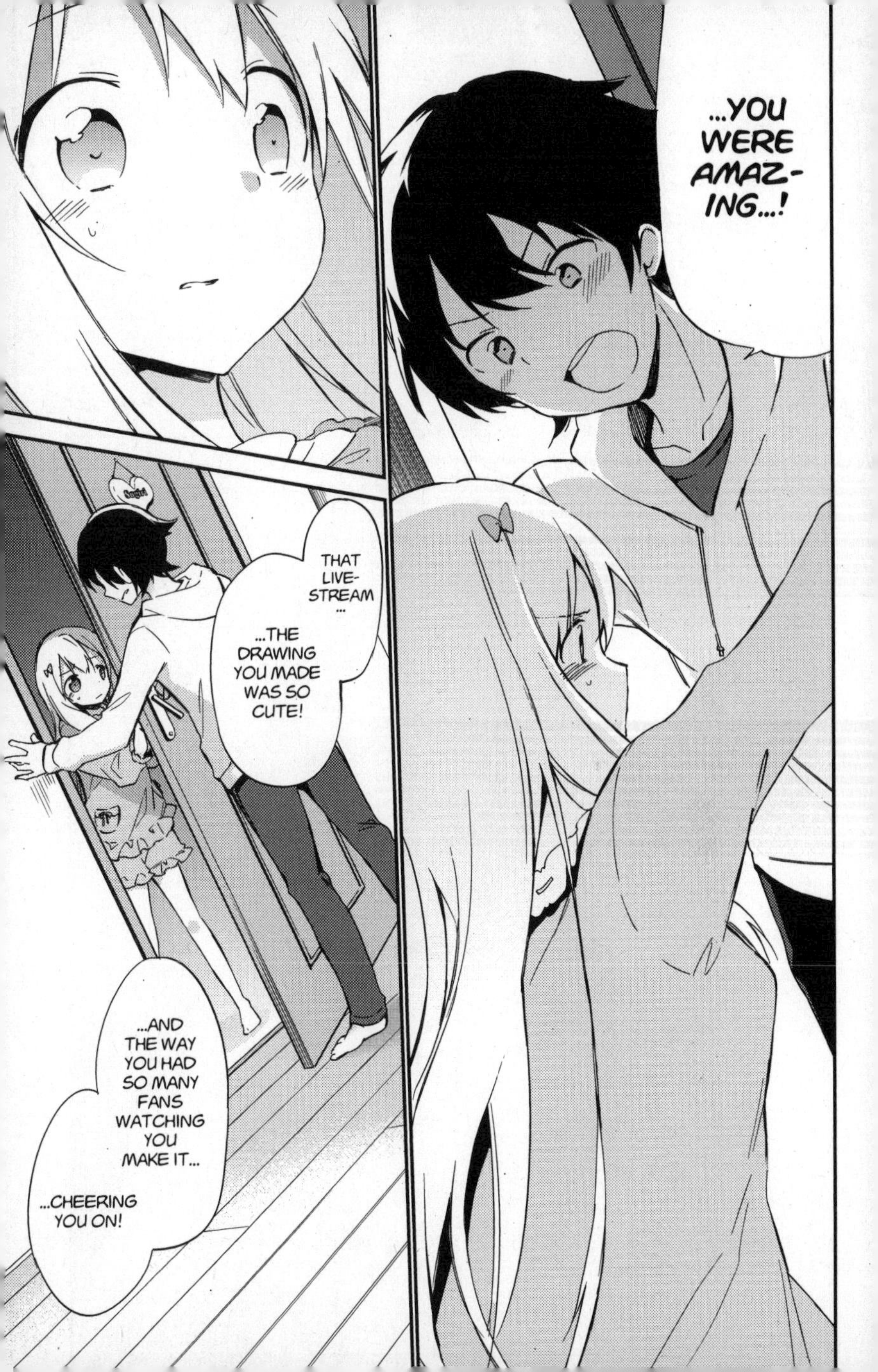
...YOU WERE AMAZ-ING...!
THAT LIVE-STREAM...
...THE DRAWING YOU MADE WAS SO CUTE!
...AND THE WAY YOU HAD SO MANY FANS WATCHING YOU MAKE IT...
...CHEERING YOU ON!

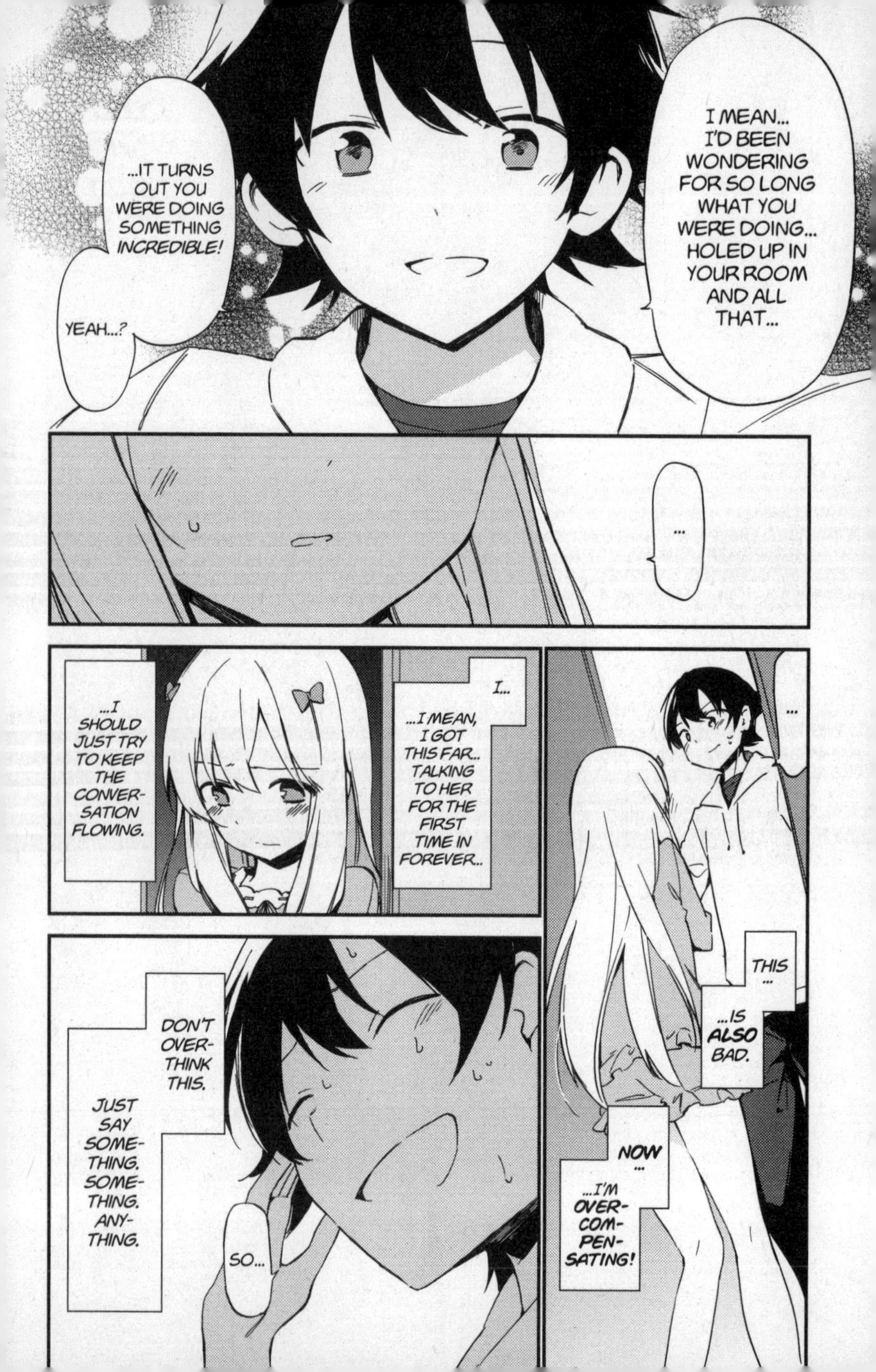
I MEAN... I'D BEEN WONDERING FOR SO LONG WHAT YOU WERE DOING... HOLED UP IN YOUR ROOM AND ALL THAT...
...IT TURNS OUT YOU WERE DOING SOMETHING INCREDIBLE!
YEAH...?
...
...
THIS ...
...IS ALSO BAD.
NOW ...
...I'M OVERCOMPENSATING!
I...
...I MEAN, I GOT THIS FAR.. TALKING TO HER FOR THE FIRST TIME IN FOREVER..
...I SHOULD JUST TRY TO KEEP THE CONVERSATION FLOWING.
DON'T OVERTHINK THIS.
JUST SAY SOMETHING. SOMETHING. ANYTHING.
SO...

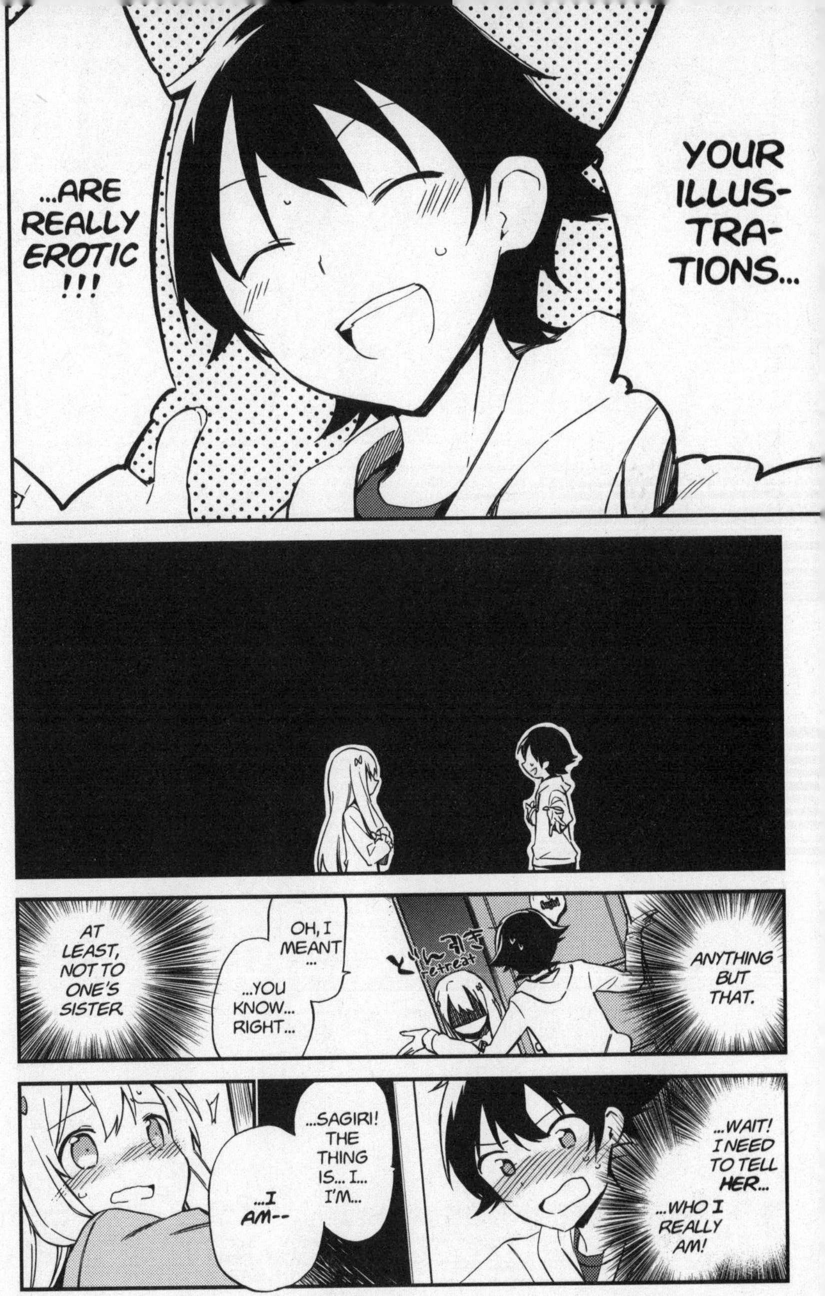
YOUR ILLUSTRATIONS...
...ARE REALLY EROTIC!!!
ANYTHING BUT THAT.
retreat
OH, I MEANT...
...YOU KNOW... RIGHT...
AT LEAST, NOT TO ONE'S SISTER.
...WAIT! I NEED TO TELL HER...
...WHO I REALLY AM!
...SAGIRI! THE THING IS... I... I'M...
...I AM--

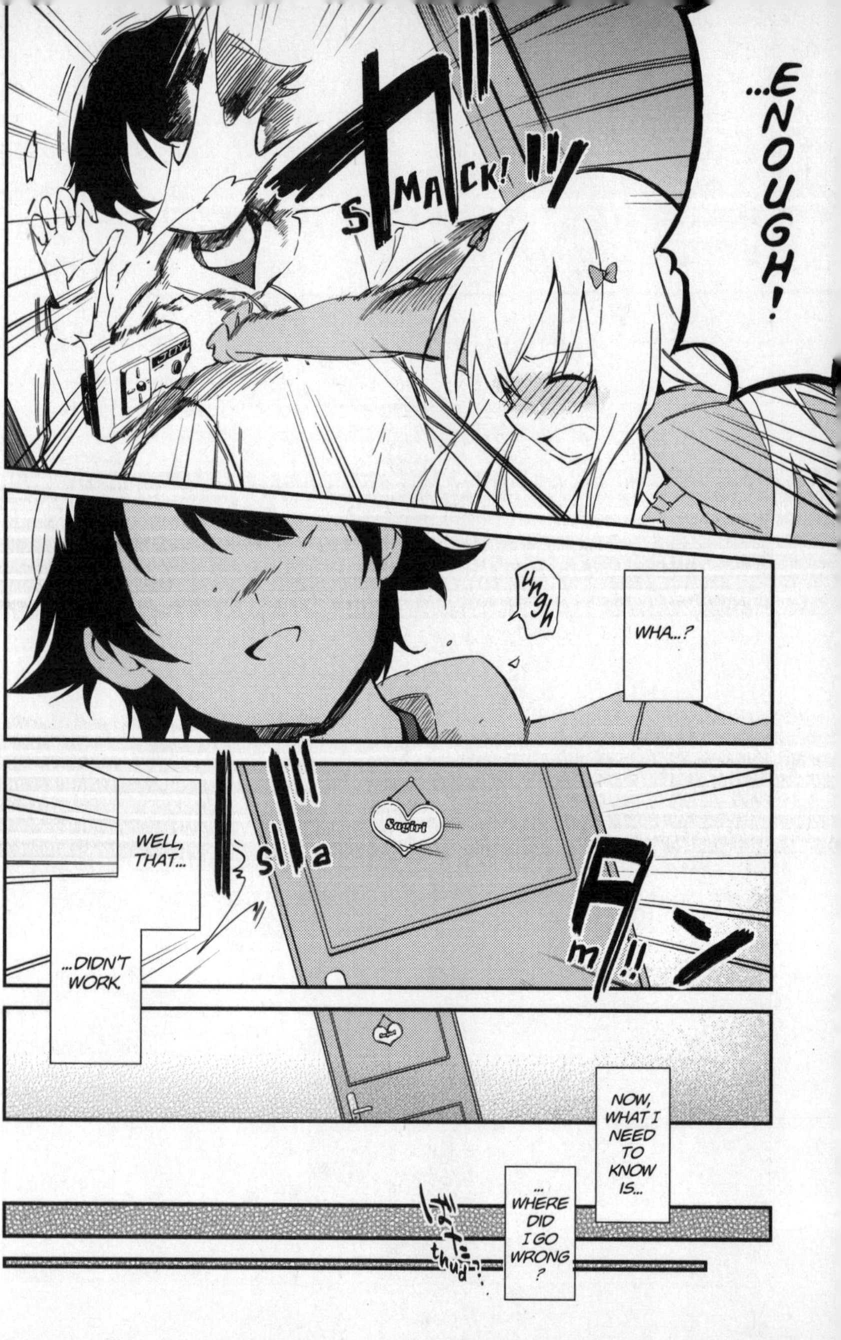
...ENOUGH!
SMACK!
WHA...?
ungh
m!!
sla
Sagiri
WELL, THAT...
...DIDN'T WORK.
NOW, WHAT I NEED TO KNOW IS...
...WHERE DID I GO WRONG?
thud...

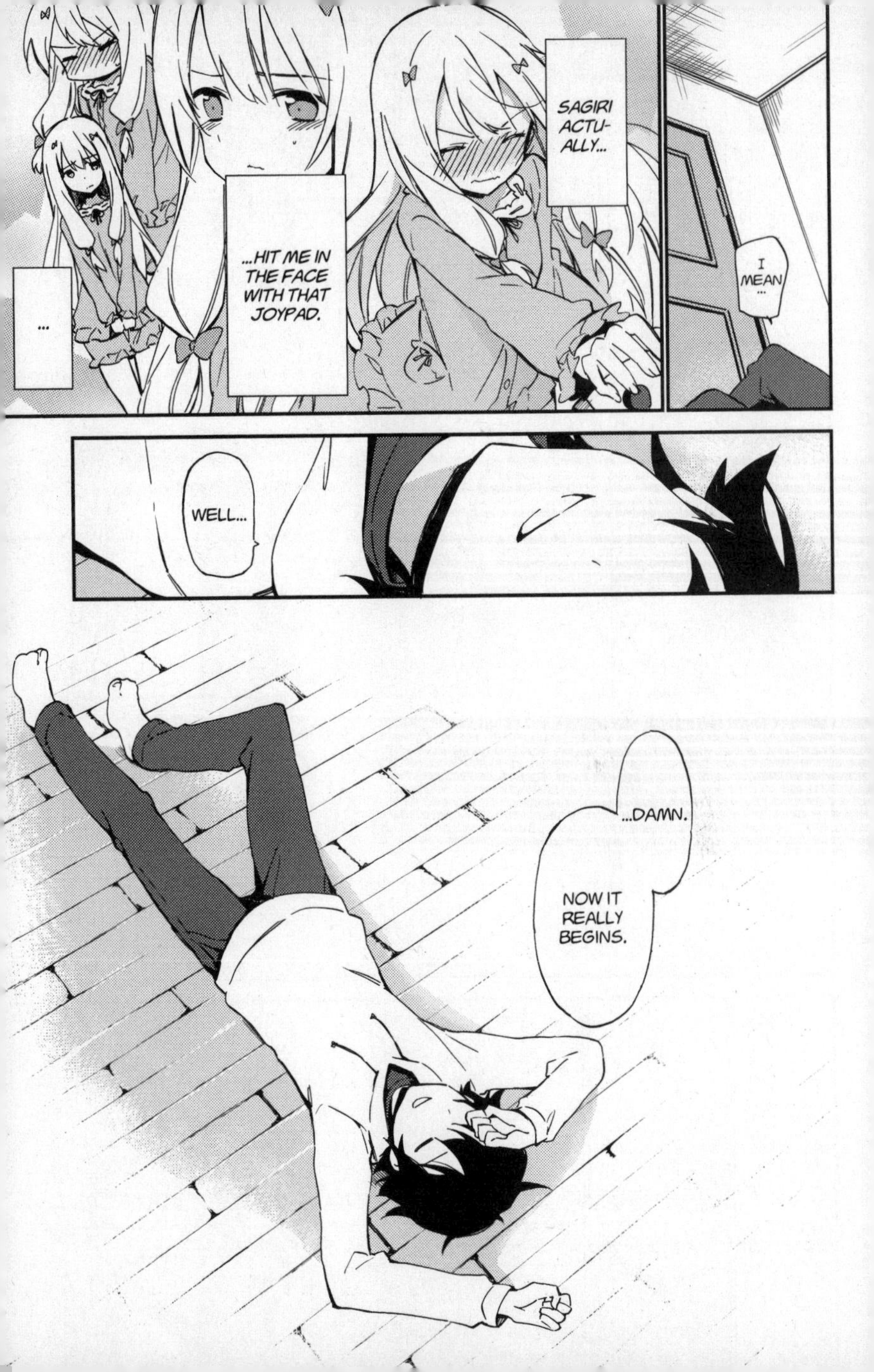
I MEAN ...
SAGIRI ACTU-ALLY...
...HIT ME IN THE FACE WITH THAT JOYPAD.
...
WELL...
...DAMN.
NOW IT REALLY BEGINS.

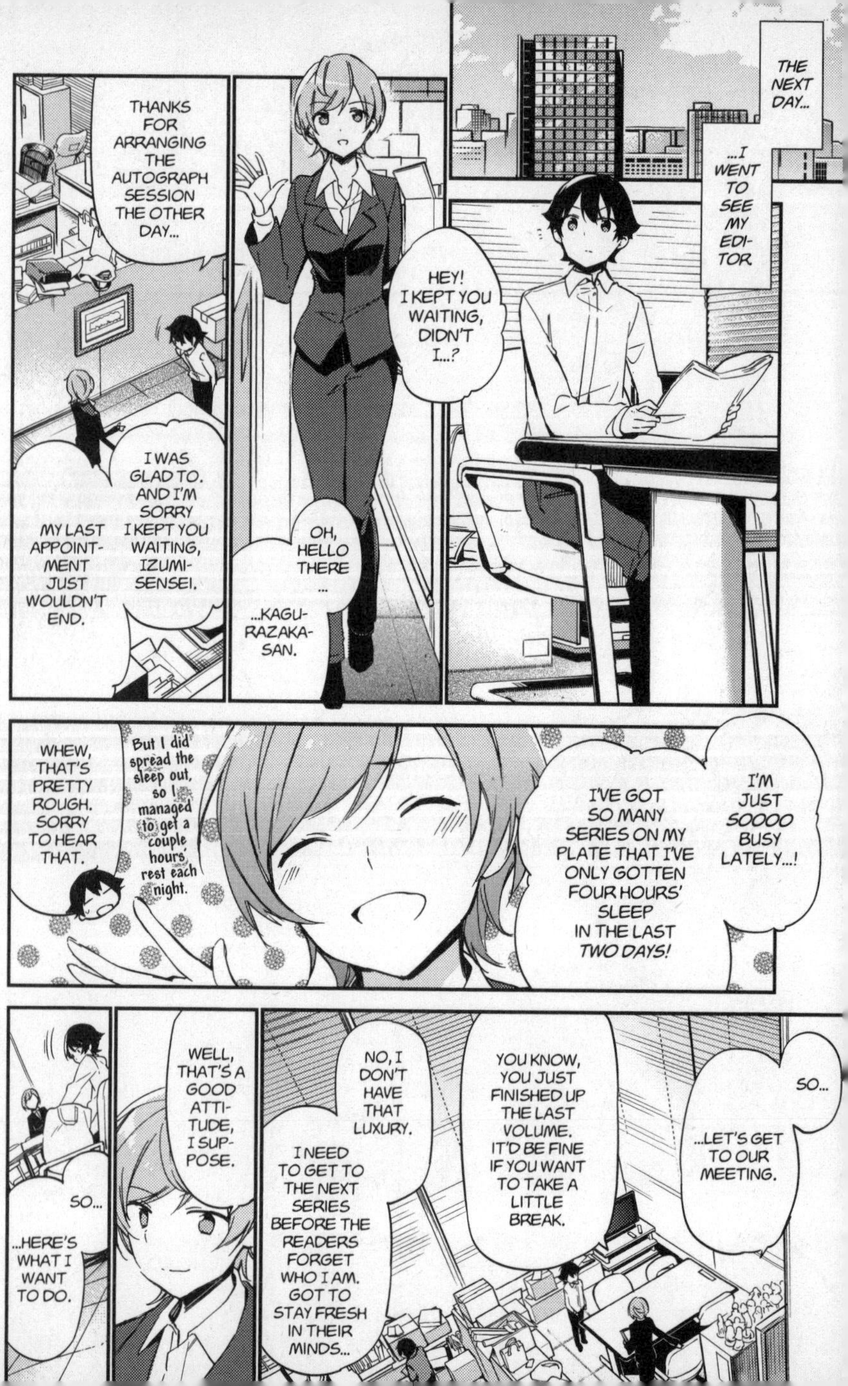
THE NEXT DAY...
...I WENT TO SEE MY EDITOR.
HEY! I KEPT YOU WAITING, DIDN'T I...?
OH, HELLO THERE ...
...KAGURAZAKA-SAN.
THANKS FOR ARRANGING THE AUTOGRAPH SESSION THE OTHER DAY...
I WAS GLAD TO. AND I'M SORRY I KEPT YOU WAITING, IZUMI-SENSEI.
MY LAST APPOINTMENT JUST WOULDN'T END.
I'M JUST SOOOO BUSY LATELY...!
I'VE GOT SO MANY SERIES ON MY PLATE THAT I'VE ONLY GOTTEN FOUR HOURS' SLEEP IN THE LAST TWO DAYS!
WHEW, THAT'S PRETTY ROUGH. SORRY TO HEAR THAT.
But I did spread the sleep out, so I managed to get a couple hours' rest each night.
SO...
...LET'S GET TO OUR MEETING.
YOU KNOW, YOU JUST FINISHED UP THE LAST VOLUME. IT'D BE FINE IF YOU WANT TO TAKE A LITTLE BREAK.
NO, I DON'T HAVE THAT LUXURY.
I NEED TO GET TO THE NEXT SERIES BEFORE THE READERS FORGET WHO I AM. GOT TO STAY FRESH IN THEIR MINDS...
WELL, THAT'S A GOOD ATTITUDE, I SUPPOSE.
SO...
...HERE'S WHAT I WANT TO DO.

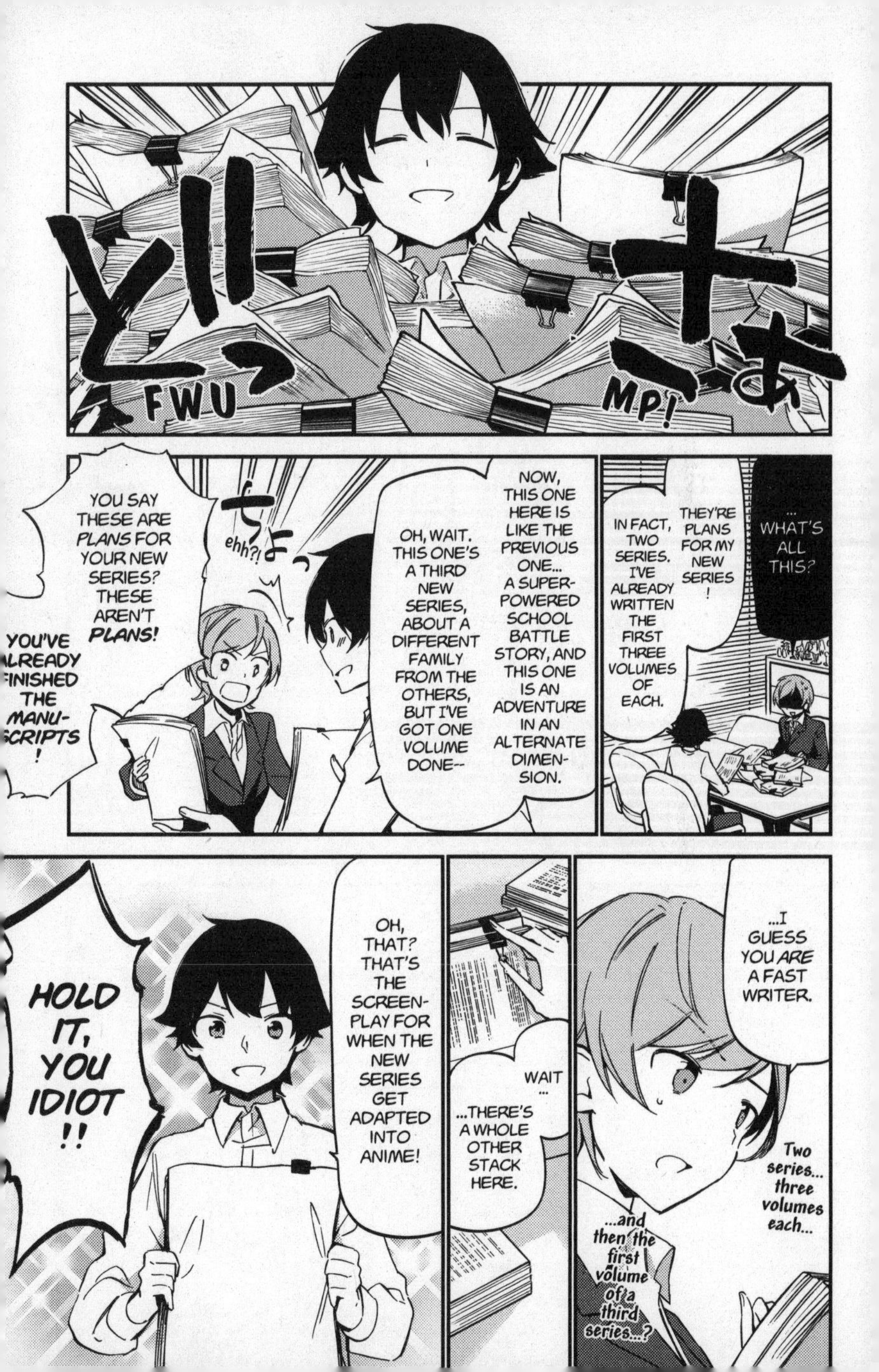
FWU MP!
...WHAT'S ALL THIS?
THEY'RE PLANS FOR MY NEW SERIES!
IN FACT, TWO SERIES. I'VE ALREADY WRITTEN THE FIRST THREE VOLUMES OF EACH.
NOW, THIS ONE HERE IS LIKE THE PREVIOUS ONE... A SUPER-POWERED SCHOOL BATTLE STORY, AND THIS ONE IS AN ADVENTURE IN AN ALTERNATE DIMENSION.
OH, WAIT. THIS ONE'S A THIRD NEW SERIES, ABOUT A DIFFERENT FAMILY FROM THE OTHERS, BUT I'VE GOT ONE VOLUME DONE--
ehh?!
YOU SAY THESE ARE PLANS FOR YOUR NEW SERIES? THESE AREN'T PLANS!
YOU'VE ALREADY FINISHED THE MANUSCRIPTS!
...I GUESS YOU ARE A FAST WRITER.
Two series... three volumes each...
...and then the first volume of a third series...?
WAIT...
...THERE'S A WHOLE OTHER STACK HERE.
OH, THAT? THAT'S THE SCREENPLAY FOR WHEN THE NEW SERIES GET ADAPTED INTO ANIME!
HOLD IT, YOU IDIOT!!

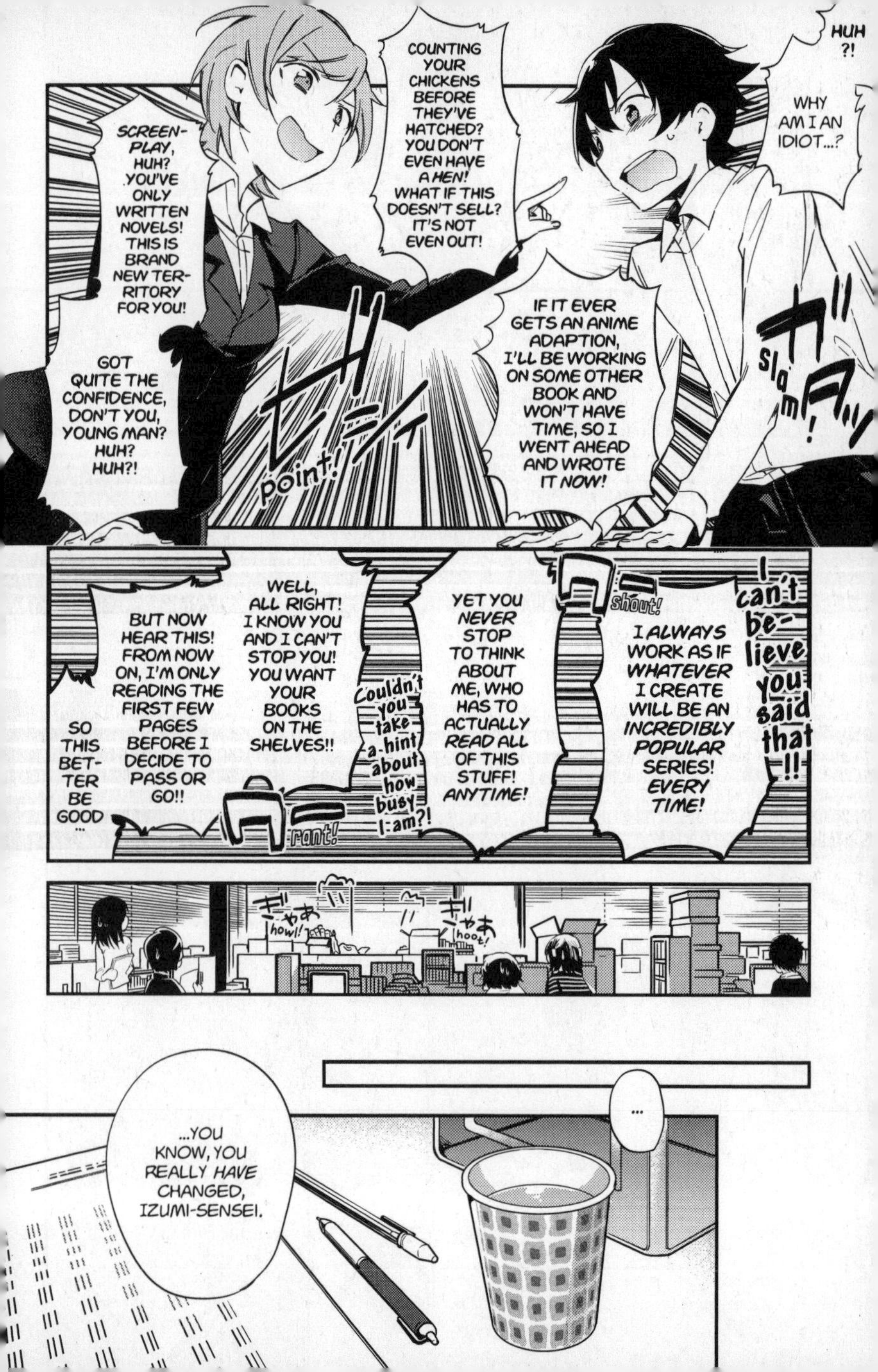
HUH ?!
WHY AM I AN IDIOT...?
COUNTING YOUR CHICKENS BEFORE THEY'VE HATCHED? YOU DON'T EVEN HAVE A HEN! WHAT IF THIS DOESN'T SELL? IT'S NOT EVEN OUT!
IF IT EVER GETS AN ANIME ADAPTION, I'LL BE WORKING ON SOME OTHER BOOK AND WON'T HAVE TIME, SO I WENT AHEAD AND WROTE IT NOW!
slam!
point!
SCREEN-PLAY, HUH? YOU'VE ONLY WRITTEN NOVELS! THIS IS BRAND NEW TER-RITORY FOR YOU!
GOT QUITE THE CONFIDENCE, DON'T YOU, YOUNG MAN? HUH? HUH?!
I can't be-lieve you said that!!
shout!
I ALWAYS WORK AS IF WHATEVER I CREATE WILL BE AN INCREDIBLY POPULAR SERIES! EVERY TIME!
YET YOU NEVER STOP TO THINK ABOUT ME, WHO HAS TO ACTUALLY READ ALL OF THIS STUFF! ANYTIME!
Couldn't you take a hint about how busy I am?!
rant!
WELL, ALL RIGHT! I KNOW YOU AND I CAN'T STOP YOU! YOU WANT YOUR BOOKS ON THE SHELVES!!
BUT NOW HEAR THIS! FROM NOW ON, I'M ONLY READING THE FIRST FEW PAGES BEFORE I DECIDE TO PASS OR GO!!
SO THIS BET-TER BE GOOD...
hoot!
howl!
...
...YOU KNOW, YOU REALLY HAVE CHANGED, IZUMI-SENSEI.

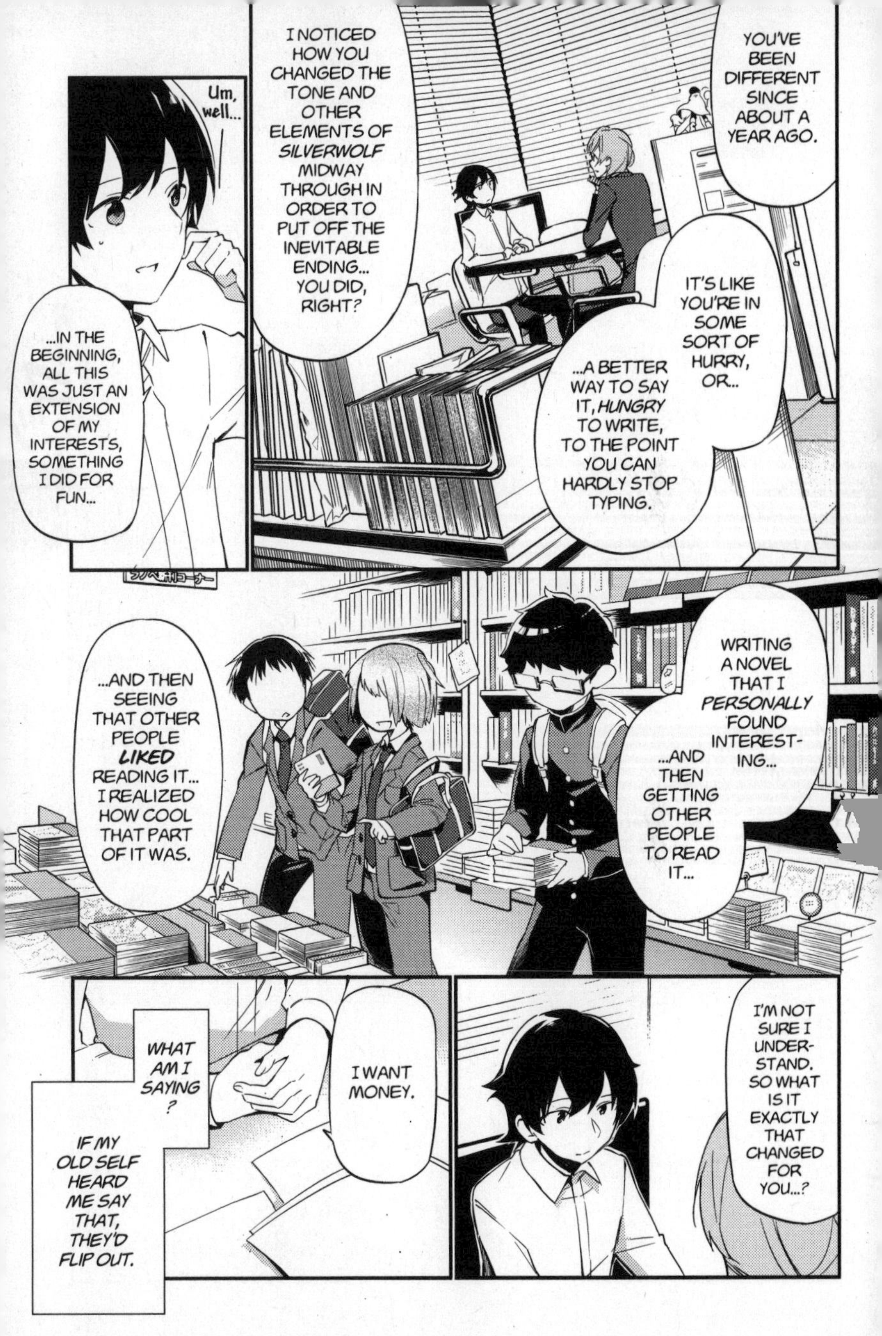
YOU'VE BEEN DIFFERENT SINCE ABOUT A YEAR AGO.
IT'S LIKE YOU'RE IN SOME SORT OF HURRY, OR...
...A BETTER WAY TO SAY IT, *HUNGRY* TO WRITE, TO THE POINT YOU CAN HARDLY STOP TYPING.
I NOTICED HOW YOU CHANGED THE TONE AND OTHER ELEMENTS OF *SILVERWOLF* MIDWAY THROUGH IN ORDER TO PUT OFF THE INEVITABLE ENDING... YOU DID, RIGHT?
Um, well...
...IN THE BEGINNING, ALL THIS WAS JUST AN EXTENSION OF MY INTERESTS, SOMETHING I DID FOR FUN...
WRITING A NOVEL THAT I *PERSONALLY* FOUND INTEREST-ING...
...AND THEN GETTING OTHER PEOPLE TO READ IT...
...AND THEN SEEING THAT OTHER PEOPLE **LIKED** READING IT... I REALIZED HOW COOL THAT PART OF IT WAS.
I'M NOT SURE I UNDER-STAND. SO WHAT IS IT EXACTLY THAT CHANGED FOR YOU...?
I WANT MONEY.
WHAT AM I SAYING?
IF MY OLD SELF HEARD ME SAY THAT, THEY'D FLIP OUT.

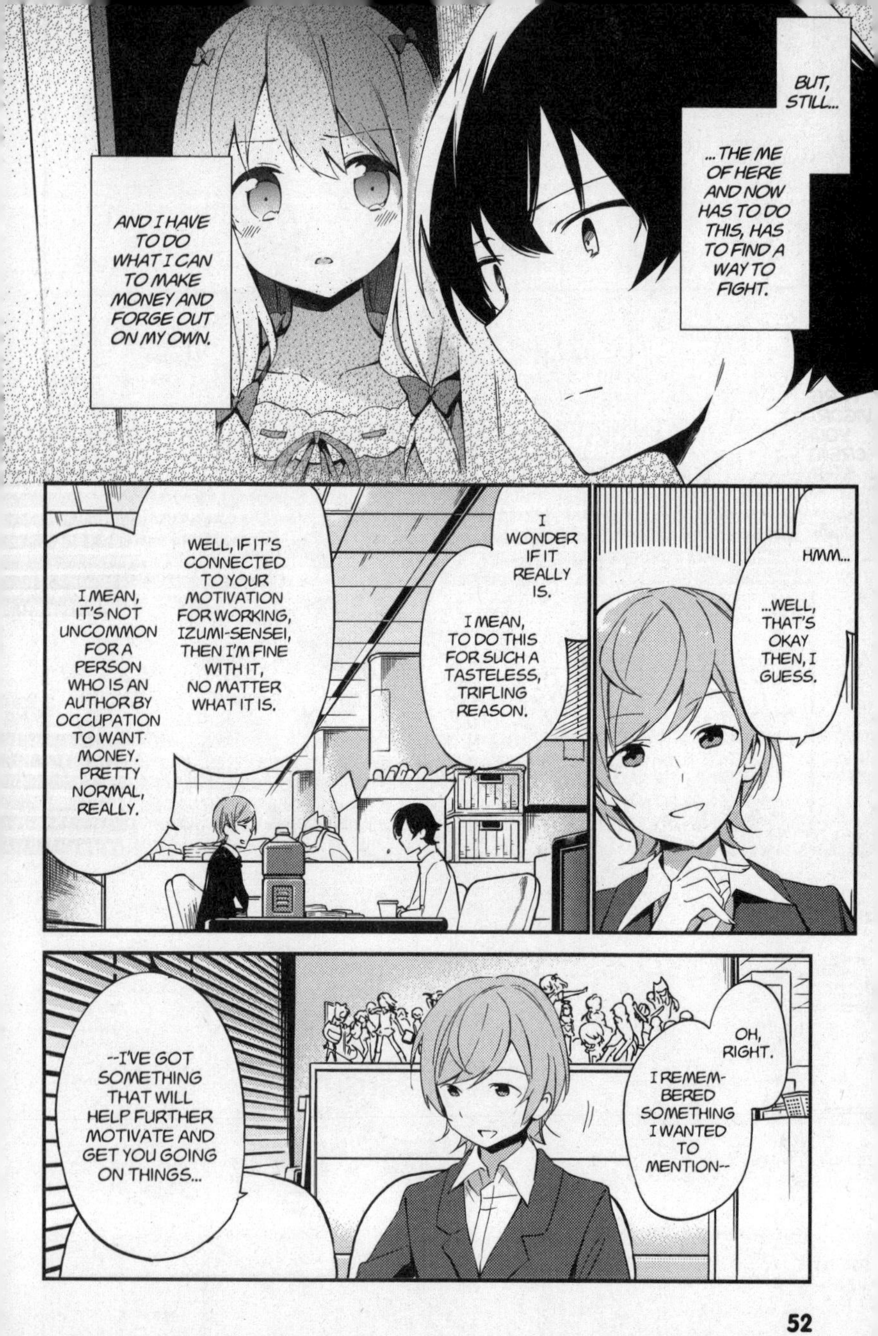
BUT, STILL...
...THE ME OF HERE AND NOW HAS TO DO THIS, HAS TO FIND A WAY TO FIGHT.
AND I HAVE TO DO WHAT I CAN TO MAKE MONEY AND FORGE OUT ON MY OWN.
HMM...
...WELL, THAT'S OKAY THEN, I GUESS.
I WONDER IF IT REALLY IS.
I MEAN, TO DO THIS FOR SUCH A TASTELESS, TRIFLING REASON.
WELL, IF IT'S CONNECTED TO YOUR MOTIVATION FOR WORKING, IZUMI-SENSEI, THEN I'M FINE WITH IT, NO MATTER WHAT IT IS.
I MEAN, IT'S NOT UNCOMMON FOR A PERSON WHO IS AN AUTHOR BY OCCUPATION TO WANT MONEY. PRETTY NORMAL, REALLY.
OH, RIGHT.
I REMEMBERED SOMETHING I WANTED TO MENTION--
--I'VE GOT SOMETHING THAT WILL HELP FURTHER MOTIVATE AND GET YOU GOING ON THINGS...

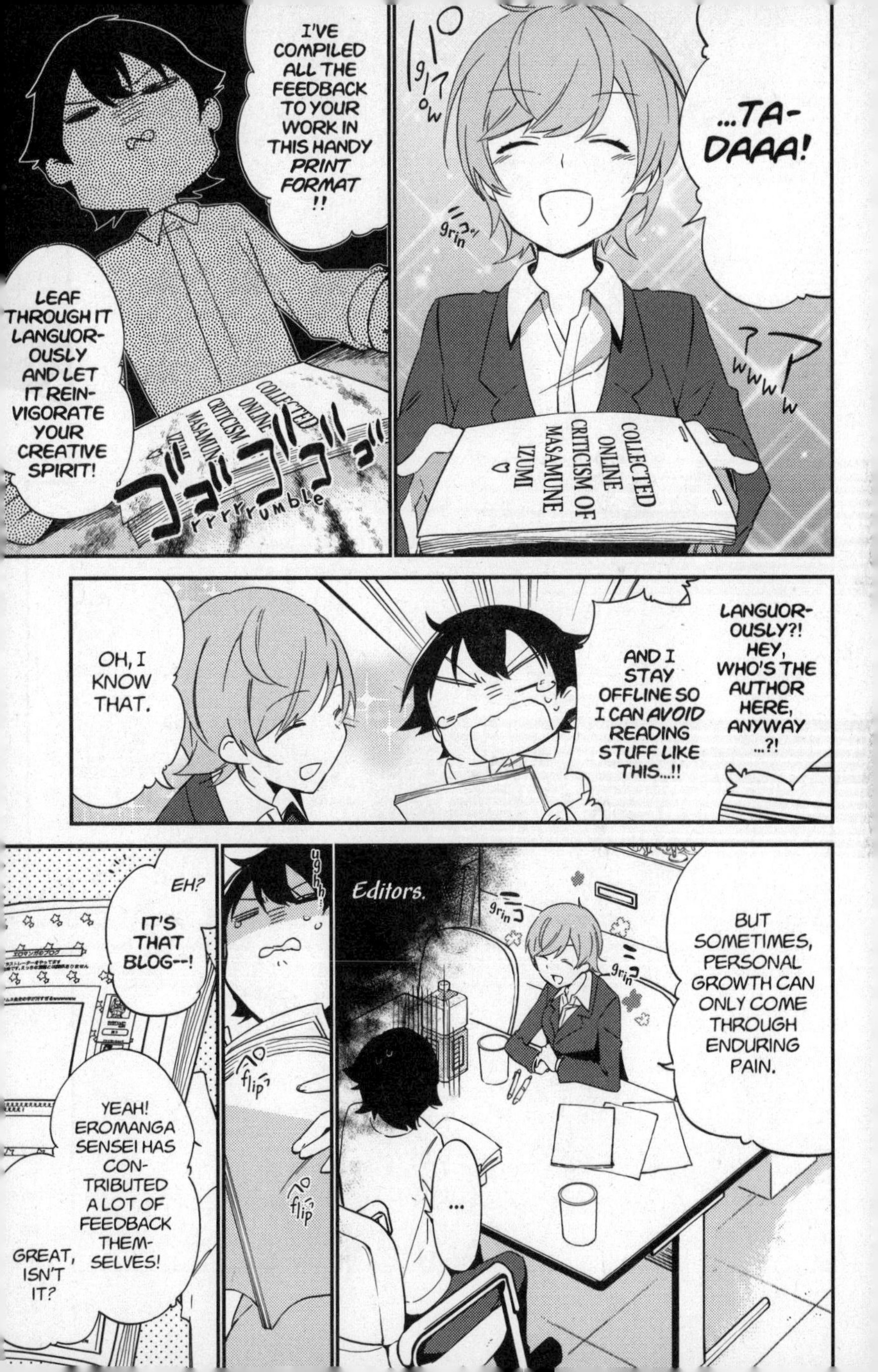

...TA-DAAA!
grin
COLLECTED ONLINE CRITICISM OF MASAMUNE IZUMI
wwww
glow
I'VE COMPILED ALL THE FEEDBACK TO YOUR WORK IN THIS HANDY PRINT FORMAT!!
LEAF THROUGH IT LANGUOROUSLY AND LET IT REINVIGORATE YOUR CREATIVE SPIRIT!
rrrrrumble
LANGUOROUSLY?! HEY, WHO'S THE AUTHOR HERE, ANYWAY...?!
AND I STAY OFFLINE SO I CAN AVOID READING STUFF LIKE THIS...!!
OH, I KNOW THAT.
BUT SOMETIMES, PERSONAL GROWTH CAN ONLY COME THROUGH ENDURING PAIN.
grin
grin
...
Editors.
ughh...
flip
flip
EH?
IT'S THAT BLOG--!
YEAH! EROMANGA SENSEI HAS CONTRIBUTED A LOT OF FEEDBACK THEMSELVES!
GREAT, ISN'T IT?

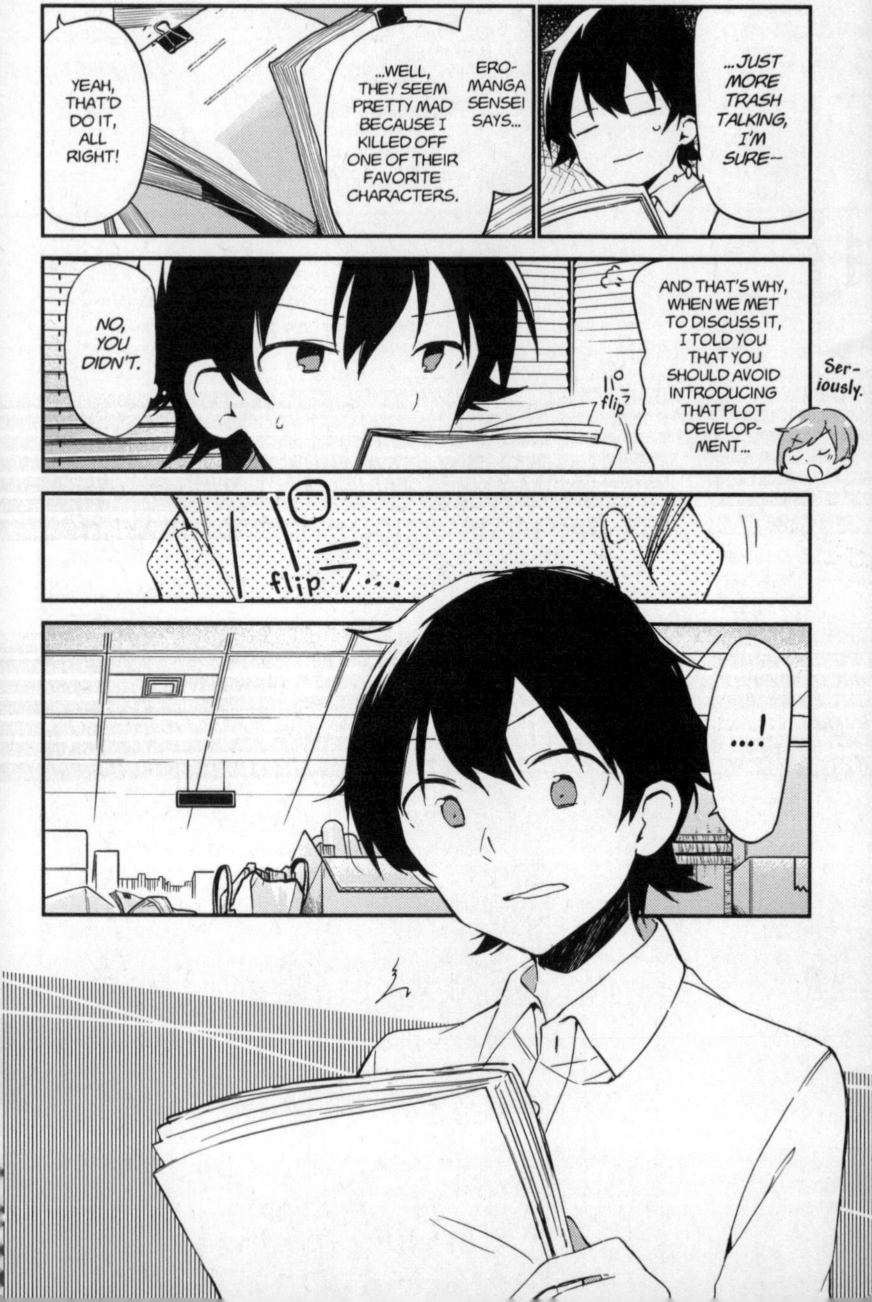
...JUST MORE TRASH TALKING, I'M SURE--
ERO-MANGA SENSEI SAYS...
...WELL, THEY SEEM PRETTY MAD BECAUSE I KILLED OFF ONE OF THEIR FAVORITE CHARACTERS.
YEAH, THAT'D DO IT, ALL RIGHT!
Ser-iously.
AND THAT'S WHY, WHEN WE MET TO DISCUSS IT, I TOLD YOU THAT YOU SHOULD AVOID INTRODUCING THAT PLOT DEVELOPMENT...
flip
NO, YOU DIDN'T.
flip...
...!

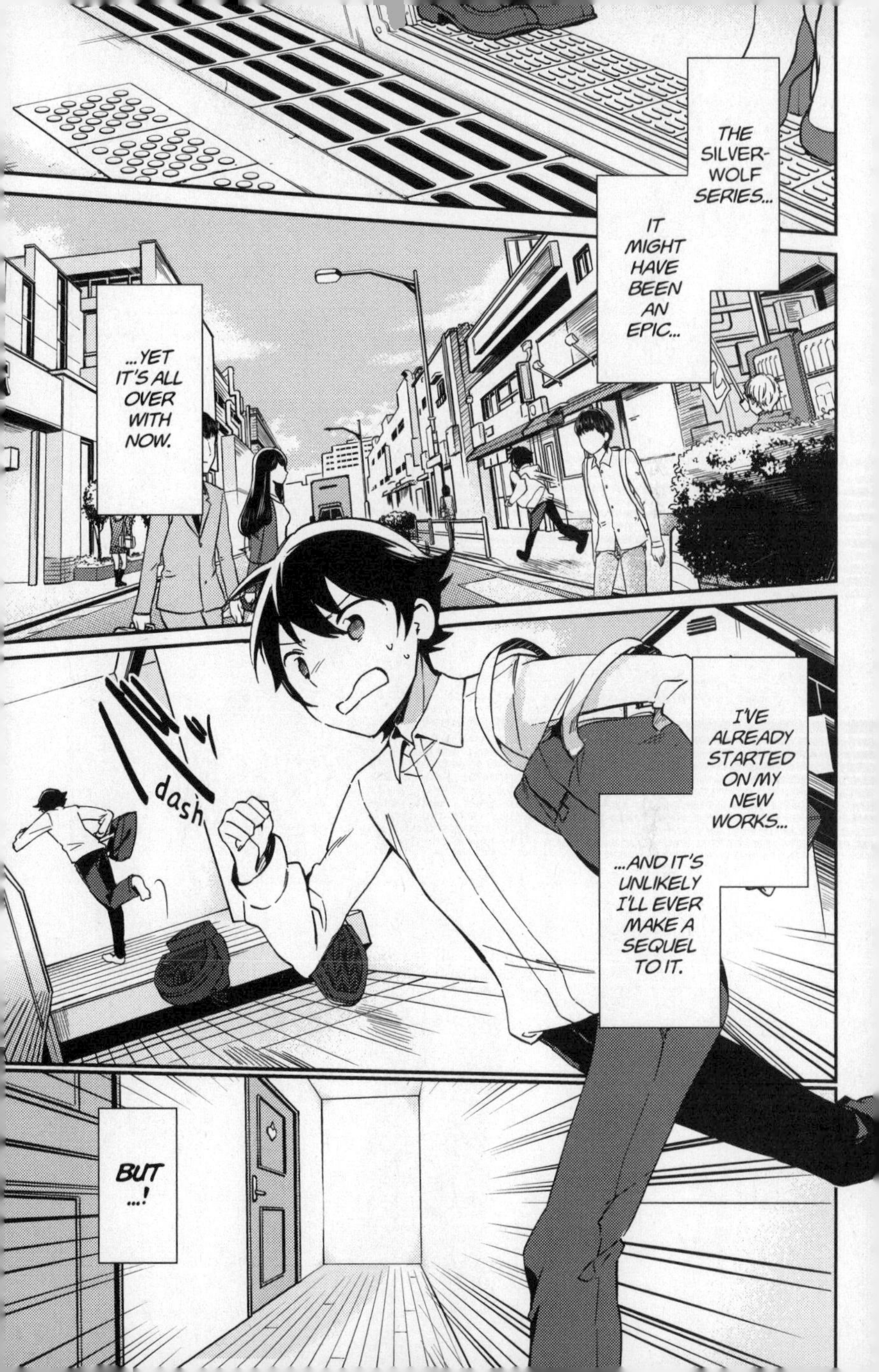
THE SILVER-WOLF SERIES...
IT MIGHT HAVE BEEN AN EPIC...
...YET IT'S ALL OVER WITH NOW.
I'VE ALREADY STARTED ON MY NEW WORKS...
...AND IT'S UNLIKELY I'LL EVER MAKE A SEQUEL TO IT.
dash
BUT ...!

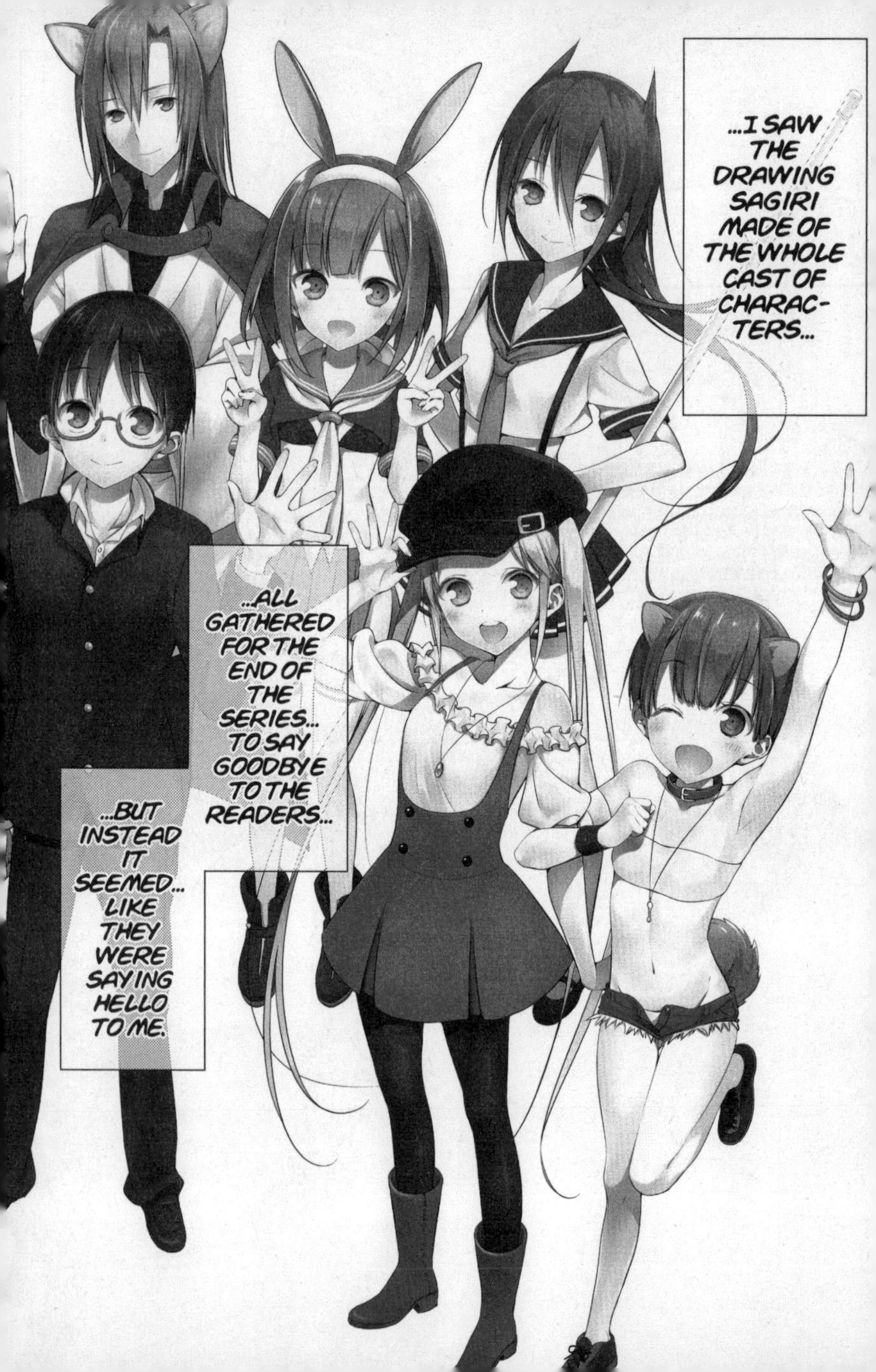
...I SAW THE DRAWING SAGIRI MADE OF THE WHOLE CAST OF CHARACTERS...
...ALL GATHERED FOR THE END OF THE SERIES... TO SAY GOODBYE TO THE READERS...
...BUT INSTEAD IT SEEMED... LIKE THEY WERE SAYING HELLO TO ME.

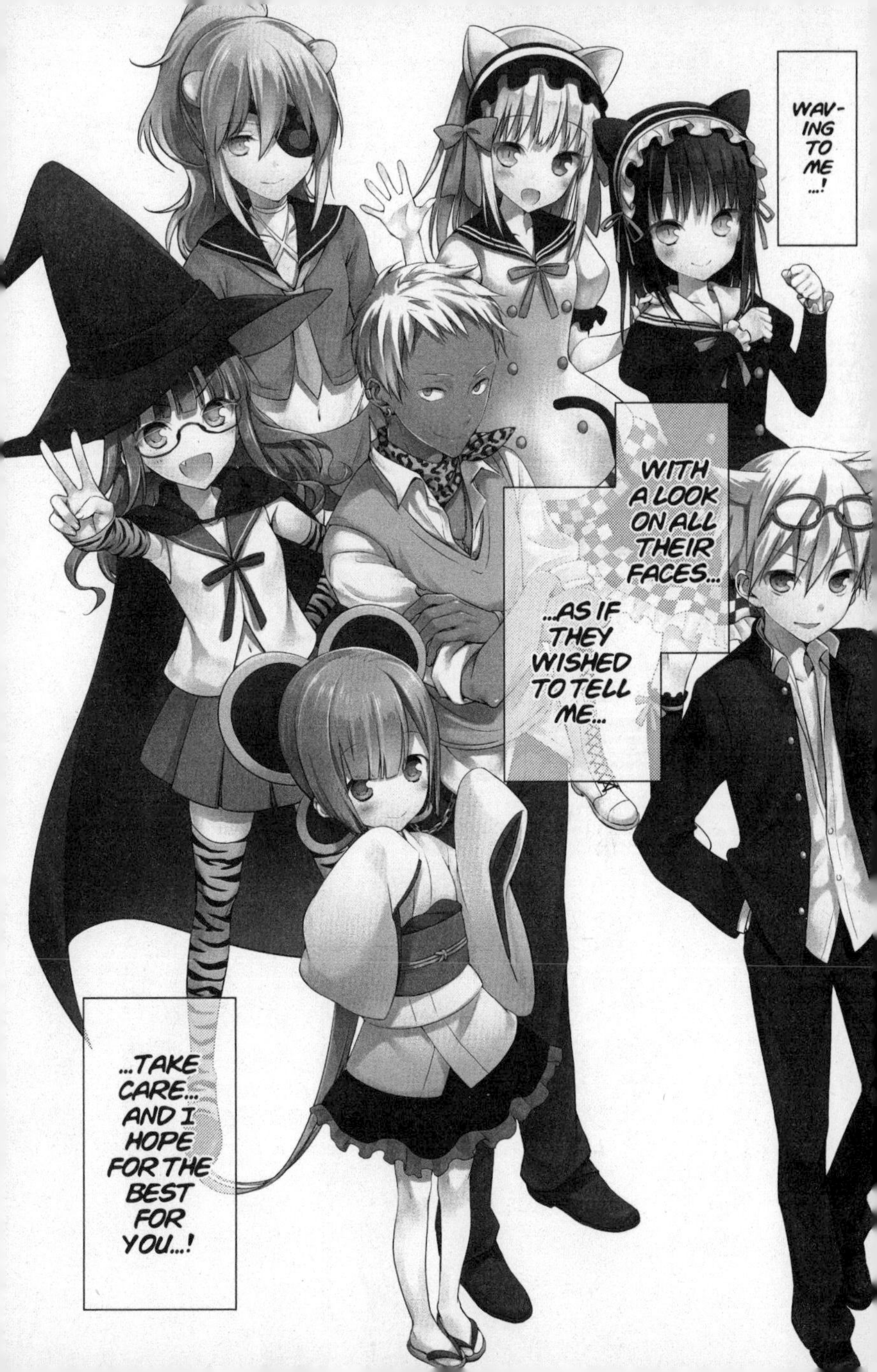
WAVING TO ME...!
WITH A LOOK ON ALL THEIR FACES...
...AS IF THEY WISHED TO TELL ME...
...TAKE CARE... AND I HOPE FOR THE BEST FOR YOU...!

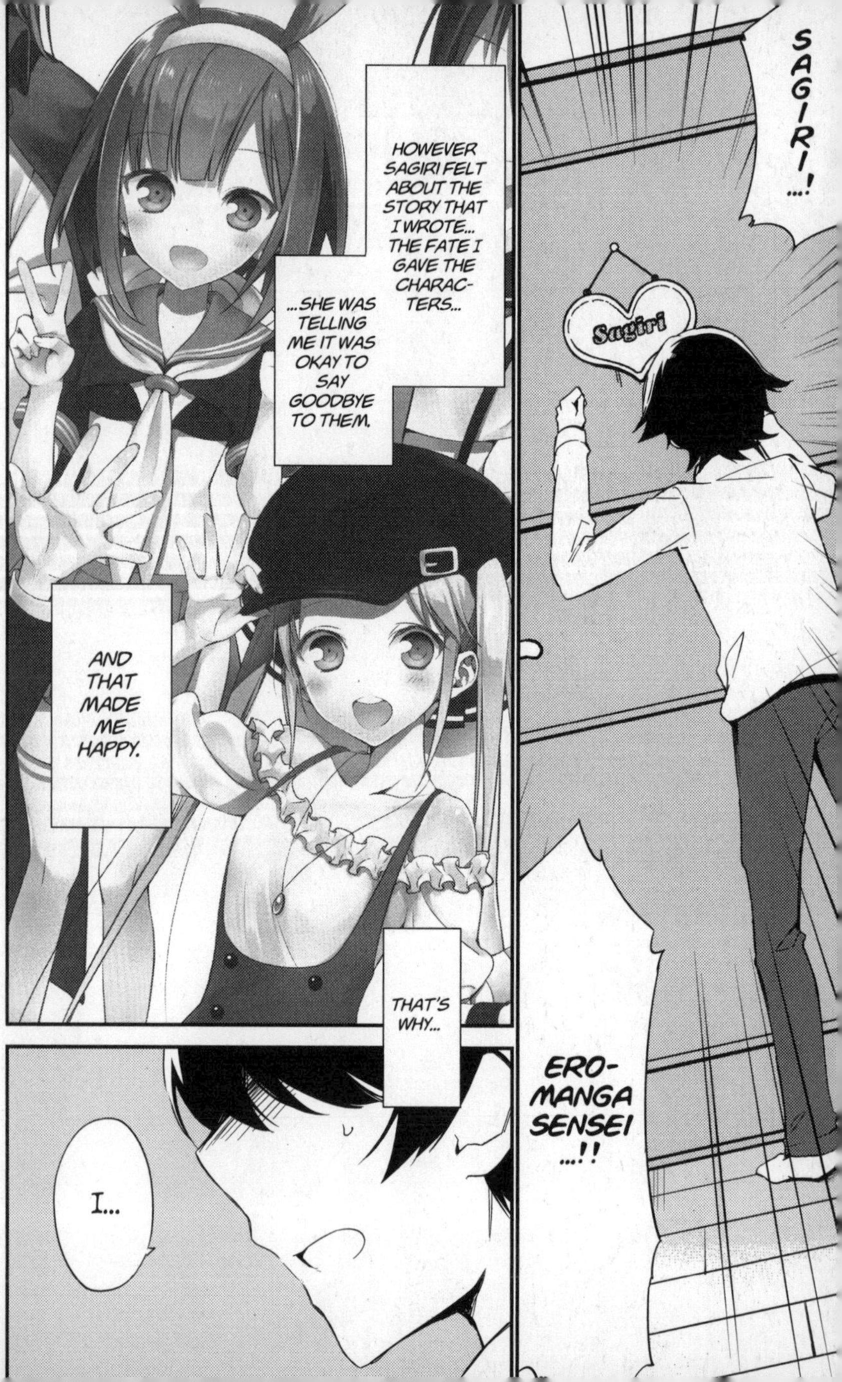
SAGIRI...!
Sagiri
ERO-MANGA SENSEI...!!
HOWEVER SAGIRI FELT ABOUT THE STORY THAT I WROTE... THE FATE I GAVE THE CHARACTERS...
...SHE WAS TELLING ME IT WAS OKAY TO SAY GOODBYE TO THEM.
AND THAT MADE ME HAPPY.
THAT'S WHY...
I...

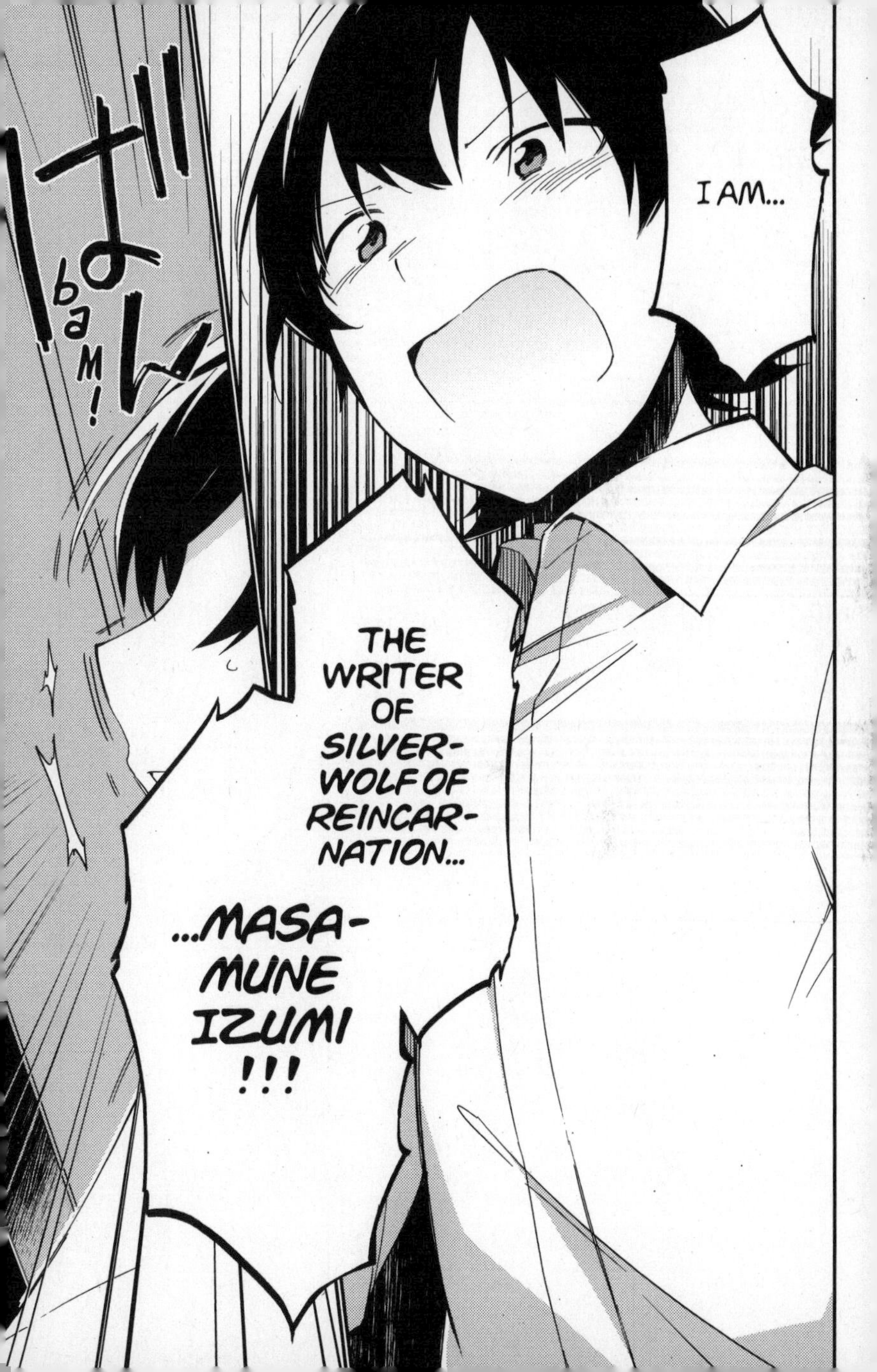
I AM...
THE WRITER OF SILVER-WOLF OF REINCAR-NATION...
...MASA-MUNE IZUMI !!!
bam!

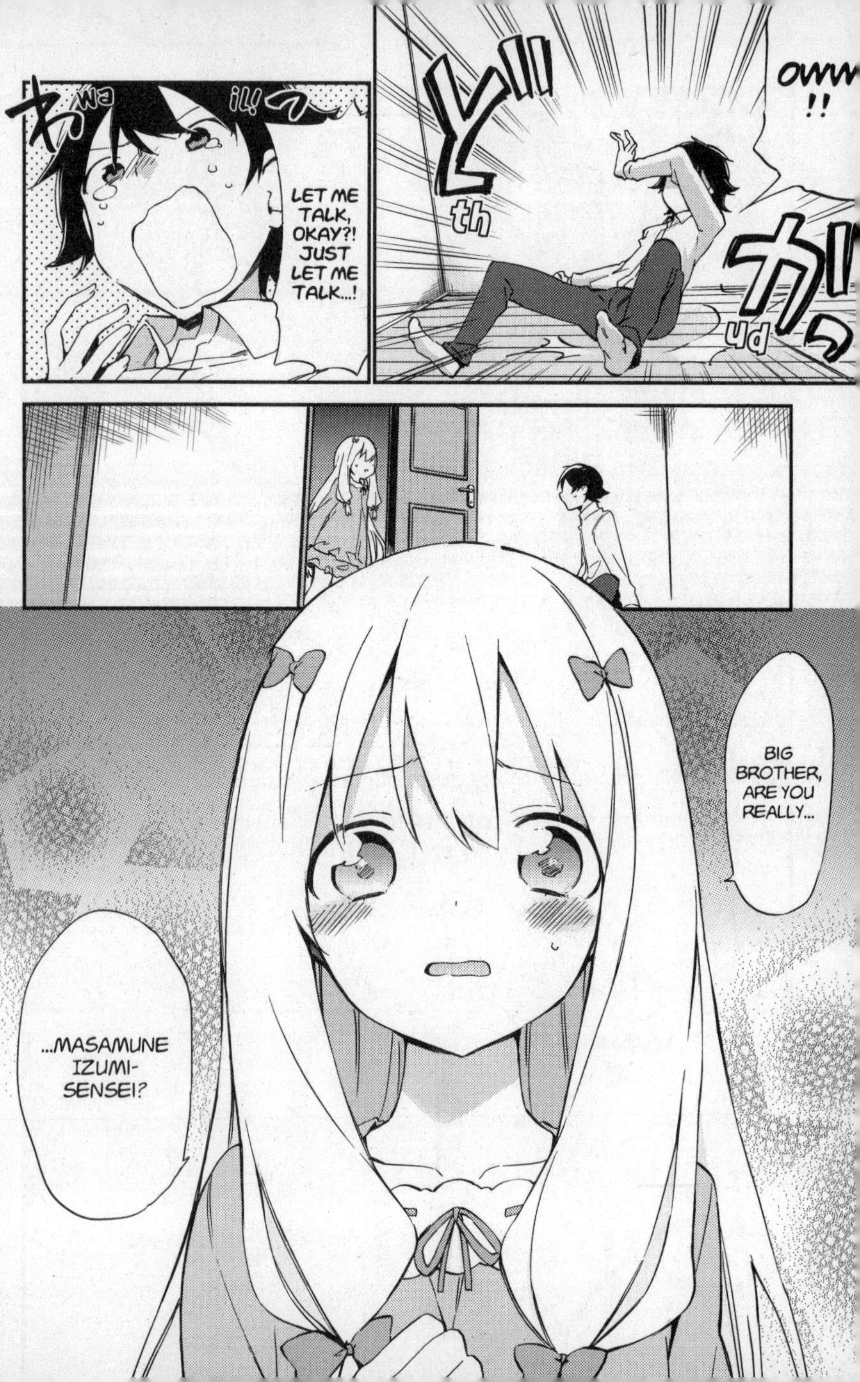
OWW!!
th
ud
wa
il!
LET ME TALK, OKAY?! JUST LET ME TALK...!
BIG BROTHER, ARE YOU REALLY...
...MASAMUNE IZUMI-SENSEI?

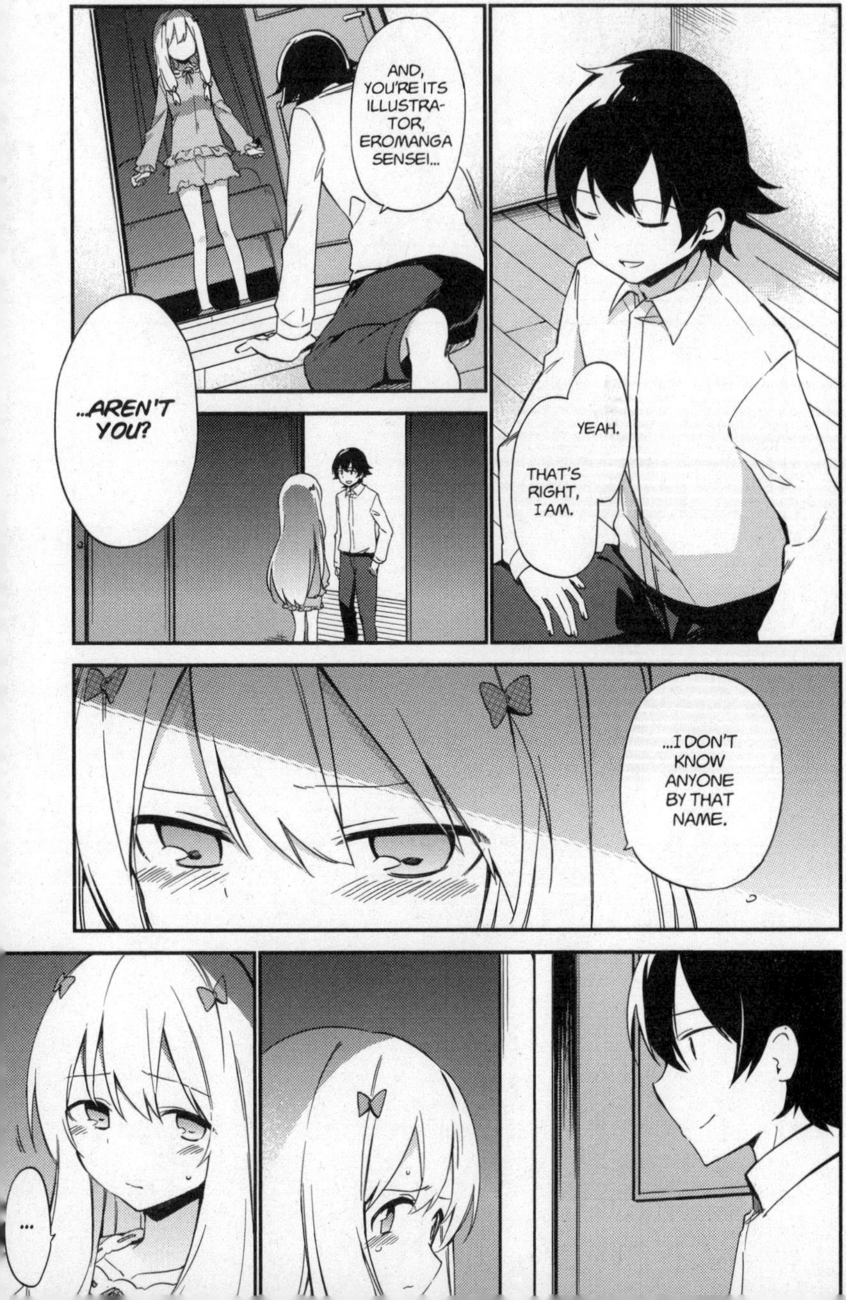
YEAH.
THAT'S RIGHT, I AM.
AND, YOU'RE ITS ILLUSTRATOR, EROMANGA SENSEI...
...AREN'T YOU?
...I DON'T KNOW ANYONE BY THAT NAME.
...

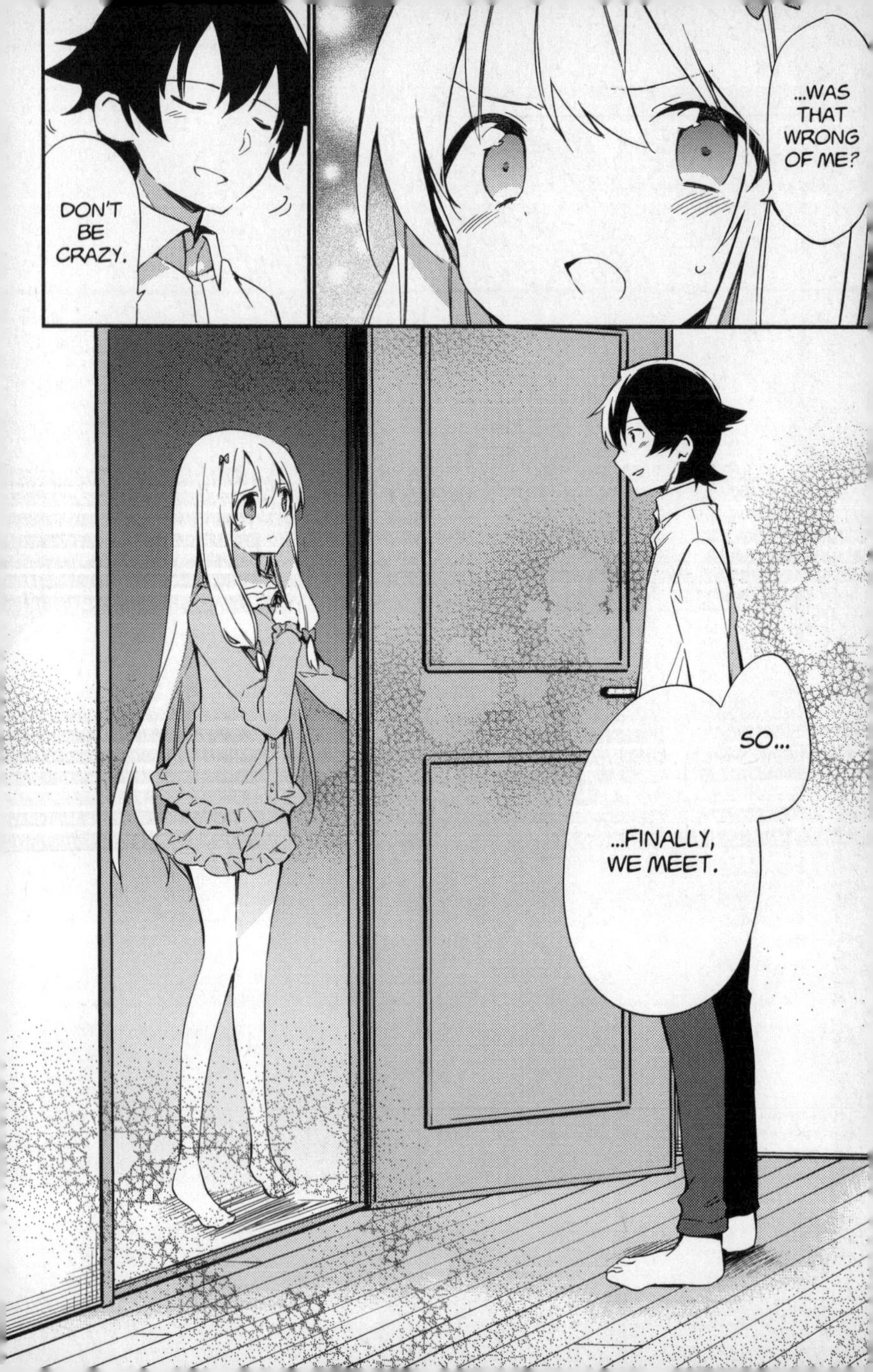
...WAS THAT WRONG OF ME?
DON'T BE CRAZY.
SO...
...FINALLY, WE MEET.

eromanga sensei

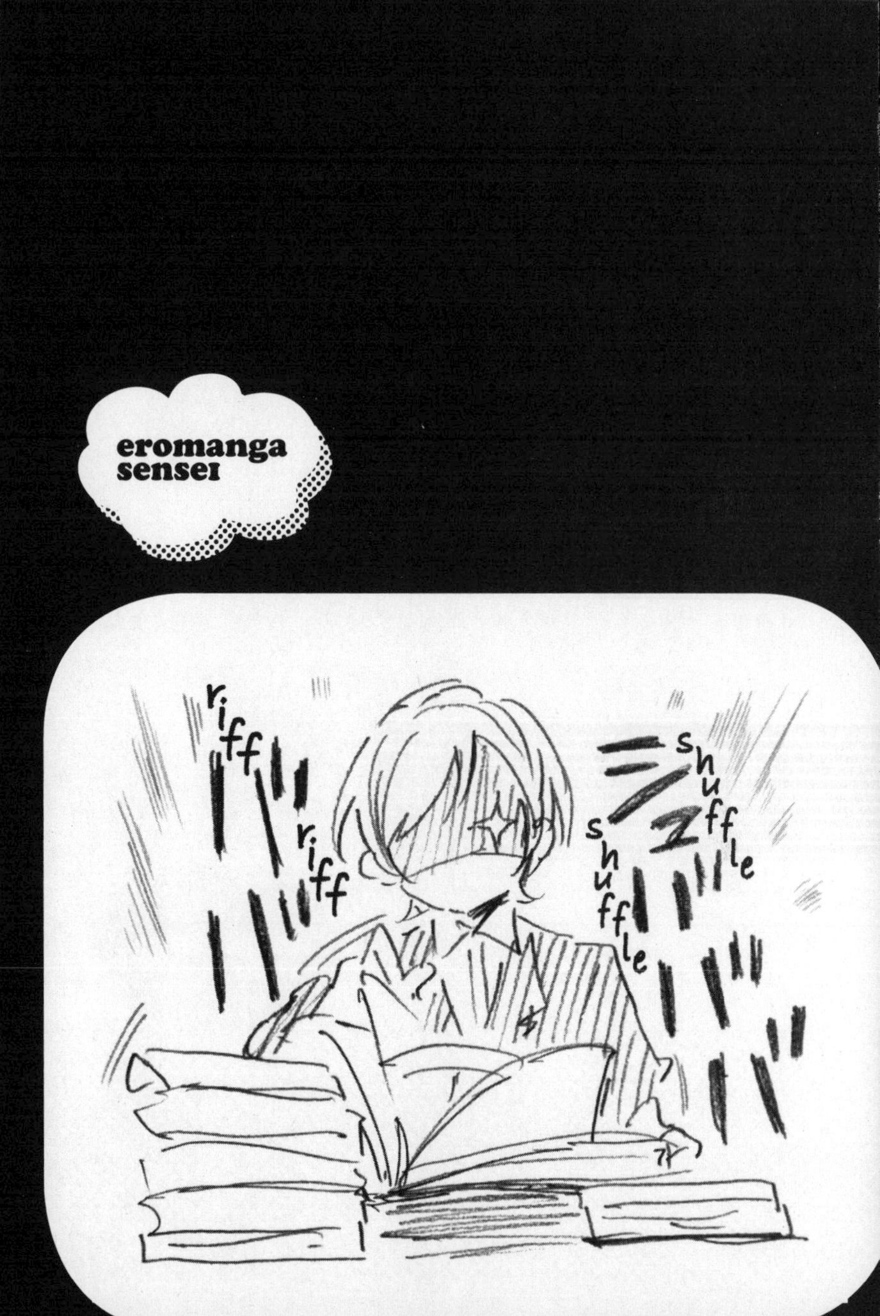
shuffle
shuffle
riff
riff

eromanga
sensei

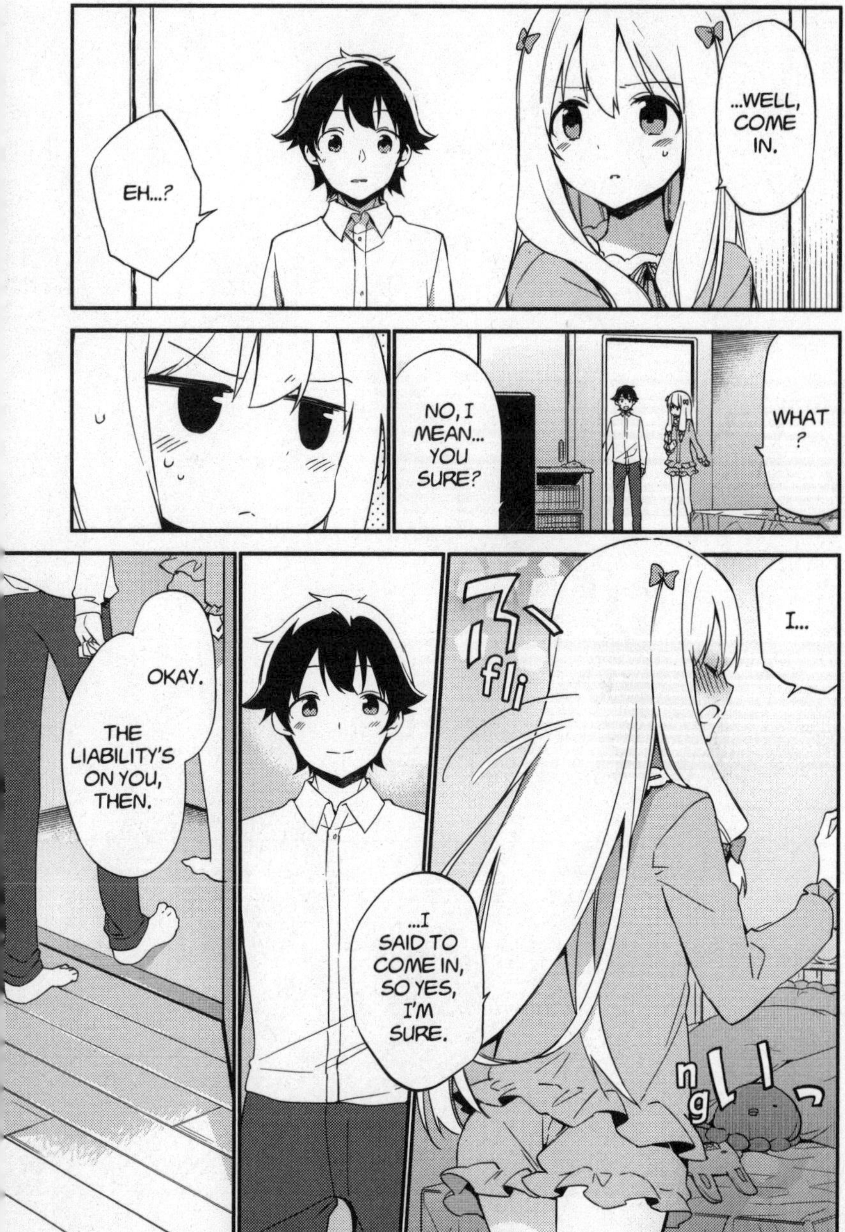
...WELL, COME IN.
EH...?
WHAT?
NO, I MEAN... YOU SURE?
I...
fli
...I SAID TO COME IN, SO YES, I'M SURE.
ng
OKAY.
THE LIABILITY'S ON YOU, THEN.

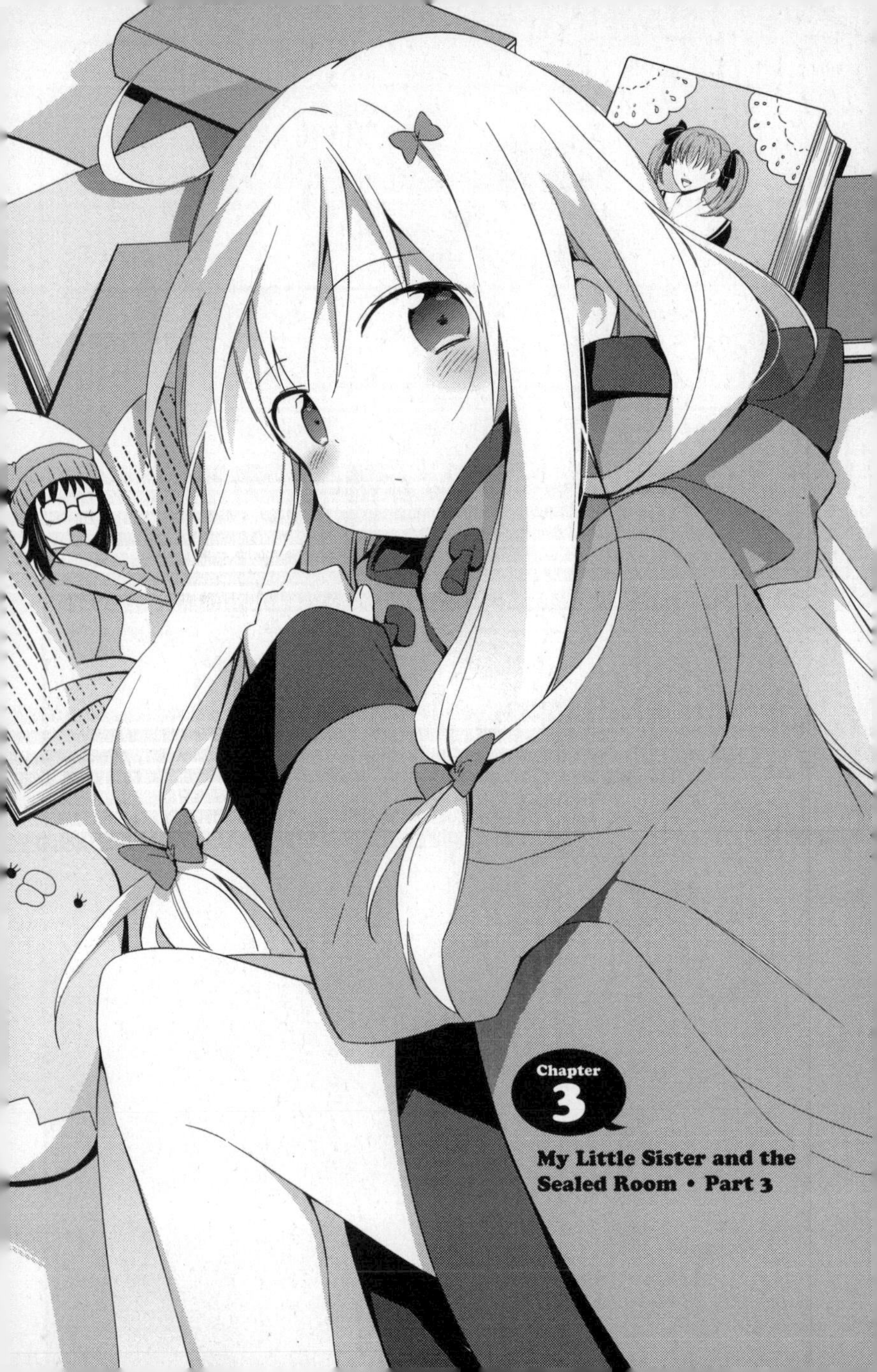

Chapter 3

My Little Sister and the Sealed Room • Part 3

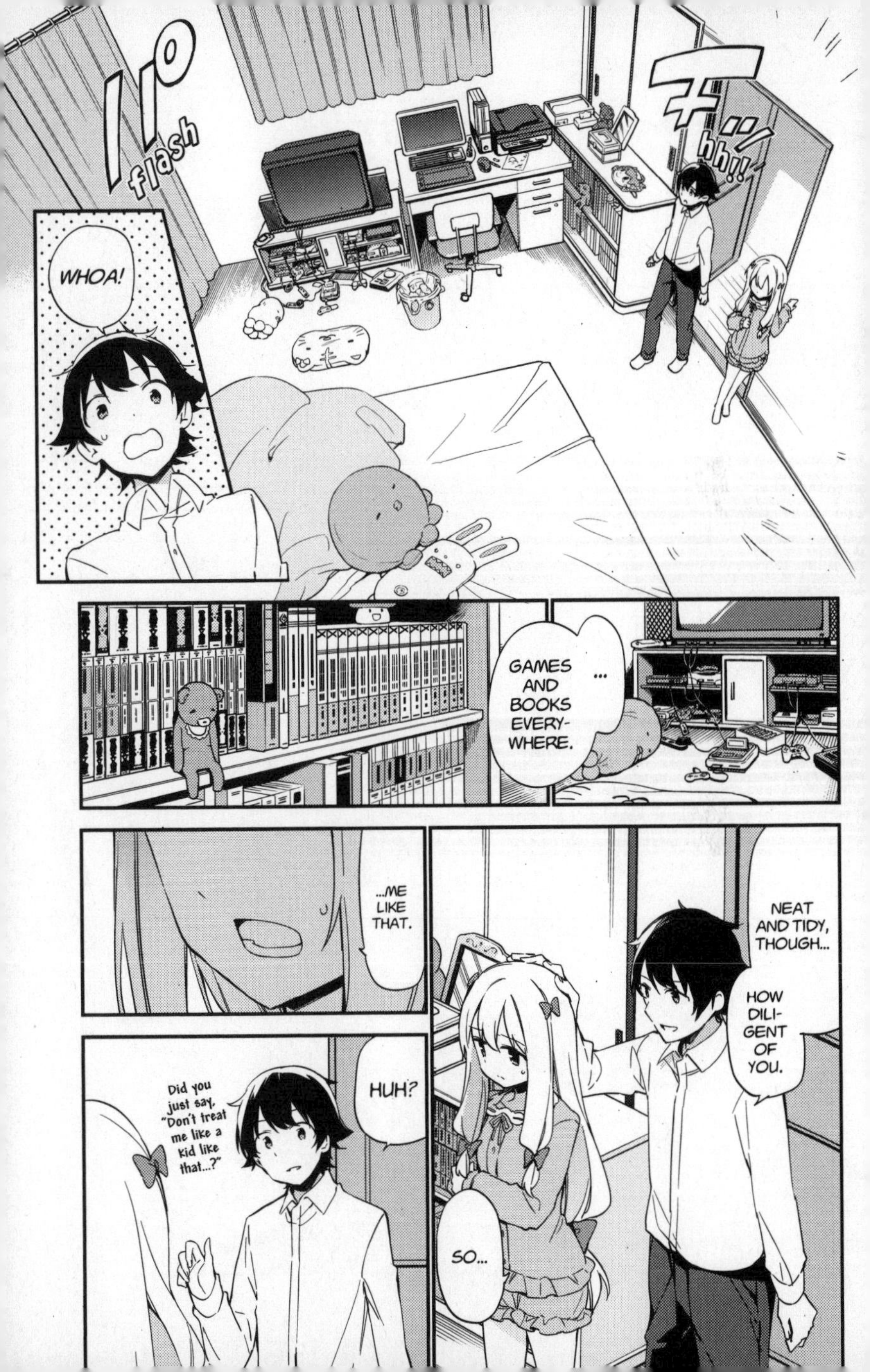

hh!!
flash
WHOA!
GAMES AND BOOKS EVERY-WHERE.
...
NEAT AND TIDY, THOUGH...
HOW DILI-GENT OF YOU.
SO...
...ME LIKE THAT.
HUH?
Did you just say, "Don't treat me like a kid like that...?"

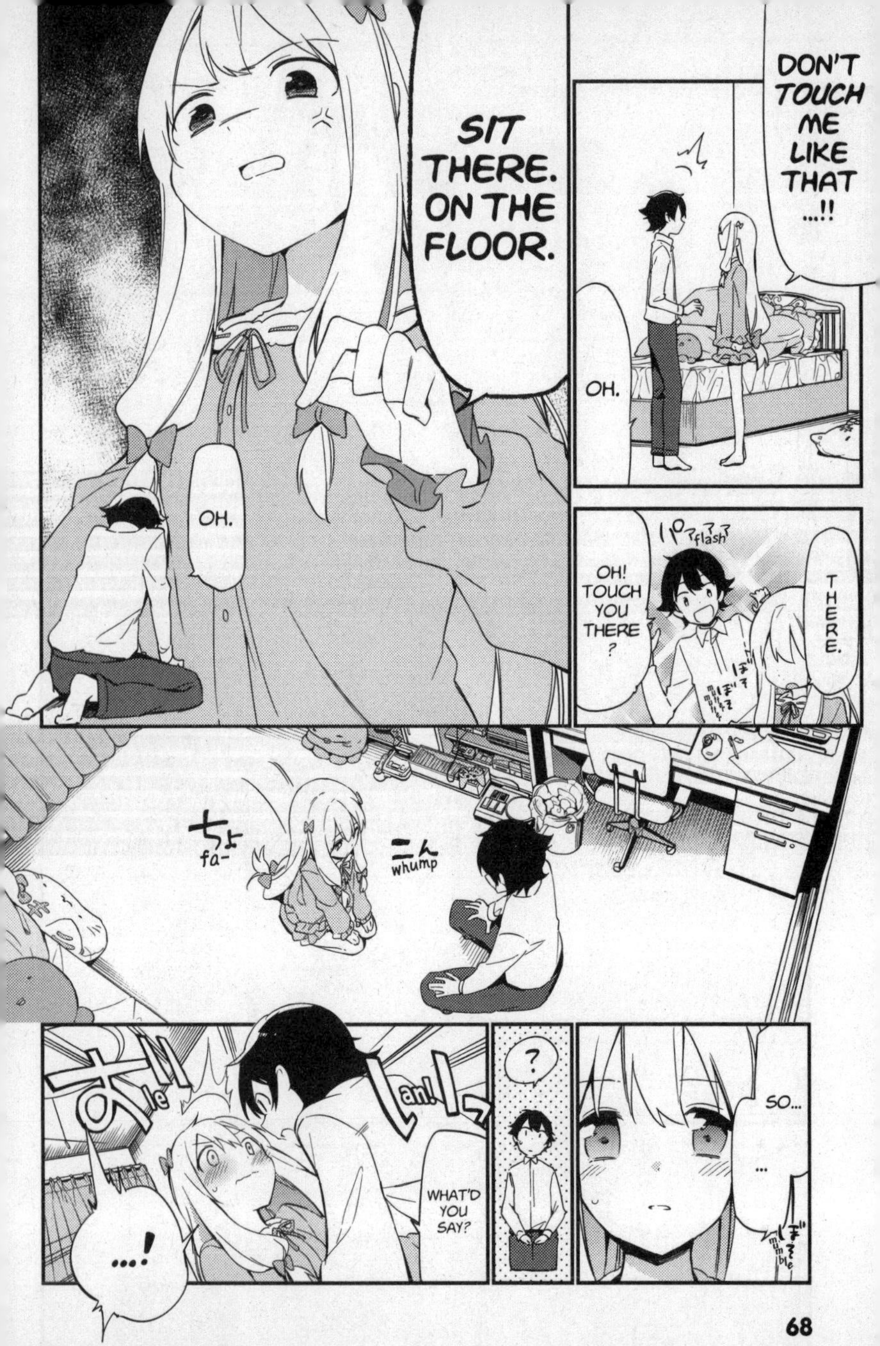
DON'T TOUCH ME LIKE THAT ...!!
OH.
THERE.
パァァ flash
OH! TOUCH YOU THERE?
ぼそぼそ mumble mumble
SIT THERE. ON THE FLOOR.
OH.
ちょ fa-
こん whump
SO...
...
ぼそ mumble
?
WHAT'D YOU SAY?
しan!
すle
...!

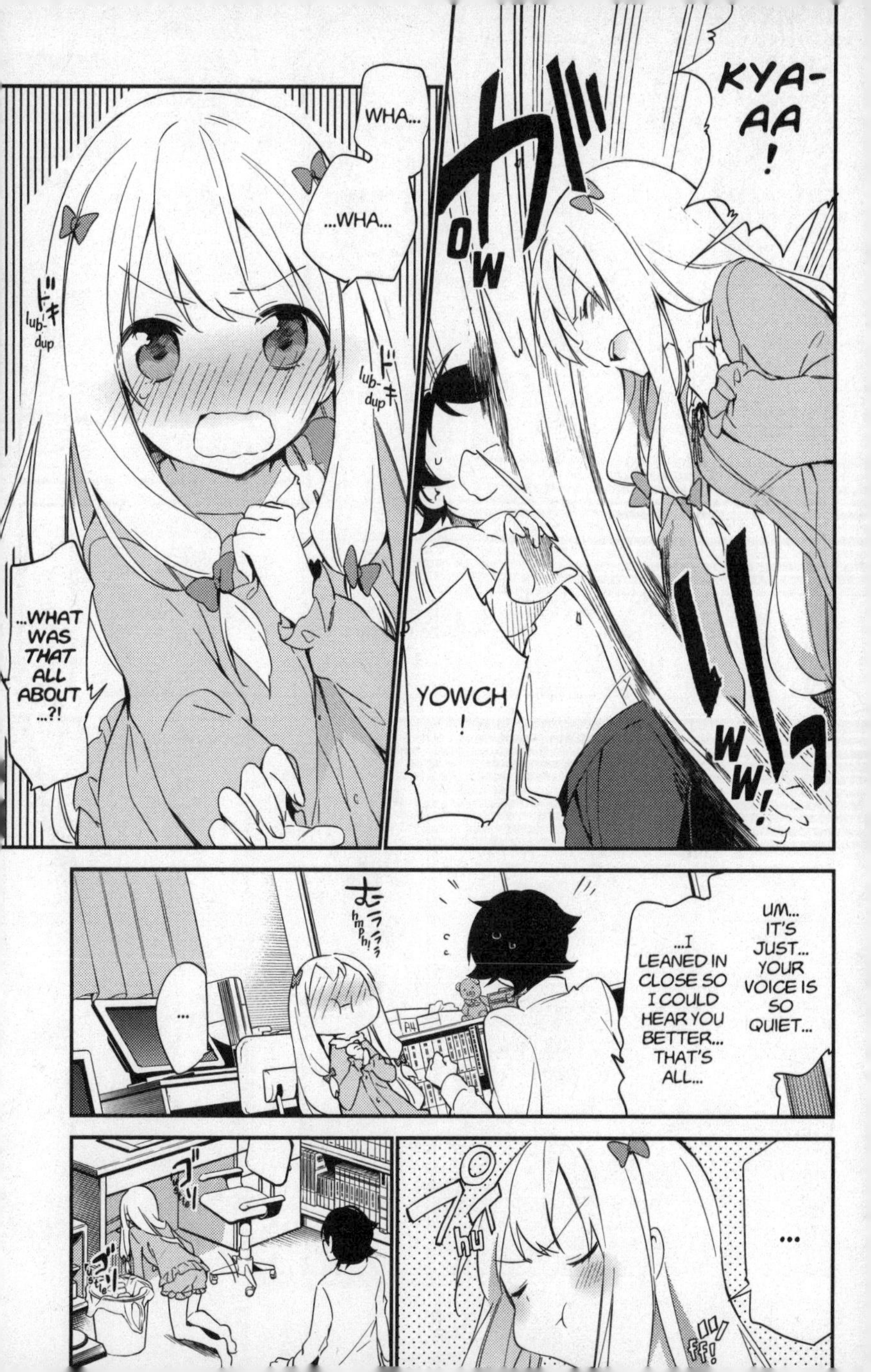
KYA-AA!
OW
WWW!
YOWCH!
WHA...
...WHA...
lub-dup
lub-dup
...WHAT WAS THAT ALL ABOUT...?!
UM... IT'S JUST... YOUR VOICE IS SO QUIET...
...I LEANED IN CLOSE SO I COULD HEAR YOU BETTER... THAT'S ALL...
hmph!
...
hu
fff!
...
rustle
rustle

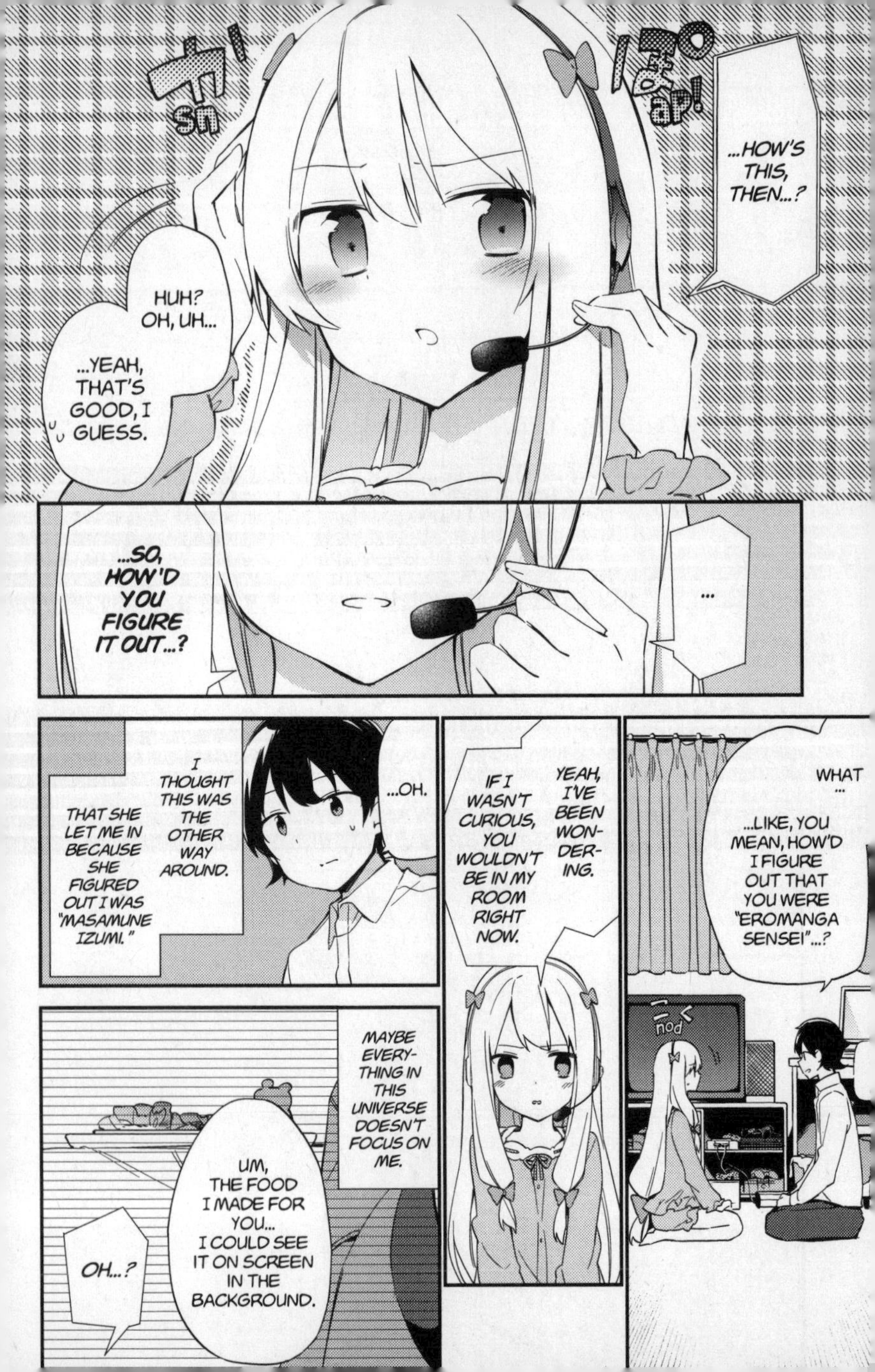
...HOW'S THIS, THEN...?
ap!
sn
HUH? OH, UH...
...YEAH, THAT'S GOOD, I GUESS.
...
...SO, HOW'D YOU FIGURE IT OUT...?
WHAT ...
...LIKE, YOU MEAN, HOW'D I FIGURE OUT THAT YOU WERE "EROMANGA SENSEI"...?
nod
YEAH, I'VE BEEN WON-DER-ING.
IF I WASN'T CURIOUS, YOU WOULDN'T BE IN MY ROOM RIGHT NOW.
...OH.
I THOUGHT THIS WAS THE OTHER WAY AROUND.
THAT SHE LET ME IN BECAUSE SHE FIGURED OUT I WAS "MASAMUNE IZUMI."
MAYBE EVERY-THING IN THIS UNIVERSE DOESN'T FOCUS ON ME.
UM, THE FOOD I MADE FOR YOU... I COULD SEE IT ON SCREEN IN THE BACKGROUND.
OH...?

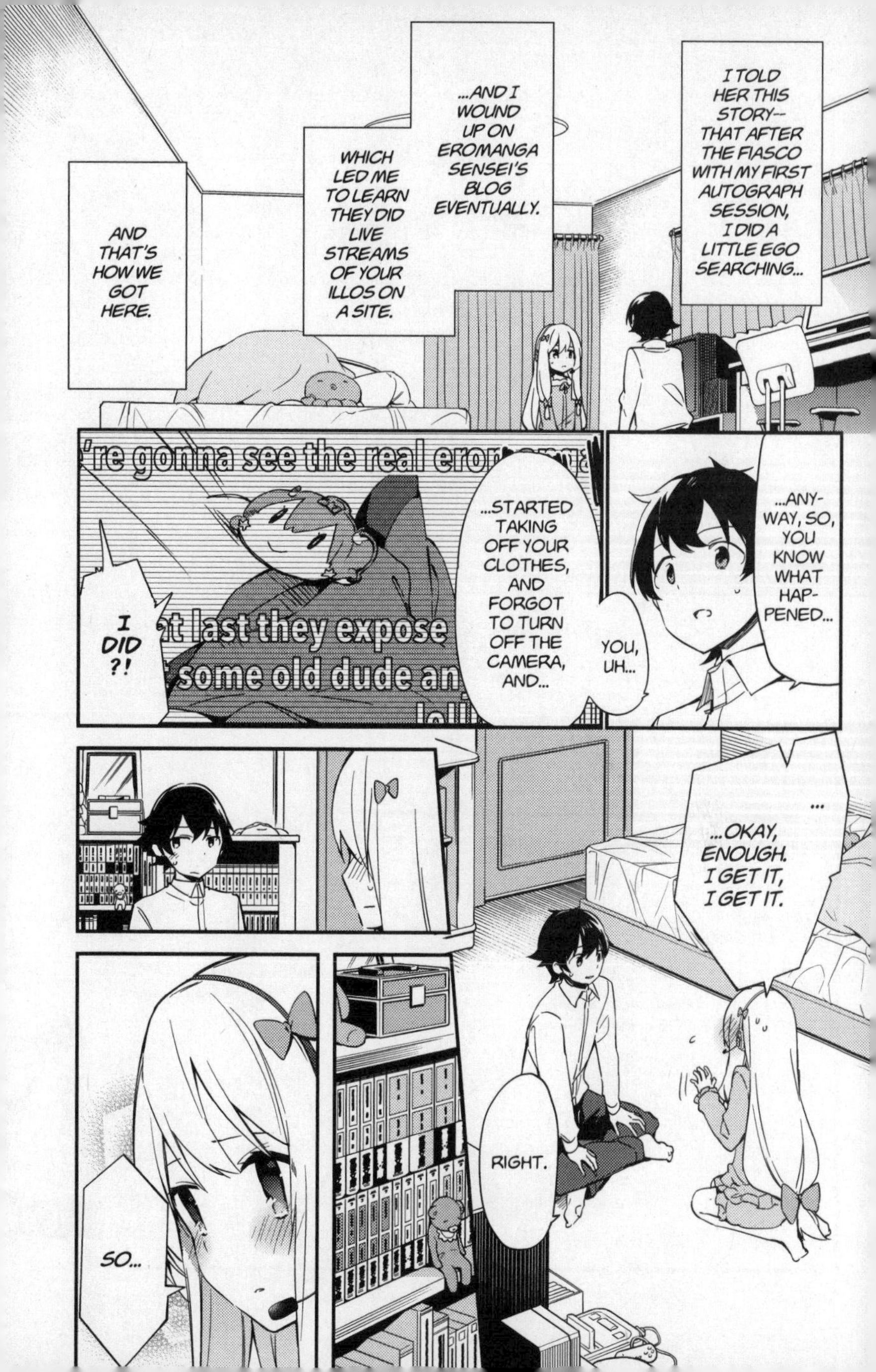
I TOLD HER THIS STORY--THAT AFTER THE FIASCO WITH MY FIRST AUTOGRAPH SESSION, I DID A LITTLE EGO SEARCHING...
...AND I WOUND UP ON EROMANGA SENSEI'S BLOG EVENTUALLY.
WHICH LED ME TO LEARN THEY DID LIVE STREAMS OF YOUR ILLOS ON A SITE.
AND THAT'S HOW WE GOT HERE.
...ANY-WAY, SO, YOU KNOW WHAT HAP-PENED...
YOU, UH...
...STARTED TAKING OFF YOUR CLOTHES, AND FORGOT TO TURN OFF THE CAMERA, AND...
're gonna see the real erom
t last they expose
some old dude an
I DID?!
...
...OKAY, ENOUGH. I GET IT, I GET IT.
RIGHT.
SO...

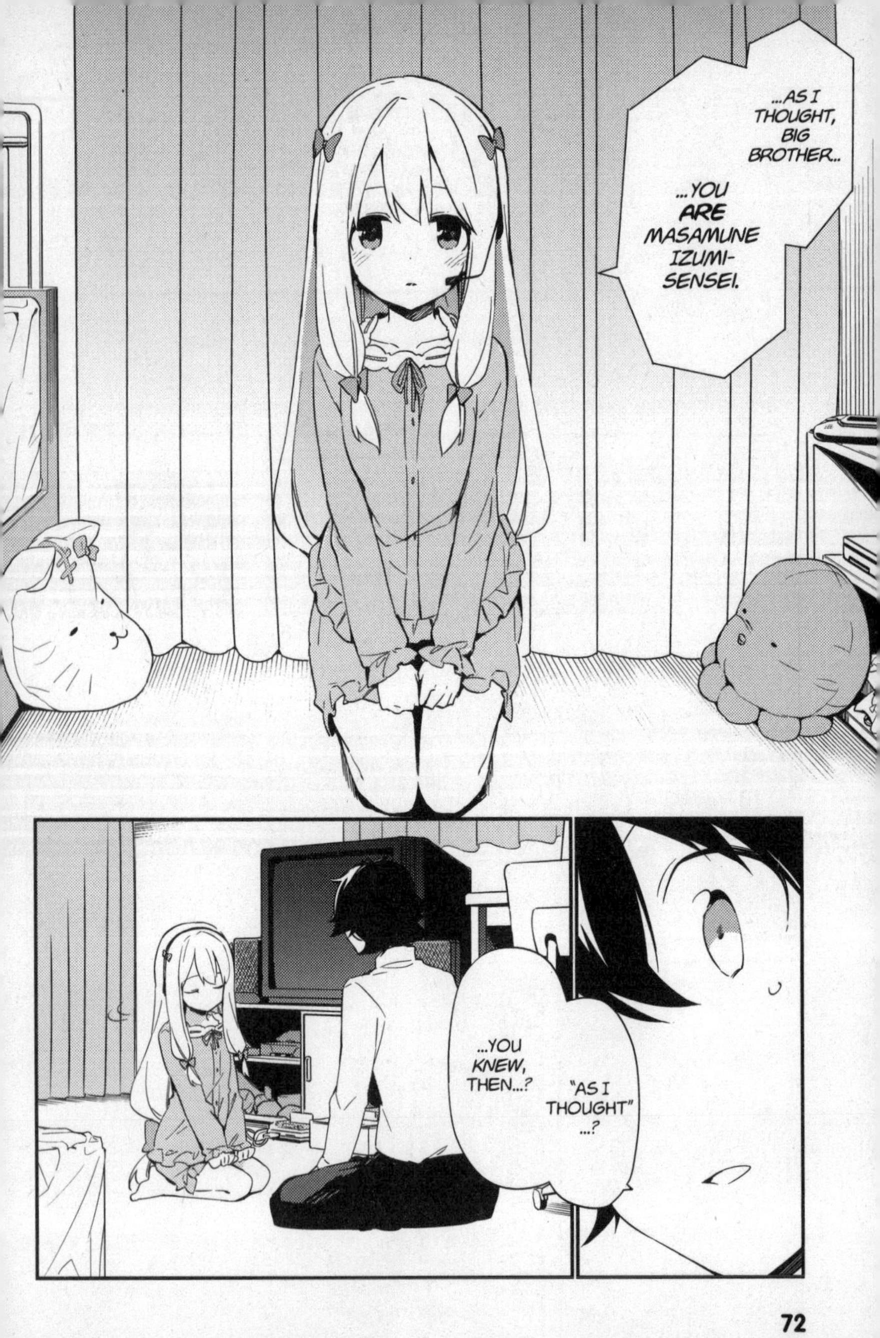
...AS I THOUGHT, BIG BROTHER...
...YOU ARE MASAMUNE IZUMI-SENSEI.
"AS I THOUGHT" ...?
...YOU KNEW, THEN...?

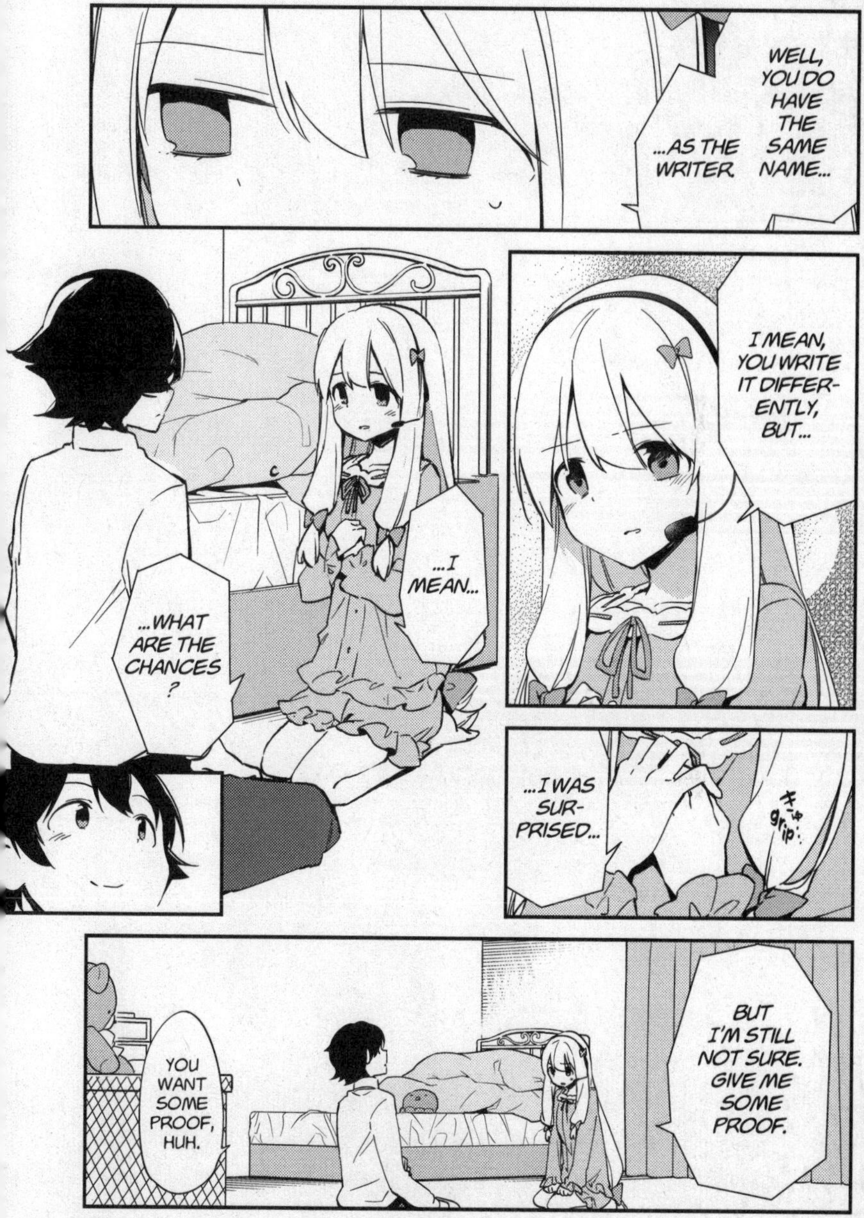
WELL, YOU DO HAVE THE SAME NAME...
...AS THE WRITER.
I MEAN, YOU WRITE IT DIFFER-ENTLY, BUT...
...I WAS SUR-PRISED...
grip
...I MEAN...
...WHAT ARE THE CHANCES?
BUT I'M STILL NOT SURE. GIVE ME SOME PROOF.
YOU WANT SOME PROOF, HUH.

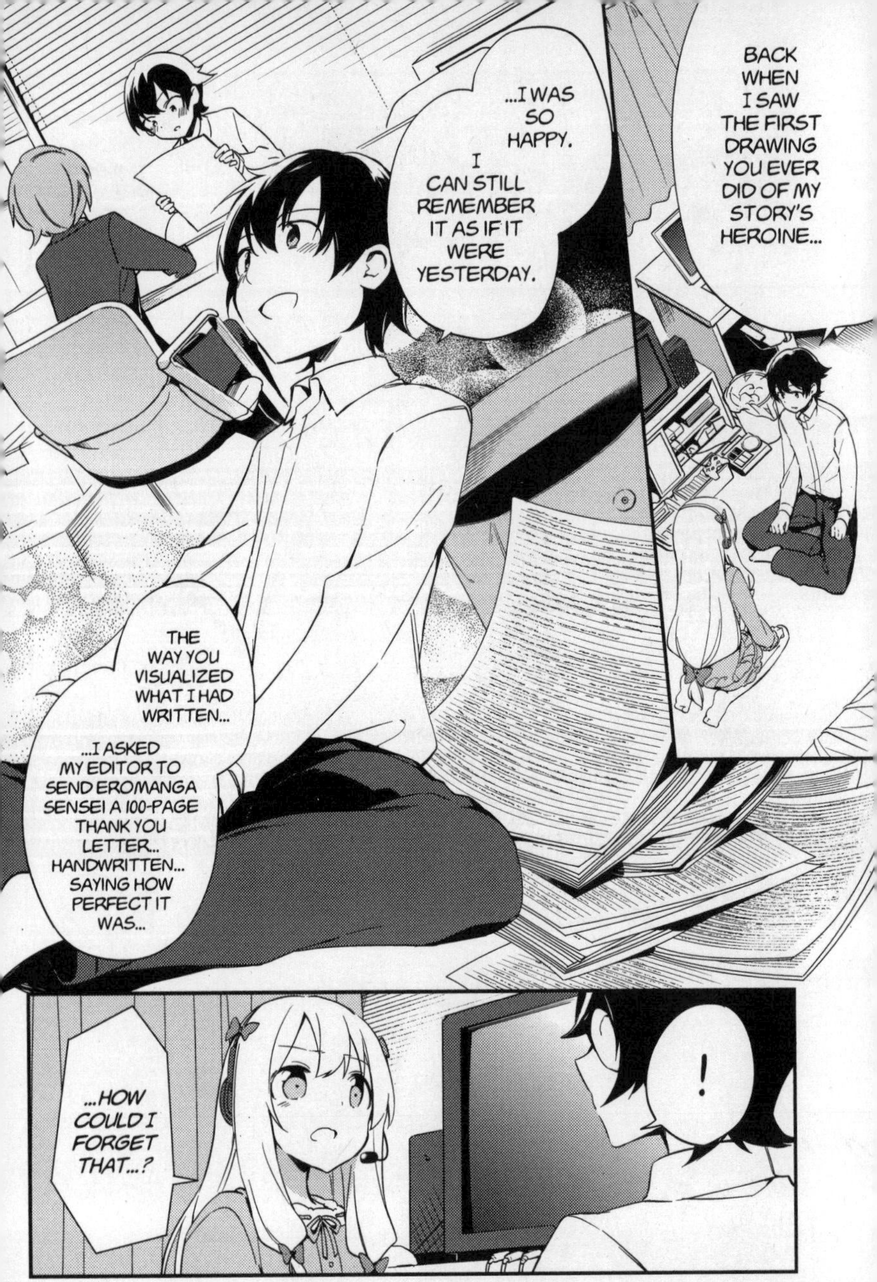
BACK WHEN I SAW THE FIRST DRAWING YOU EVER DID OF MY STORY'S HEROINE...
...I WAS SO HAPPY.
I CAN STILL REMEMBER IT AS IF IT WERE YESTERDAY.
THE WAY YOU VISUALIZED WHAT I HAD WRITTEN...
...I ASKED MY EDITOR TO SEND EROMANGA SENSEI A 100-PAGE THANK YOU LETTER... HANDWRITTEN... SAYING HOW PERFECT IT WAS...
!
...HOW COULD I FORGET THAT...?

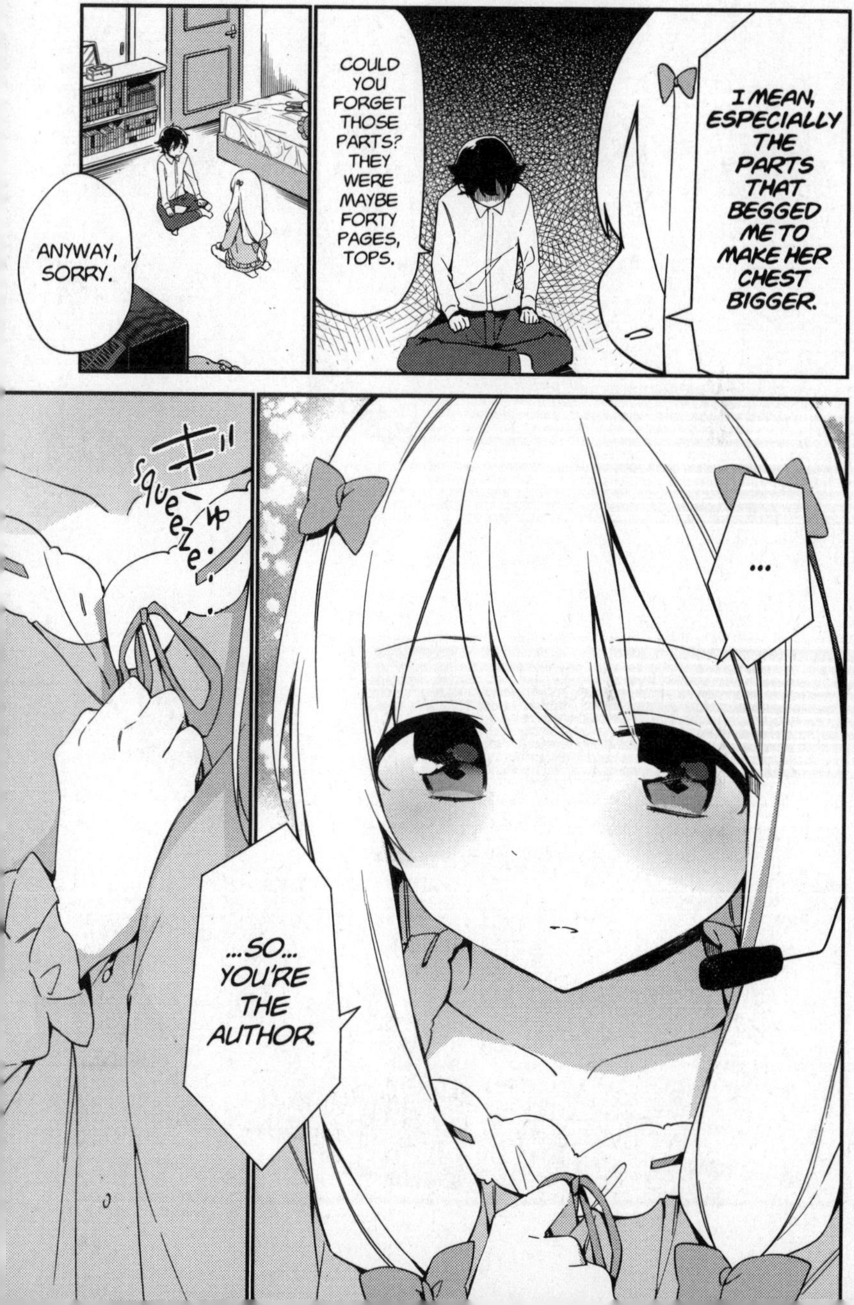
I MEAN, ESPECIALLY THE PARTS THAT BEGGED ME TO MAKE HER CHEST BIGGER.
COULD YOU FORGET THOSE PARTS? THEY WERE MAYBE FORTY PAGES, TOPS.
ANYWAY, SORRY.
...
...SO... YOU'RE THE AUTHOR.
squeeze

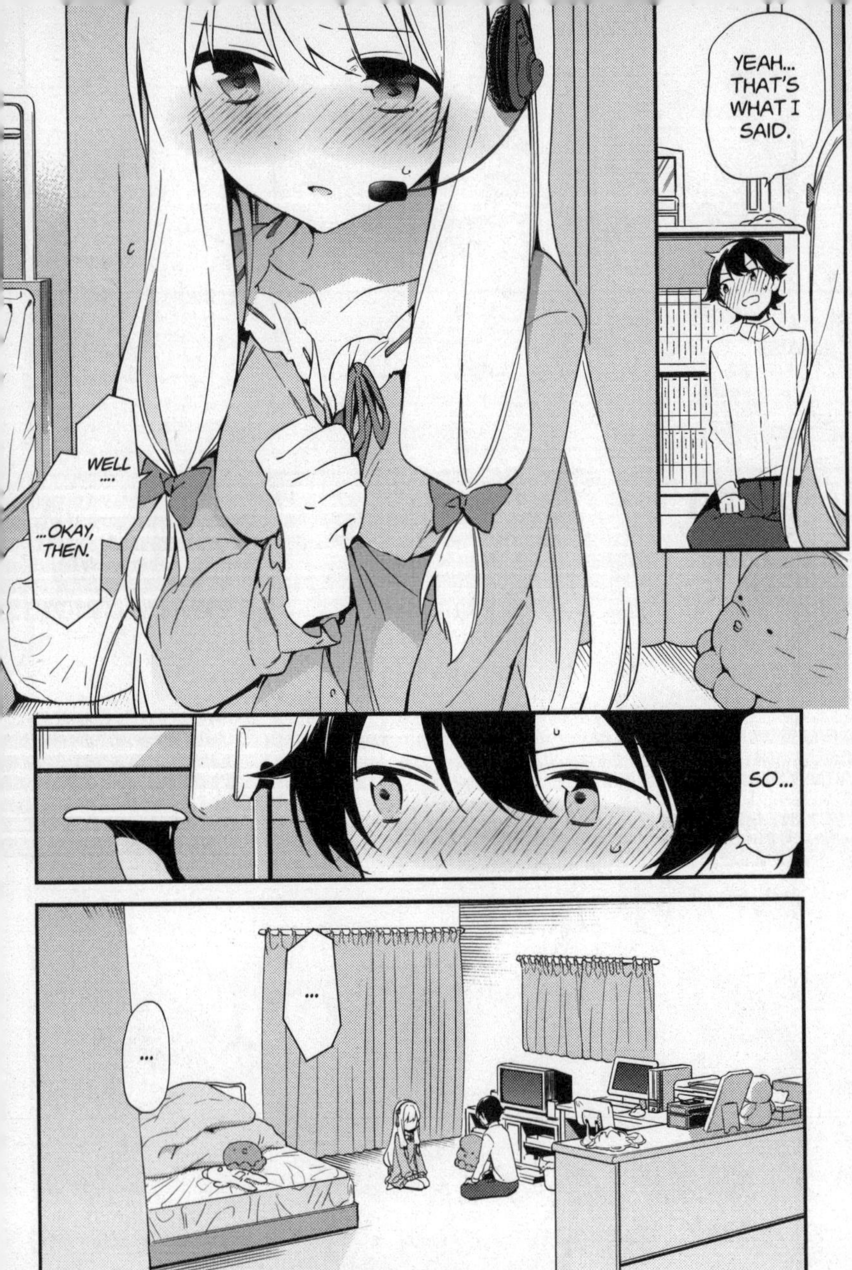
YEAH... THAT'S WHAT I SAID.
WELL ....
...OKAY, THEN.
SO...
...
...

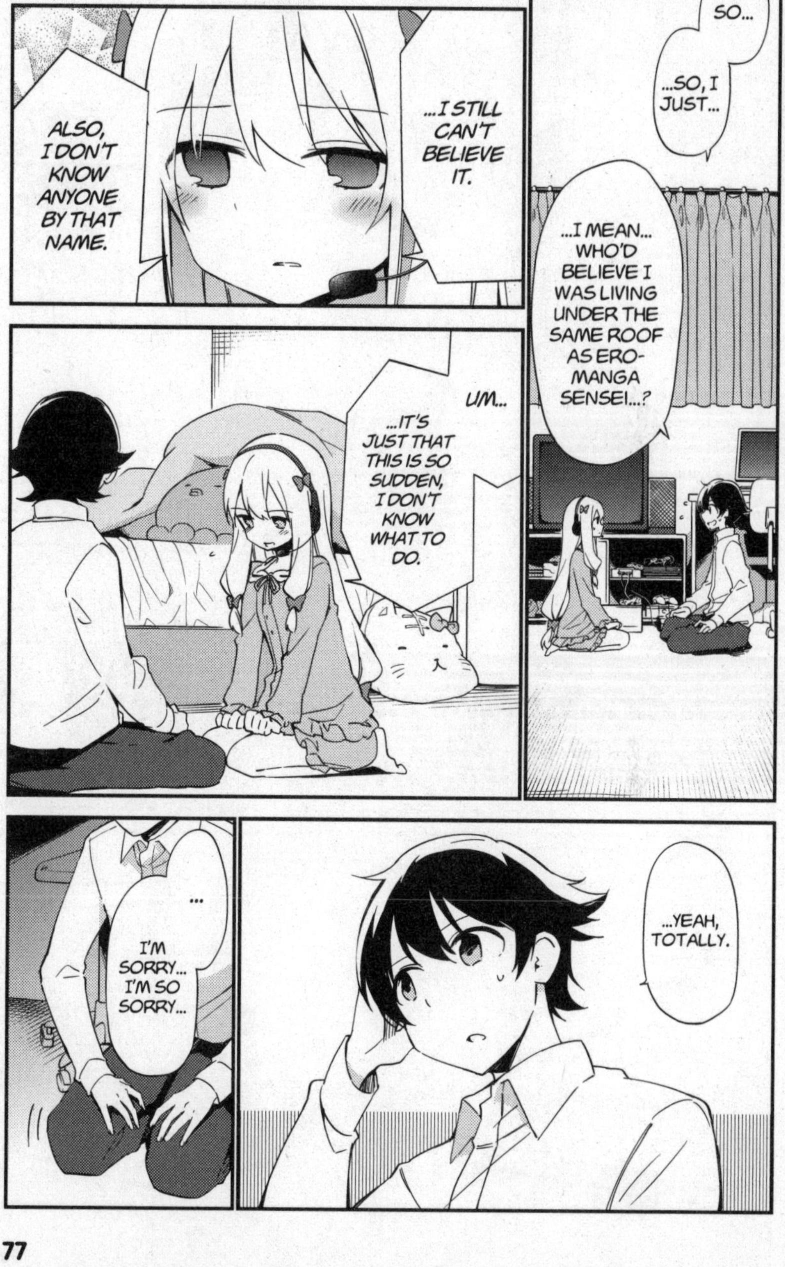
SO...
...SO, I JUST...
...I MEAN... WHO'D BELIEVE I WAS LIVING UNDER THE SAME ROOF AS ERO-MANGA SENSEI...?
...I STILL CAN'T BELIEVE IT.
ALSO, I DON'T KNOW ANYONE BY THAT NAME.
UM...
...IT'S JUST THAT THIS IS SO SUDDEN, I DON'T KNOW WHAT TO DO.
...YEAH, TOTALLY.
...
I'M SORRY... I'M SO SORRY...

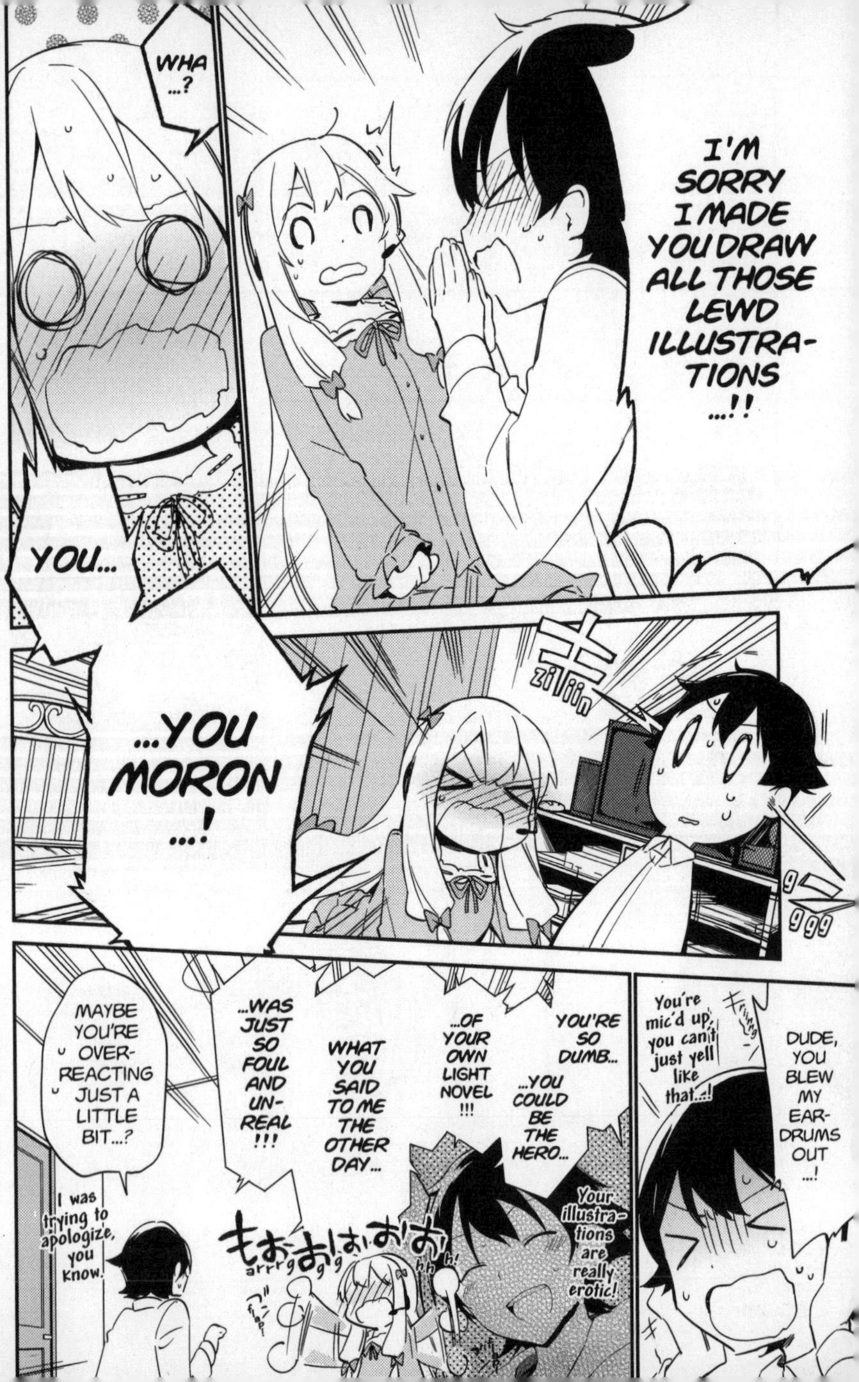
I'M SORRY I MADE YOU DRAW ALL THOSE LEWD ILLUSTRATIONS ...!!
WHA ...?
YOU...
...YOU MORON ...!
zi-iin
ggg
DUDE, YOU BLEW MY EAR-DRUMS OUT ...!
You're mic'd up, you can't just yell like that...!
Kriiing
YOU'RE SO DUMB...
...YOU COULD BE THE HERO...
...OF YOUR OWN LIGHT NOVEL !!!
Your illustrations are really erotic!
WHAT YOU SAID TO ME THE OTHER DAY...
...WAS JUST SO FOUL AND UN-REAL !!!
MAYBE YOU'RE OVER-REACTING JUST A LITTLE BIT...?
arrrggghhh
flap
I was trying to apologize, you know.

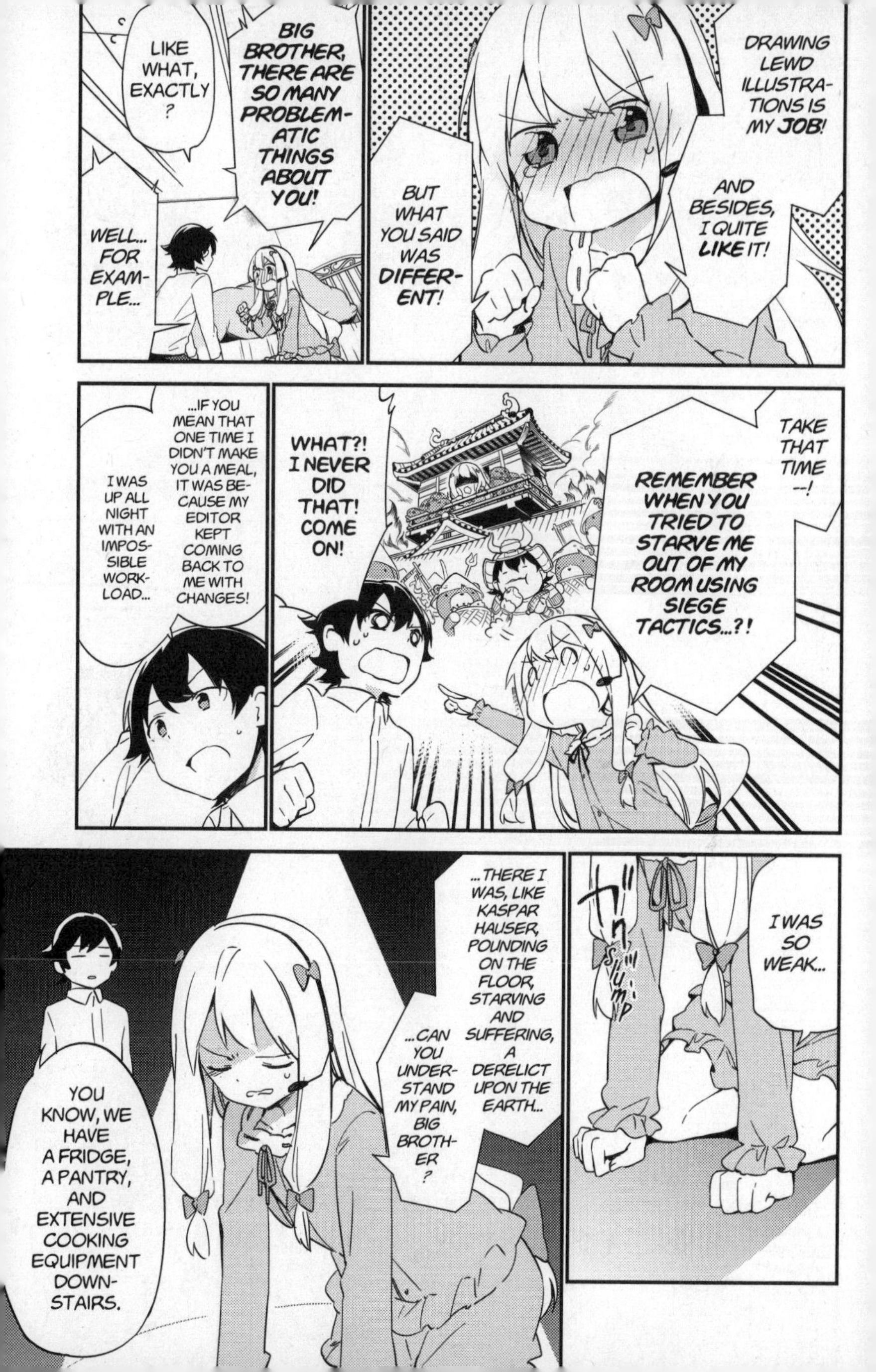
DRAWING LEWD ILLUSTRATIONS IS MY JOB!
AND BESIDES, I QUITE LIKE IT!
BUT WHAT YOU SAID WAS DIFFERENT!
BIG BROTHER, THERE ARE SO MANY PROBLEMATIC THINGS ABOUT YOU!
LIKE WHAT, EXACTLY?
WELL... FOR EXAMPLE...
TAKE THAT TIME--!
REMEMBER WHEN YOU TRIED TO STARVE ME OUT OF MY ROOM USING SIEGE TACTICS...?!
WHAT?! I NEVER DID THAT! COME ON!
...IF YOU MEAN THAT ONE TIME I DIDN'T MAKE YOU A MEAL, IT WAS BECAUSE MY EDITOR KEPT COMING BACK TO ME WITH CHANGES!
I WAS UP ALL NIGHT WITH AN IMPOSSIBLE WORKLOAD...
SLUMP
I WAS SO WEAK...
...THERE I WAS, LIKE KASPAR HAUSER, POUNDING ON THE FLOOR, STARVING AND SUFFERING, A DERELICT UPON THE EARTH...
...CAN YOU UNDERSTAND MY PAIN, BIG BROTHER?
YOU KNOW, WE HAVE A FRIDGE, A PANTRY, AND EXTENSIVE COOKING EQUIPMENT DOWNSTAIRS.

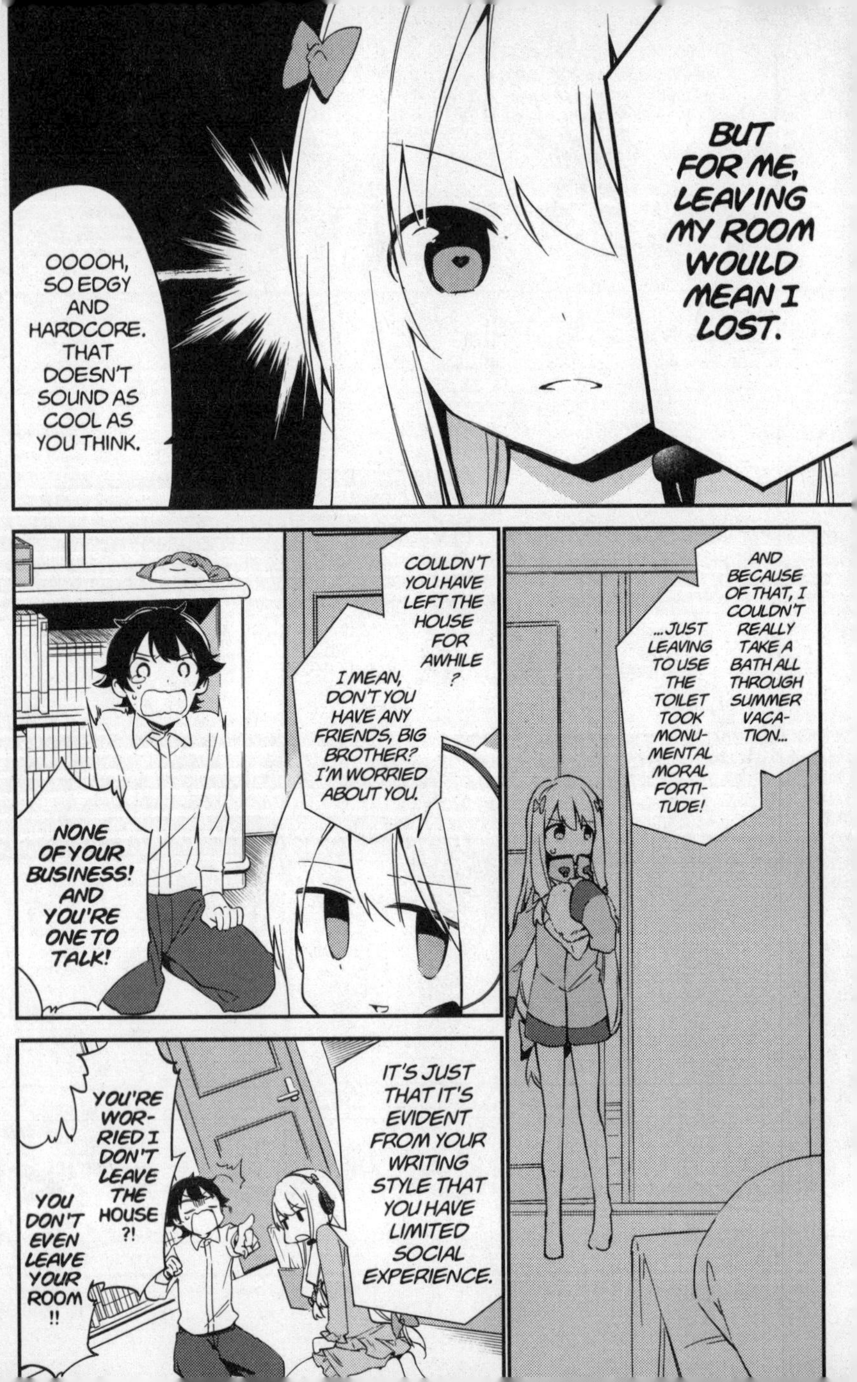
BUT FOR ME, LEAVING MY ROOM WOULD MEAN I LOST.
OOOOH, SO EDGY AND HARDCORE. THAT DOESN'T SOUND AS COOL AS YOU THINK.
...JUST LEAVING TO USE THE TOILET TOOK MONUMENTAL MORAL FORTITUDE!
AND BECAUSE OF THAT, I COULDN'T REALLY TAKE A BATH ALL THROUGH SUMMER VACATION...
COULDN'T YOU HAVE LEFT THE HOUSE FOR AWHILE?
I MEAN, DON'T YOU HAVE ANY FRIENDS, BIG BROTHER? I'M WORRIED ABOUT YOU.
NONE OF YOUR BUSINESS! AND YOU'RE ONE TO TALK!
IT'S JUST THAT IT'S EVIDENT FROM YOUR WRITING STYLE THAT YOU HAVE LIMITED SOCIAL EXPERIENCE.
YOU'RE WORRIED I DON'T LEAVE THE HOUSE?!
YOU DON'T EVEN LEAVE YOUR ROOM!!

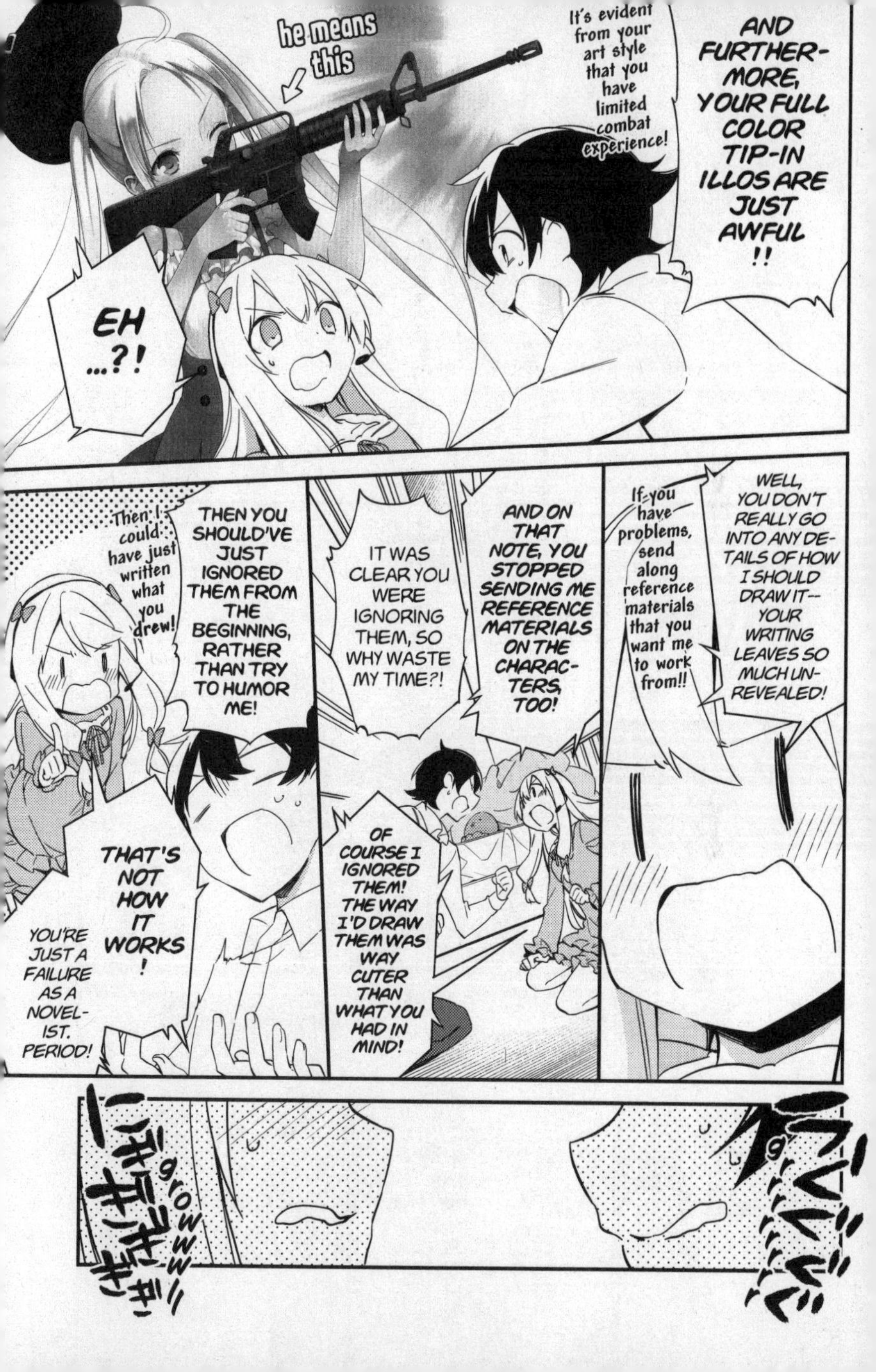
AND FURTHER-MORE, YOUR FULL COLOR TIP-IN ILLOS ARE JUST AWFUL!!
It's evident from your art style that you have limited combat experience!
he means this
EH...?!
WELL, YOU DON'T REALLY GO INTO ANY DE-TAILS OF HOW I SHOULD DRAW IT-- YOUR WRITING LEAVES SO MUCH UN-REVEALED!
If you have problems, send along reference materials that you want me to work from!!
AND ON THAT NOTE, YOU STOPPED SENDING ME REFERENCE MATERIALS ON THE CHARAC-TERS, TOO!
IT WAS CLEAR YOU WERE IGNORING THEM, SO WHY WASTE MY TIME?!
OF COURSE I IGNORED THEM! THE WAY I'D DRAW THEM WAS WAY CUTER THAN WHAT YOU HAD IN MIND!
THEN YOU SHOULD'VE JUST IGNORED THEM FROM THE BEGINNING, RATHER THAN TRY TO HUMOR ME!
Then I could have just written what you drew!
THAT'S NOT HOW IT WORKS!
YOU'RE JUST A FAILURE AS A NOVEL-IST. PERIOD!
grrrrrrr
growwww

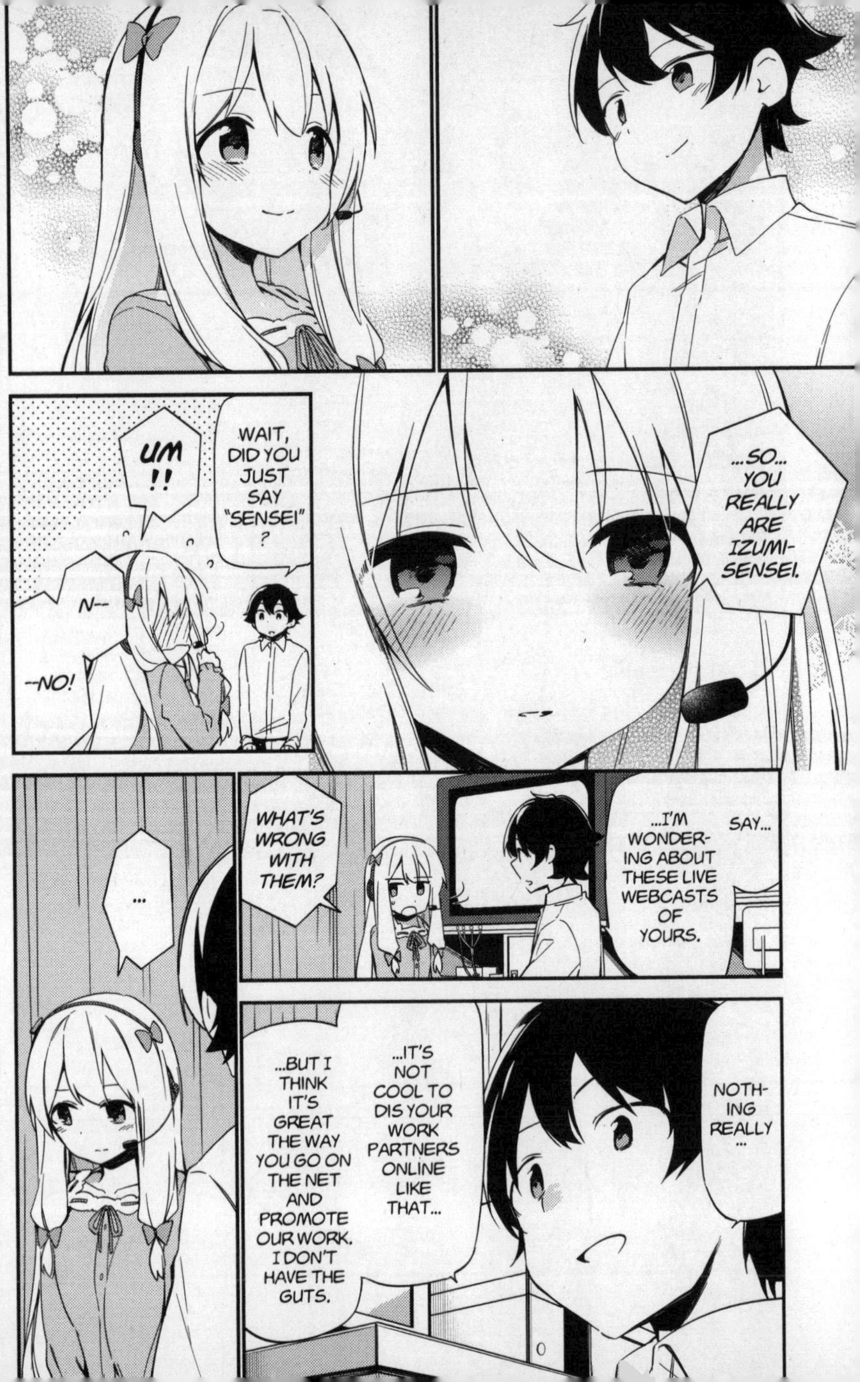
...SO... YOU REALLY ARE IZUMI-SENSEI.
WAIT, DID YOU JUST SAY "SENSEI"?
UM !!
N--
--NO!
SAY...
...I'M WONDER-ING ABOUT THESE LIVE WEBCASTS OF YOURS.
WHAT'S WRONG WITH THEM?
NOTH-ING REALLY ...
...IT'S NOT COOL TO DIS YOUR WORK PARTNERS ONLINE LIKE THAT...
...BUT I THINK IT'S GREAT THE WAY YOU GO ON THE NET AND PROMOTE OUR WORK. I DON'T HAVE THE GUTS.
...

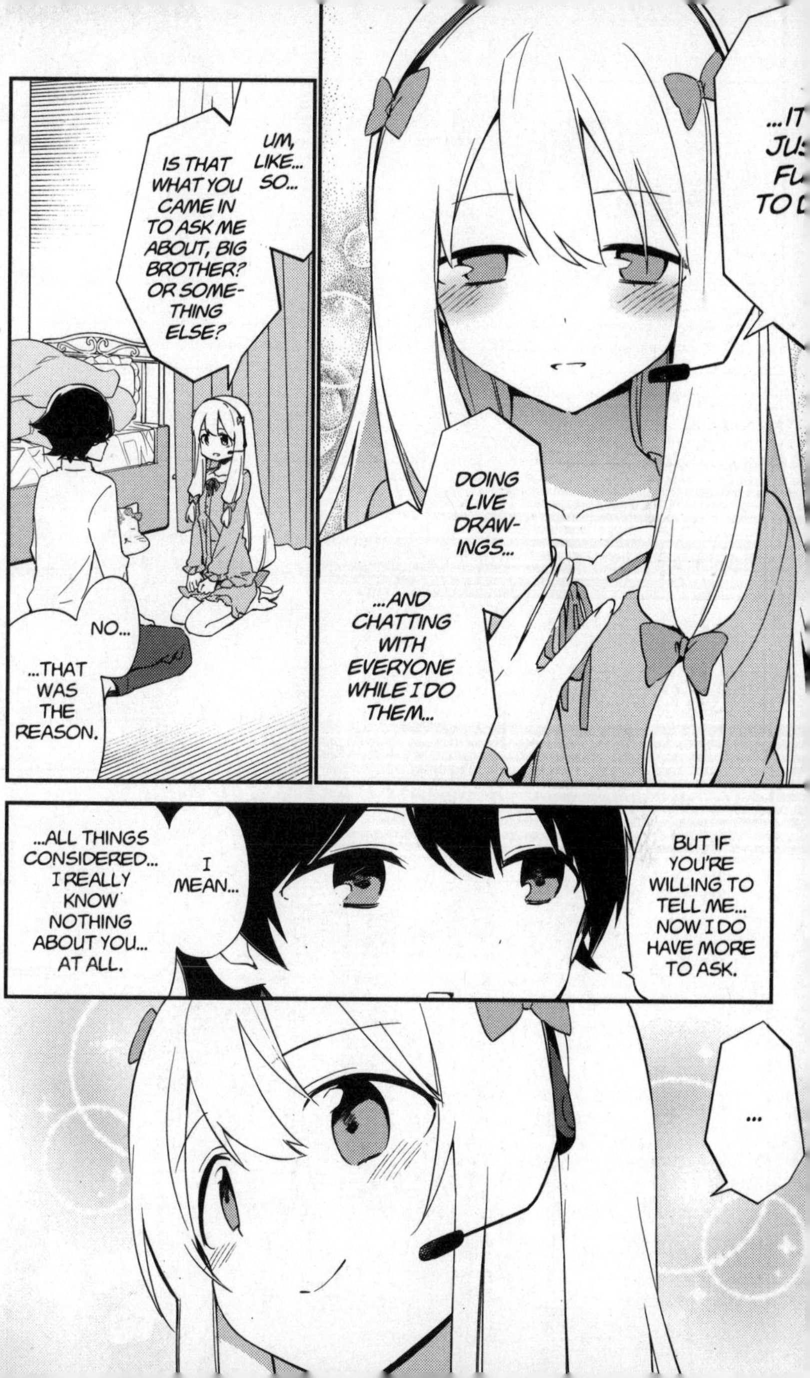
...IT
DOING LIVE DRAW-INGS...
...AND CHATTING WITH EVERYONE WHILE I DO THEM...
UM, LIKE... SO...
IS THAT WHAT YOU CAME IN TO ASK ME ABOUT, BIG BROTHER? OR SOME-THING ELSE?
NO...
...THAT WAS THE REASON.
BUT IF YOU'RE WILLING TO TELL ME... NOW I DO HAVE MORE TO ASK.
I MEAN...
...ALL THINGS CONSIDERED... I REALLY KNOW NOTHING ABOUT YOU... AT ALL.
...

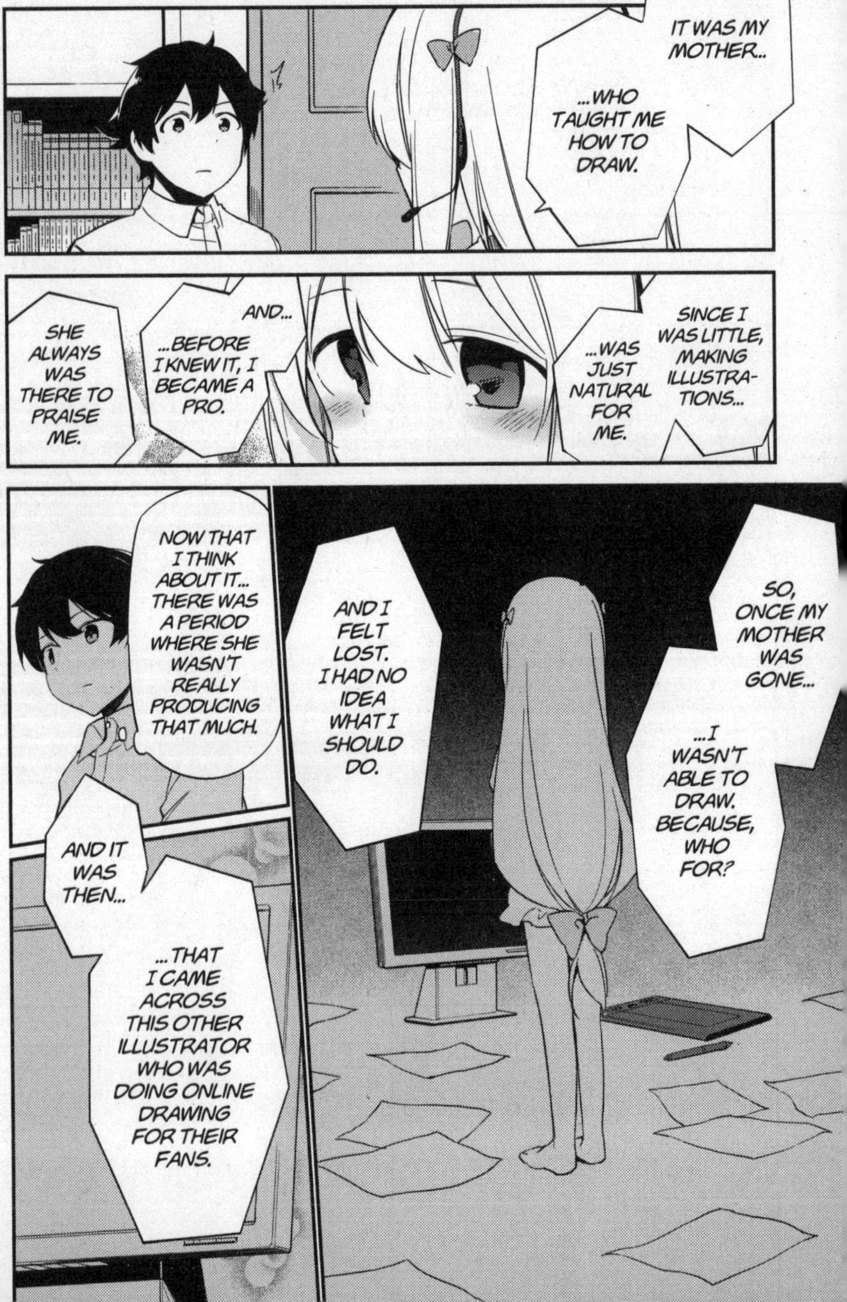
IT WAS MY MOTHER...
...WHO TAUGHT ME HOW TO DRAW.
SINCE I WAS LITTLE, MAKING ILLUSTRATIONS...
...WAS JUST NATURAL FOR ME.
AND...
...BEFORE I KNEW IT, I BECAME A PRO.
SHE ALWAYS WAS THERE TO PRAISE ME.
SO, ONCE MY MOTHER WAS GONE...
...I WASN'T ABLE TO DRAW. BECAUSE, WHO FOR?
AND I FELT LOST. I HAD NO IDEA WHAT I SHOULD DO.
NOW THAT I THINK ABOUT IT... THERE WAS A PERIOD WHERE SHE WASN'T REALLY PRODUCING THAT MUCH.
AND IT WAS THEN...
...THAT I CAME ACROSS THIS OTHER ILLUSTRATOR WHO WAS DOING ONLINE DRAWING FOR THEIR FANS.

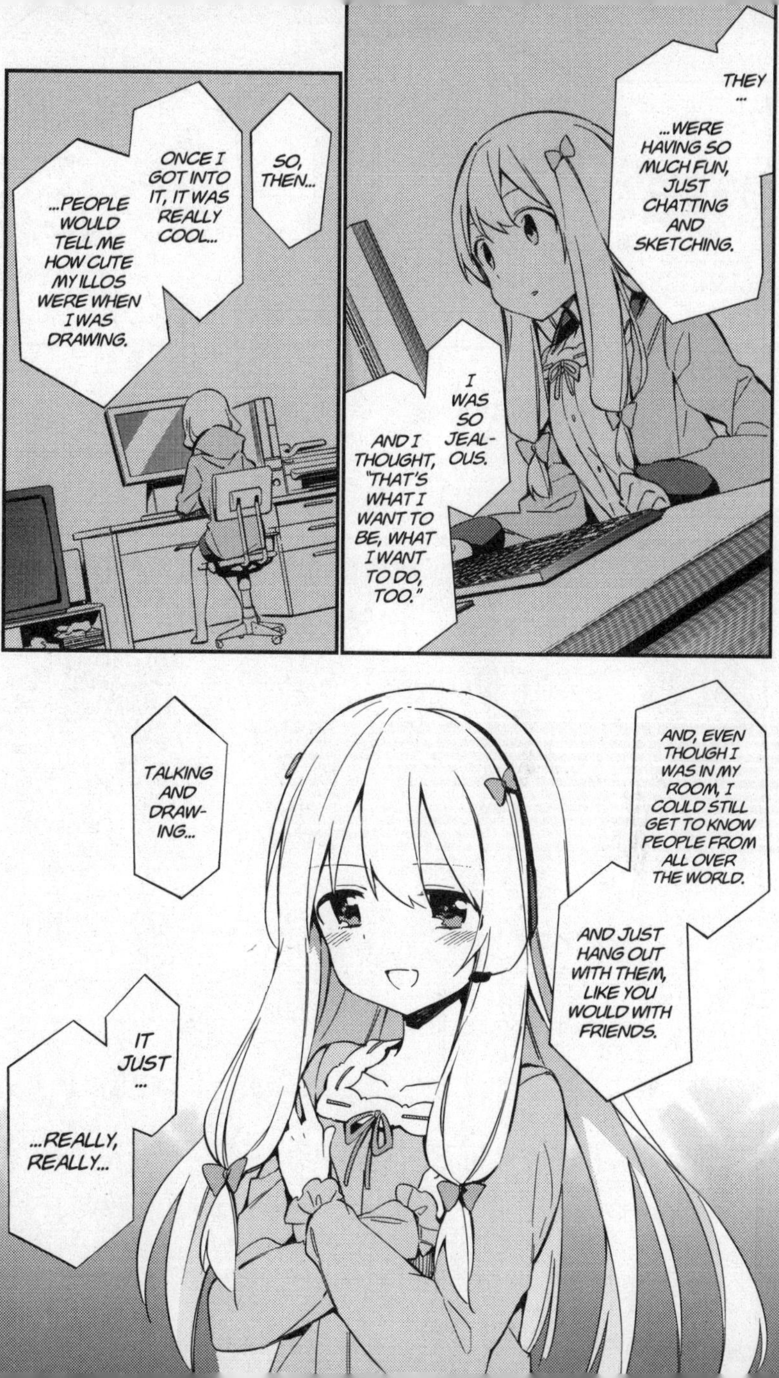
THEY ...
...WERE HAVING SO MUCH FUN, JUST CHATTING AND SKETCHING.
I WAS SO JEAL-OUS.
AND I THOUGHT, "THAT'S WHAT I WANT TO BE, WHAT I WANT TO DO, TOO."
SO, THEN...
ONCE I GOT INTO IT, IT WAS REALLY COOL...
...PEOPLE WOULD TELL ME HOW CUTE MY ILLOS WERE WHEN I WAS DRAWING.
AND, EVEN THOUGH I WAS IN MY ROOM, I COULD STILL GET TO KNOW PEOPLE FROM ALL OVER THE WORLD.
TALKING AND DRAW-ING...
AND JUST HANG OUT WITH THEM, LIKE YOU WOULD WITH FRIENDS.
IT JUST ...
...REALLY, REALLY...

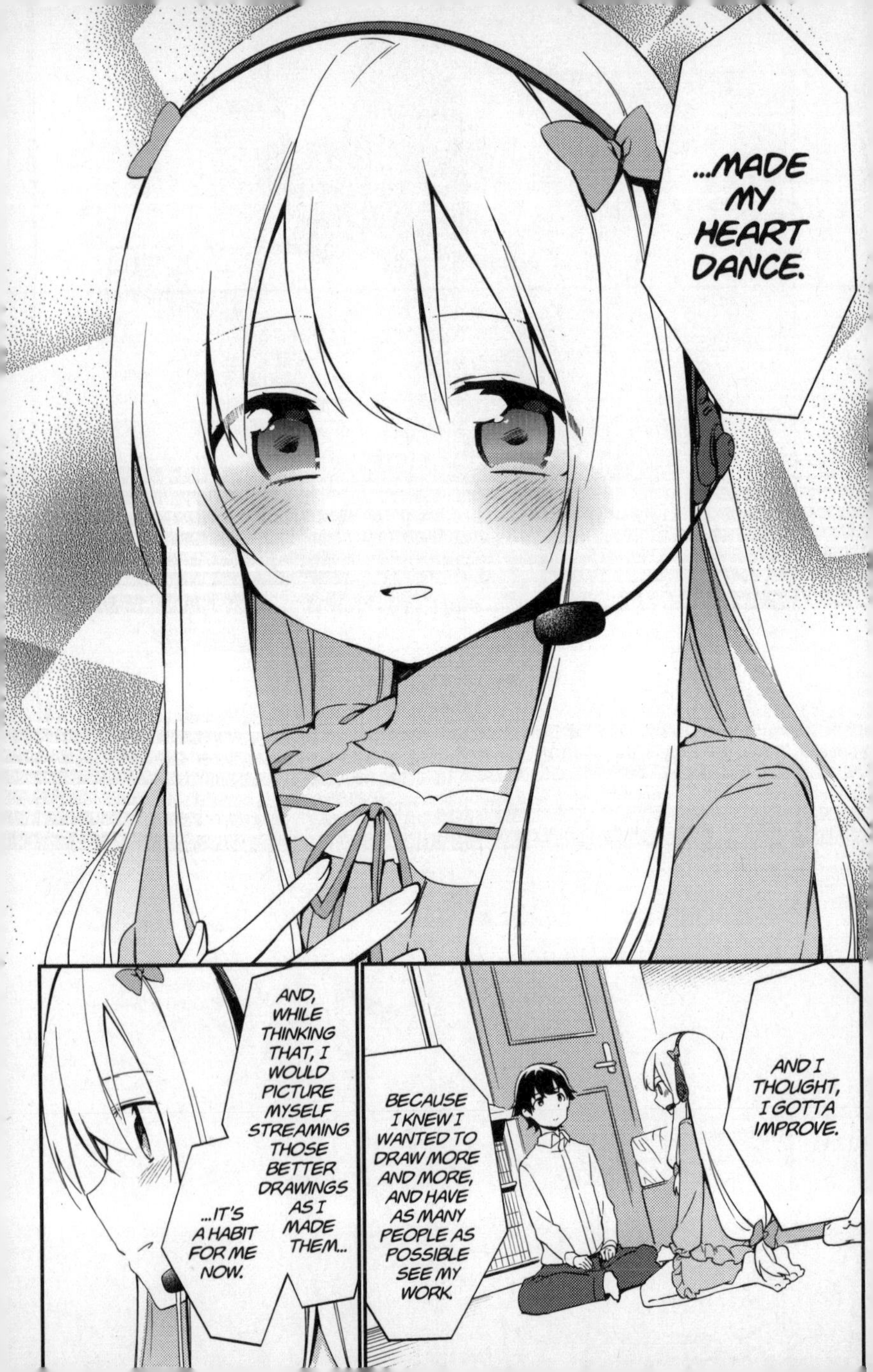
...MADE MY HEART DANCE.
AND I THOUGHT, I GOTTA IMPROVE.
BECAUSE I KNEW I WANTED TO DRAW MORE AND MORE, AND HAVE AS MANY PEOPLE AS POSSIBLE SEE MY WORK.
AND, WHILE THINKING THAT, I WOULD PICTURE MYSELF STREAMING THOSE BETTER DRAWINGS AS I MADE THEM...
...IT'S A HABIT FOR ME NOW.

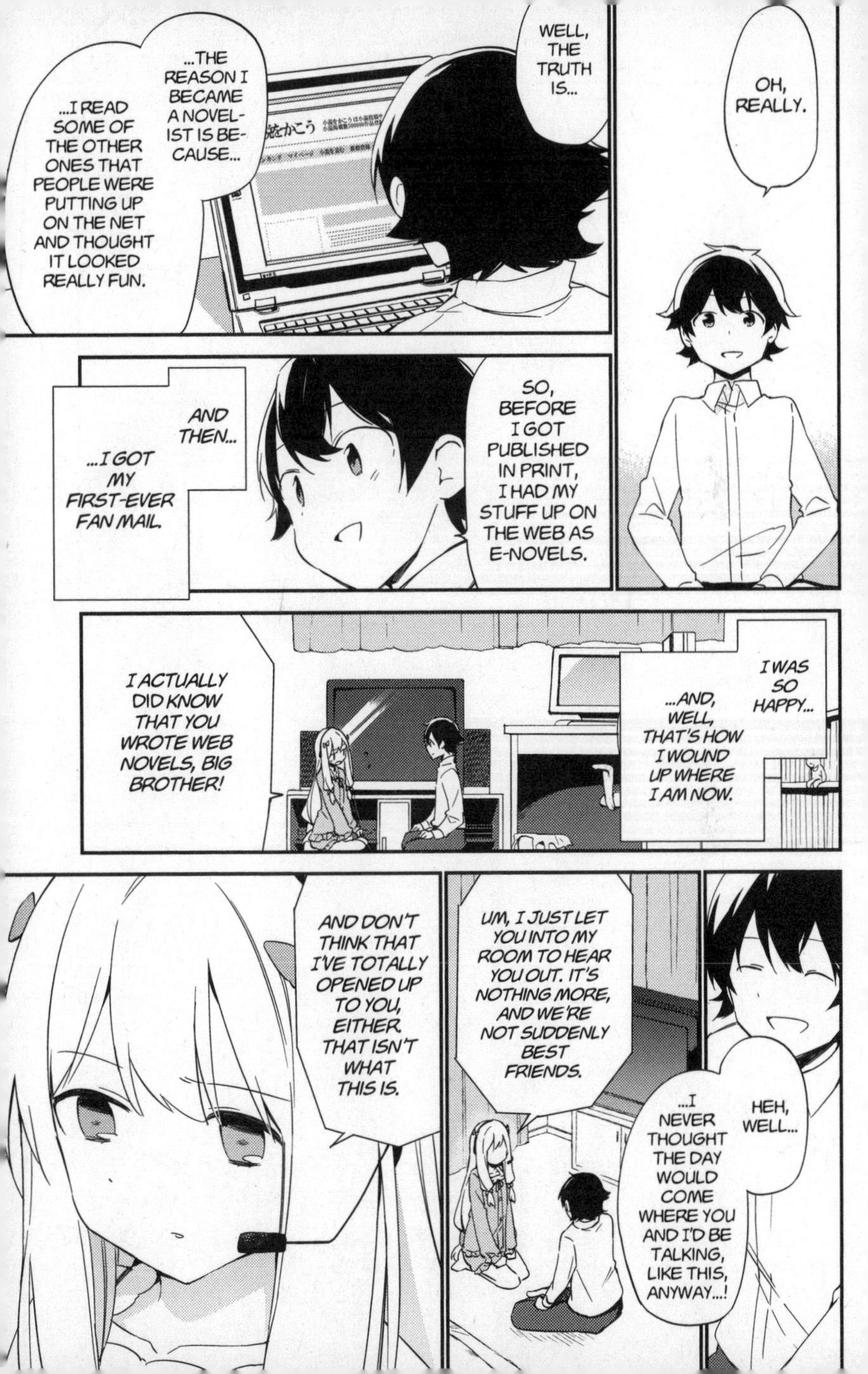
OH, REALLY.
WELL, THE TRUTH IS...
...THE REASON I BECAME A NOVELIST IS BECAUSE...
...I READ SOME OF THE OTHER ONES THAT PEOPLE WERE PUTTING UP ON THE NET AND THOUGHT IT LOOKED REALLY FUN.
SO, BEFORE I GOT PUBLISHED IN PRINT, I HAD MY STUFF UP ON THE WEB AS E-NOVELS.
AND THEN...
...I GOT MY FIRST-EVER FAN MAIL.
I WAS SO HAPPY...
...AND, WELL, THAT'S HOW I WOUND UP WHERE I AM NOW.
I ACTUALLY DID KNOW THAT YOU WROTE WEB NOVELS, BIG BROTHER!
HEH, WELL...
...I NEVER THOUGHT THE DAY WOULD COME WHERE YOU AND I'D BE TALKING, LIKE THIS, ANYWAY...!
UM, I JUST LET YOU INTO MY ROOM TO HEAR YOU OUT. IT'S NOTHING MORE, AND WE'RE NOT SUDDENLY BEST FRIENDS.
AND DON'T THINK THAT I'VE TOTALLY OPENED UP TO YOU, EITHER. THAT ISN'T WHAT THIS IS.

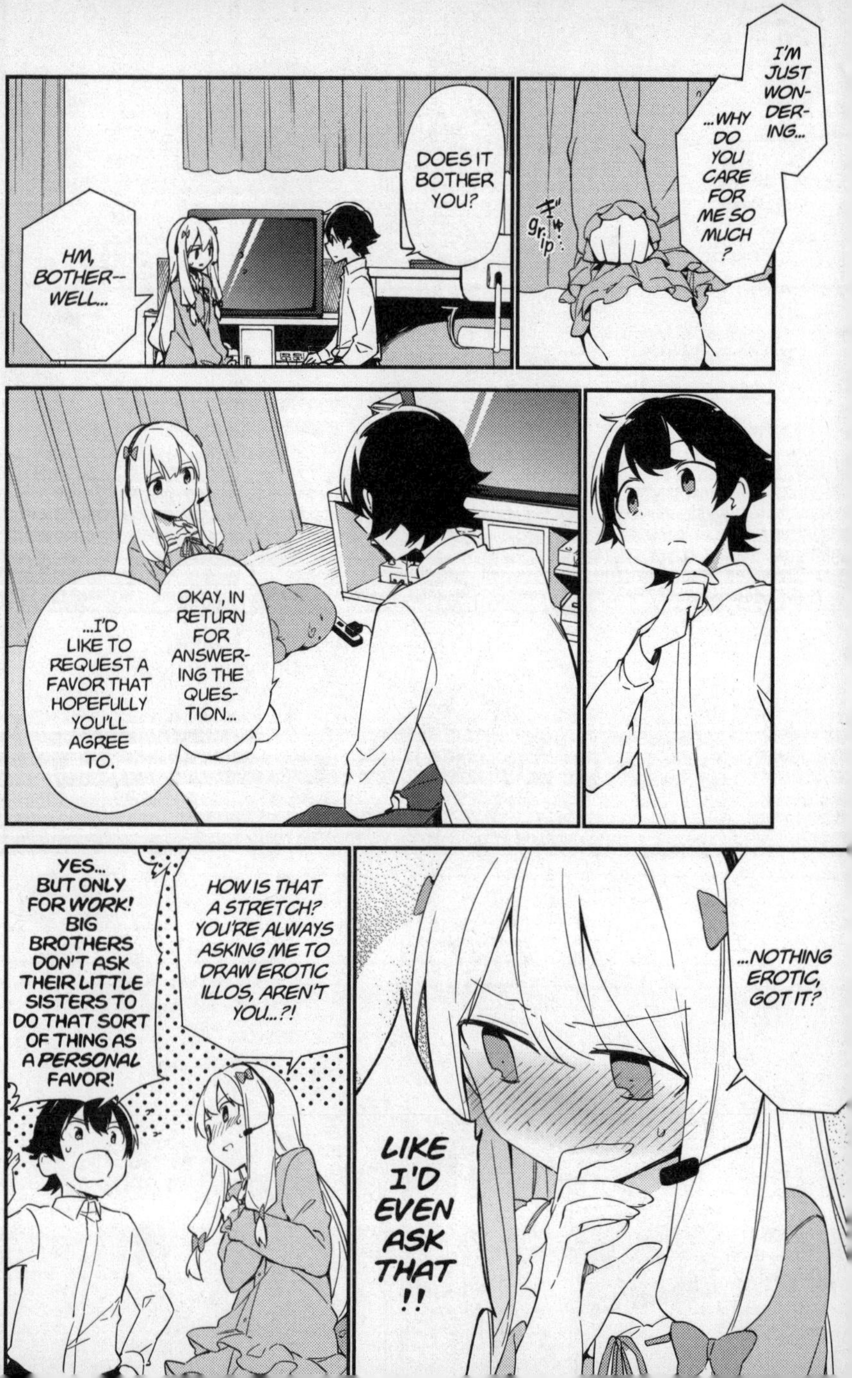
I'M JUST WONDERING...
...WHY DO YOU CARE FOR ME SO MUCH?
ぎゅ grip
DOES IT BOTHER YOU?
HM, BOTHER-- WELL...
OKAY, IN RETURN FOR ANSWERING THE QUESTION...
...I'D LIKE TO REQUEST A FAVOR THAT HOPEFULLY YOU'LL AGREE TO.
...NOTHING EROTIC, GOT IT?
LIKE I'D EVEN ASK THAT!!
HOW IS THAT A STRETCH? YOU'RE ALWAYS ASKING ME TO DRAW EROTIC ILLOS, AREN'T YOU...?!
YES... BUT ONLY FOR WORK! BIG BROTHERS DON'T ASK THEIR LITTLE SISTERS TO DO THAT SORT OF THING AS A PERSONAL FAVOR!

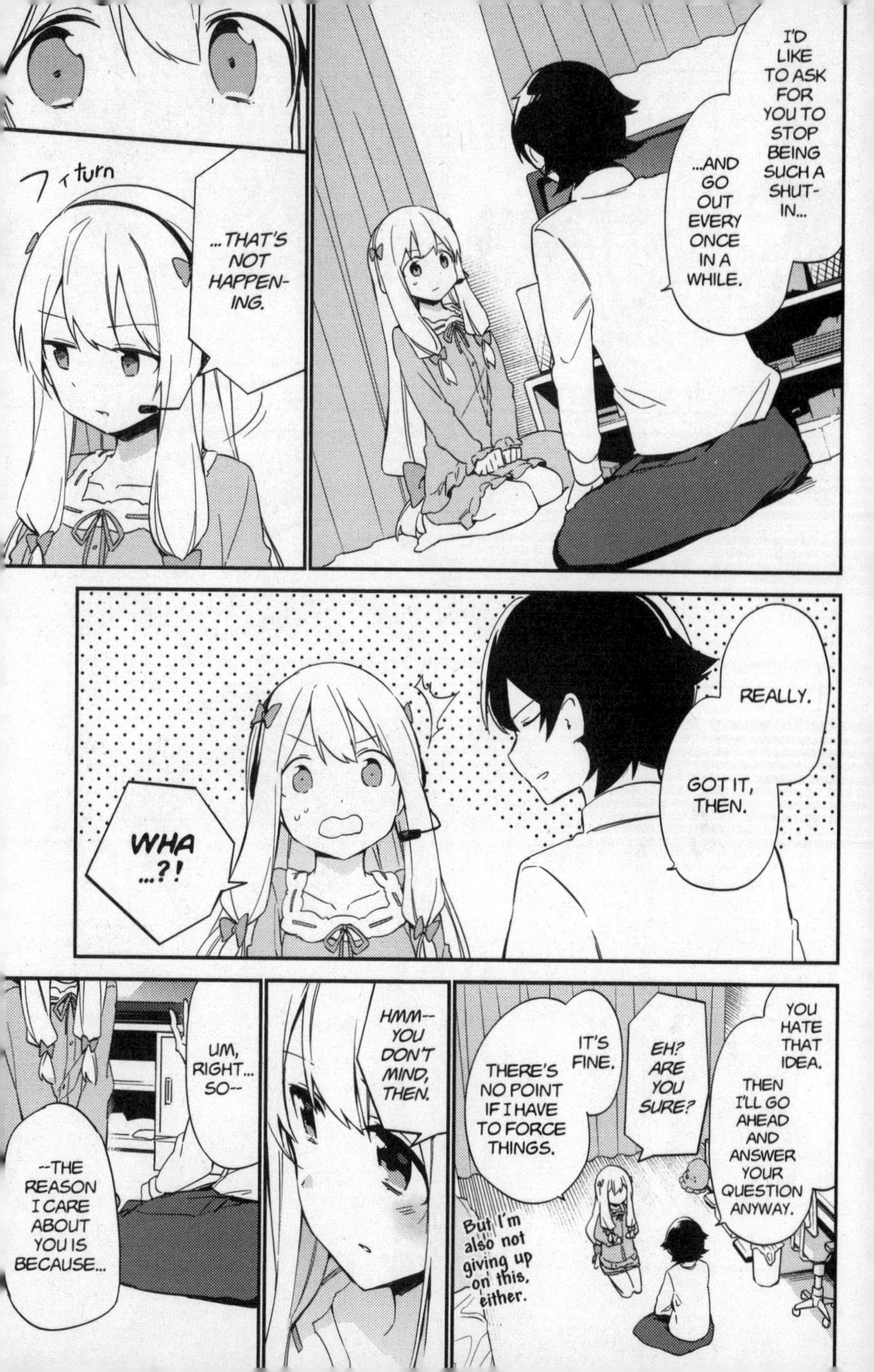
I'D LIKE TO ASK FOR YOU TO STOP BEING SUCH A SHUT-IN...
...AND GO OUT EVERY ONCE IN A WHILE.
フィ turn
...THAT'S NOT HAPPENING.
REALLY.
GOT IT, THEN.
WHA ...?!
YOU HATE THAT IDEA.
THEN I'LL GO AHEAD AND ANSWER YOUR QUESTION ANYWAY.
EH? ARE YOU SURE?
IT'S FINE.
THERE'S NO POINT IF I HAVE TO FORCE THINGS.
But I'm also not giving up on this, either.
HMM-- YOU DON'T MIND, THEN.
UM, RIGHT... SO--
--THE REASON I CARE ABOUT YOU IS BECAUSE...

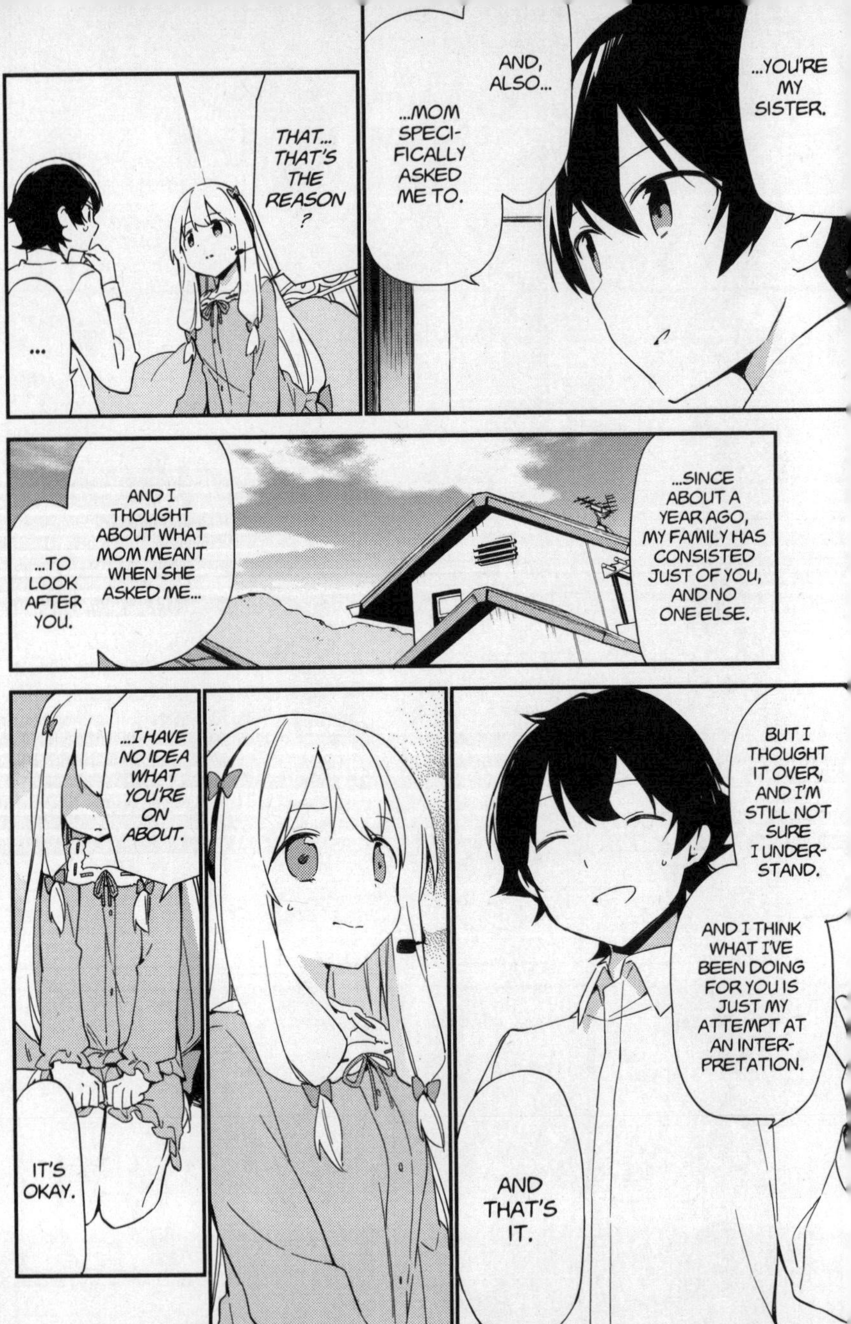
...YOU'RE MY SISTER.
AND, ALSO...
...MOM SPECI-FICALLY ASKED ME TO.
THAT... THAT'S THE REASON ?
...
...SINCE ABOUT A YEAR AGO, MY FAMILY HAS CONSISTED JUST OF YOU, AND NO ONE ELSE.
AND I THOUGHT ABOUT WHAT MOM MEANT WHEN SHE ASKED ME...
...TO LOOK AFTER YOU.
BUT I THOUGHT IT OVER, AND I'M STILL NOT SURE I UNDER-STAND.
AND I THINK WHAT I'VE BEEN DOING FOR YOU IS JUST MY ATTEMPT AT AN INTER-PRETATION.
AND THAT'S IT.
...I HAVE NO IDEA WHAT YOU'RE ON ABOUT.
IT'S OKAY.

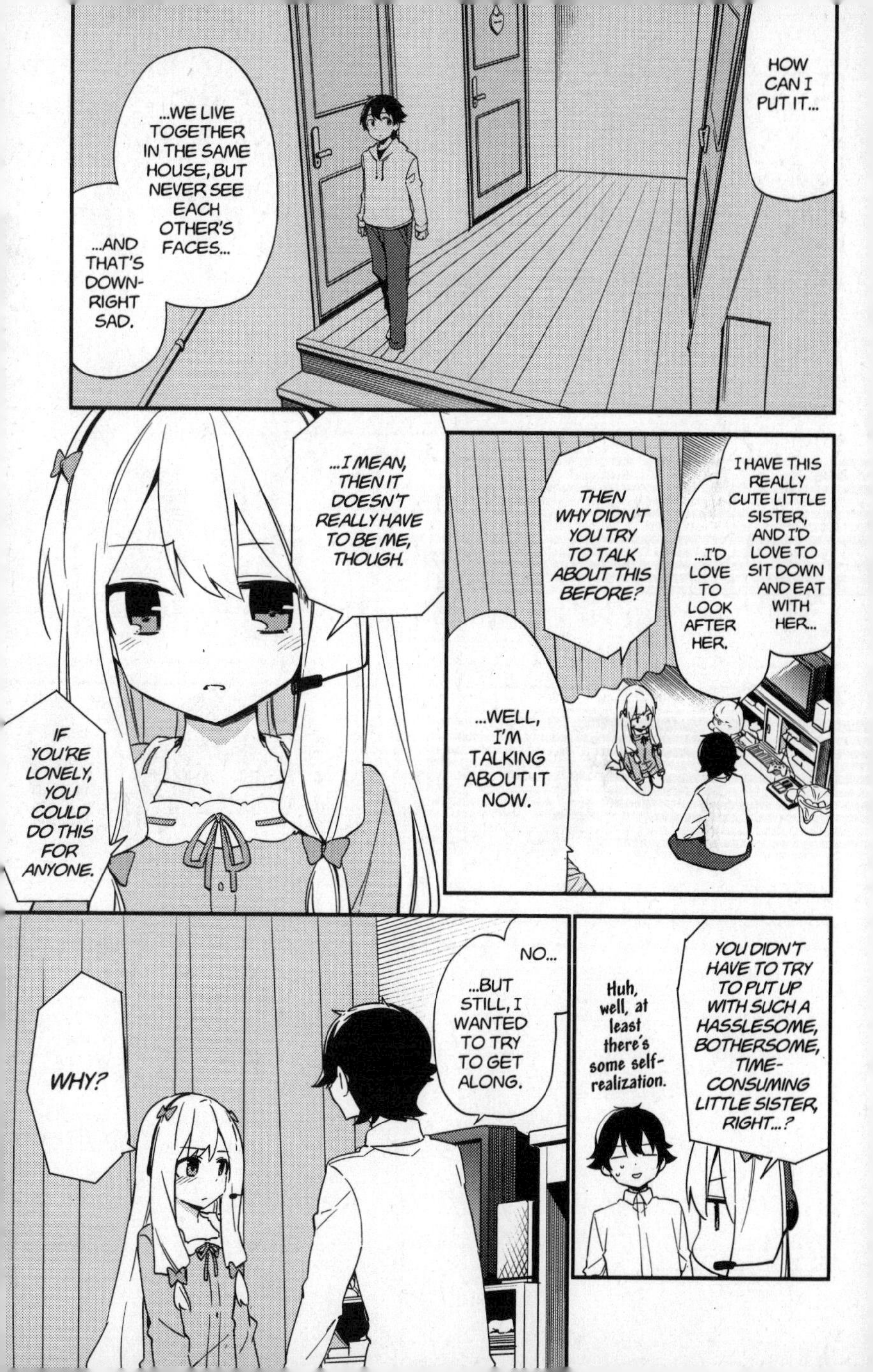
HOW CAN I PUT IT...
...WE LIVE TOGETHER IN THE SAME HOUSE, BUT NEVER SEE EACH OTHER'S FACES...
...AND THAT'S DOWN-RIGHT SAD.
I HAVE THIS REALLY CUTE LITTLE SISTER, AND I'D LOVE TO SIT DOWN AND EAT WITH HER...
...I'D LOVE TO LOOK AFTER HER.
THEN WHY DIDN'T YOU TRY TO TALK ABOUT THIS BEFORE?
...WELL, I'M TALKING ABOUT IT NOW.
...I MEAN, THEN IT DOESN'T REALLY HAVE TO BE ME, THOUGH.
IF YOU'RE LONELY, YOU COULD DO THIS FOR ANYONE.
YOU DIDN'T HAVE TO TRY TO PUT UP WITH SUCH A HASSLESOME, BOTHERSOME, TIME-CONSUMING LITTLE SISTER, RIGHT...?
Huh, well, at least there's some self-realization.
NO...
...BUT STILL, I WANTED TO TRY TO GET ALONG.
WHY?

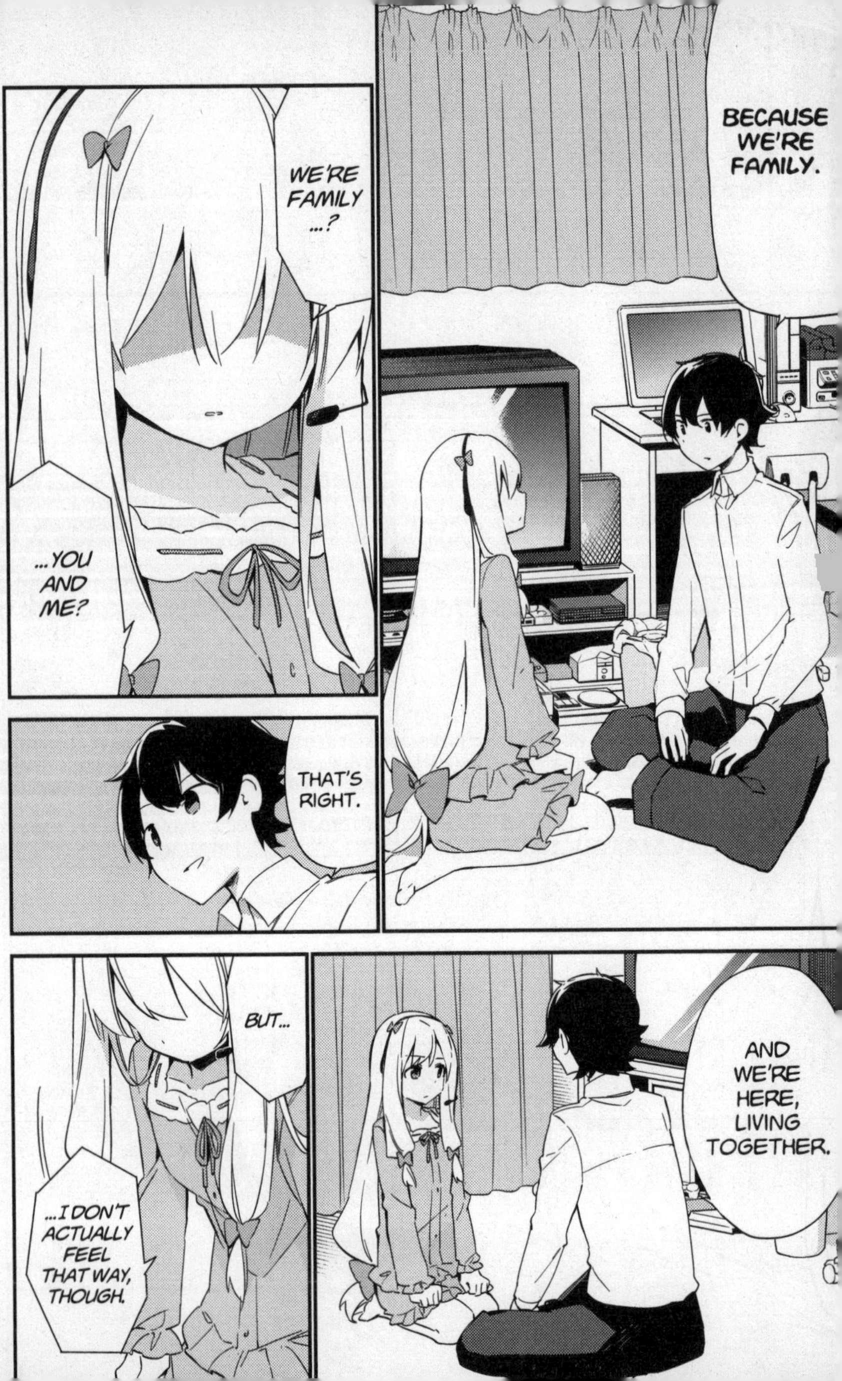
BECAUSE WE'RE FAMILY.
WE'RE FAMILY ...?
...YOU AND ME?
THAT'S RIGHT.
AND WE'RE HERE, LIVING TOGETHER.
BUT...
...I DON'T ACTUALLY FEEL THAT WAY, THOUGH.

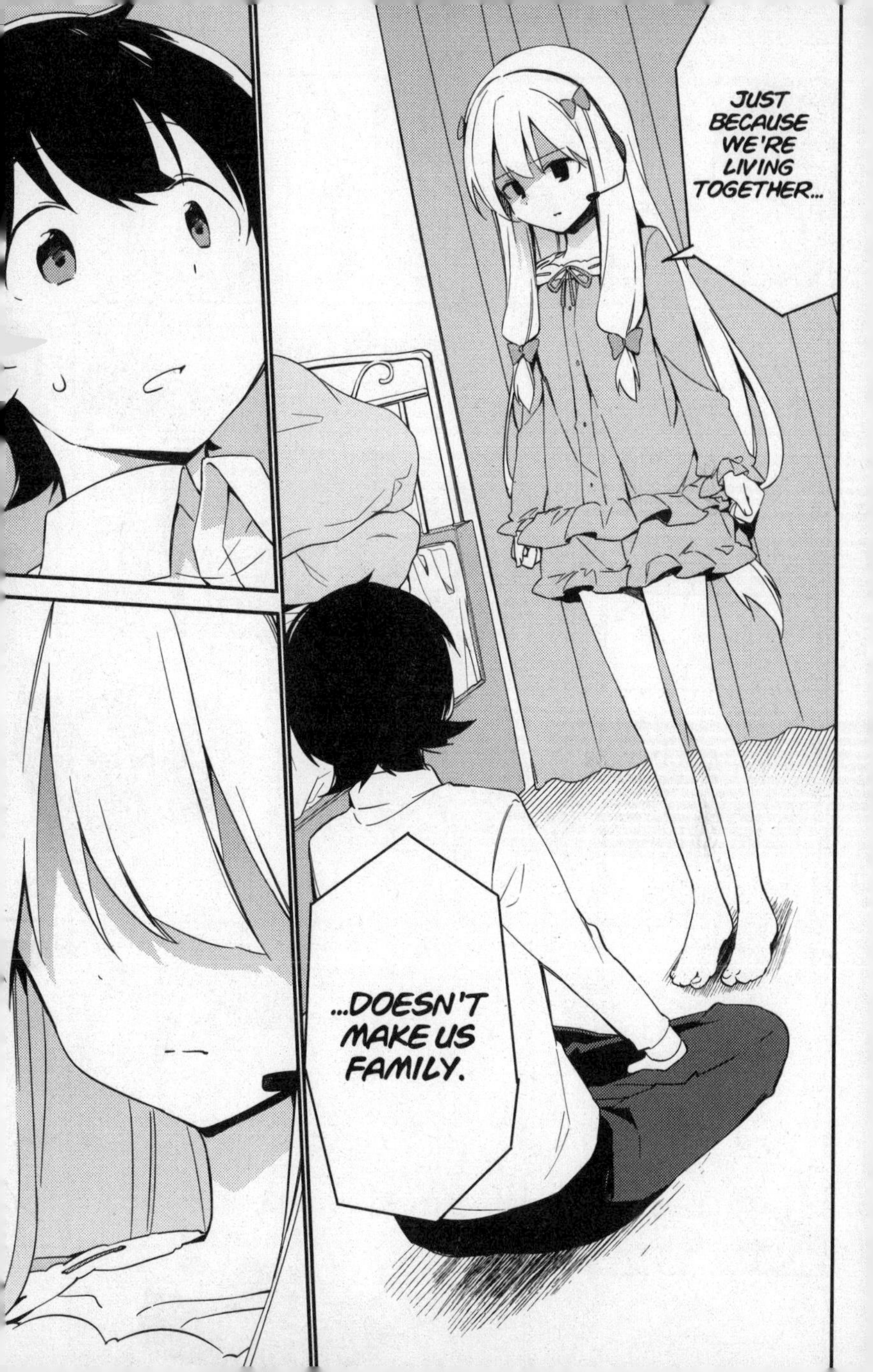
JUST BECAUSE WE'RE LIVING TOGETHER...
...DOESN'T MAKE US FAMILY.

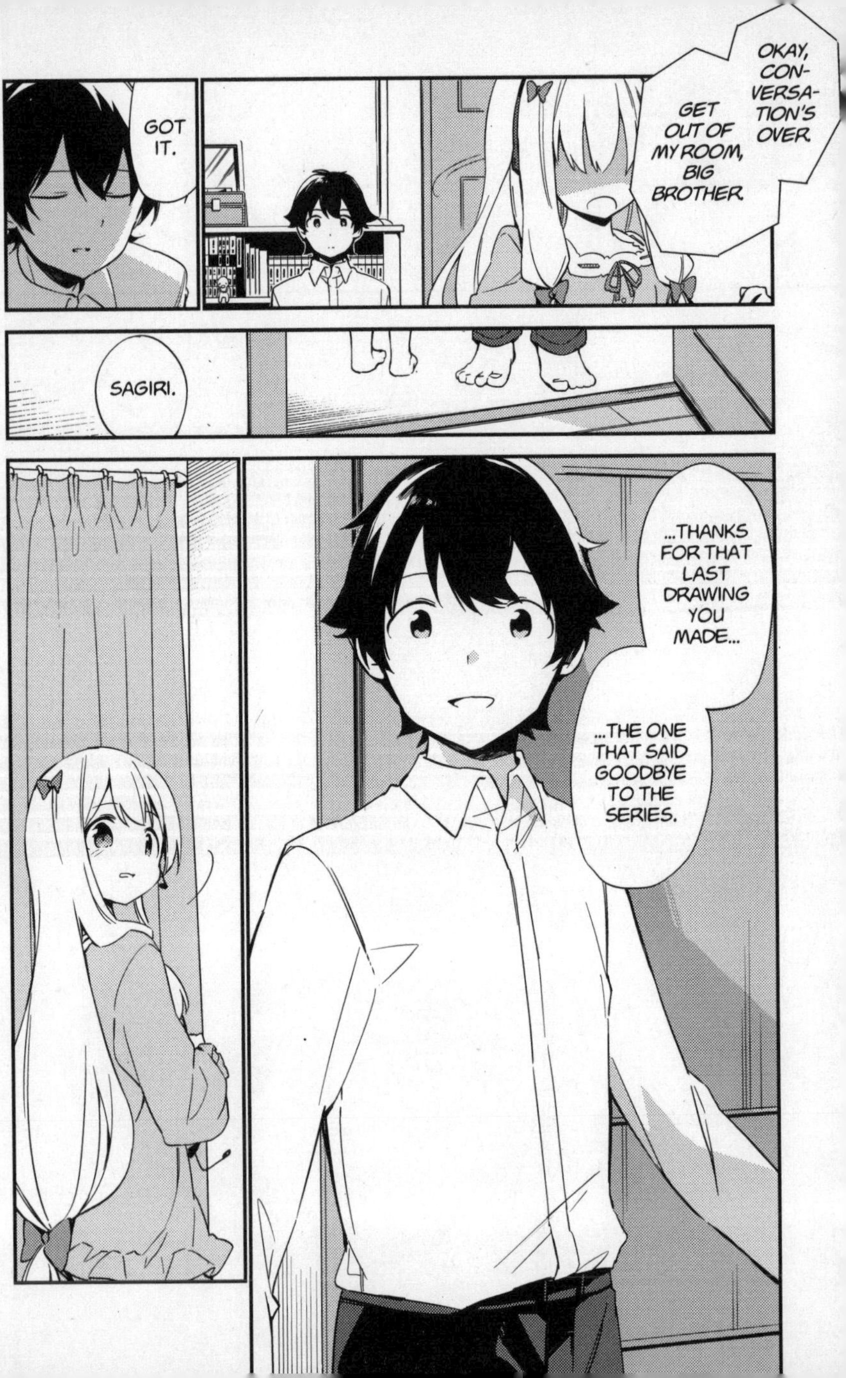
OKAY, CON-VERSA-TION'S OVER.
GET OUT OF MY ROOM, BIG BROTHER.
GOT IT.
SAGIRI.
...THANKS FOR THAT LAST DRAWING YOU MADE...
...THE ONE THAT SAID GOODBYE TO THE SERIES.

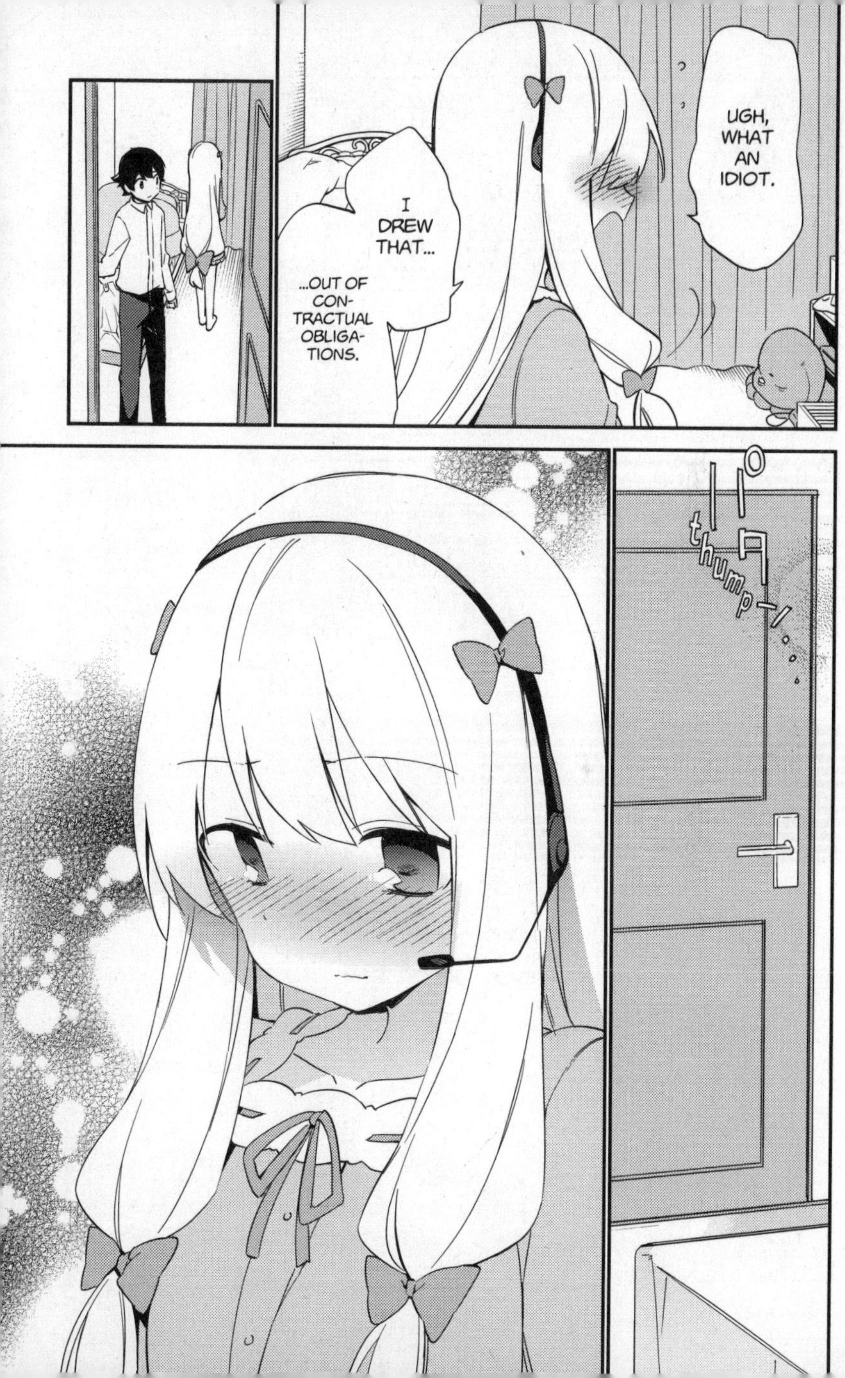
UGH, WHAT AN IDIOT.
I DREW THAT...
...OUT OF CON-TRACTUAL OBLIGA-TIONS.
thump-!

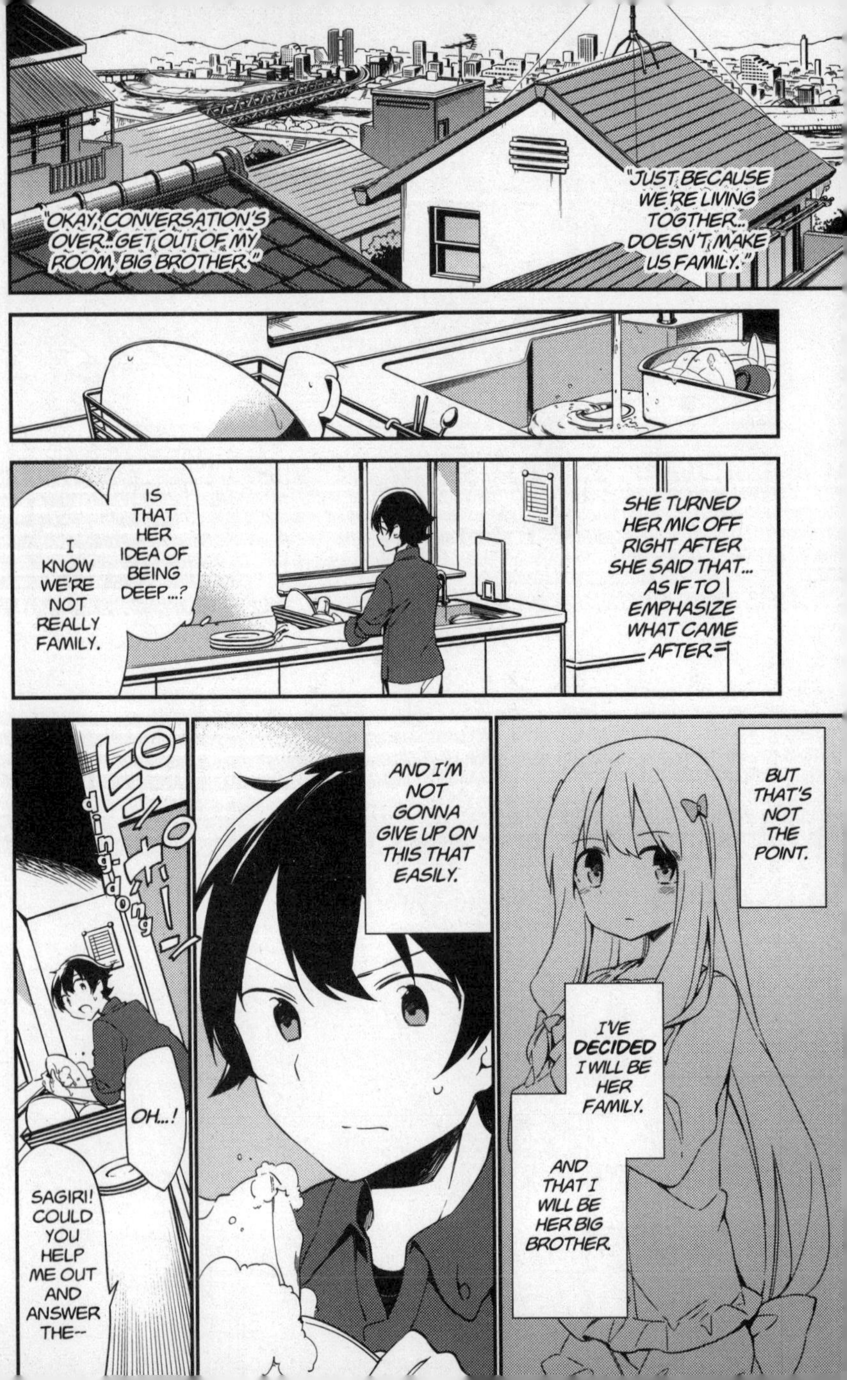
"JUST BECAUSE WE'RE LIVING TOGTHER... DOESN'T MAKE US FAMILY."
"OKAY, CONVERSATION'S OVER... GET OUT OF MY ROOM, BIG BROTHER."
SHE TURNED HER MIC OFF RIGHT AFTER SHE SAID THAT... AS IF TO EMPHASIZE WHAT CAME AFTER.
IS THAT HER IDEA OF BEING DEEP...? I KNOW WE'RE NOT REALLY FAMILY.
BUT THAT'S NOT THE POINT.
I'VE **DECIDED** I WILL BE HER FAMILY.
AND THAT I WILL BE HER BIG BROTHER.
AND I'M NOT GONNA GIVE UP ON THIS THAT EASILY.
ding-dong
OH...!
SAGIRI! COULD YOU HELP ME OUT AND ANSWER THE--

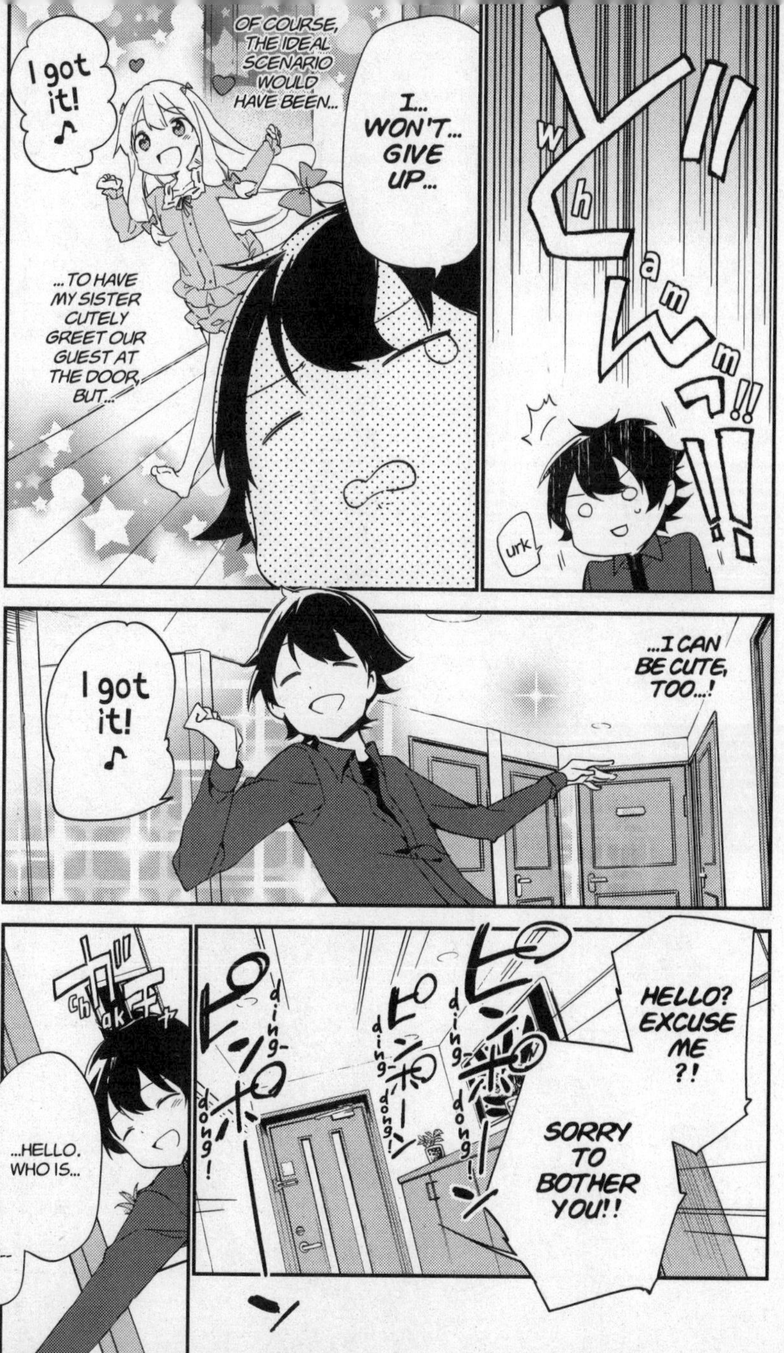
Wham!!
urk
I... WON'T... GIVE UP...
OF COURSE, THE IDEAL SCENARIO WOULD HAVE BEEN...
I got it! ♪
...TO HAVE MY SISTER CUTELY GREET OUR GUEST AT THE DOOR, BUT...
...I CAN BE CUTE, TOO...!
I got it! ♪
HELLO? EXCUSE ME?!
SORRY TO BOTHER YOU!!
ding-dong!
ding-dong!
ding-dong!
Chak
...HELLO. WHO IS...
...IT--

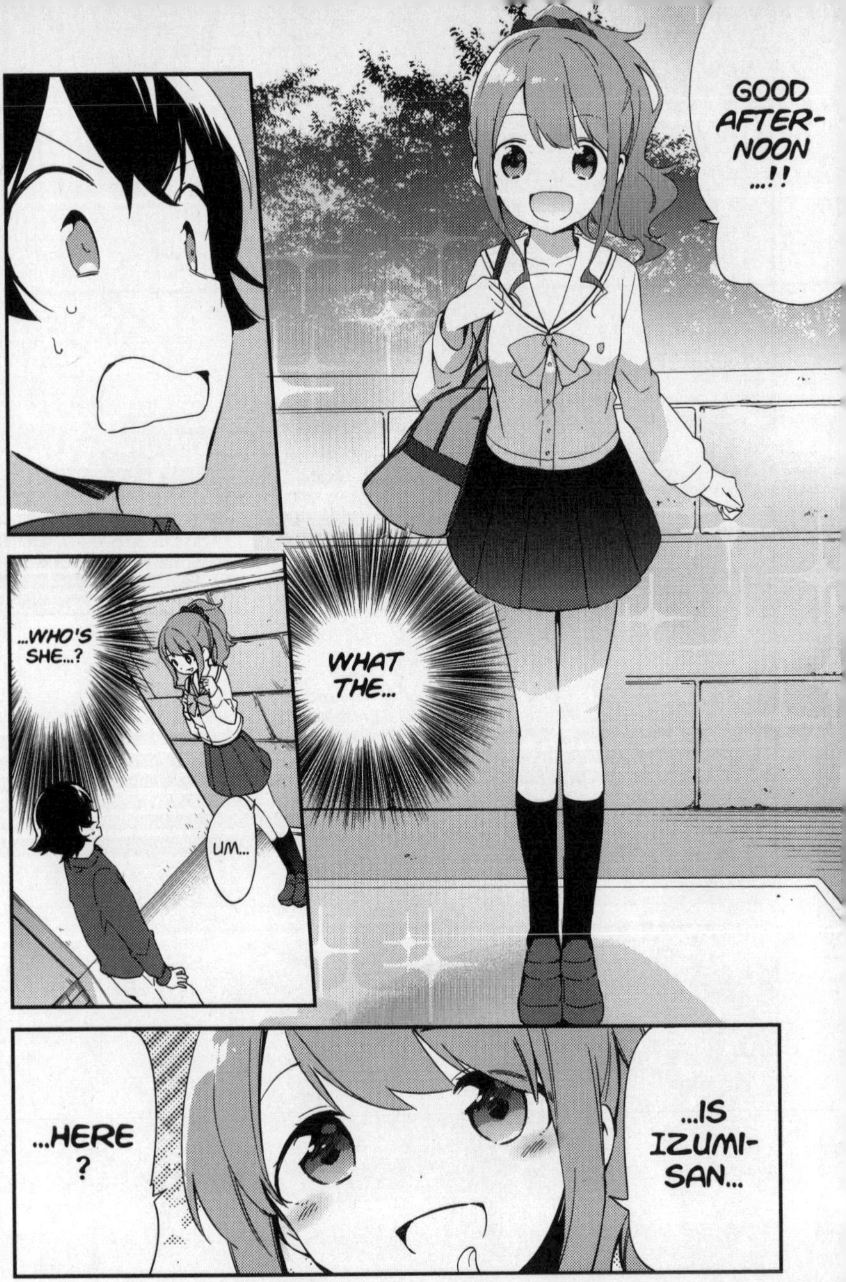
GOOD AFTER-NOON ...!!
WHAT THE...
...WHO'S SHE...?
UM...
...IS IZUMI-SAN...
...HERE ?

eromanga sensei

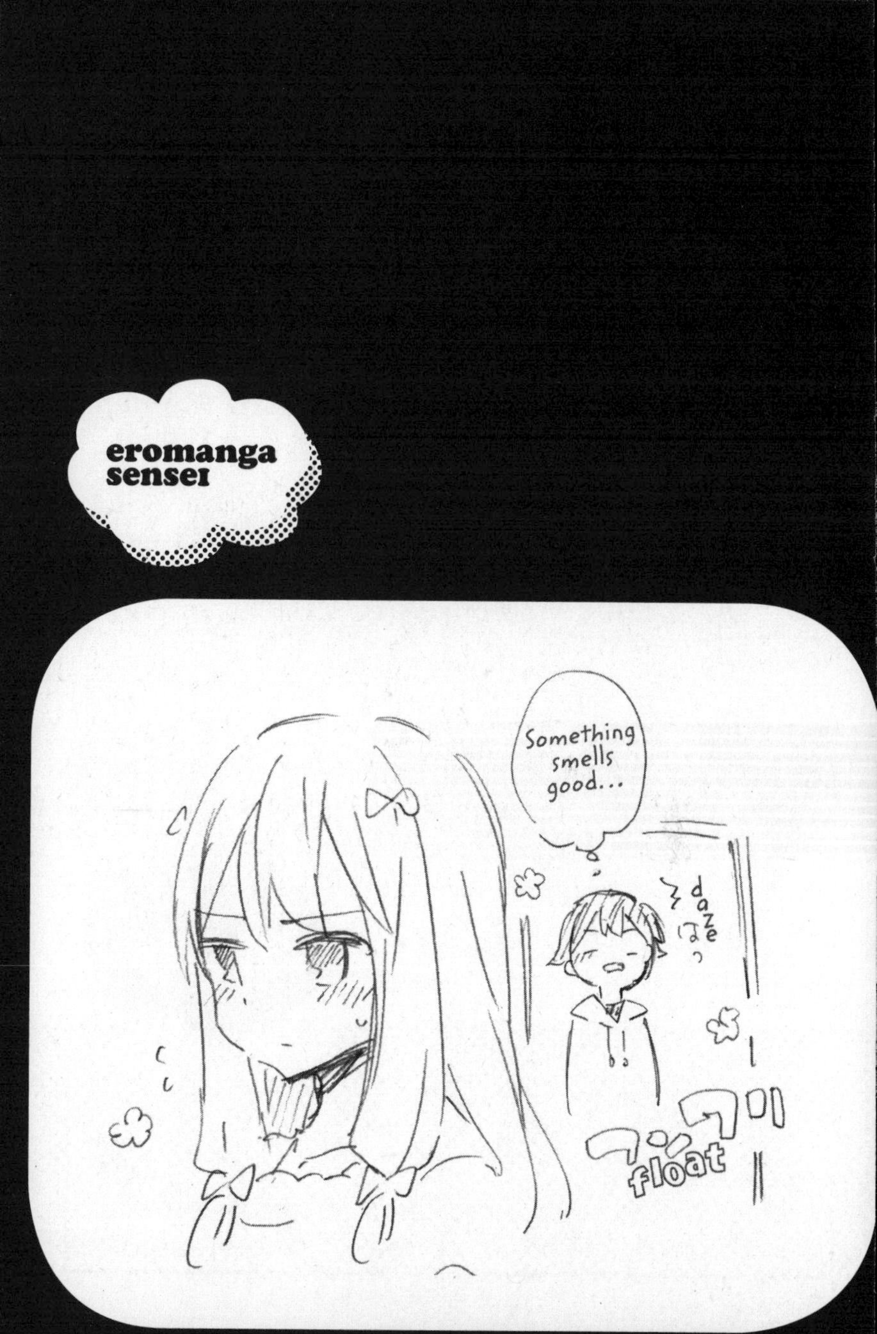
Something smells good...
daze
はっ
float
フワリ

eromanga
sensei

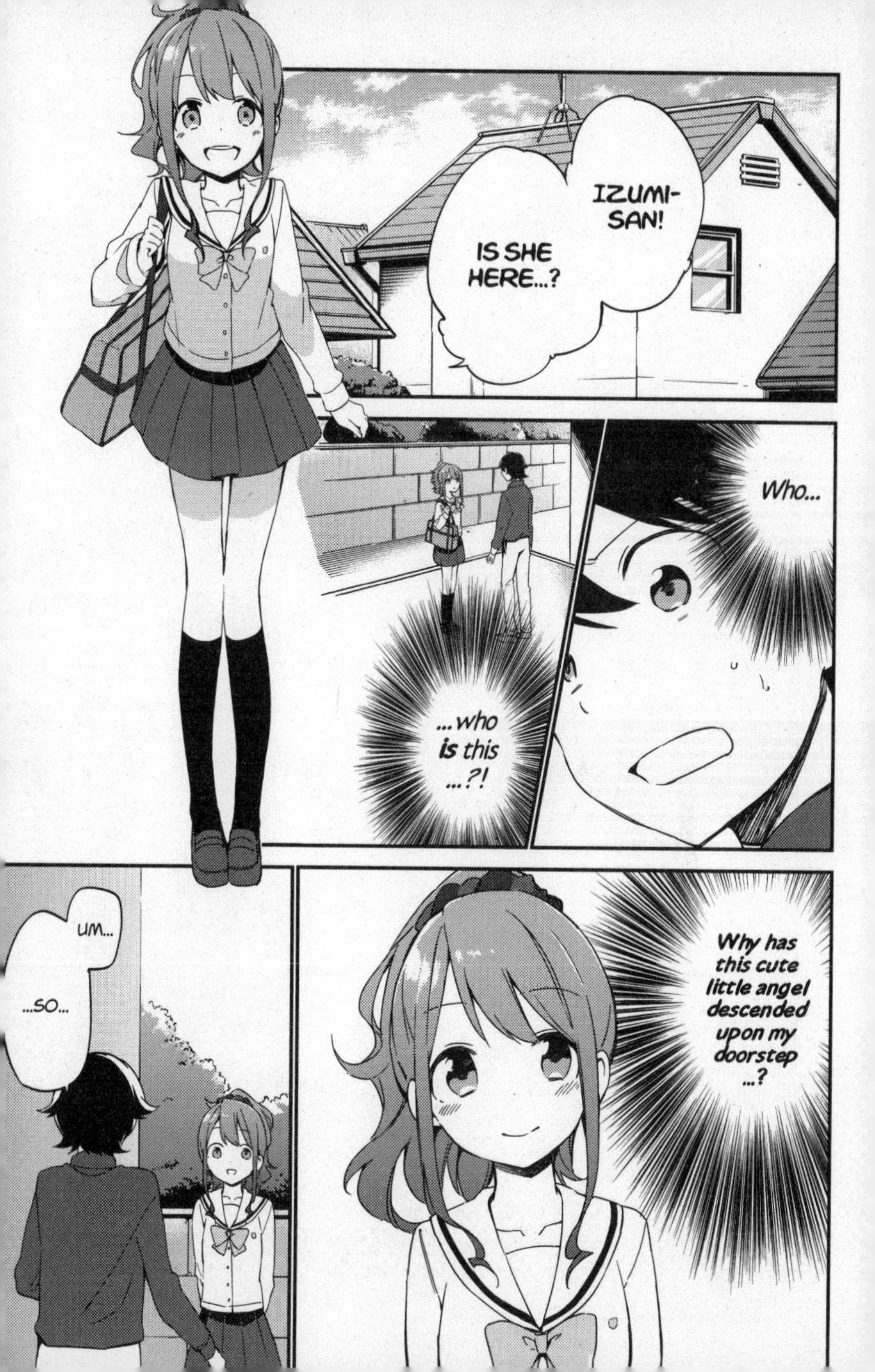
IZUMI-SAN!
IS SHE HERE...?
Who...
...who is this ...?!
Why has this cute little angel descended upon my doorstep ...?
um...
...so...

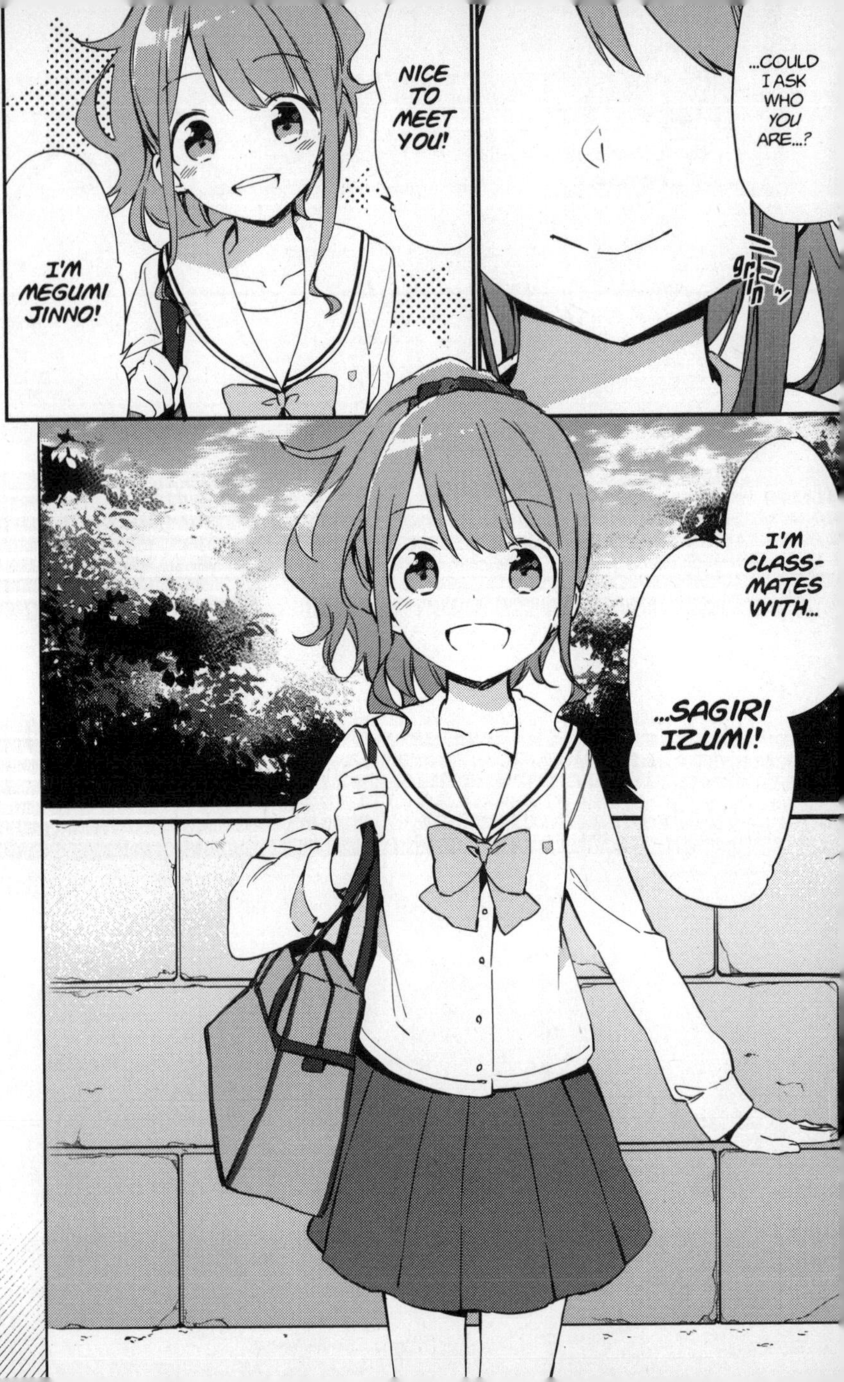
...COULD I ASK WHO YOU ARE...?
grin
ニコッ
NICE TO MEET YOU!
I'M MEGUMI JINNO!
I'M CLASSMATES WITH...
...SAGIRI IZUMI!

Chapter 4

My Little Sister and the Sealed Room • Part 4

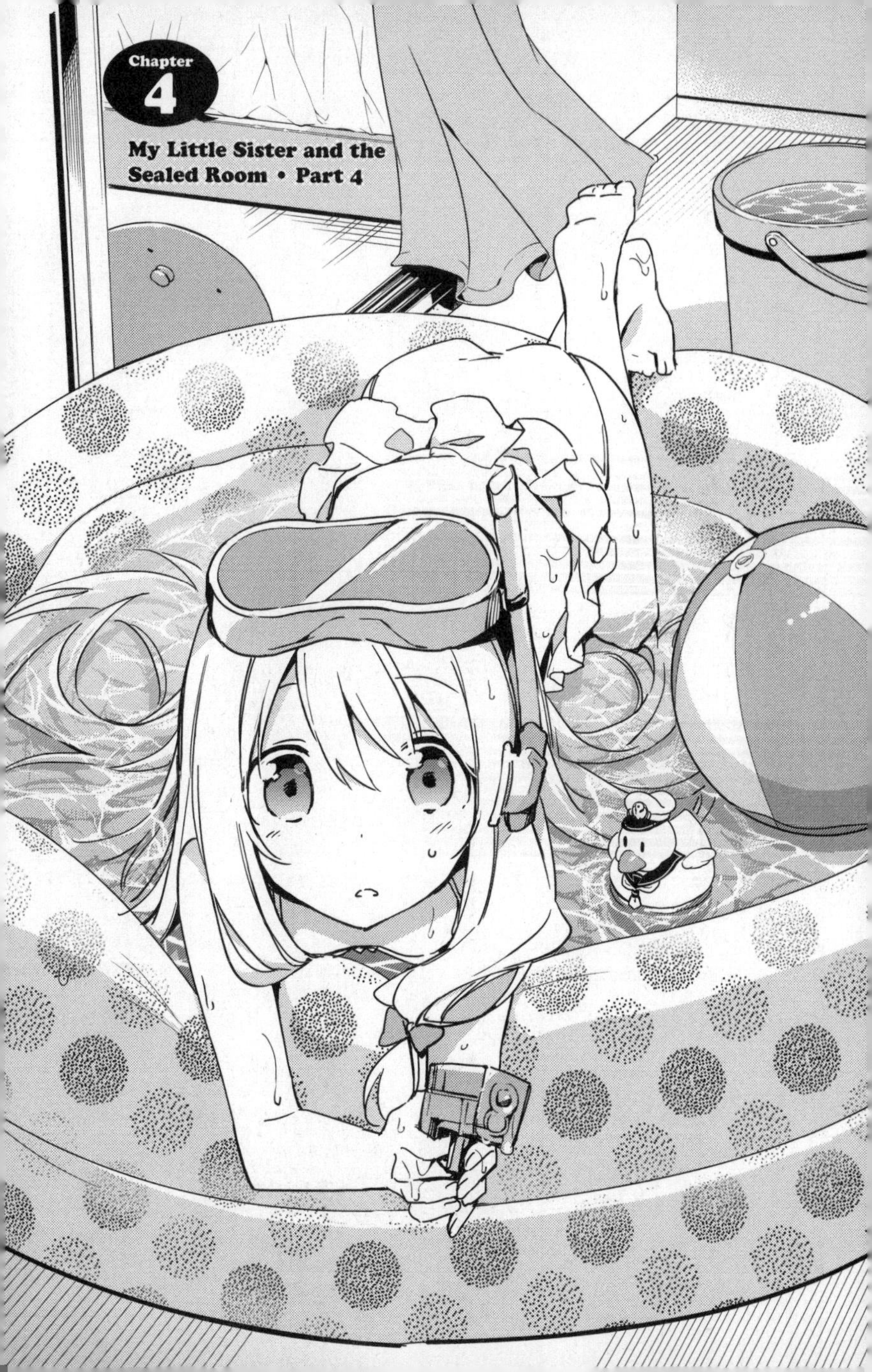

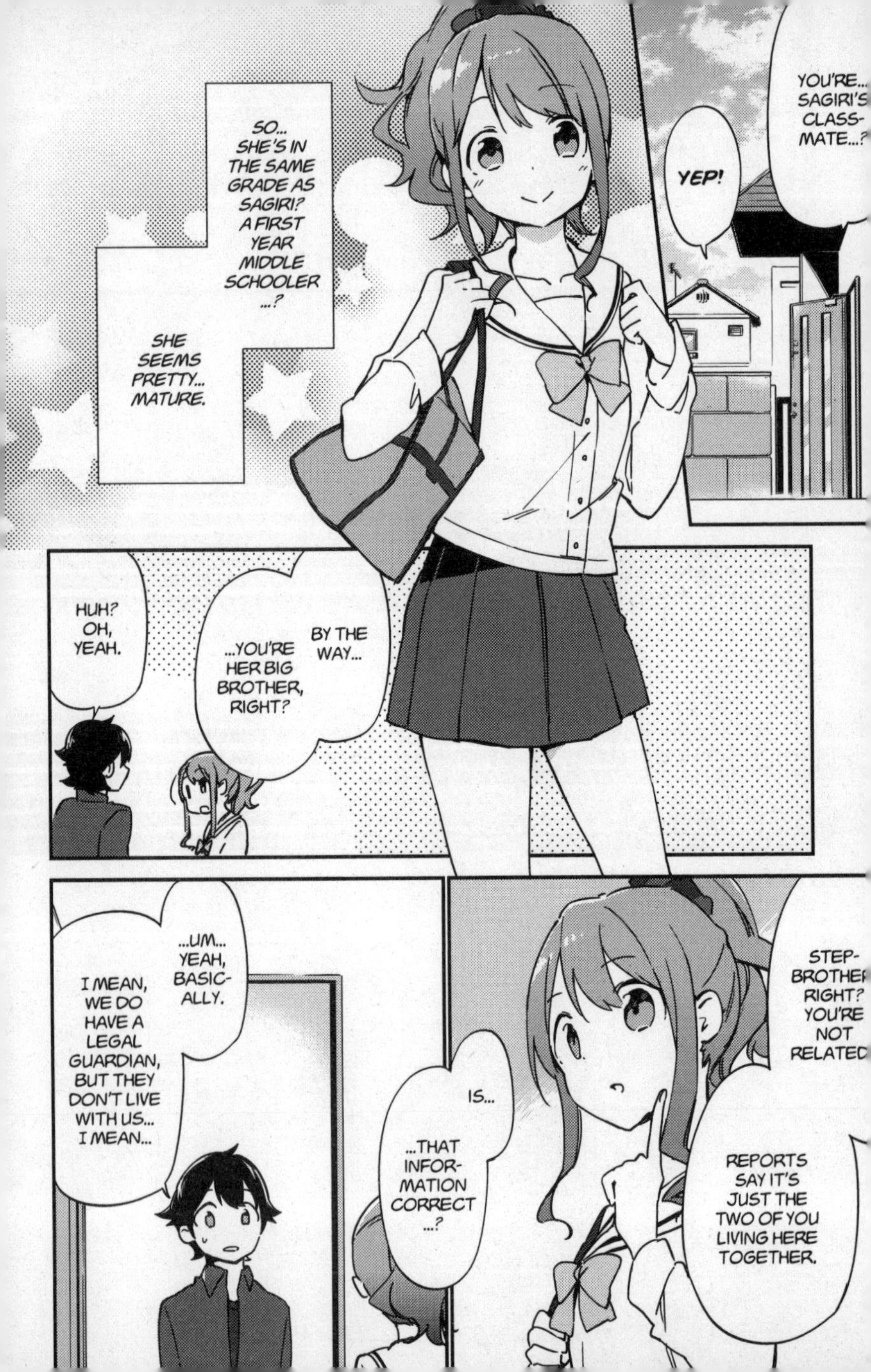
YOU'RE... SAGIRI'S CLASS-MATE...?
YEP!
SO... SHE'S IN THE SAME GRADE AS SAGIRI? A FIRST YEAR MIDDLE SCHOOLER ...?
SHE SEEMS PRETTY... MATURE.
BY THE WAY...
...YOU'RE HER BIG BROTHER, RIGHT?
HUH? OH, YEAH.
STEP-BROTHER RIGHT? YOU'RE NOT RELATED
REPORTS SAY IT'S JUST THE TWO OF YOU LIVING HERE TOGETHER.
IS...
...THAT INFORMATION CORRECT ...?
...UM... YEAH, BASIC-ALLY.
I MEAN, WE DO HAVE A LEGAL GUARDIAN, BUT THEY DON'T LIVE WITH US... I MEAN...

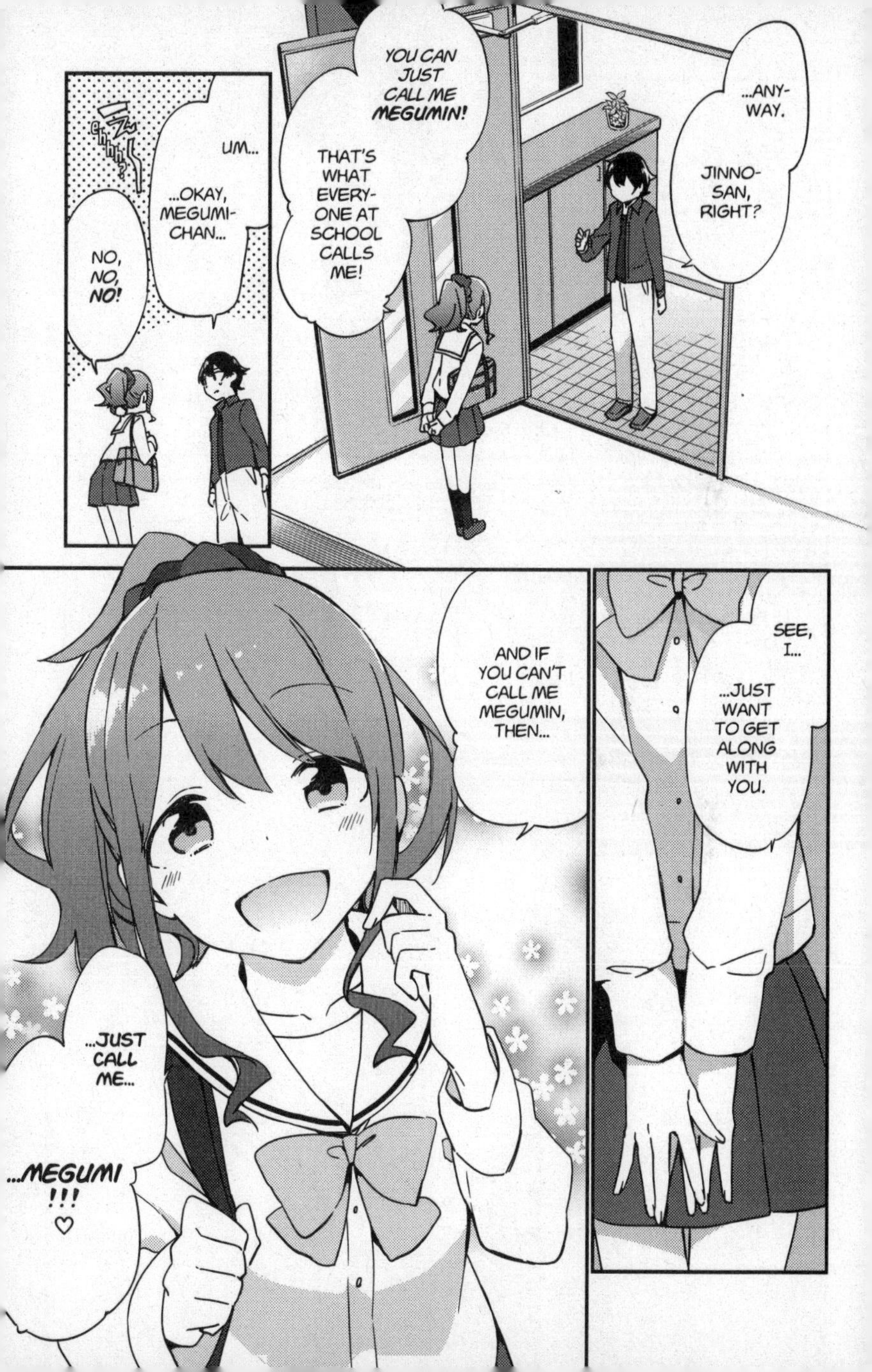
...ANY-WAY.
JINNO-SAN, RIGHT?
YOU CAN JUST CALL ME **MEGUMIN!**
THAT'S WHAT EVERY-ONE AT SCHOOL CALLS ME!
UM...
...OKAY, MEGUMI-CHAN...
NO, NO, **NO!**
SEE, I...
...JUST WANT TO GET ALONG WITH YOU.
AND IF YOU CAN'T CALL ME MEGUMIN, THEN...
...JUST CALL ME...
...MEGUMI!!! ♡

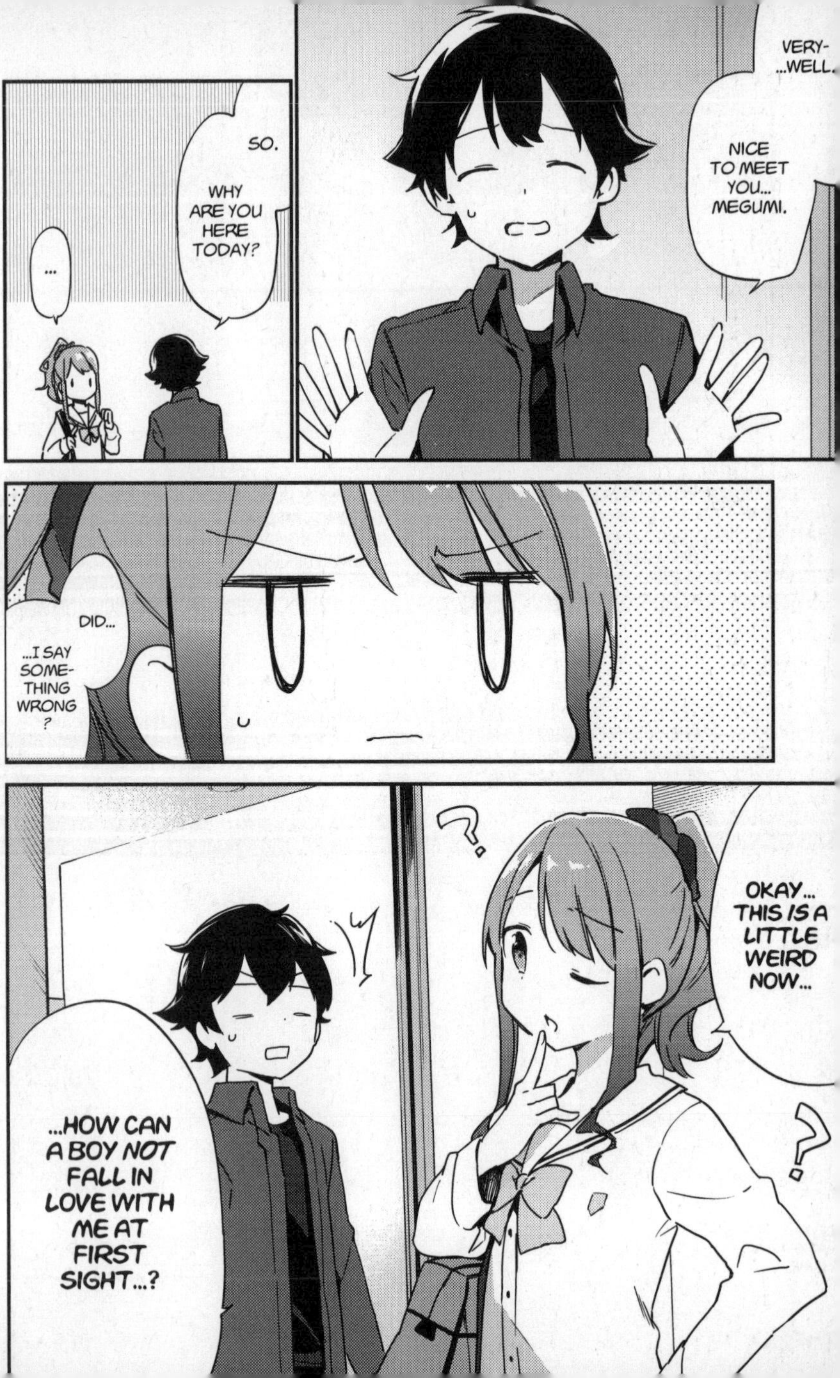
VERY- ...WELL.
NICE TO MEET YOU... MEGUMI.
SO.
WHY ARE YOU HERE TODAY?
...
DID...
...I SAY SOMETHING WRONG?
OKAY... THIS IS A LITTLE WEIRD NOW...
...HOW CAN A BOY NOT FALL IN LOVE WITH ME AT FIRST SIGHT...?

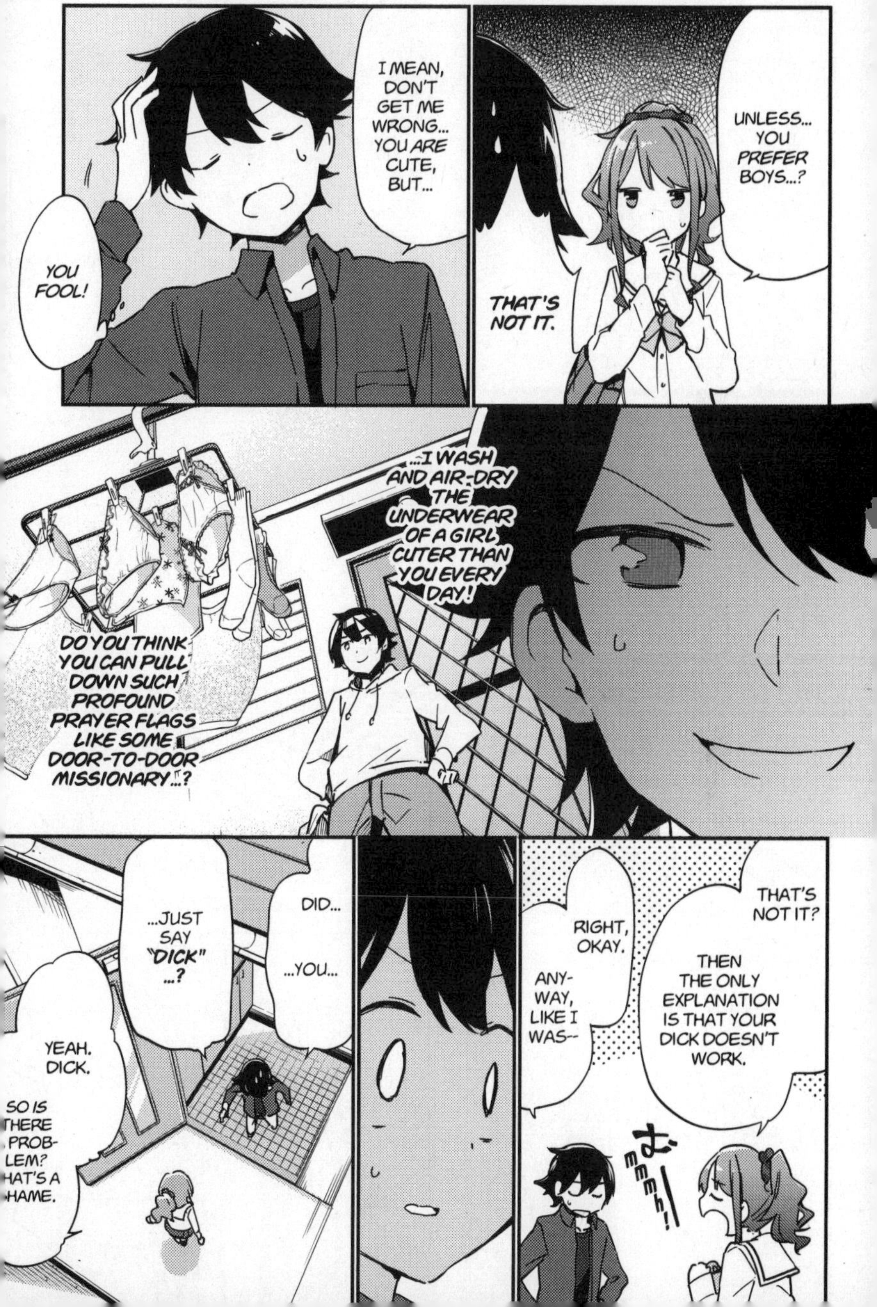
UNLESS... YOU PREFER BOYS...?
THAT'S NOT IT.
I MEAN, DON'T GET ME WRONG... YOU ARE CUTE, BUT...
YOU FOOL!
...I WASH AND AIR-DRY THE UNDERWEAR OF A GIRL CUTER THAN YOU EVERY DAY!
DO YOU THINK YOU CAN PULL DOWN SUCH PROFOUND PRAYER FLAGS LIKE SOME DOOR-TO-DOOR MISSIONARY...!?
THAT'S NOT IT?
THEN THE ONLY EXPLANATION IS THAT YOUR DICK DOESN'T WORK.
RIGHT, OKAY.
ANY-WAY, LIKE I WAS--
mmmh!
DID...
...YOU...
...JUST SAY "DICK" ...?
YEAH. DICK.
SO IS THERE PROB-LEM? HAT'S A HAME.

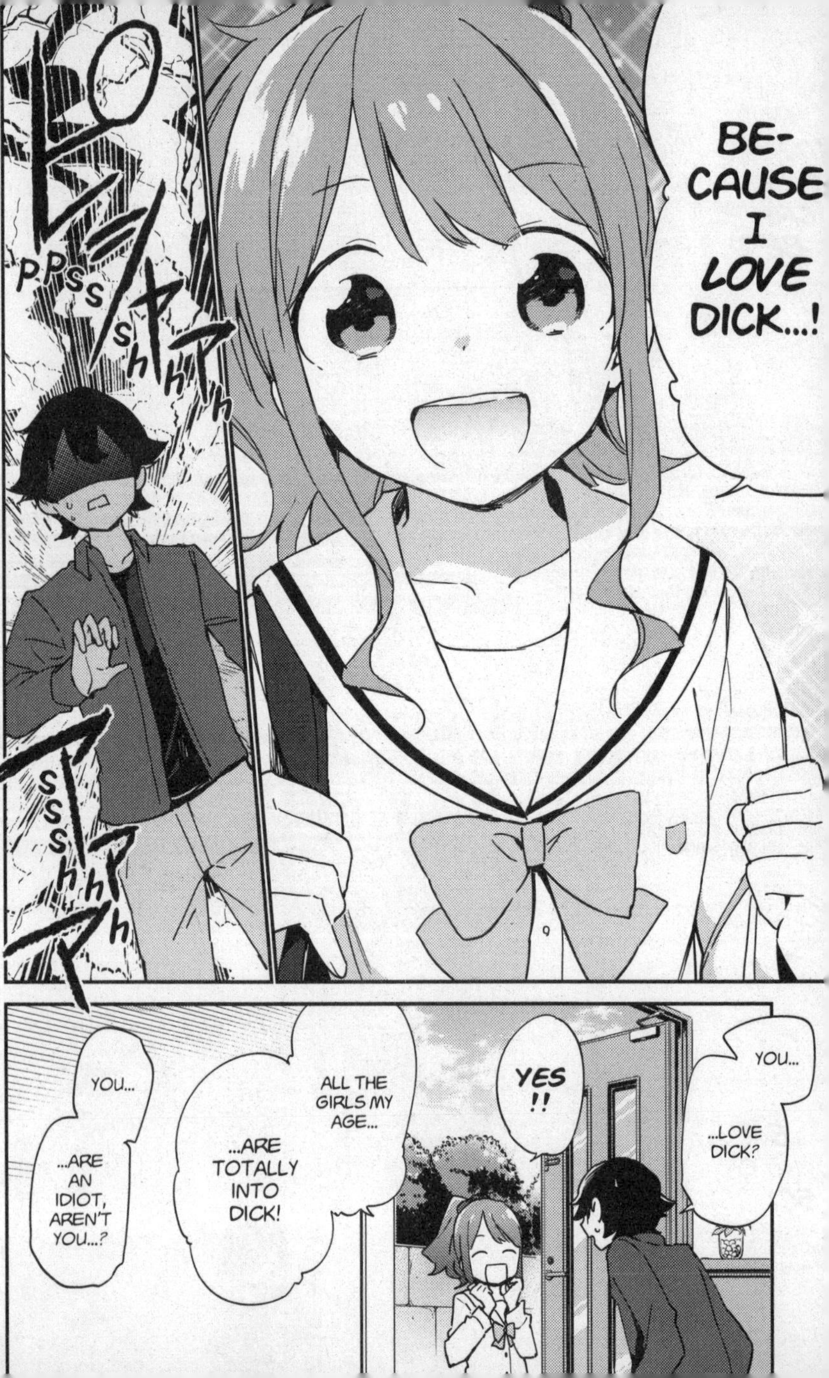
BE-CAUSE I LOVE DICK...!
PPSSShhhh
SSShhhh
YOU... ...LOVE DICK?
YES!!
ALL THE GIRLS MY AGE... ...ARE TOTALLY INTO DICK!
YOU... ...ARE AN IDIOT, AREN'T YOU...?

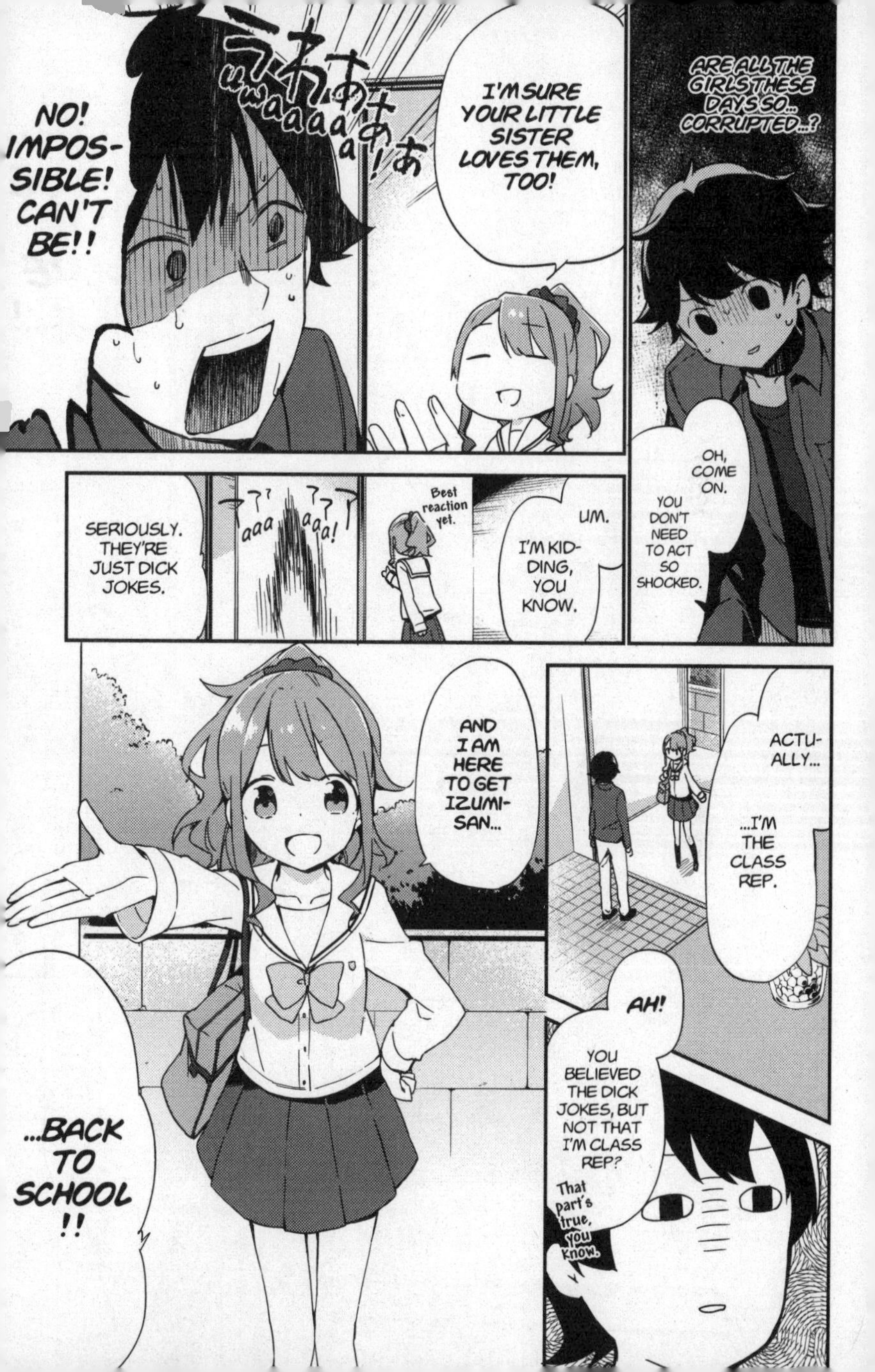
ARE ALL THE GIRLS THESE DAYS SO... CORRUPTED...?
OH, COME ON. YOU DON'T NEED TO ACT SO SHOCKED.
I'M SURE YOUR LITTLE SISTER LOVES THEM, TOO!
uwaaaaaaa!
NO! IMPOSSIBLE! CAN'T BE!!
UM. I'M KIDDING, YOU KNOW.
Best reaction yet.
aaa aaa!
SERIOUSLY. THEY'RE JUST DICK JOKES.
ACTUALLY... ...I'M THE CLASS REP.
AH! YOU BELIEVED THE DICK JOKES, BUT NOT THAT I'M CLASS REP?
That part's true, you know.
AND I AM HERE TO GET IZUMI-SAN...
...BACK TO SCHOOL!!

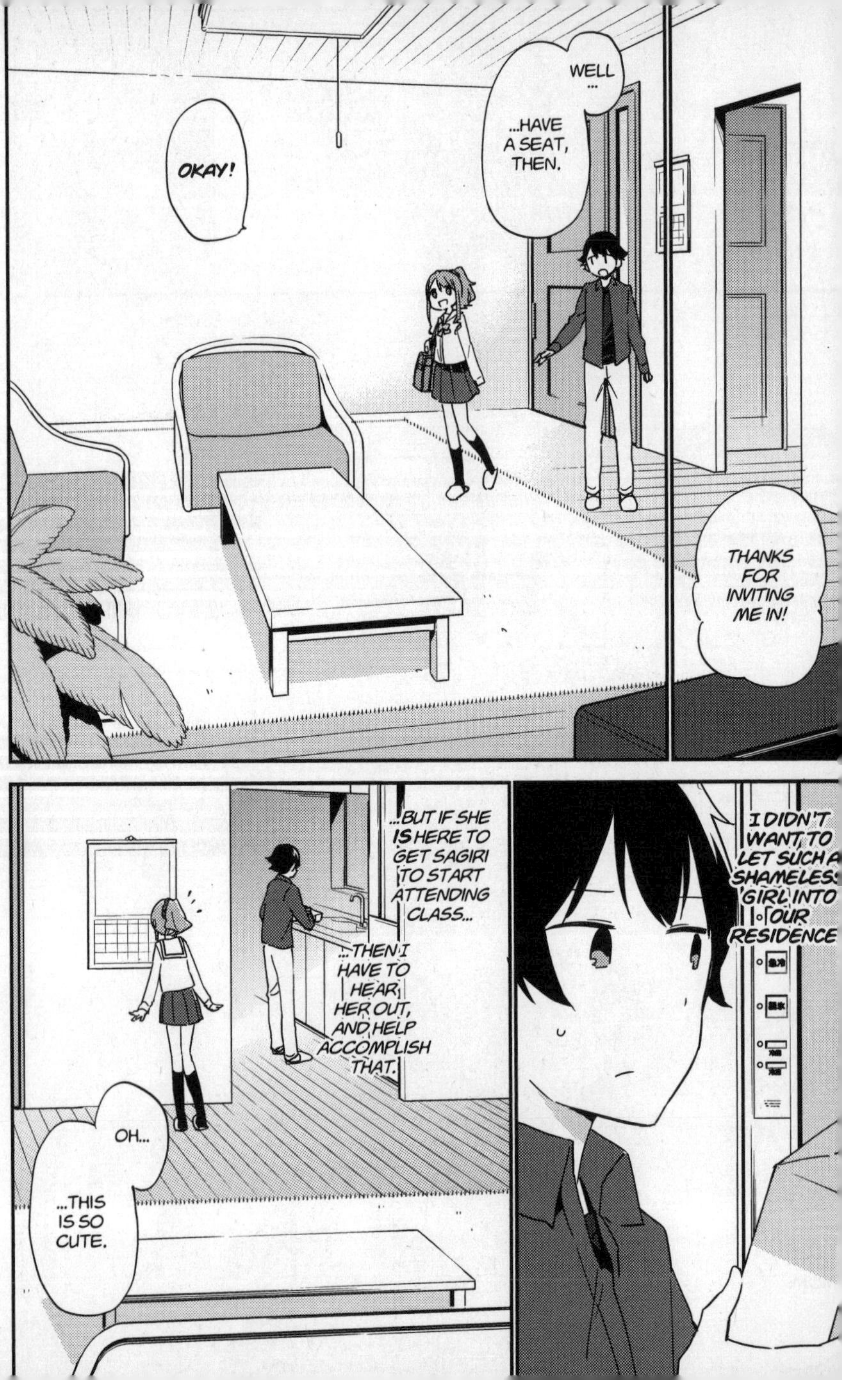
WELL...
...HAVE A SEAT, THEN.
THANKS FOR INVITING ME IN!
OKAY!
I DIDN'T WANT TO LET SUCH A SHAMELESS GIRL INTO OUR RESIDENCE
...BUT IF SHE IS HERE TO GET SAGIRI TO START ATTENDING CLASS...
...THEN I HAVE TO HEAR HER OUT, AND HELP ACCOMPLISH THAT.
OH...
...THIS IS SO CUTE.

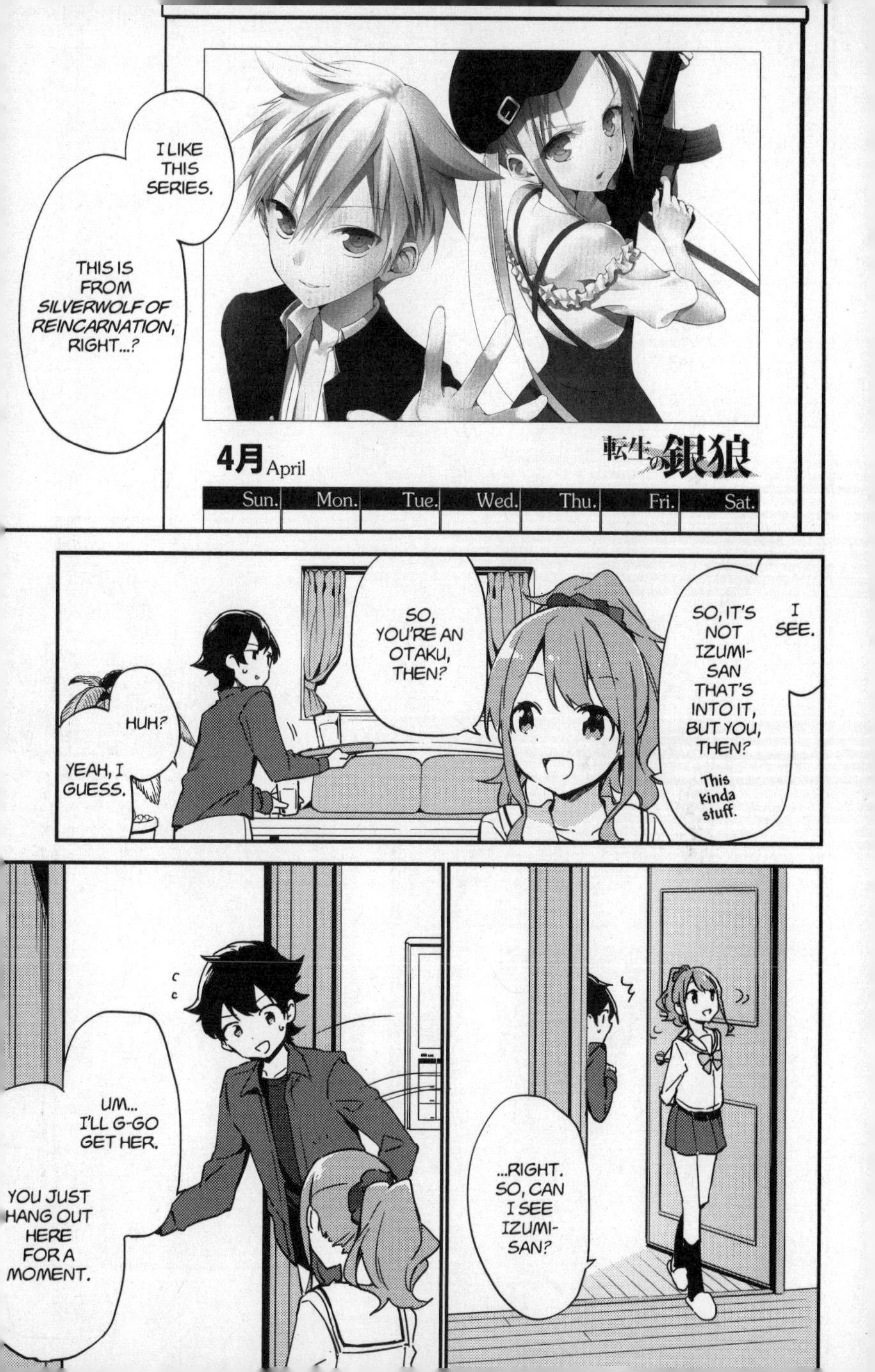
I LIKE THIS SERIES.
THIS IS FROM SILVERWOLF OF REINCARNATION, RIGHT...?
転生の銀狼
4月 April
Sun. Mon. Tue. Wed. Thu. Fri. Sat.
I SEE.
SO, IT'S NOT IZUMI-SAN THAT'S INTO IT, BUT YOU, THEN?
This kinda stuff.
SO, YOU'RE AN OTAKU, THEN?
HUH?
YEAH, I GUESS.
...RIGHT. SO, CAN I SEE IZUMI-SAN?
UM... I'LL G-GO GET HER.
YOU JUST HANG OUT HERE FOR A MOMENT.

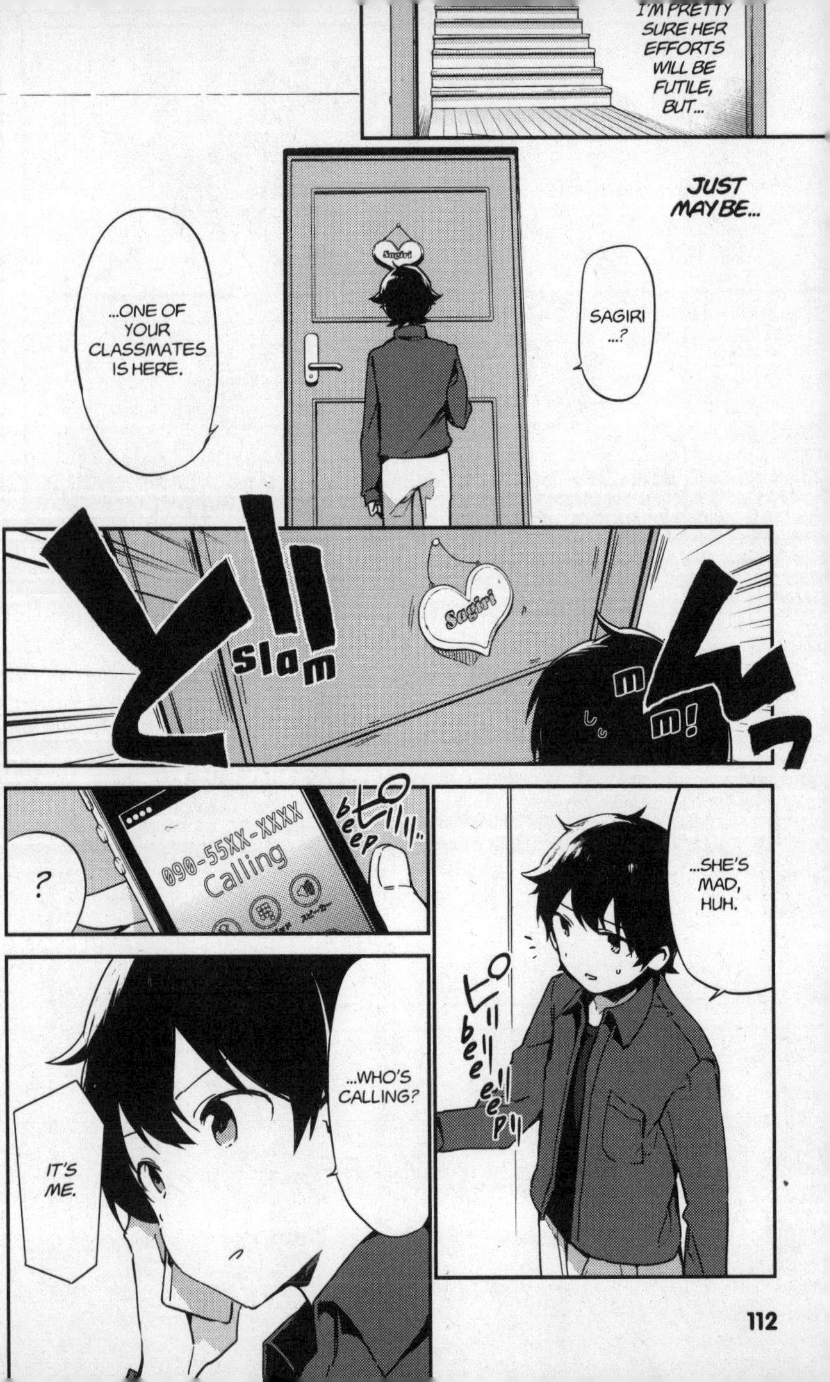
I'M PRETTY SURE HER EFFORTS WILL BE FUTILE, BUT...
JUST MAYBE...
SAGIRI ...?
...ONE OF YOUR CLASSMATES IS HERE.
mm!
slam
...SHE'S MAD, HUH.
beeeeep
beep
090-55XX-XXXX
Calling
?
...WHO'S CALLING?
IT'S ME.

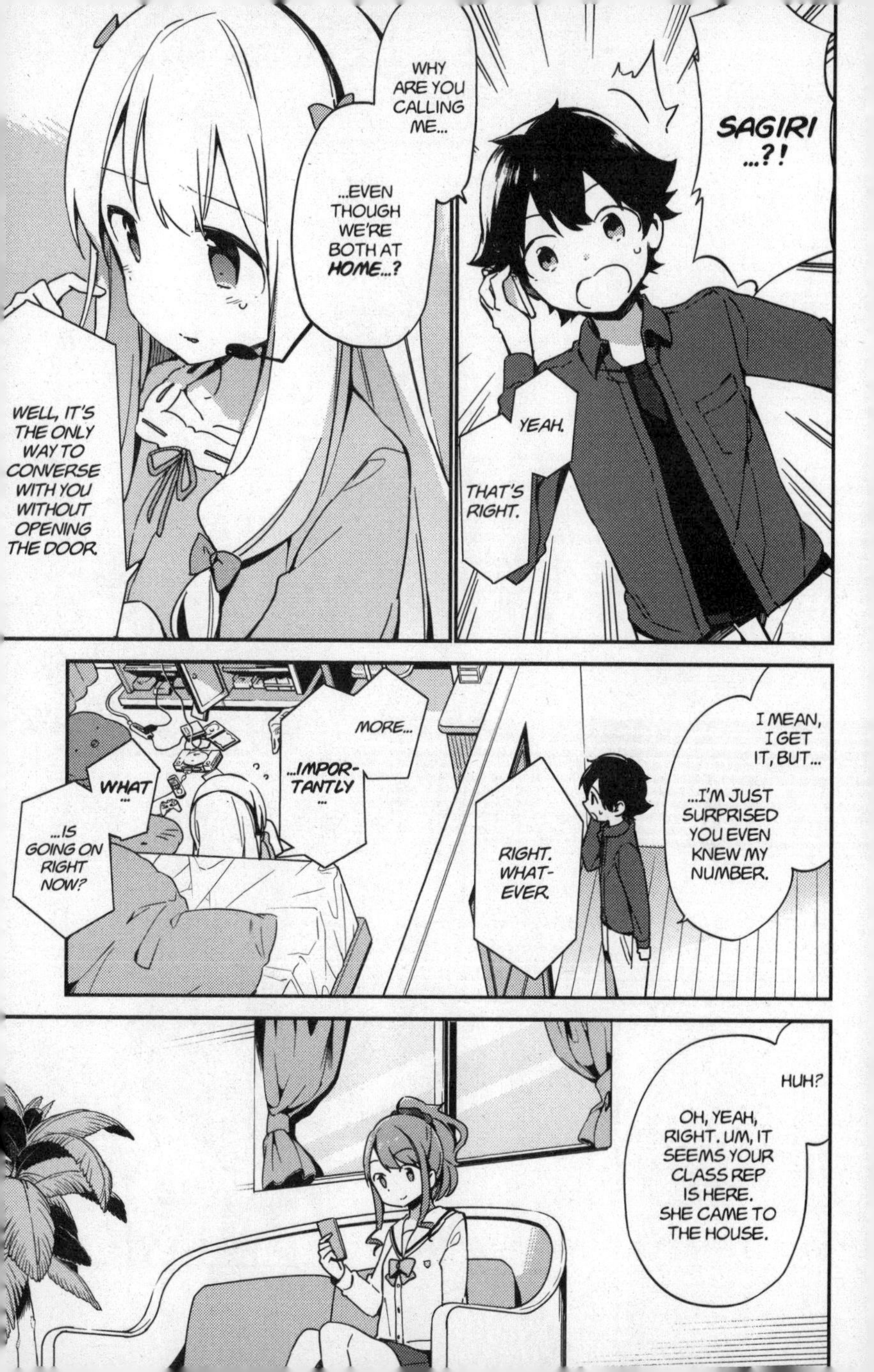
SAGIRI ...?!
WHY ARE YOU CALLING ME...
...EVEN THOUGH WE'RE BOTH AT HOME...?
YEAH.
THAT'S RIGHT.
WELL, IT'S THE ONLY WAY TO CONVERSE WITH YOU WITHOUT OPENING THE DOOR.
I MEAN, I GET IT, BUT...
...I'M JUST SURPRISED YOU EVEN KNEW MY NUMBER.
RIGHT. WHATEVER.
MORE...
...IMPORTANTLY...
WHAT...
...IS GOING ON RIGHT NOW?
HUH?
OH, YEAH, RIGHT. UM, IT SEEMS YOUR CLASS REP IS HERE. SHE CAME TO THE HOUSE.

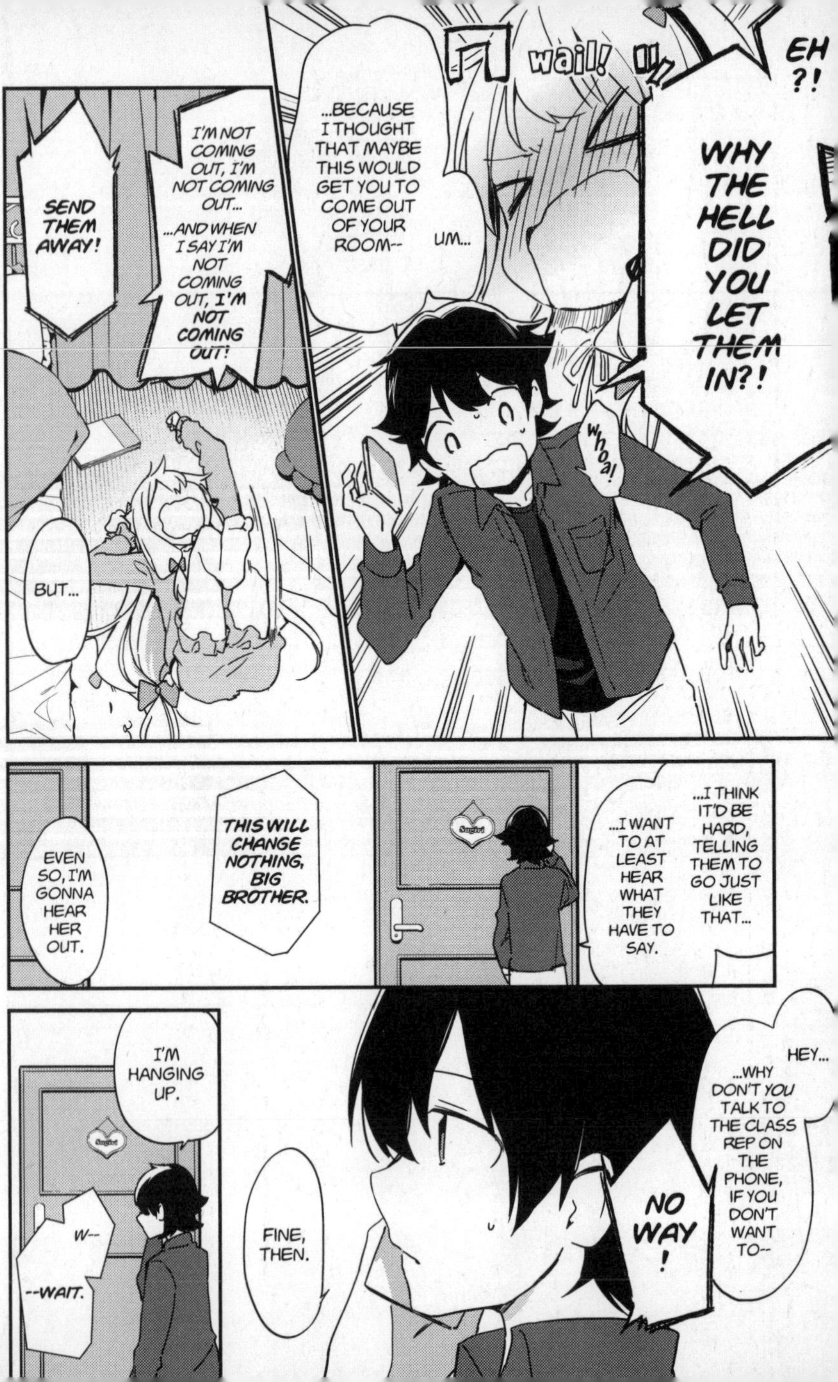
EH ?!
wail!
WHY THE HELL DID YOU LET THEM IN?!
whoa!
UM...
...BECAUSE I THOUGHT THAT MAYBE THIS WOULD GET YOU TO COME OUT OF YOUR ROOM--
I'M NOT COMING OUT, I'M NOT COMING OUT... ...AND WHEN I SAY I'M NOT COMING OUT, I'M NOT COMING OUT!
SEND THEM AWAY!
BUT...
...I THINK IT'D BE HARD, TELLING THEM TO GO JUST LIKE THAT...
...I WANT TO AT LEAST HEAR WHAT THEY HAVE TO SAY.
THIS WILL CHANGE NOTHING, BIG BROTHER.
EVEN SO, I'M GONNA HEAR HER OUT.
HEY...
...WHY DON'T YOU TALK TO THE CLASS REP ON THE PHONE, IF YOU DON'T WANT TO--
NO WAY!
FINE, THEN.
I'M HANGING UP.
W--
--WAIT.

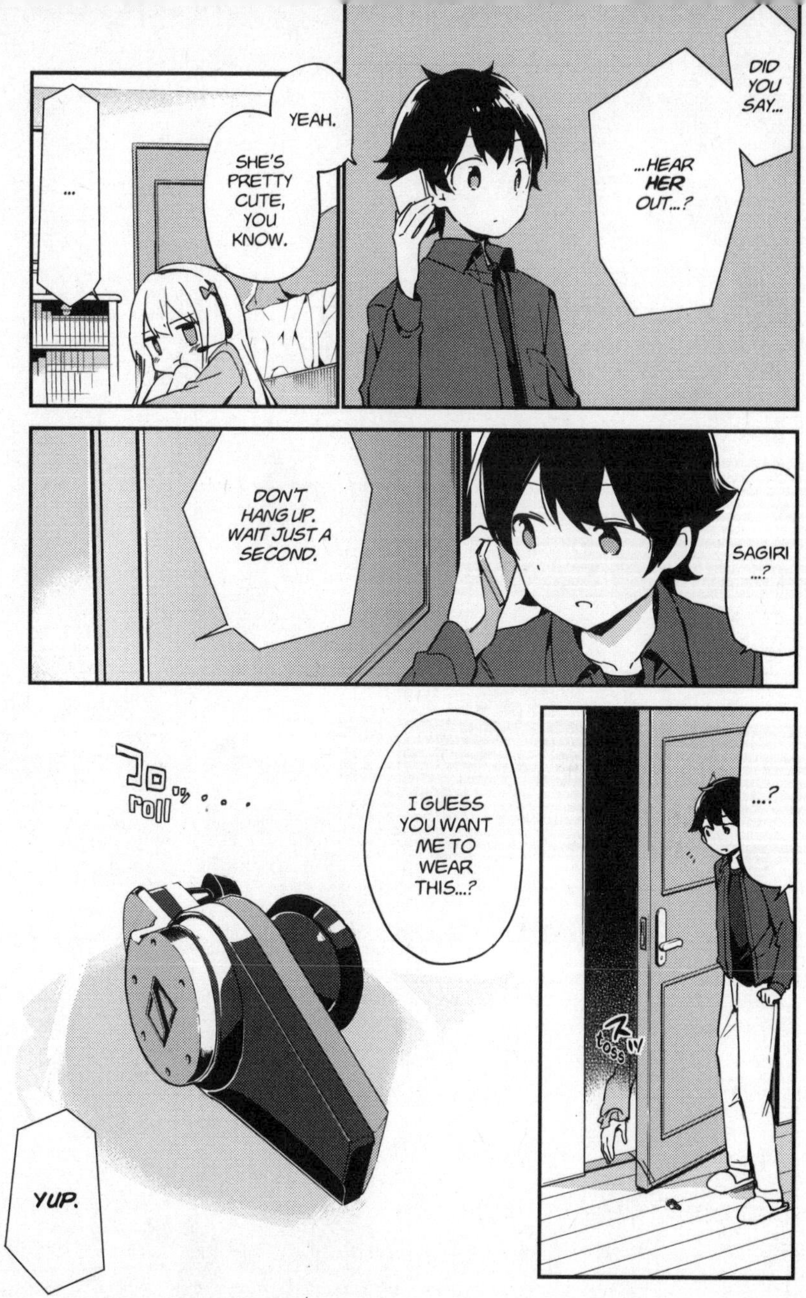
DID YOU SAY...
...HEAR HER OUT...?
YEAH.
SHE'S PRETTY CUTE, YOU KNOW.
...
SAGIRI ...?
DON'T HANG UP. WAIT JUST A SECOND.
...?
ス toss
I GUESS YOU WANT ME TO WEAR THIS...?
コロッ roll
YUP.

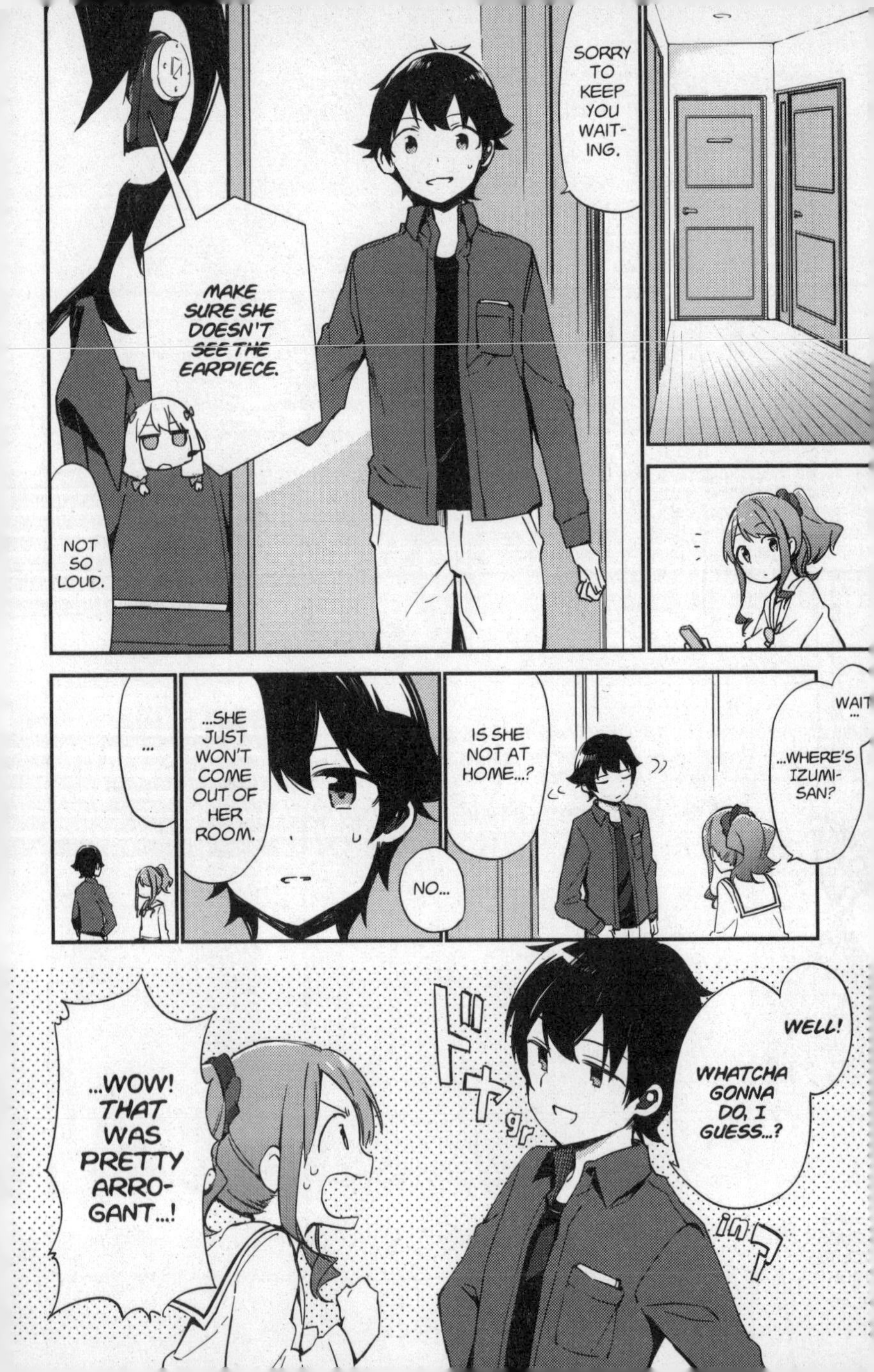
SORRY TO KEEP YOU WAIT-ING.
MAKE SURE SHE DOESN'T SEE THE EARPIECE.
NOT SO LOUD.
WAIT...
...WHERE'S IZUMI-SAN?
IS SHE NOT AT HOME...?
NO...
...SHE JUST WON'T COME OUT OF HER ROOM.
...
WELL!
WHATCHA GONNA DO, I GUESS...?
ドヤ
gr
in
...WOW! THAT WAS PRETTY ARRO-GANT...!

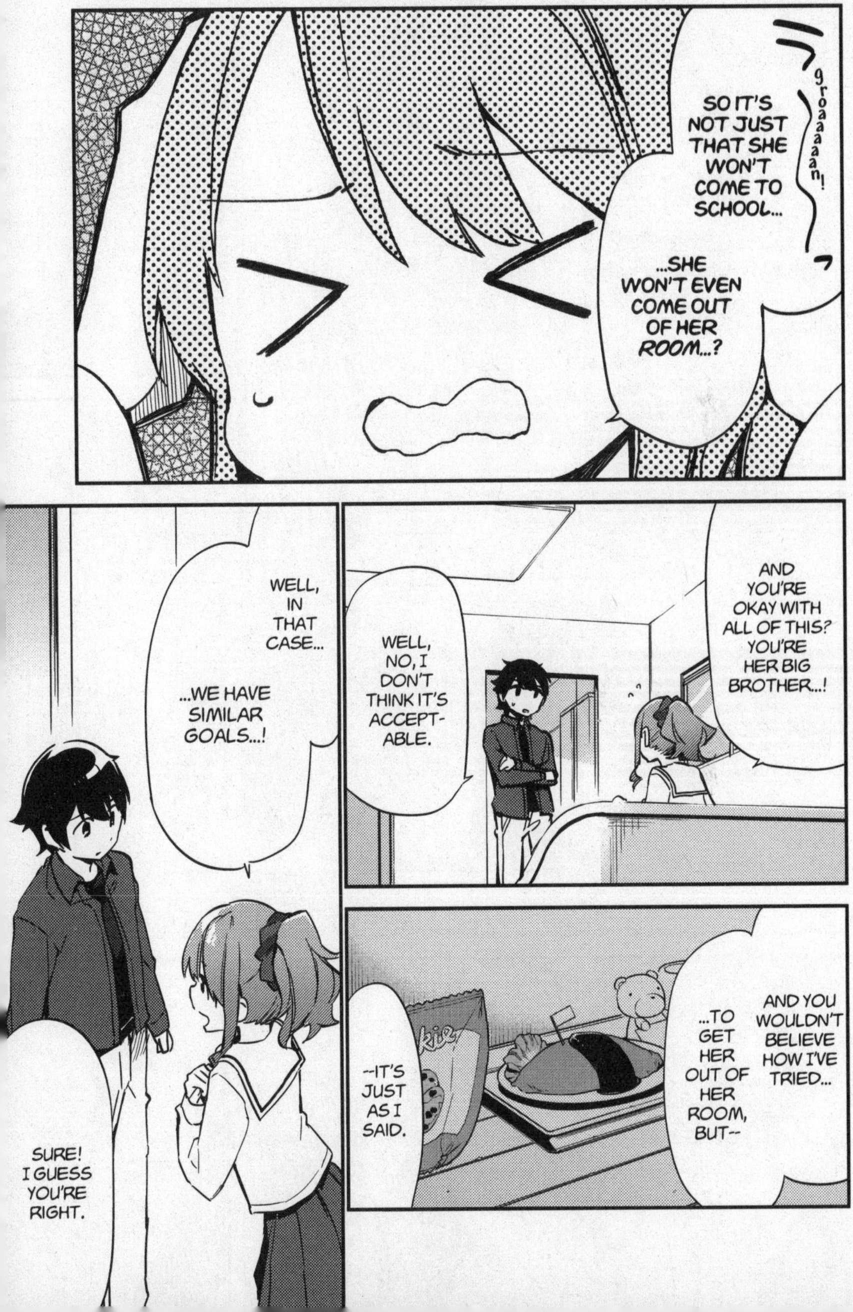
groaaaaan!
SO IT'S NOT JUST THAT SHE WON'T COME TO SCHOOL...
...SHE WON'T EVEN COME OUT OF HER *ROOM*...?
AND YOU'RE OKAY WITH ALL OF THIS? YOU'RE HER BIG BROTHER...!
WELL, NO, I DON'T THINK IT'S ACCEPTABLE.
AND YOU WOULDN'T BELIEVE HOW I'VE TRIED...
...TO GET HER OUT OF HER ROOM, BUT--
--IT'S JUST AS I SAID.
WELL, IN THAT CASE...
...WE HAVE SIMILAR GOALS...!
SURE! I GUESS YOU'RE RIGHT.

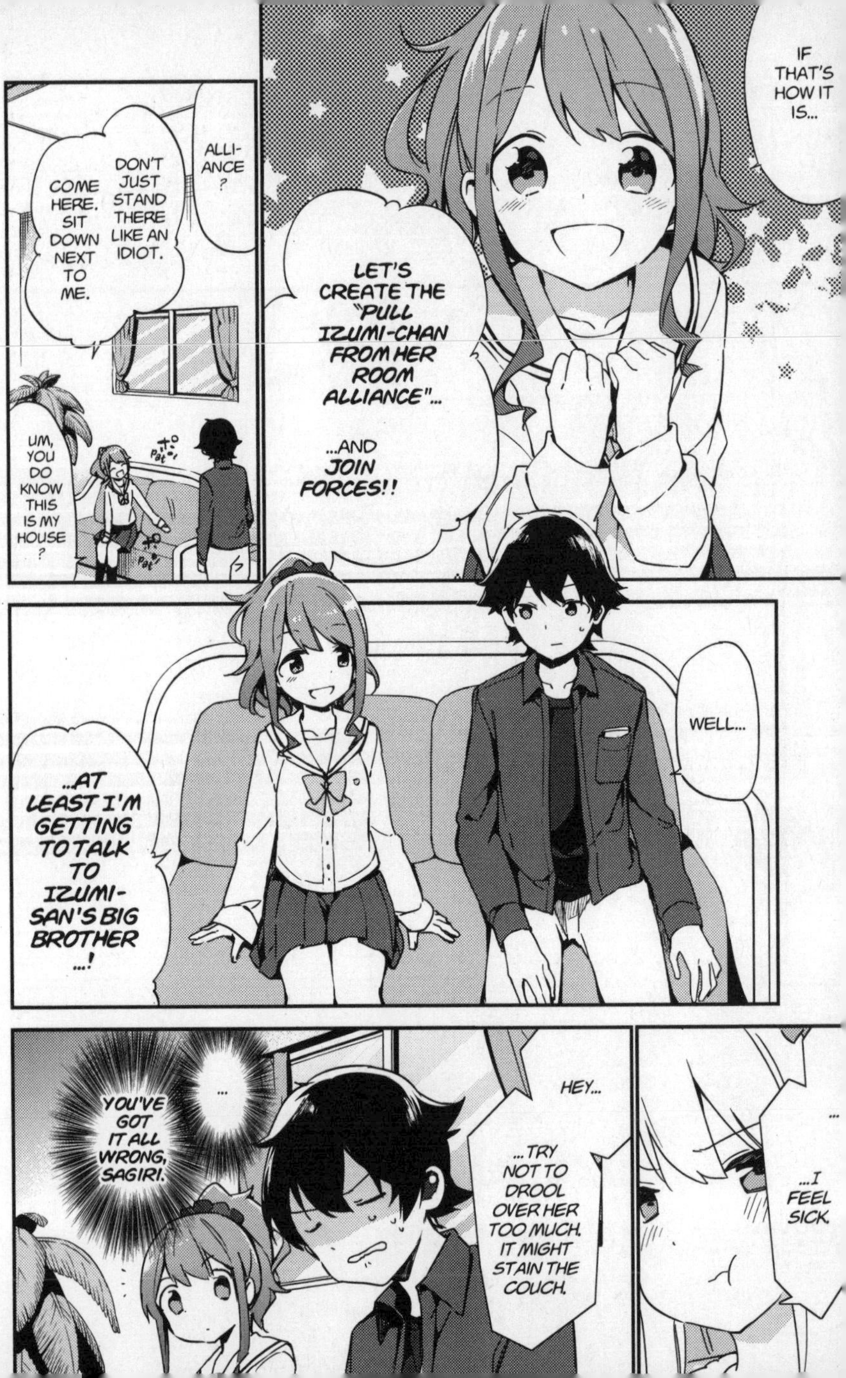
IF THAT'S HOW IT IS...
LET'S CREATE THE "PULL IZUMI-CHAN FROM HER ROOM ALLIANCE"...
...AND JOIN FORCES!!
ALLIANCE?
DON'T JUST STAND THERE LIKE AN IDIOT.
COME HERE. SIT DOWN NEXT TO ME.
UM, YOU DO KNOW THIS IS MY HOUSE?
WELL...
...AT LEAST I'M GETTING TO TALK TO IZUMI-SAN'S BIG BROTHER...!
...
...I FEEL SICK.
HEY...
...TRY NOT TO DROOL OVER HER TOO MUCH. IT MIGHT STAIN THE COUCH.
...
YOU'VE GOT IT ALL WRONG, SAGIRI.

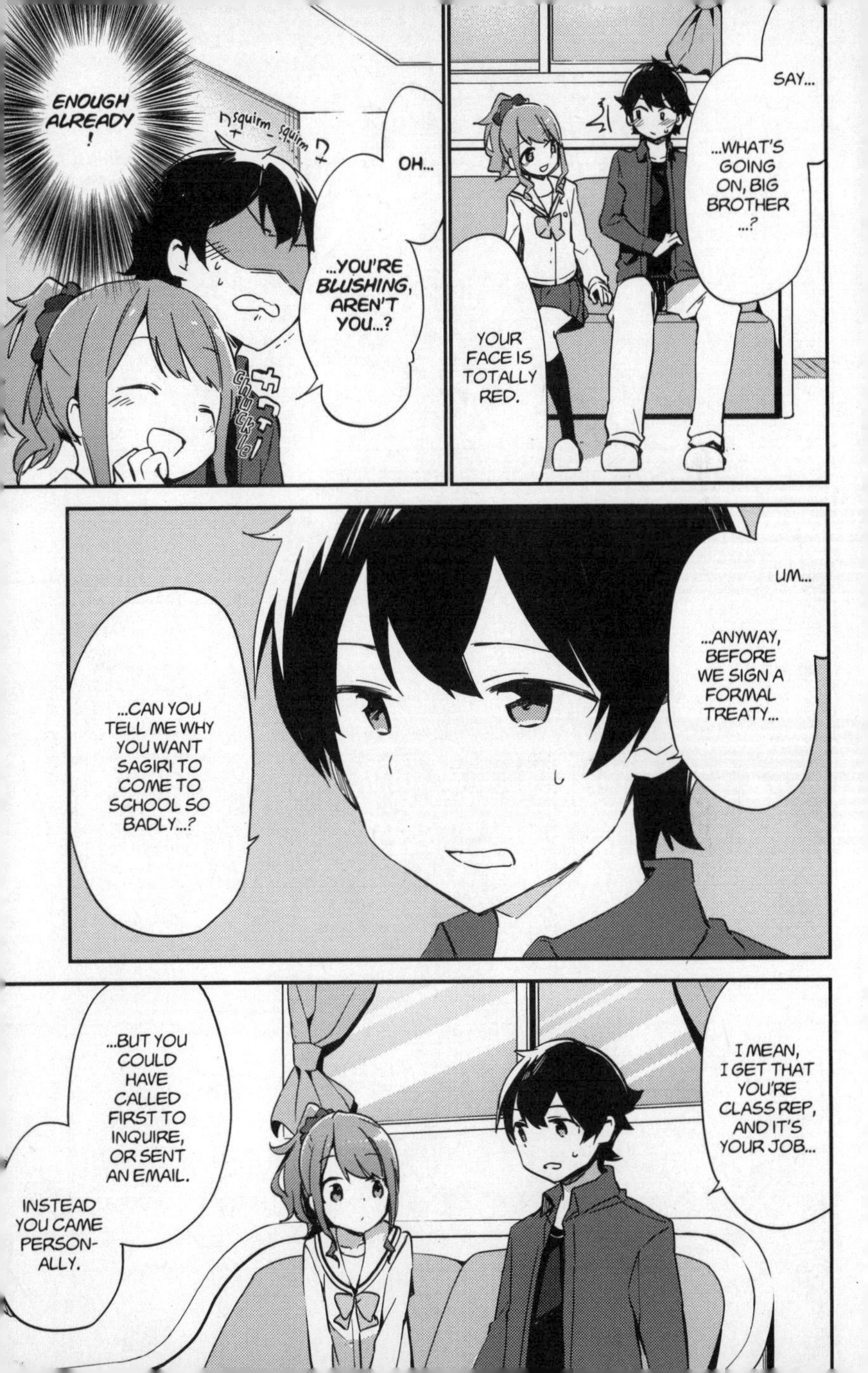
SAY...
...WHAT'S GOING ON, BIG BROTHER ...?
YOUR FACE IS TOTALLY RED.
OH...
...YOU'RE *BLUSHING*, AREN'T YOU...?
squirm squirm
ENOUGH ALREADY!
chuckle
UM...
...ANYWAY, BEFORE WE SIGN A FORMAL TREATY...
...CAN YOU TELL ME WHY YOU WANT SAGIRI TO COME TO SCHOOL SO BADLY...?
I MEAN, I GET THAT YOU'RE CLASS REP, AND IT'S YOUR JOB...
...BUT YOU COULD HAVE CALLED FIRST TO INQUIRE, OR SENT AN EMAIL.
INSTEAD YOU CAME PERSON-ALLY.

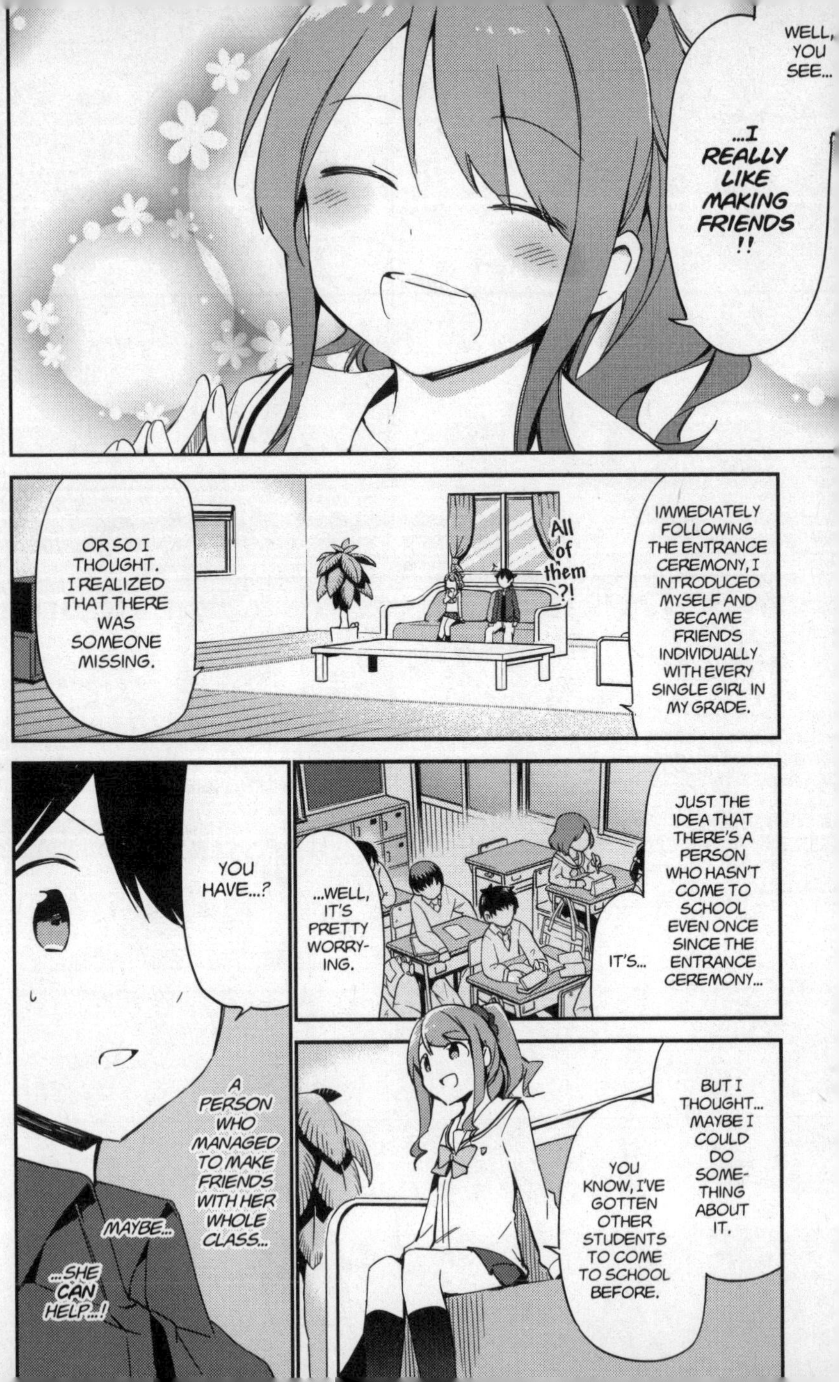
WELL, YOU SEE...
...I REALLY LIKE MAKING FRIENDS!!
IMMEDIATELY FOLLOWING THE ENTRANCE CEREMONY, I INTRODUCED MYSELF AND BECAME FRIENDS INDIVIDUALLY WITH EVERY SINGLE GIRL IN MY GRADE.
All of them?!
OR SO I THOUGHT. I REALIZED THAT THERE WAS SOMEONE MISSING.
JUST THE IDEA THAT THERE'S A PERSON WHO HASN'T COME TO SCHOOL EVEN ONCE SINCE THE ENTRANCE CEREMONY...
IT'S...
...WELL, IT'S PRETTY WORRY-ING.
BUT I THOUGHT... MAYBE I COULD DO SOME-THING ABOUT IT.
YOU KNOW, I'VE GOTTEN OTHER STUDENTS TO COME TO SCHOOL BEFORE.
YOU HAVE...?
A PERSON WHO MANAGED TO MAKE FRIENDS WITH HER WHOLE CLASS...
MAYBE...
...SHE CAN HELP...!

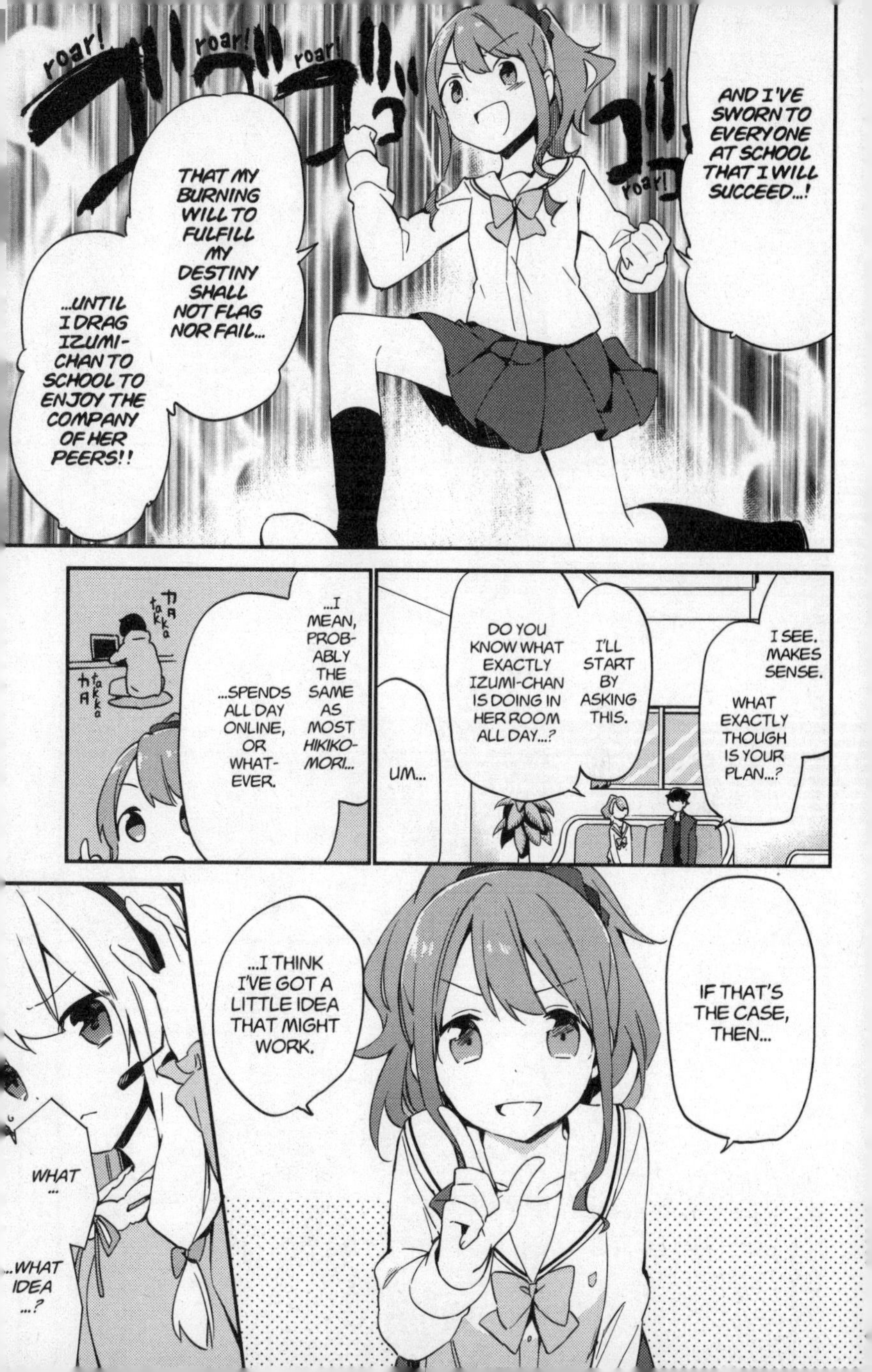
roar! roar! roar!
AND I'VE SWORN TO EVERYONE AT SCHOOL THAT I WILL SUCCEED...!
roar!
THAT MY BURNING WILL TO FULFILL MY DESTINY SHALL NOT FLAG NOR FAIL...
...UNTIL I DRAG IZUMI-CHAN TO SCHOOL TO ENJOY THE COMPANY OF HER PEERS!!
I SEE. MAKES SENSE.
WHAT EXACTLY THOUGH IS YOUR PLAN...?
I'LL START BY ASKING THIS.
DO YOU KNOW WHAT EXACTLY IZUMI-CHAN IS DOING IN HER ROOM ALL DAY...?
UM...
...I MEAN, PROBABLY THE SAME AS MOST HIKIKOMORI...
...SPENDS ALL DAY ONLINE, OR WHATEVER.
takka takka
IF THAT'S THE CASE, THEN...
...I THINK I'VE GOT A LITTLE IDEA THAT MIGHT WORK.
WHAT...
...WHAT IDEA...?

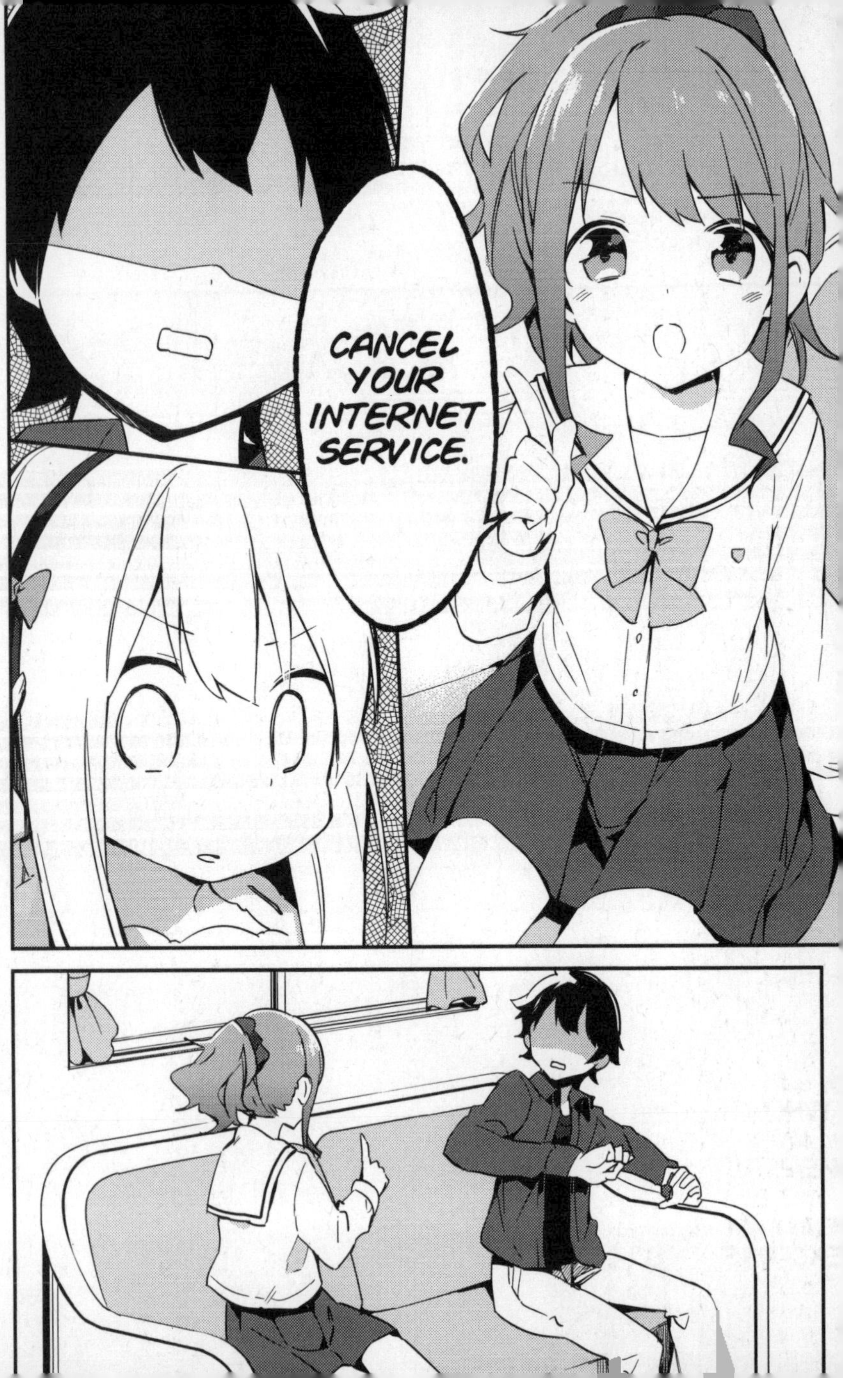
CANCEL YOUR INTERNET SERVICE.

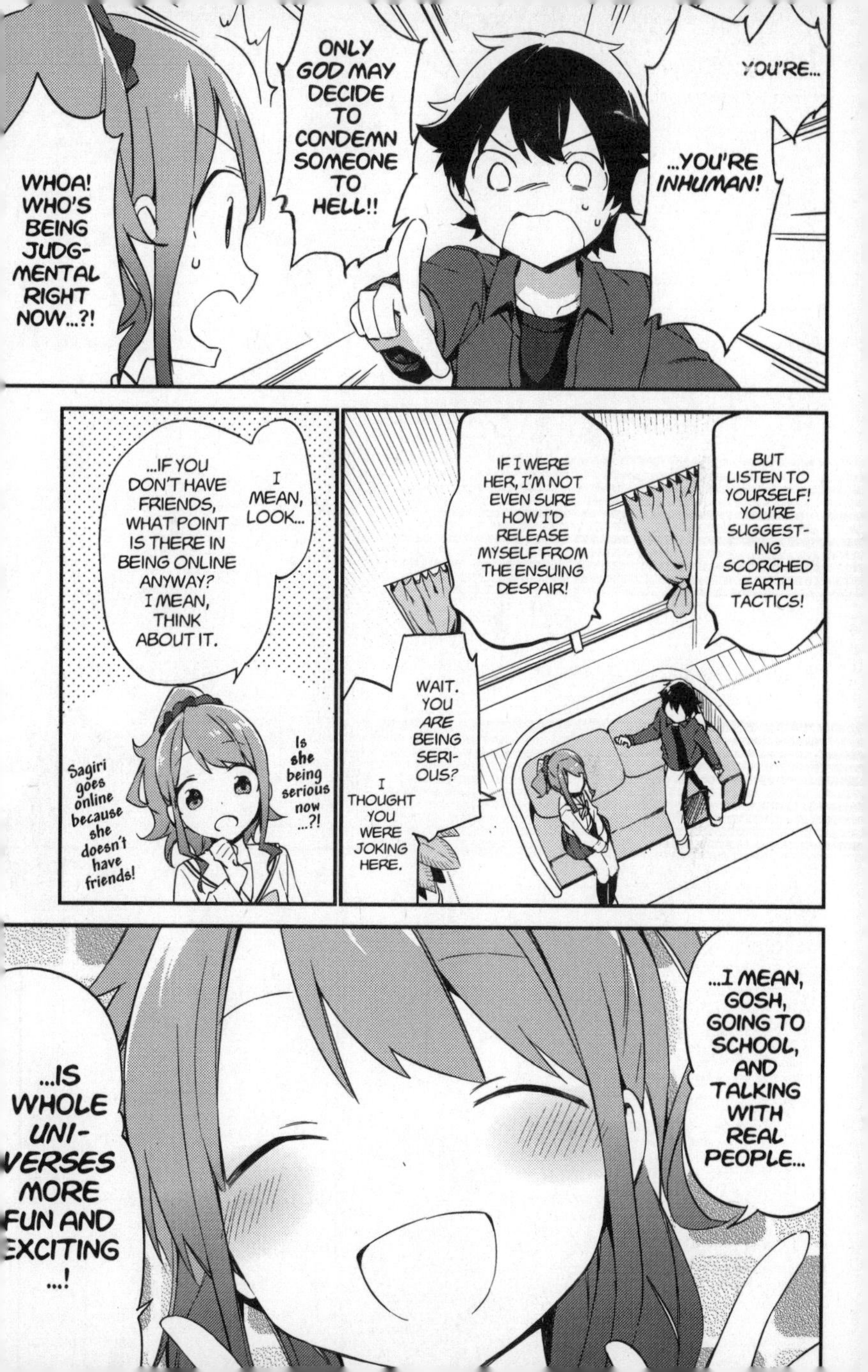
YOU'RE...
...YOU'RE INHUMAN!
ONLY GOD MAY DECIDE TO CONDEMN SOMEONE TO HELL!!
WHOA! WHO'S BEING JUDGMENTAL RIGHT NOW...?!
BUT LISTEN TO YOURSELF! YOU'RE SUGGESTING SCORCHED EARTH TACTICS!
IF I WERE HER, I'M NOT EVEN SURE HOW I'D RELEASE MYSELF FROM THE ENSUING DESPAIR!
WAIT. YOU *ARE* BEING SERIOUS?
I THOUGHT YOU WERE JOKING HERE.
I MEAN, LOOK...
...IF YOU DON'T HAVE FRIENDS, WHAT POINT IS THERE IN BEING ONLINE ANYWAY? I MEAN, THINK ABOUT IT.
Is *she* being serious now...?!
Sagiri goes online because she doesn't have friends!
...I MEAN, GOSH, GOING TO SCHOOL, AND TALKING WITH REAL PEOPLE...
...IS WHOLE UNIVERSES MORE FUN AND EXCITING...!

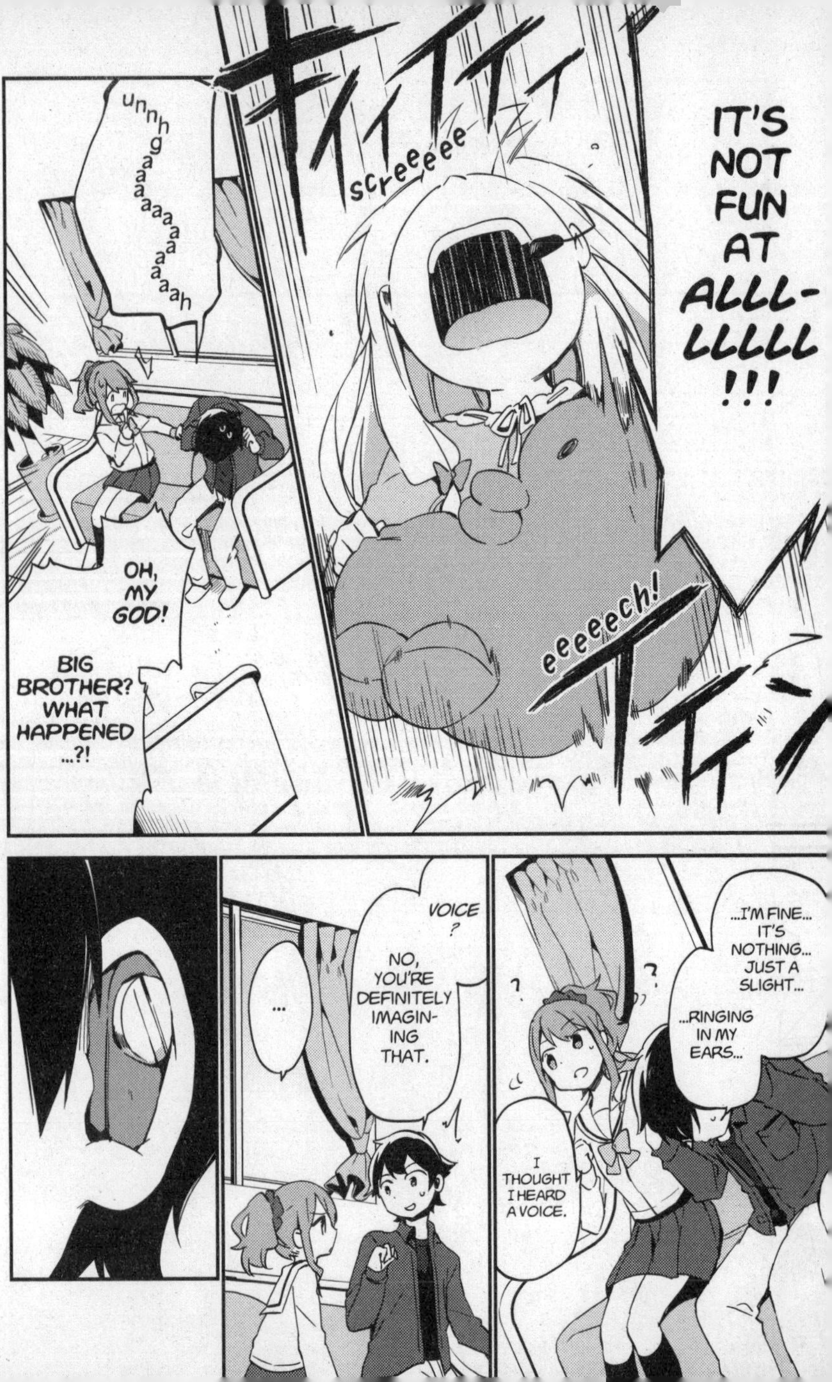
IT'S NOT FUN AT ALLLL-LLLLL!!!
screeeeee
eeeeech!
unnhgaaaaaaaaaaaah
OH, MY GOD!
BIG BROTHER? WHAT HAPPENED ...?!
...I'M FINE... IT'S NOTHING... JUST A SLIGHT...
...RINGING IN MY EARS...
? ?
I THOUGHT I HEARD A VOICE.
VOICE ?
NO, YOU'RE DEFINITELY IMAGIN-ING THAT.
...

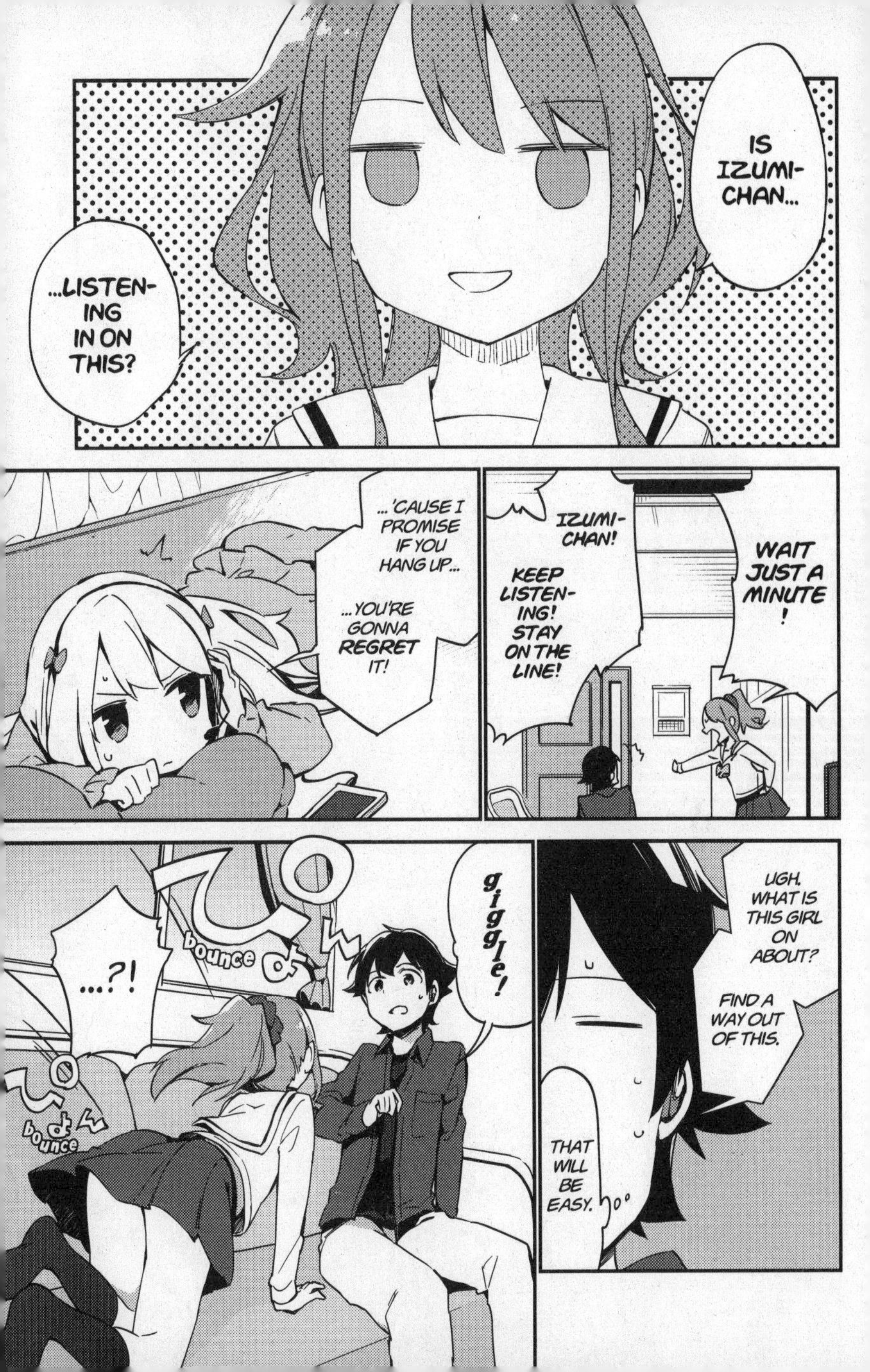
IS IZUMI-CHAN...
...LISTENING IN ON THIS?
WAIT JUST A MINUTE!
IZUMI-CHAN!
KEEP LISTENING! STAY ON THE LINE!
...'CAUSE I PROMISE IF YOU HANG UP...
...YOU'RE GONNA REGRET IT!
UGH. WHAT IS THIS GIRL ON ABOUT?
FIND A WAY OUT OF THIS.
THAT WILL BE EASY.
giggle!
bounce
...?!
bounce

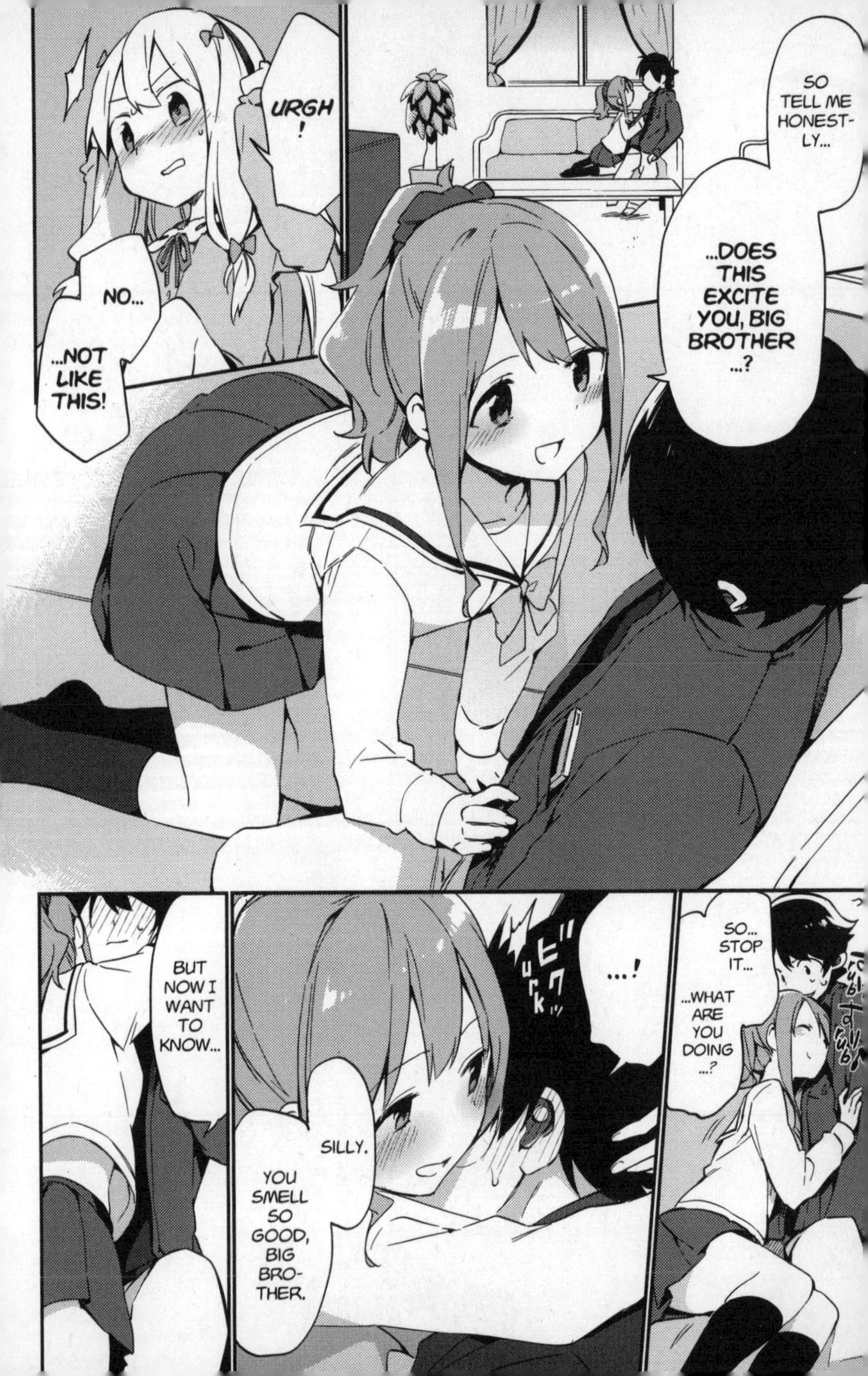
SO TELL ME HONEST-LY...
...DOES THIS EXCITE YOU, BIG BROTHER ...?
URGH!
NO...
...NOT LIKE THIS!
SO... STOP IT...
...WHAT ARE YOU DOING ...?
rub rub
...!
urk
SILLY.
YOU SMELL SO GOOD, BIG BRO-THER.
BUT NOW I WANT TO KNOW...

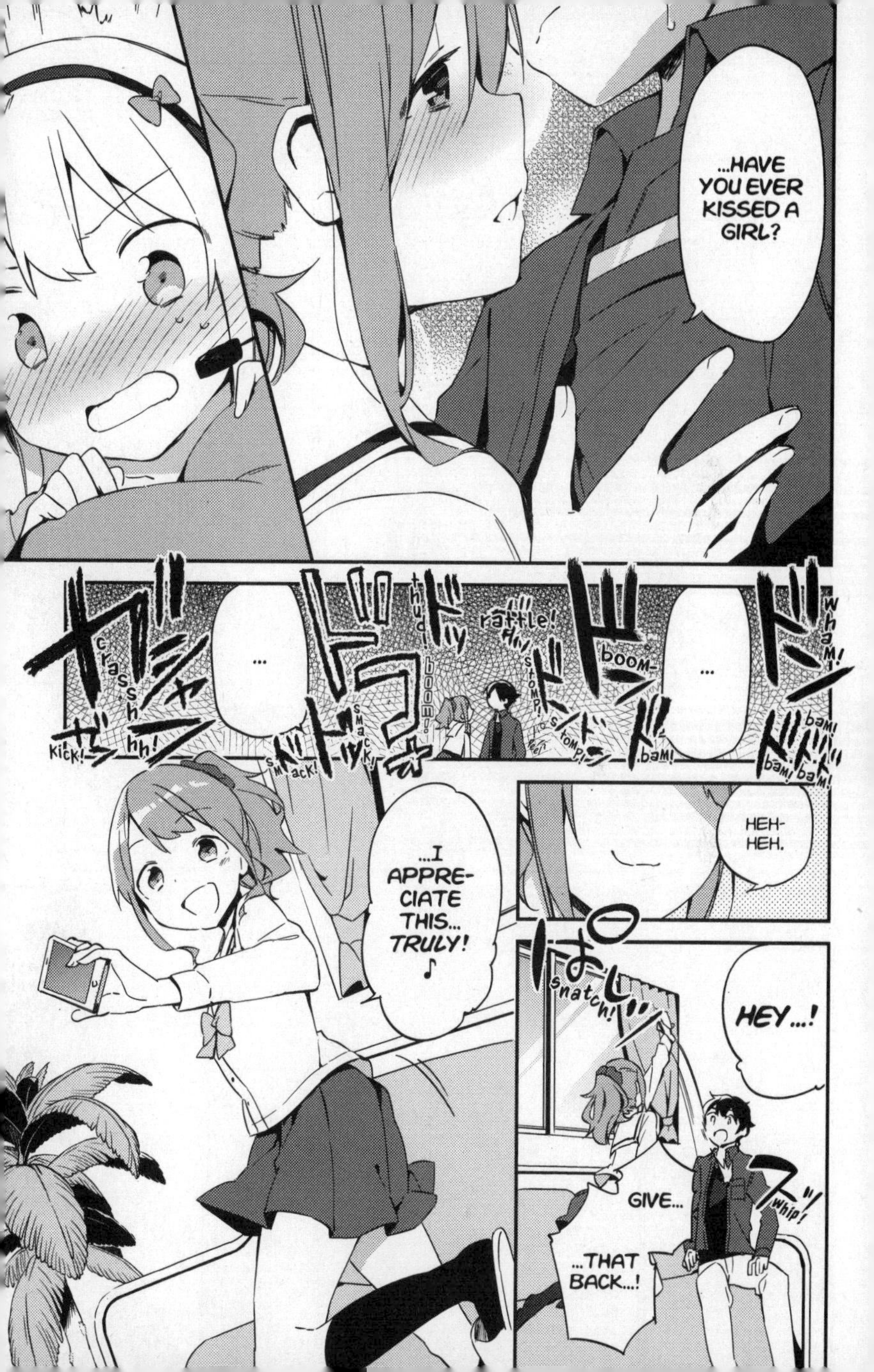
...HAVE YOU EVER KISSED A GIRL?
wham!
bam!
bam! bam!
...
bam!
boom-
stomp!
stomp!
rattle!
thud!
boom!
smack!
smack!
...
crash
kick!
HEH-HEH.
snatch!
HEY...!
whip!
GIVE...
...THAT BACK...!
...I APPRECIATE THIS... TRULY! ♪

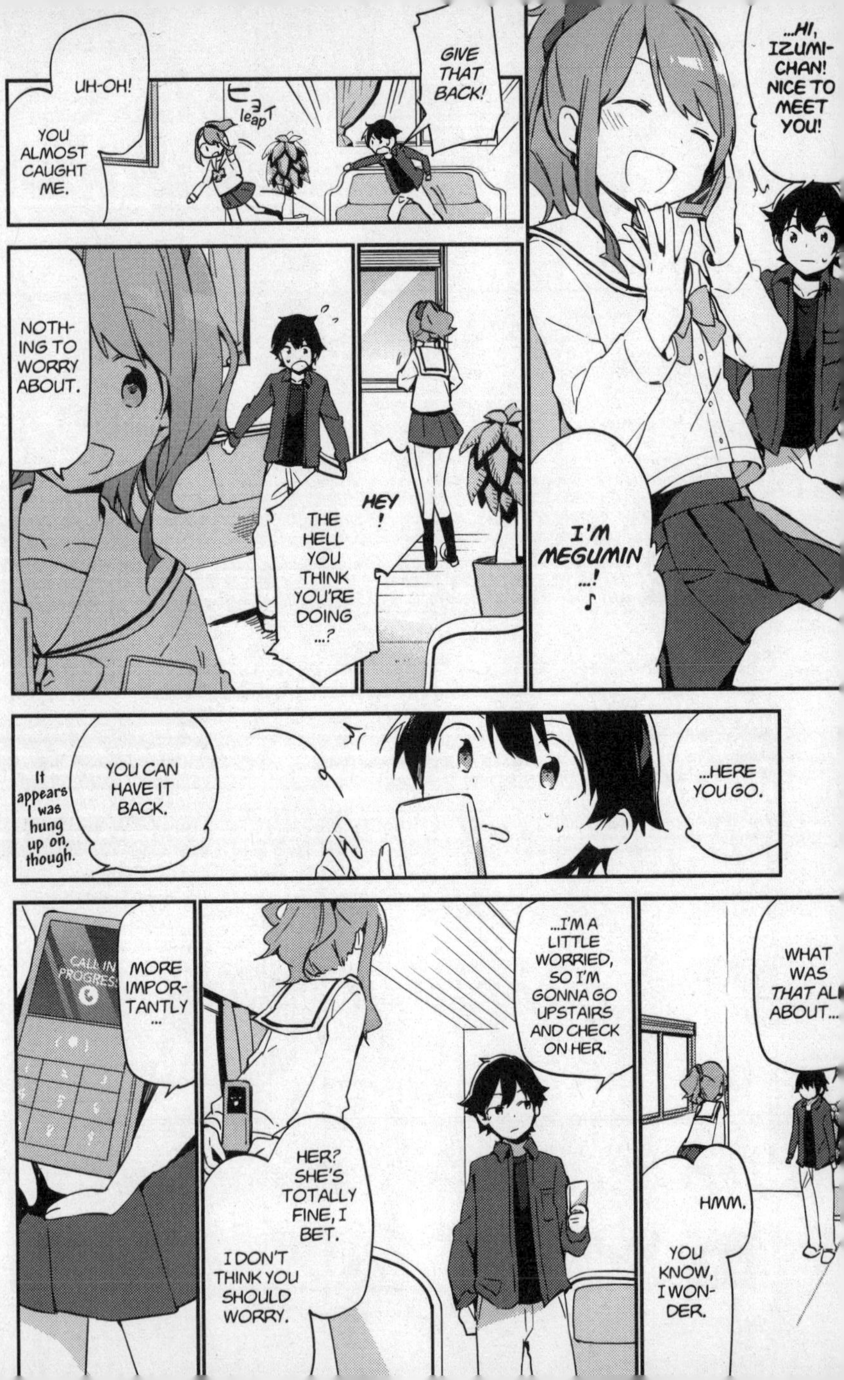
...HI, IZUMI-CHAN! NICE TO MEET YOU!
I'M MEGUMIN...! ♪
GIVE THAT BACK!
ヒョイ leap
UH-OH!
YOU ALMOST CAUGHT ME.
HEY!
THE HELL YOU THINK YOU'RE DOING...?
NOTHING TO WORRY ABOUT.
...HERE YOU GO.
YOU CAN HAVE IT BACK.
It appears I was hung up on, though.
WHAT WAS THAT AL ABOUT...
HMM.
YOU KNOW, I WONDER.
...I'M A LITTLE WORRIED, SO I'M GONNA GO UPSTAIRS AND CHECK ON HER.
HER? SHE'S TOTALLY FINE, I BET.
I DON'T THINK YOU SHOULD WORRY.
MORE IMPORTANTLY...
CALL IN PROGRESS

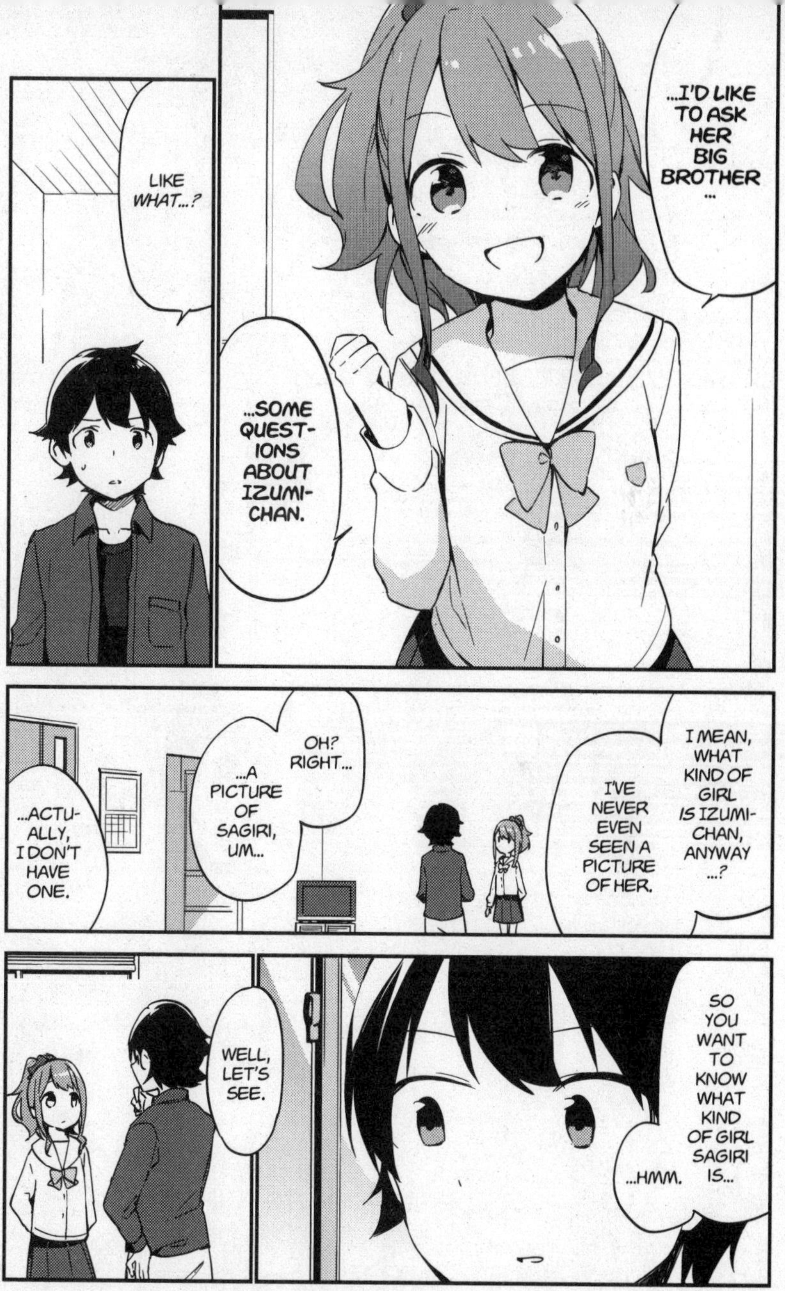
...I'D LIKE TO ASK HER BIG BROTHER ...
...SOME QUESTIONS ABOUT IZUMI-CHAN.
LIKE WHAT...?
I MEAN, WHAT KIND OF GIRL IS IZUMI-CHAN, ANYWAY ...?
I'VE NEVER EVEN SEEN A PICTURE OF HER.
OH? RIGHT...
...A PICTURE OF SAGIRI, UM...
...ACTUALLY, I DON'T HAVE ONE.
SO YOU WANT TO KNOW WHAT KIND OF GIRL SAGIRI IS...
...HMM.
WELL, LET'S SEE.

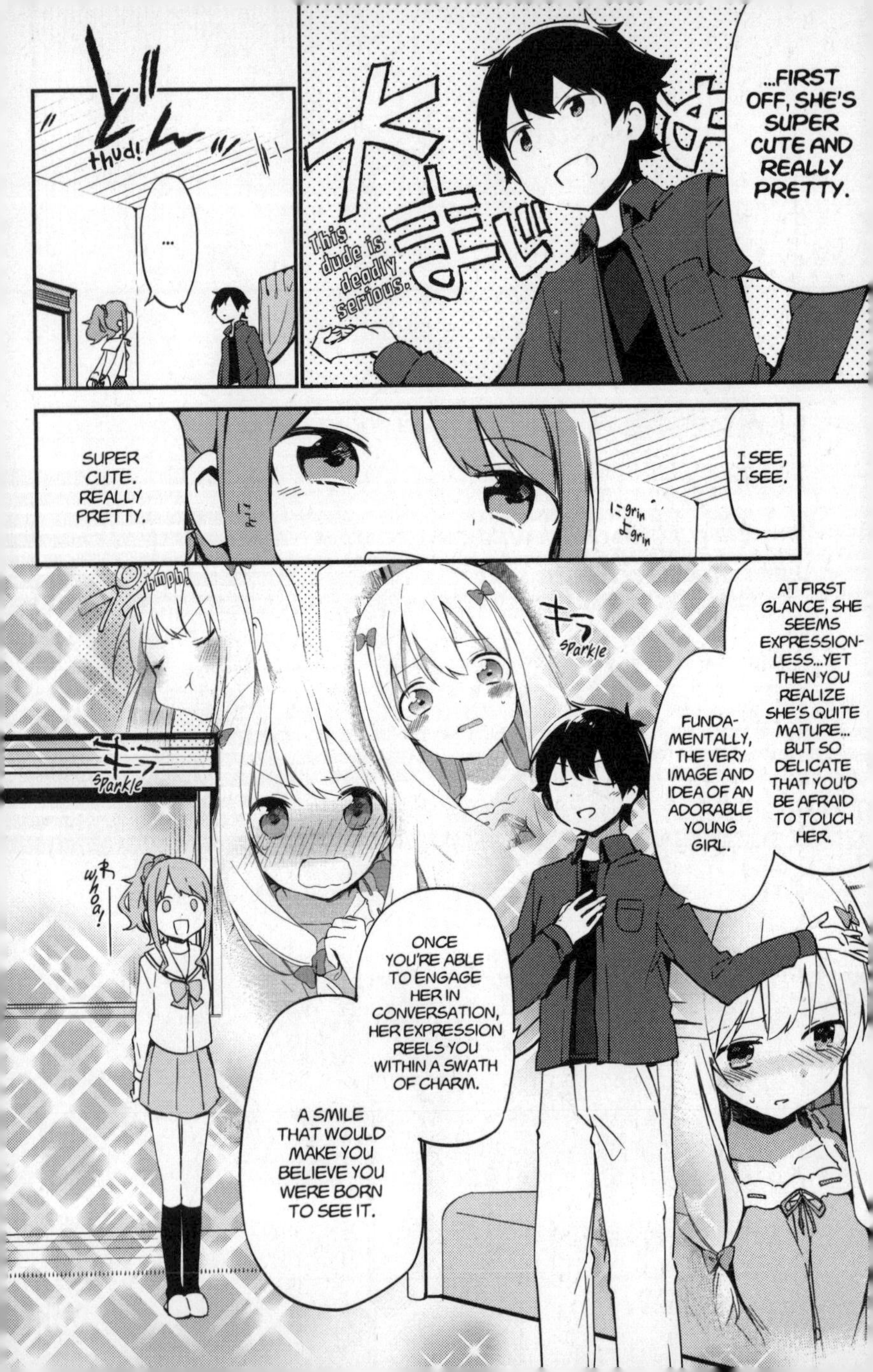
...FIRST OFF, SHE'S SUPER CUTE AND REALLY PRETTY.
This dude is deadly serious.
thud!
...
I SEE, I SEE.
grin grin
SUPER CUTE. REALLY PRETTY.
AT FIRST GLANCE, SHE SEEMS EXPRESSION-LESS...YET THEN YOU REALIZE SHE'S QUITE MATURE... BUT SO DELICATE THAT YOU'D BE AFRAID TO TOUCH HER.
sparkle
FUNDA-MENTALLY, THE VERY IMAGE AND IDEA OF AN ADORABLE YOUNG GIRL.
hmph!
sparkle
ONCE YOU'RE ABLE TO ENGAGE HER IN CONVERSATION, HER EXPRESSION REELS YOU WITHIN A SWATH OF CHARM.
A SMILE THAT WOULD MAKE YOU BELIEVE YOU WERE BORN TO SEE IT.
whoa!

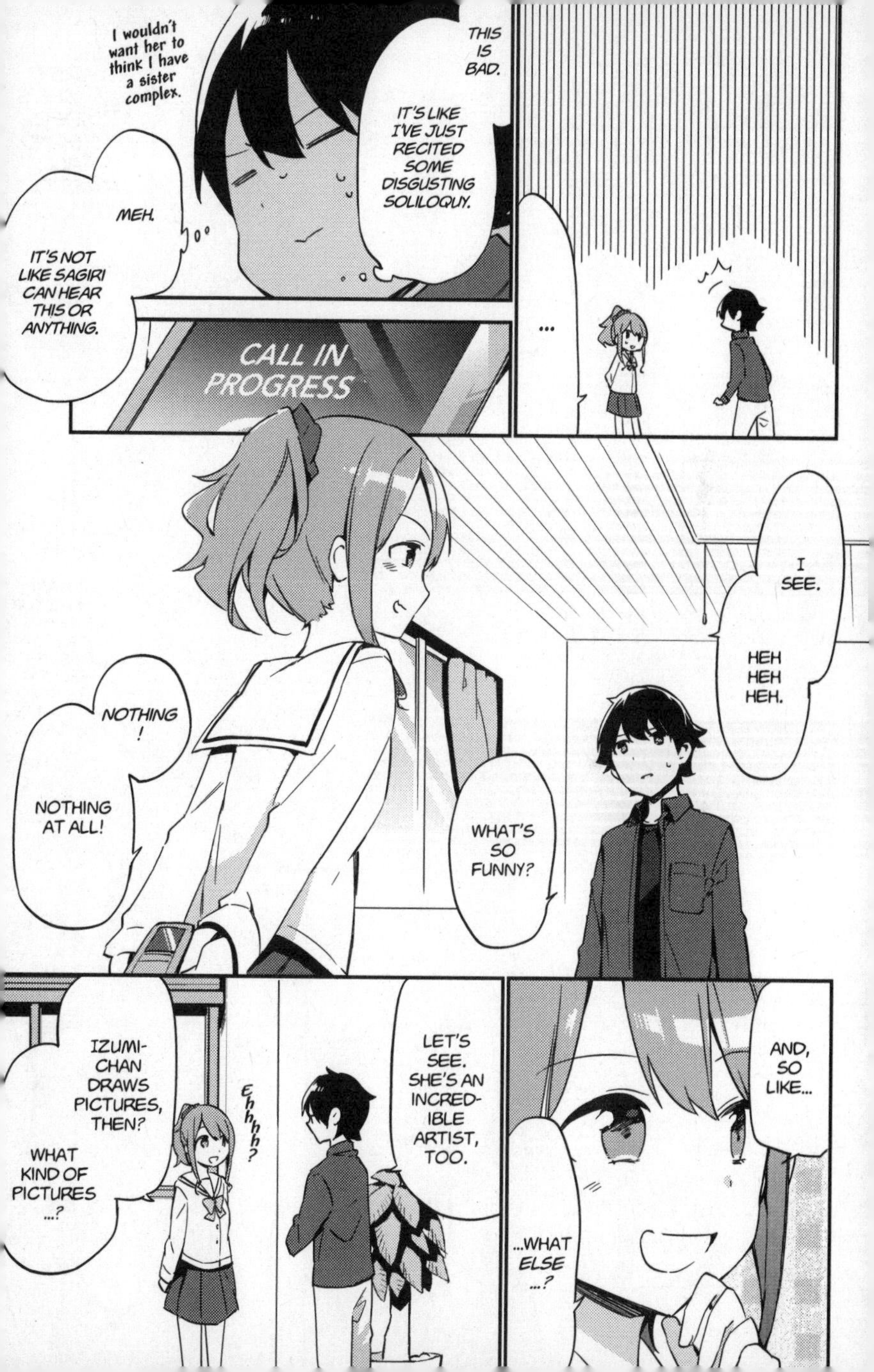
...
THIS IS BAD.
IT'S LIKE I'VE JUST RECITED SOME DISGUSTING SOLILOQUY.
I wouldn't want her to think I have a sister complex.
MEH.
IT'S NOT LIKE SAGIRI CAN HEAR THIS OR ANYTHING.
CALL IN PROGRESS
I SEE.
HEH HEH HEH.
WHAT'S SO FUNNY?
NOTHING!
NOTHING AT ALL!
AND, SO LIKE...
...WHAT ELSE ...?
LET'S SEE. SHE'S AN INCREDIBLE ARTIST, TOO.
Ehhhh?
IZUMI-CHAN DRAWS PICTURES, THEN?
WHAT KIND OF PICTURES ...?

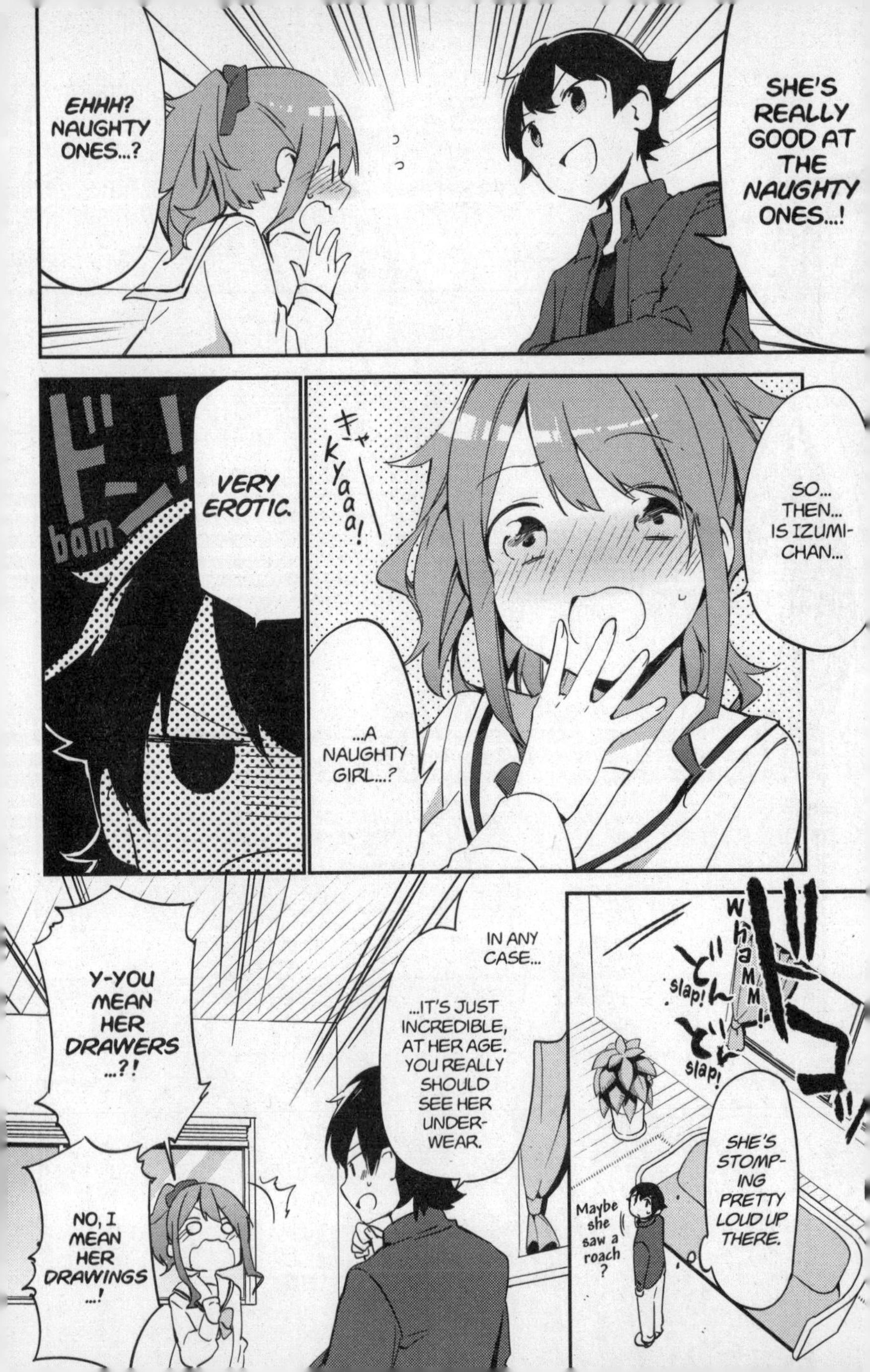
SHE'S REALLY GOOD AT THE NAUGHTY ONES...!
EHHH? NAUGHTY ONES...?
SO... THEN... IS IZUMI-CHAN...
kyaaa!
...A NAUGHTY GIRL...?
bam
VERY EROTIC.
whamm!
slap!
slap!
SHE'S STOMPING PRETTY LOUD UP THERE.
Maybe she saw a roach?
IN ANY CASE...
...IT'S JUST INCREDIBLE, AT HER AGE. YOU REALLY SHOULD SEE HER UNDERWEAR.
Y-YOU MEAN HER DRAWERS...?!
NO, I MEAN HER DRAWINGS...!

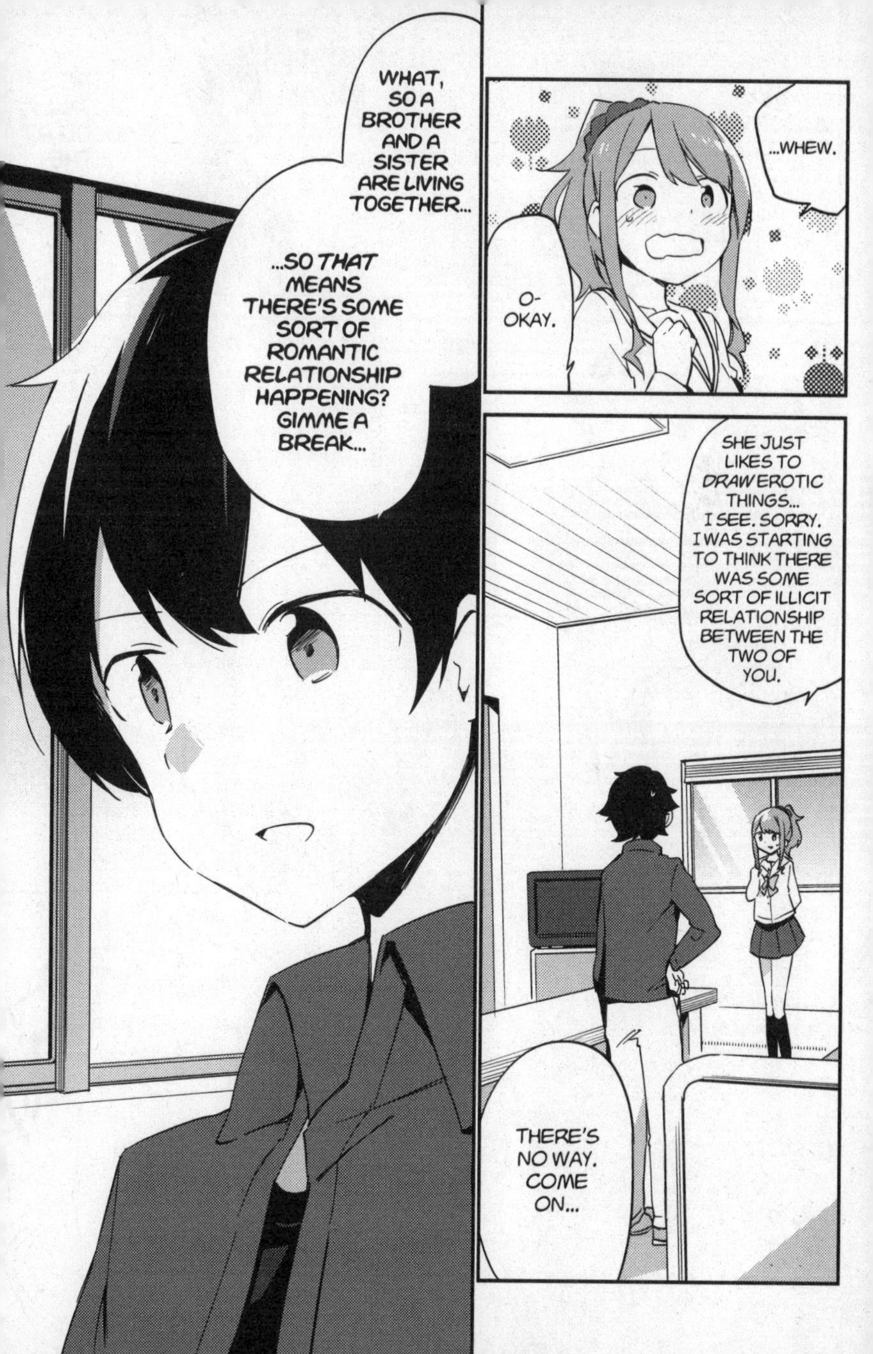
...WHEW.
O-OKAY.
SHE JUST LIKES TO DRAW EROTIC THINGS... I SEE. SORRY. I WAS STARTING TO THINK THERE WAS SOME SORT OF ILLICIT RELATIONSHIP BETWEEN THE TWO OF YOU.
THERE'S NO WAY. COME ON...
WHAT, SO A BROTHER AND A SISTER ARE LIVING TOGETHER...
...SO THAT MEANS THERE'S SOME SORT OF ROMANTIC RELATIONSHIP HAPPENING? GIMME A BREAK...

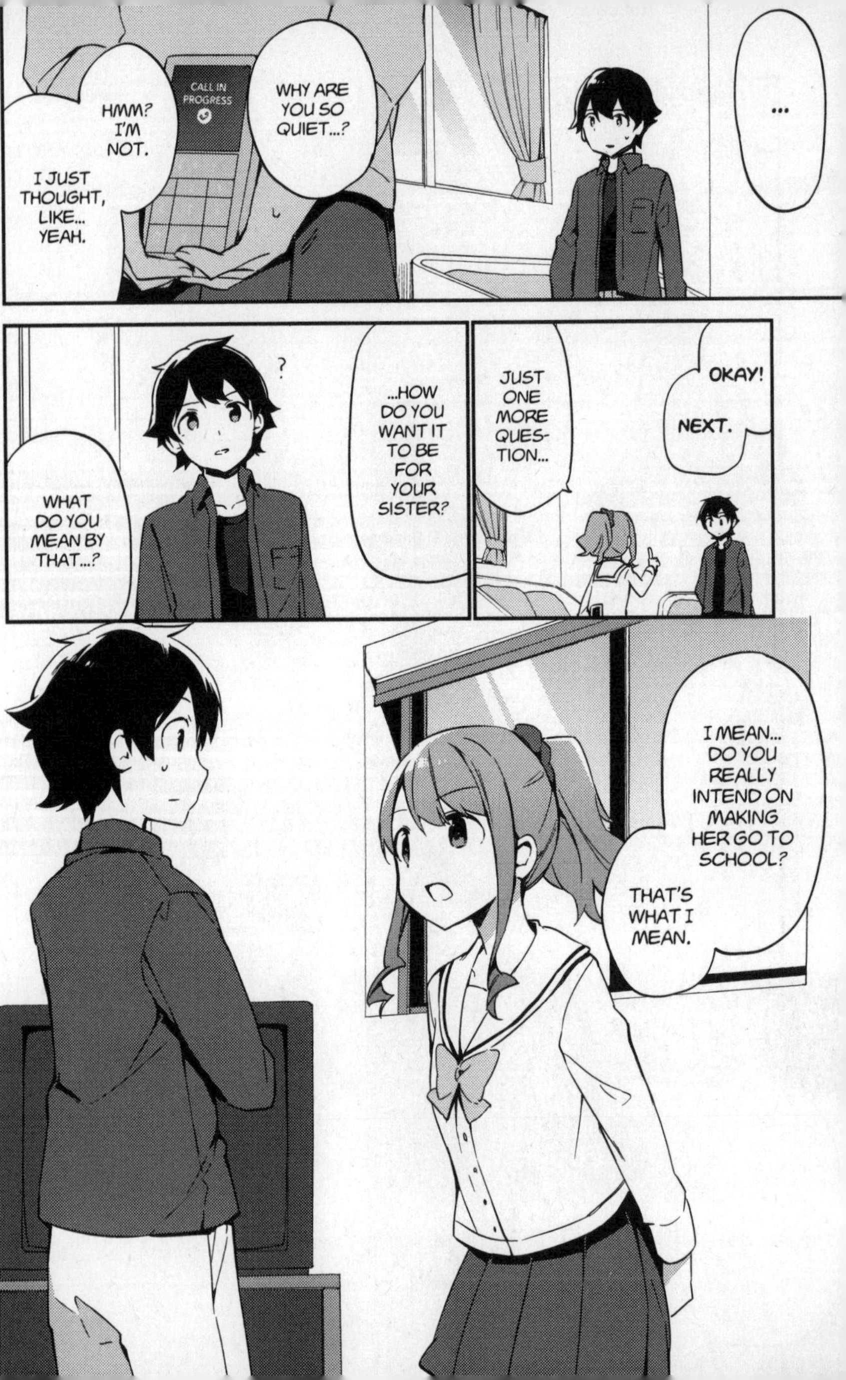
...
WHY ARE YOU SO QUIET...?
CALL IN PROGRESS
HMM? I'M NOT.
I JUST THOUGHT, LIKE... YEAH.
OKAY!
NEXT.
JUST ONE MORE QUESTION...
...HOW DO YOU WANT IT TO BE FOR YOUR SISTER?
?
WHAT DO YOU MEAN BY THAT...?
I MEAN... DO YOU REALLY INTEND ON MAKING HER GO TO SCHOOL?
THAT'S WHAT I MEAN.

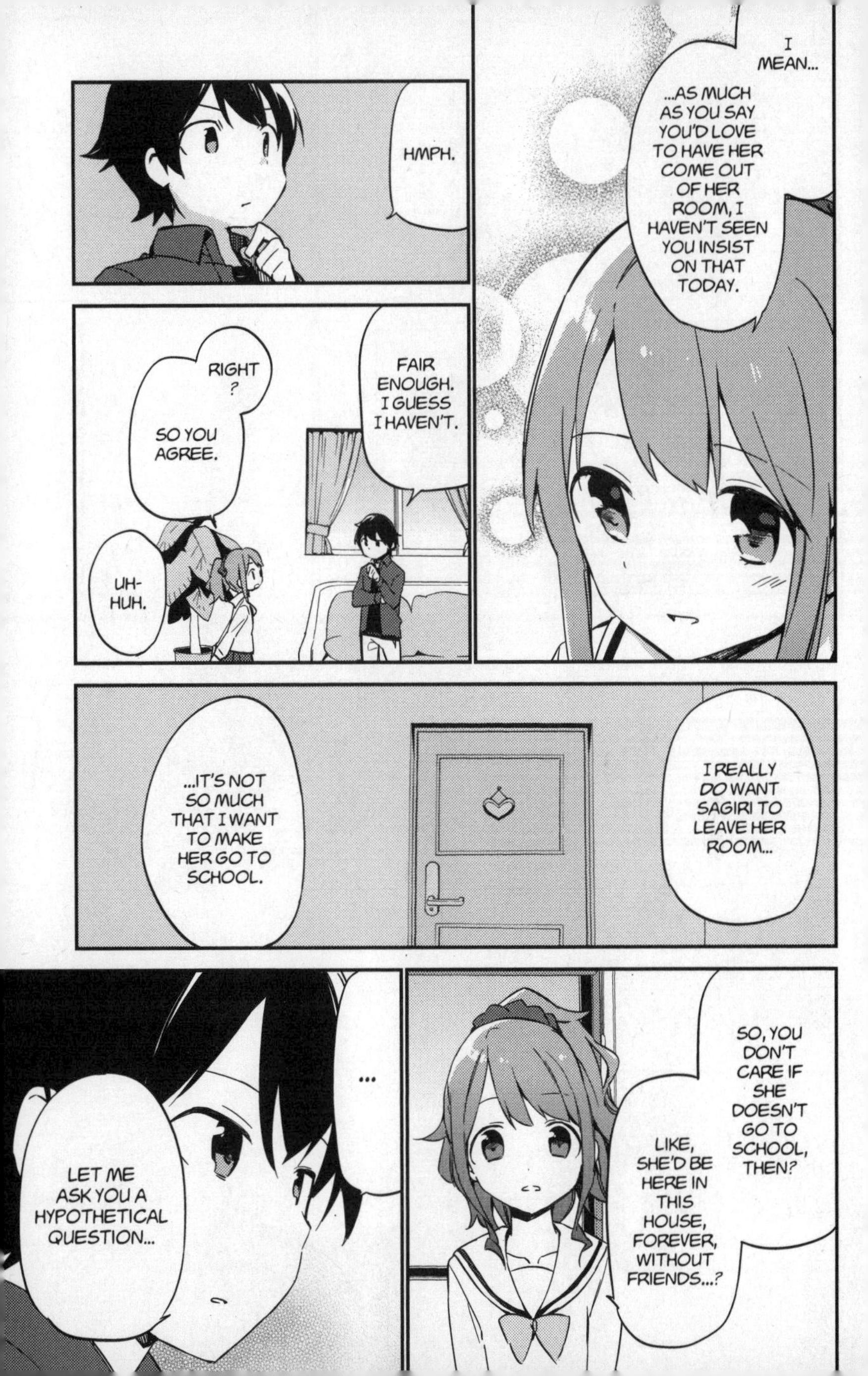
I MEAN...
...AS MUCH AS YOU SAY YOU'D LOVE TO HAVE HER COME OUT OF HER ROOM, I HAVEN'T SEEN YOU INSIST ON THAT TODAY.
HMPH.
FAIR ENOUGH. I GUESS I HAVEN'T.
RIGHT? SO YOU AGREE.
UH-HUH.
I REALLY DO WANT SAGIRI TO LEAVE HER ROOM...
...IT'S NOT SO MUCH THAT I WANT TO MAKE HER GO TO SCHOOL.
SO, YOU DON'T CARE IF SHE DOESN'T GO TO SCHOOL, THEN?
LIKE, SHE'D BE HERE IN THIS HOUSE, FOREVER, WITHOUT FRIENDS...?
...
LET ME ASK YOU A HYPOTHETICAL QUESTION...

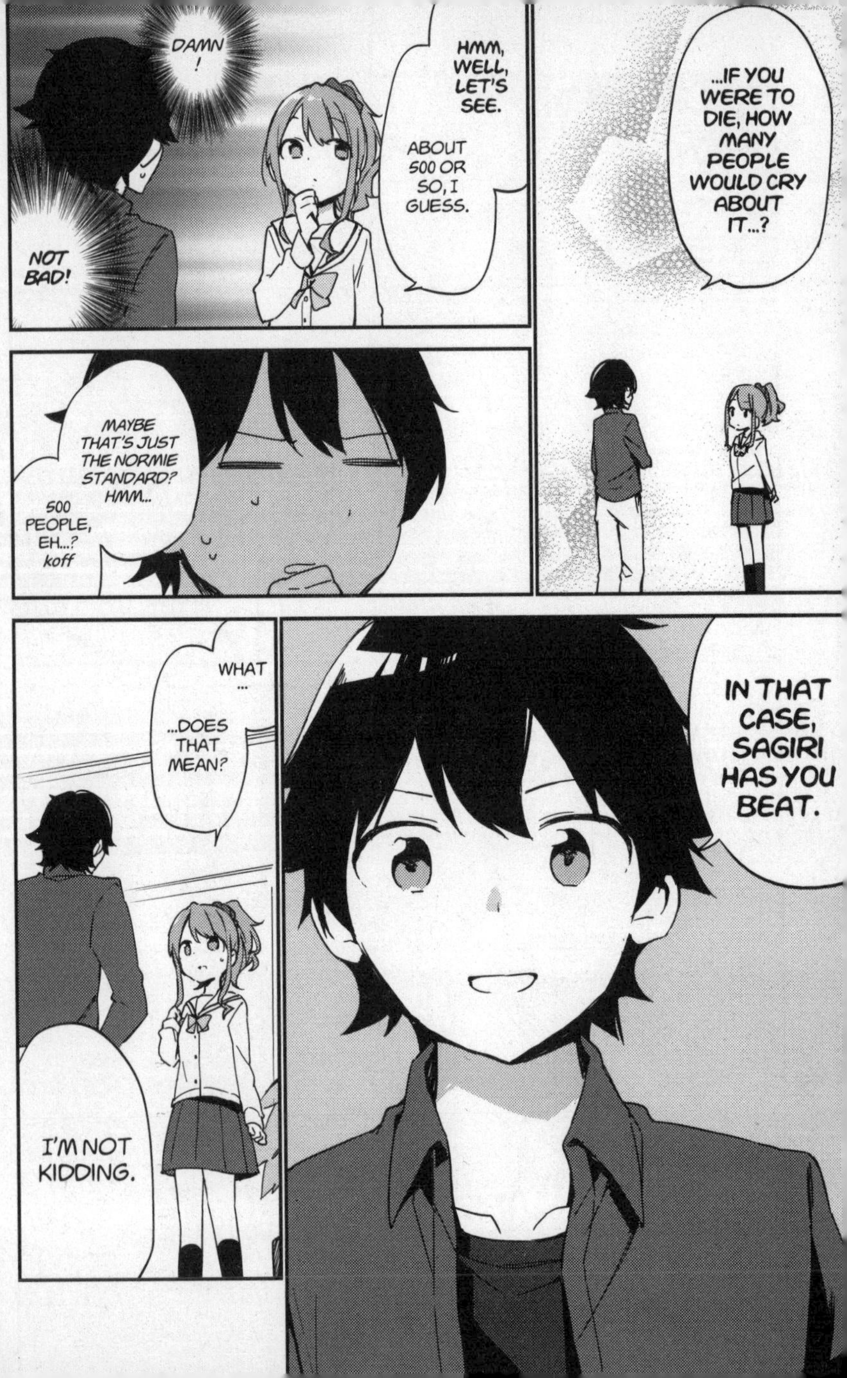
...IF YOU WERE TO DIE, HOW MANY PEOPLE WOULD CRY ABOUT IT...?
HMM, WELL, LET'S SEE.
ABOUT 500 OR SO, I GUESS.
DAMN!
NOT BAD!
MAYBE THAT'S JUST THE NORMIE STANDARD? HMM...
500 PEOPLE, EH...? koff
IN THAT CASE, SAGIRI HAS YOU BEAT.
WHAT...
...DOES THAT MEAN?
I'M NOT KIDDING.

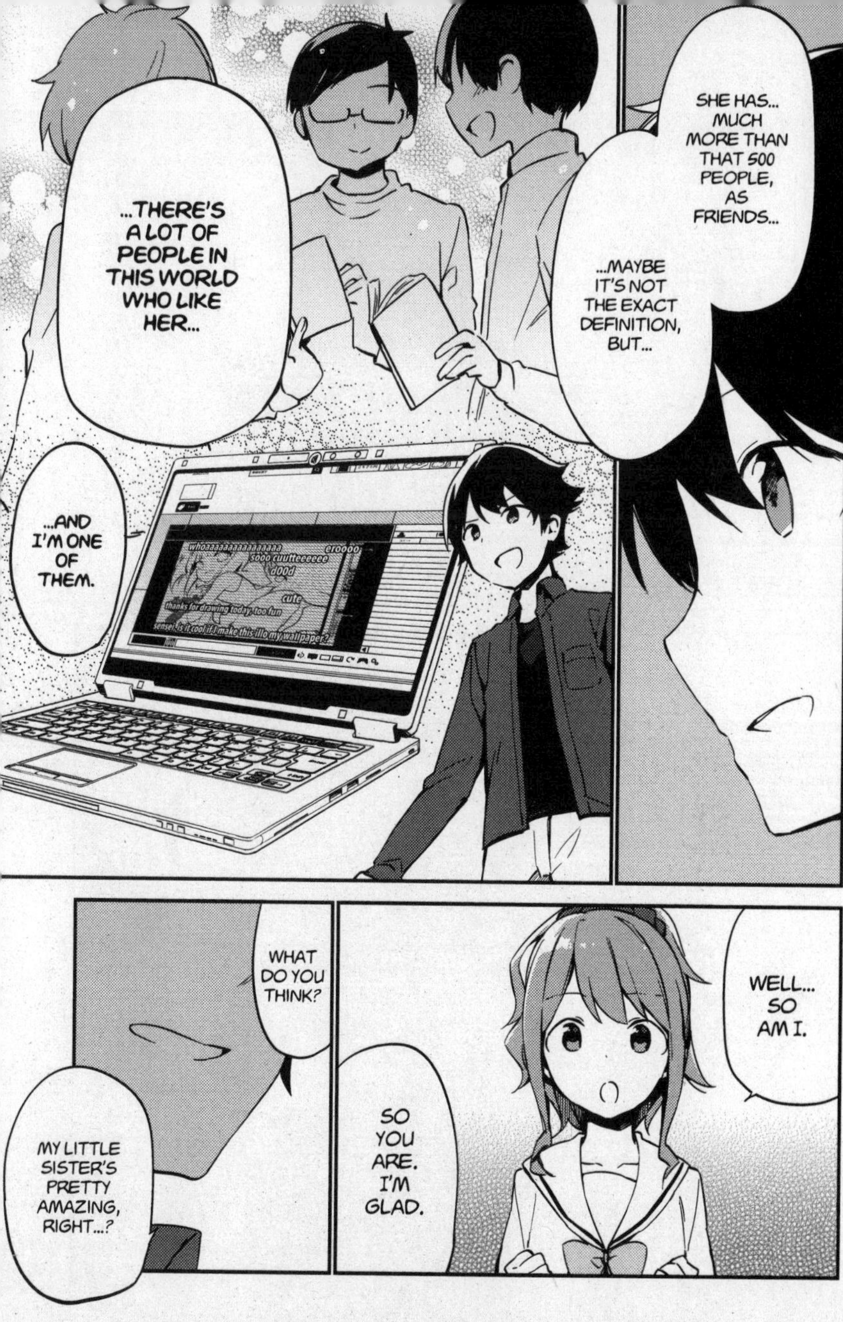
SHE HAS... MUCH MORE THAN THAT 500 PEOPLE, AS FRIENDS...
...MAYBE IT'S NOT THE EXACT DEFINITION, BUT...
...THERE'S A LOT OF PEOPLE IN THIS WORLD WHO LIKE HER...
...AND I'M ONE OF THEM.
whoaaaaaaaaaaaaaaaa
eroooo
sooo cuutteeeeee
d00d
cute
thanks for drawing today, too fun
sensei, is it cool if I make this illo my wallpaper?
WELL... SO AM I.
SO YOU ARE. I'M GLAD.
WHAT DO YOU THINK?
MY LITTLE SISTER'S PRETTY AMAZING, RIGHT...?

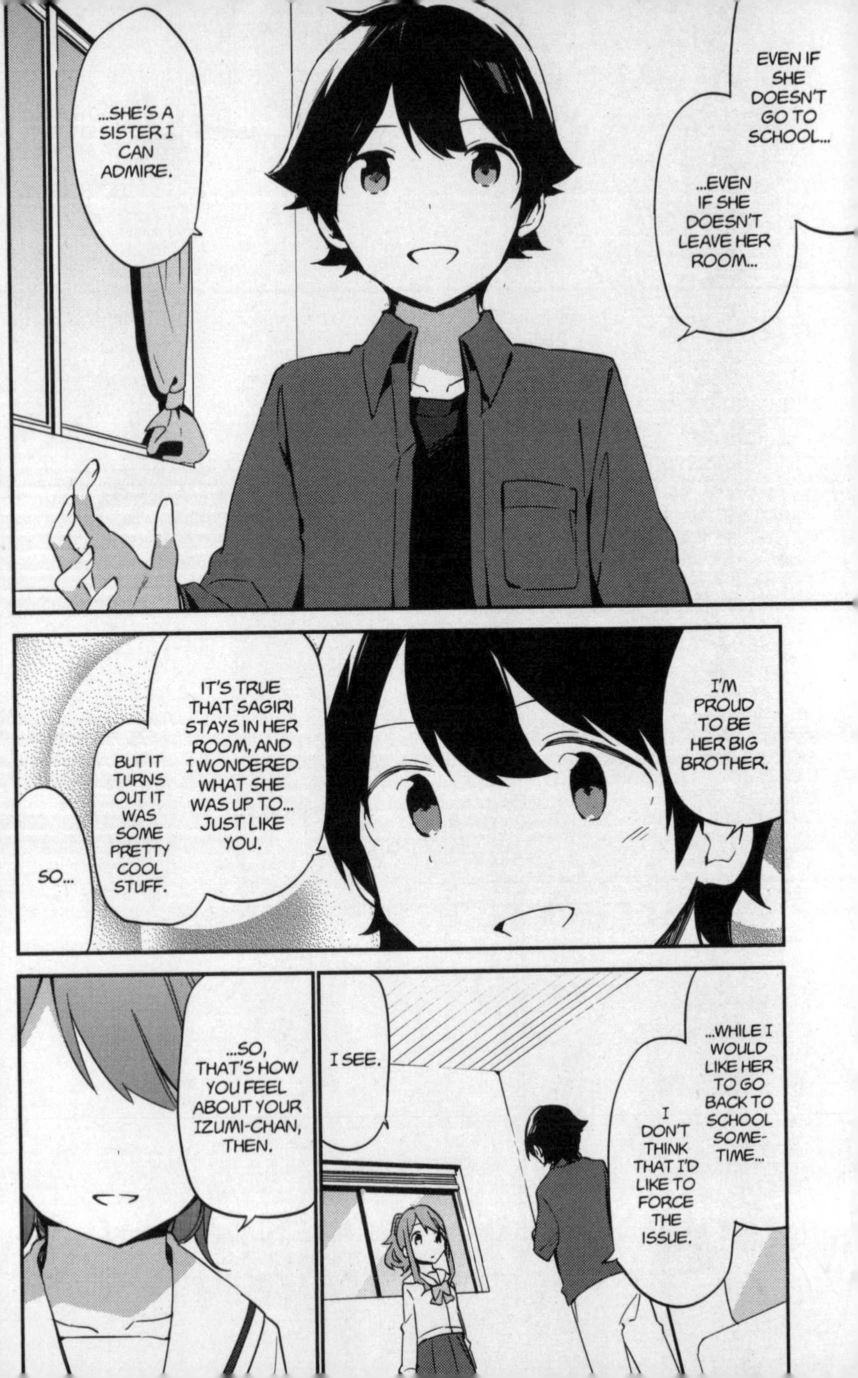
EVEN IF SHE DOESN'T GO TO SCHOOL...
...EVEN IF SHE DOESN'T LEAVE HER ROOM...
...SHE'S A SISTER I CAN ADMIRE.
I'M PROUD TO BE HER BIG BROTHER.
IT'S TRUE THAT SAGIRI STAYS IN HER ROOM, AND I WONDERED WHAT SHE WAS UP TO... JUST LIKE YOU.
BUT IT TURNS OUT IT WAS SOME PRETTY COOL STUFF.
SO...
...WHILE I WOULD LIKE HER TO GO BACK TO SCHOOL SOME-TIME...
I DON'T THINK THAT I'D LIKE TO FORCE THE ISSUE.
I SEE.
...SO, THAT'S HOW YOU FEEL ABOUT YOUR IZUMI-CHAN, THEN.

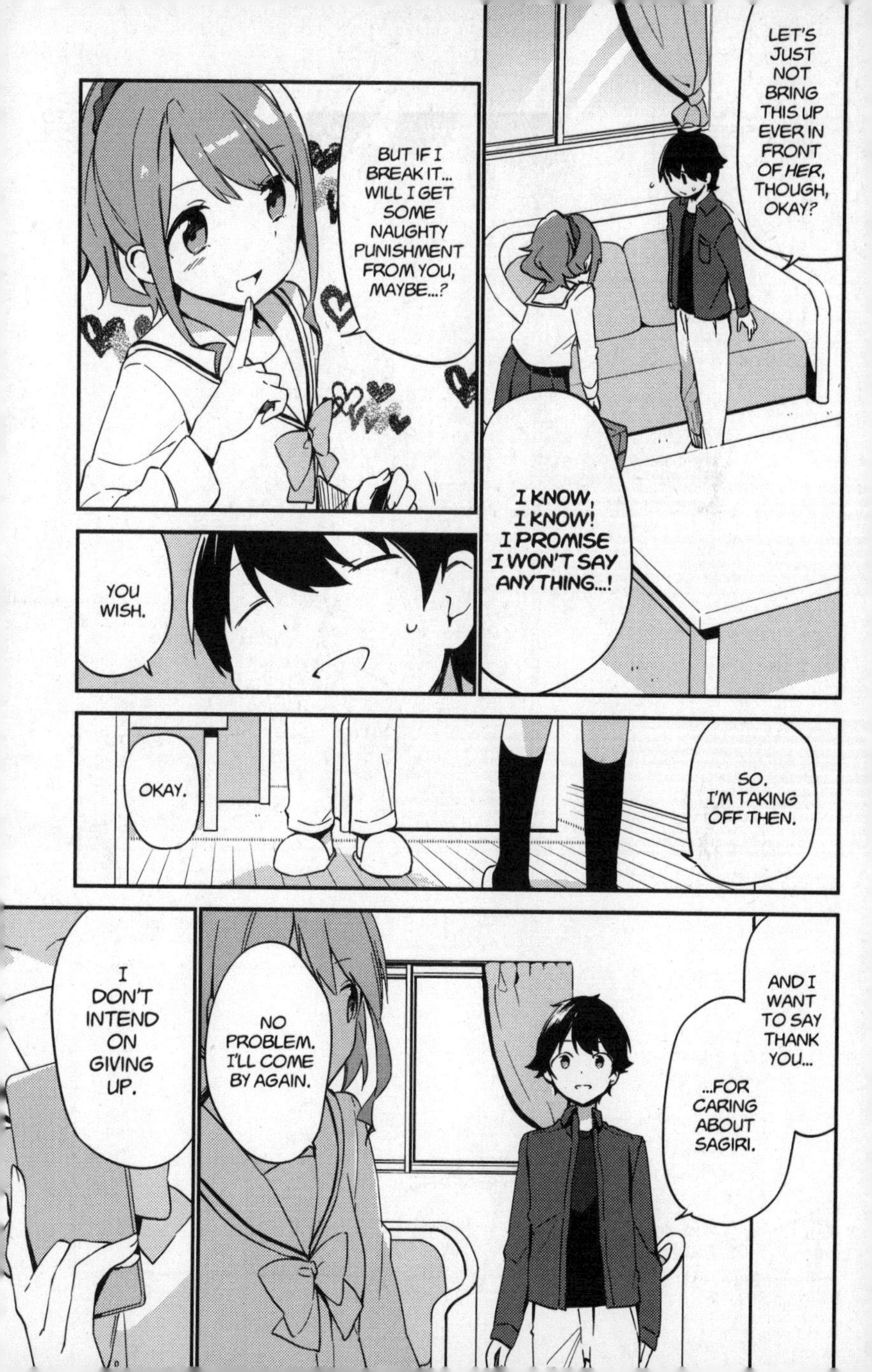
LET'S JUST NOT BRING THIS UP EVER IN FRONT OF *HER*, THOUGH, OKAY?
I KNOW, I KNOW! I PROMISE I WON'T SAY ANYTHING...!
BUT IF I BREAK IT... WILL I GET SOME NAUGHTY PUNISHMENT FROM YOU, MAYBE...?
YOU WISH.
SO. I'M TAKING OFF THEN.
OKAY.
AND I WANT TO SAY THANK YOU...
...FOR CARING ABOUT SAGIRI.
NO PROBLEM. I'LL COME BY AGAIN.
I DON'T INTEND ON GIVING UP.

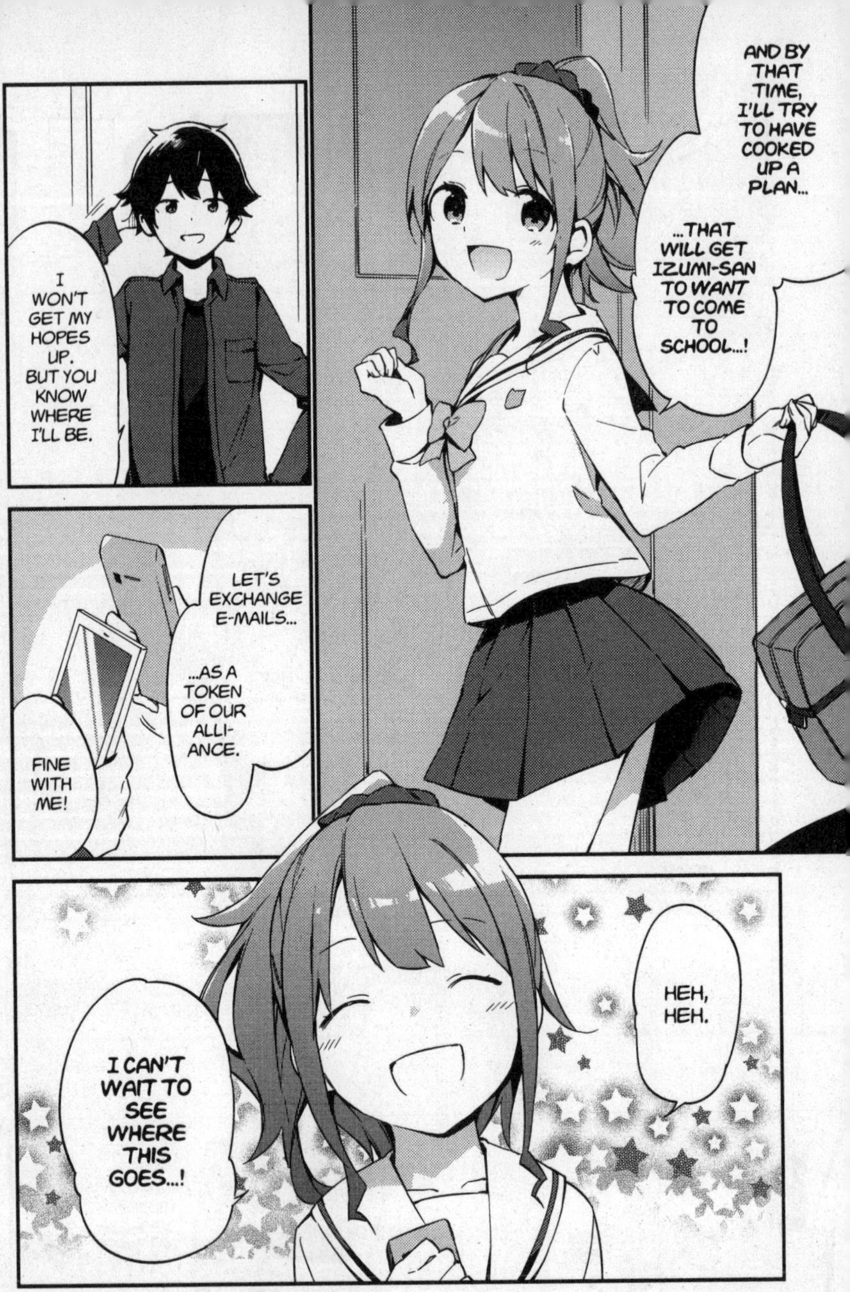
AND BY THAT TIME, I'LL TRY TO HAVE COOKED UP A PLAN...
...THAT WILL GET IZUMI-SAN TO WANT TO COME TO SCHOOL...!
I WON'T GET MY HOPES UP. BUT YOU KNOW WHERE I'LL BE.
LET'S EXCHANGE E-MAILS...
...AS A TOKEN OF OUR ALLI-ANCE.
FINE WITH ME!
HEH, HEH.
I CAN'T WAIT TO SEE WHERE THIS GOES...!

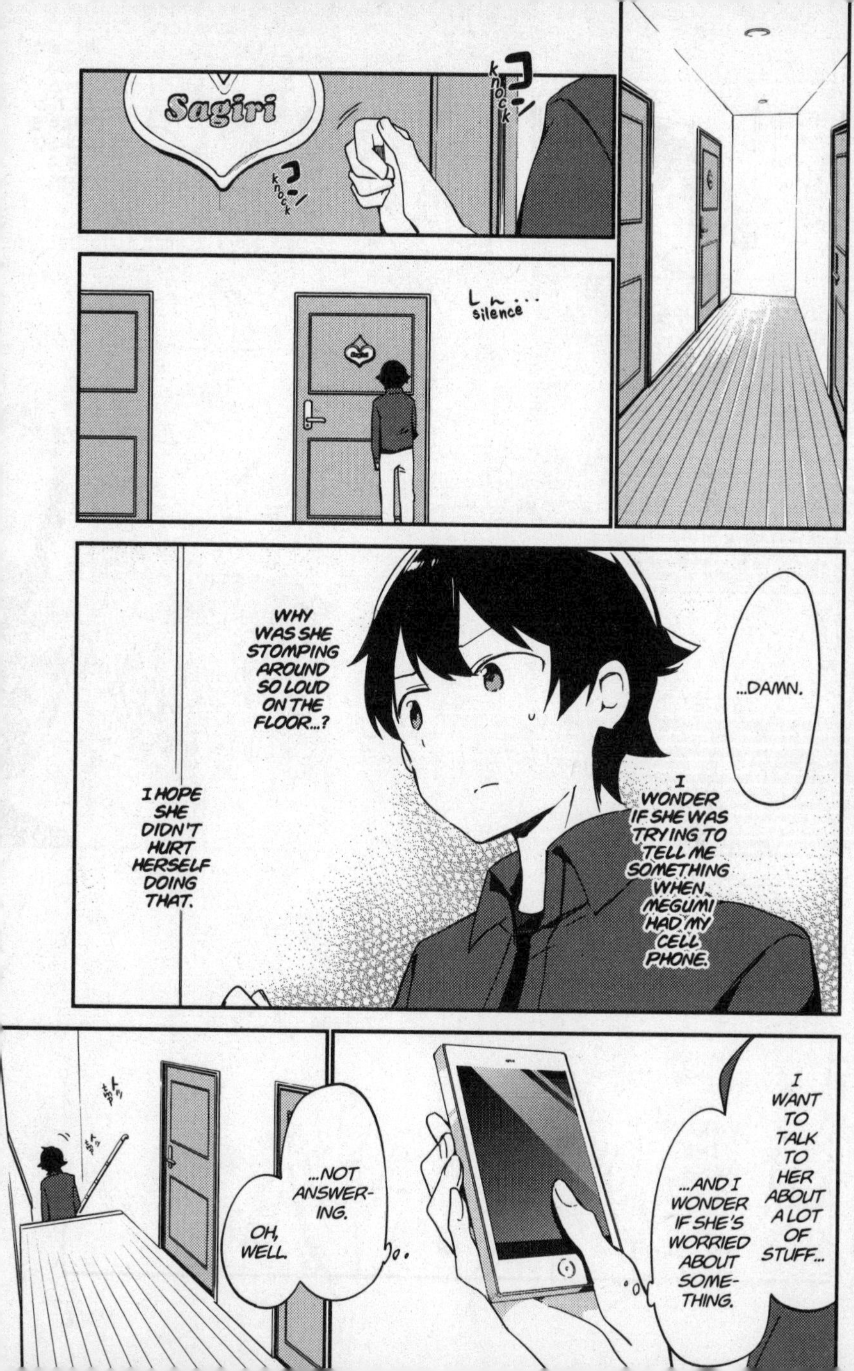
Sagiri
knock
knock
silence
...DAMN.
I WONDER IF SHE WAS TRYING TO TELL ME SOMETHING WHEN MEGUMI HAD MY CELL PHONE.
WHY WAS SHE STOMPING AROUND SO LOUD ON THE FLOOR...?
I HOPE SHE DIDN'T HURT HERSELF DOING THAT.
I WANT TO TALK TO HER ABOUT A LOT OF STUFF...
...AND I WONDER IF SHE'S WORRIED ABOUT SOMETHING.
...NOT ANSWERING.
OH, WELL.

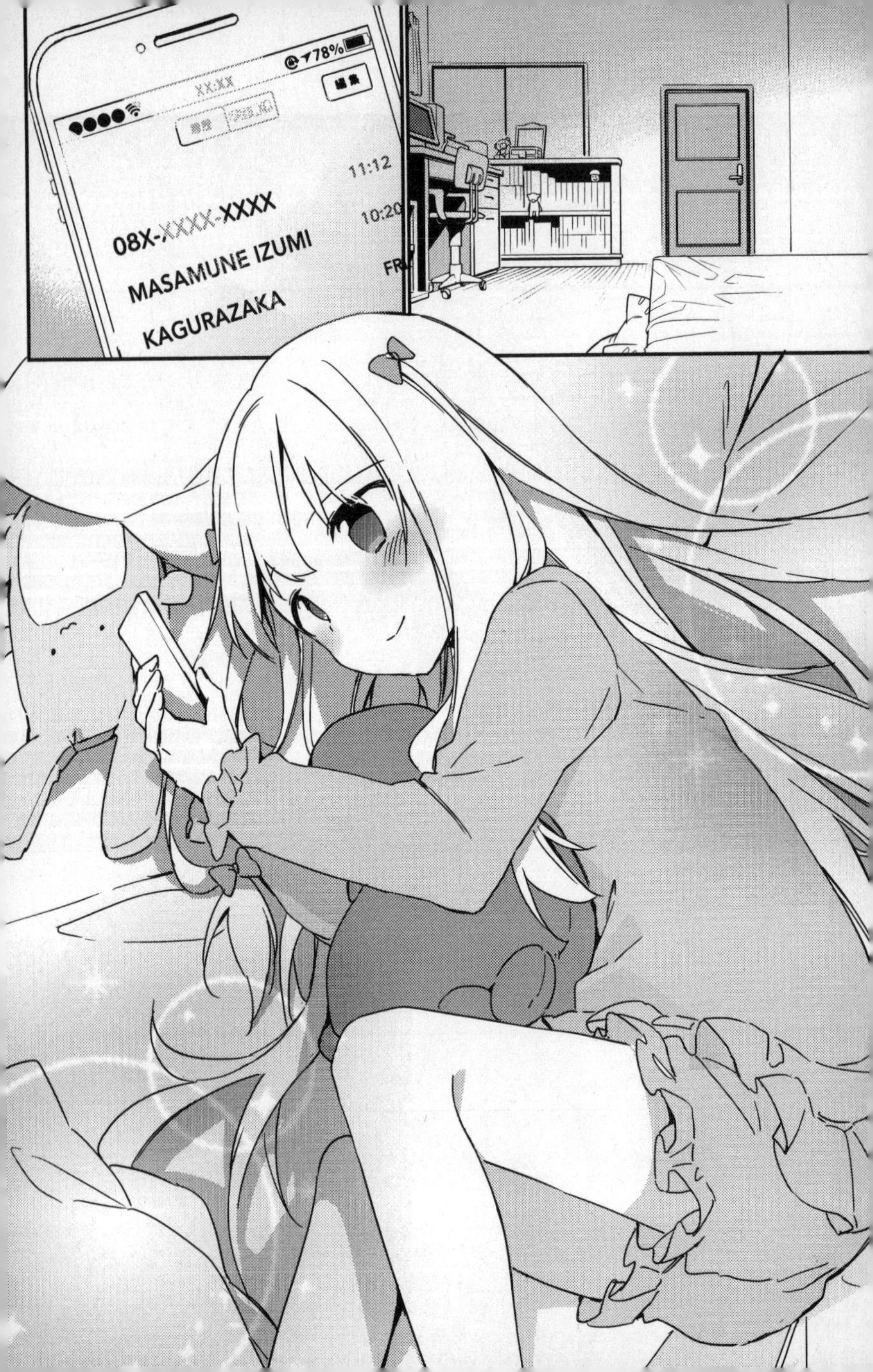
78%
XX:XX
11:12
10:20
08X-XXXX-XXXX
MASAMUNE IZUMI
KAGURAZAKA

eromanga sensei

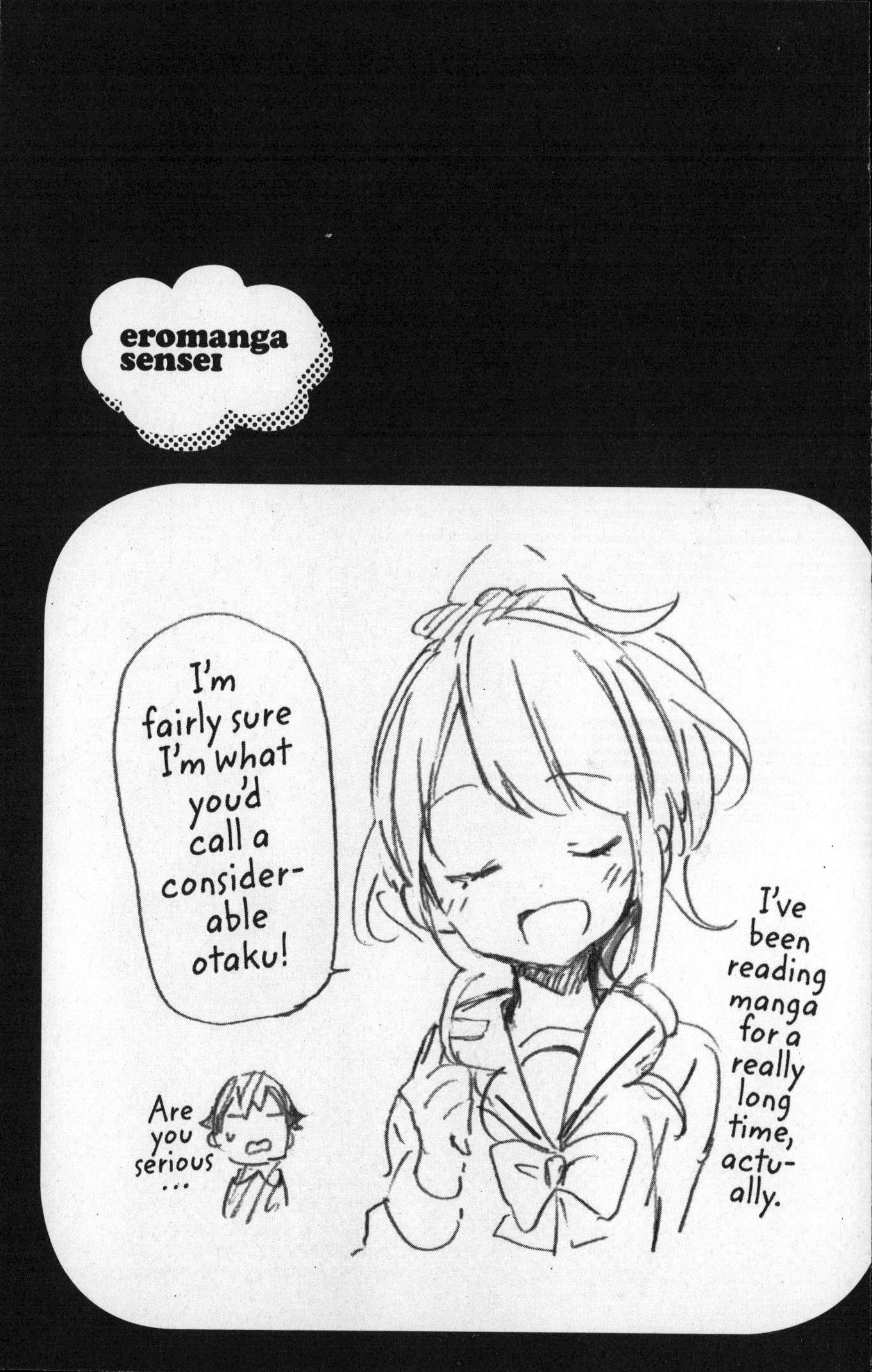
I'm fairly sure I'm what you'd call a consider-able otaku!
I've been reading manga for a really long time, actu-ally.
Are you serious...

eromanga
sensei

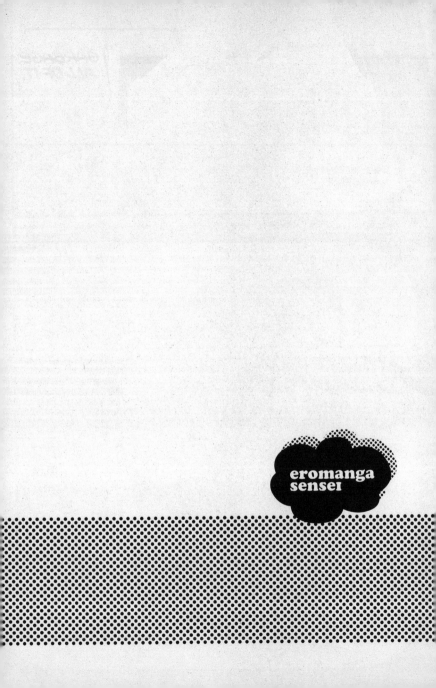

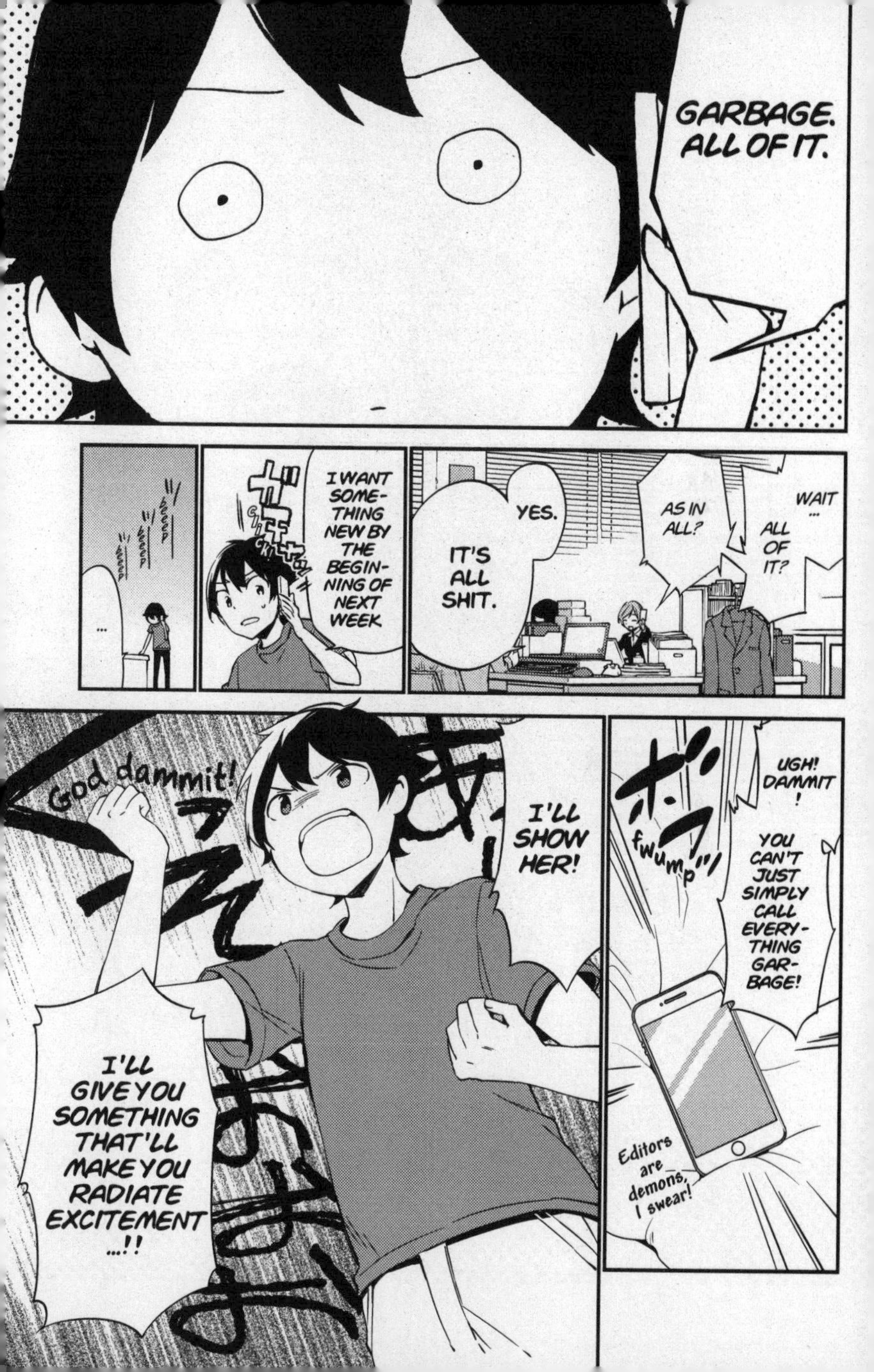
GARBAGE. ALL OF IT.
WAIT ... ALL OF IT?
AS IN ALL?
YES.
IT'S ALL SHIT.
I WANT SOME-THING NEW BY THE BEGIN-NING OF NEXT WEEK
beeep
beeep
beeep
...
UGH! DAMMIT!
YOU CAN'T JUST SIMPLY CALL EVERY-THING GAR-BAGE!
fwump
Editors are demons, I swear!
I'LL SHOW HER!
God dammit!
I'LL GIVE YOU SOMETHING THAT'LL MAKE YOU RADIATE EXCITEMENT ...!!

Chapter 5

My Little Sister and the Sealed Room • Part 5

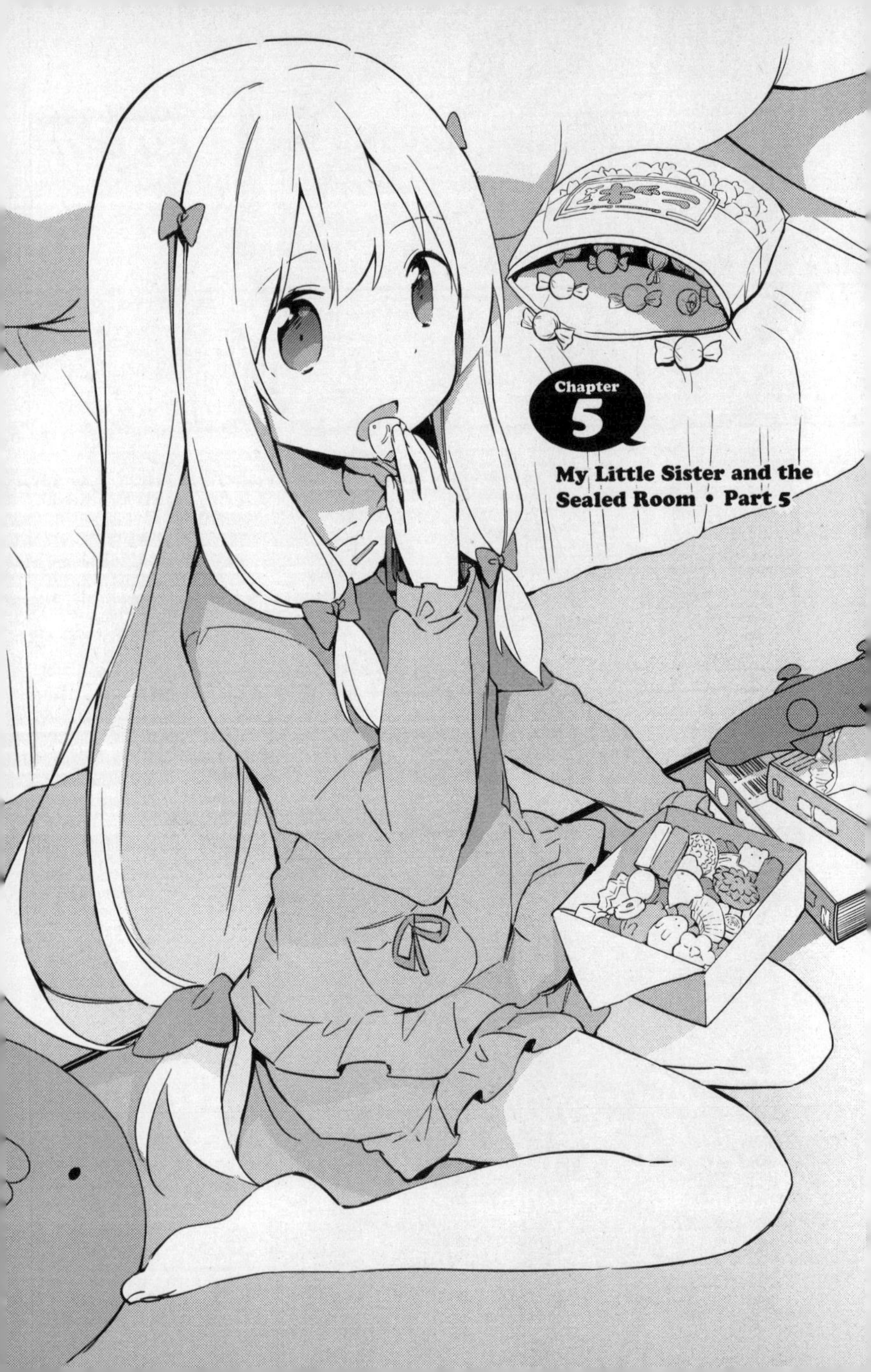

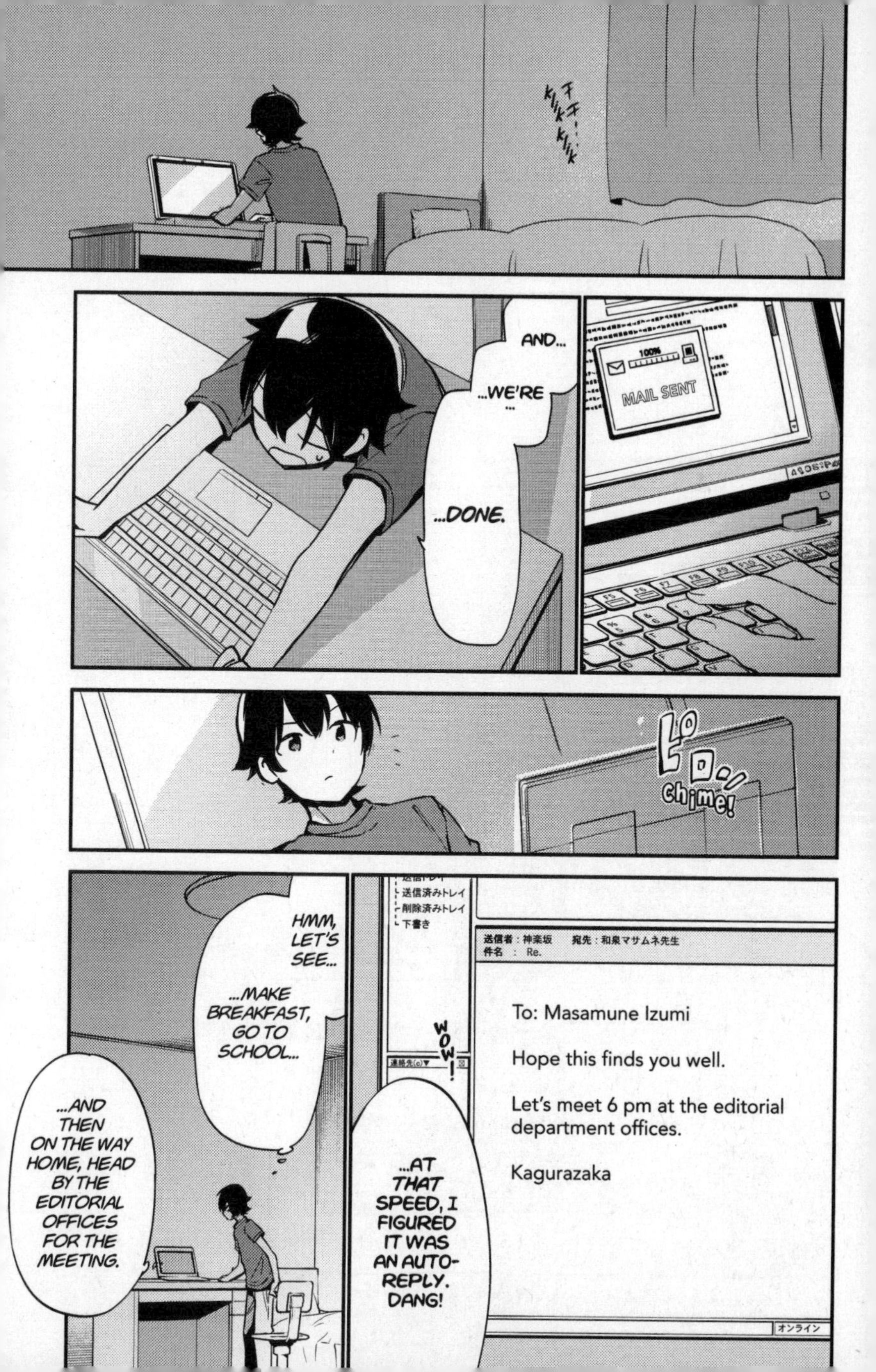
klik klik
100%
MAIL SENT
AND...
...WE'RE...
...DONE.
chime!
送信済みトレイ
削除済みトレイ
下書き
送信者：神楽坂 宛先：和泉マサムネ先生
件名 ： Re.
To: Masamune Izumi
Hope this finds you well.
Let's meet 6 pm at the editorial department offices.
Kagurazaka
連絡先(c)▼
オンライン
WOW!
...AT THAT SPEED, I FIGURED IT WAS AN AUTO-REPLY. DANG!
HMM, LET'S SEE...
...MAKE BREAKFAST, GO TO SCHOOL...
...AND THEN ON THE WAY HOME, HEAD BY THE EDITORIAL OFFICES FOR THE MEETING.

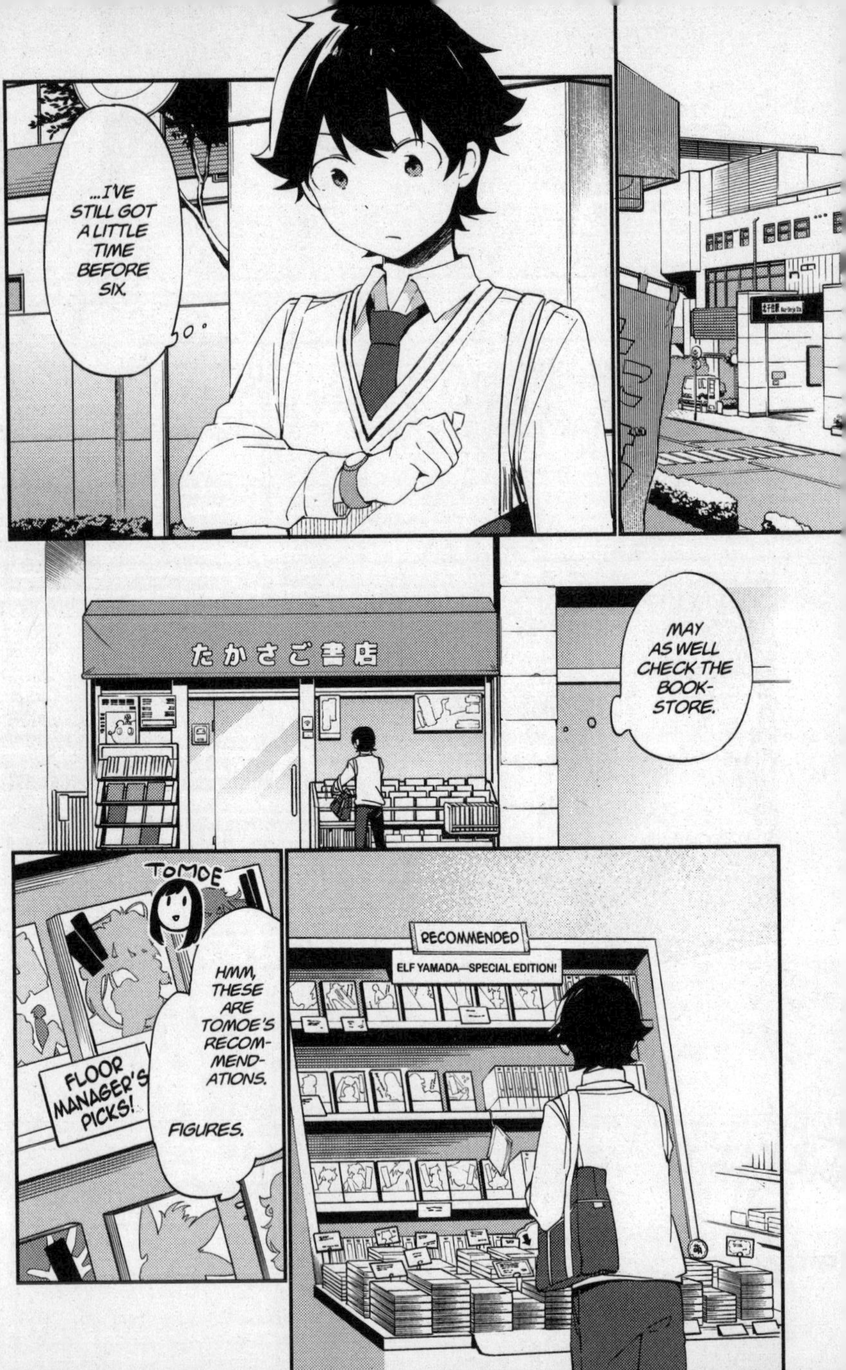
...I'VE STILL GOT A LITTLE TIME BEFORE SIX.
MAY AS WELL CHECK THE BOOK-STORE.
たかさご書店
RECOMMENDED
ELF YAMADA—SPECIAL EDITION!
TOMOE
HMM, THESE ARE TOMOE'S RECOM-MEND-ATIONS.
FIGURES.
FLOOR MANAGER'S PICKS!

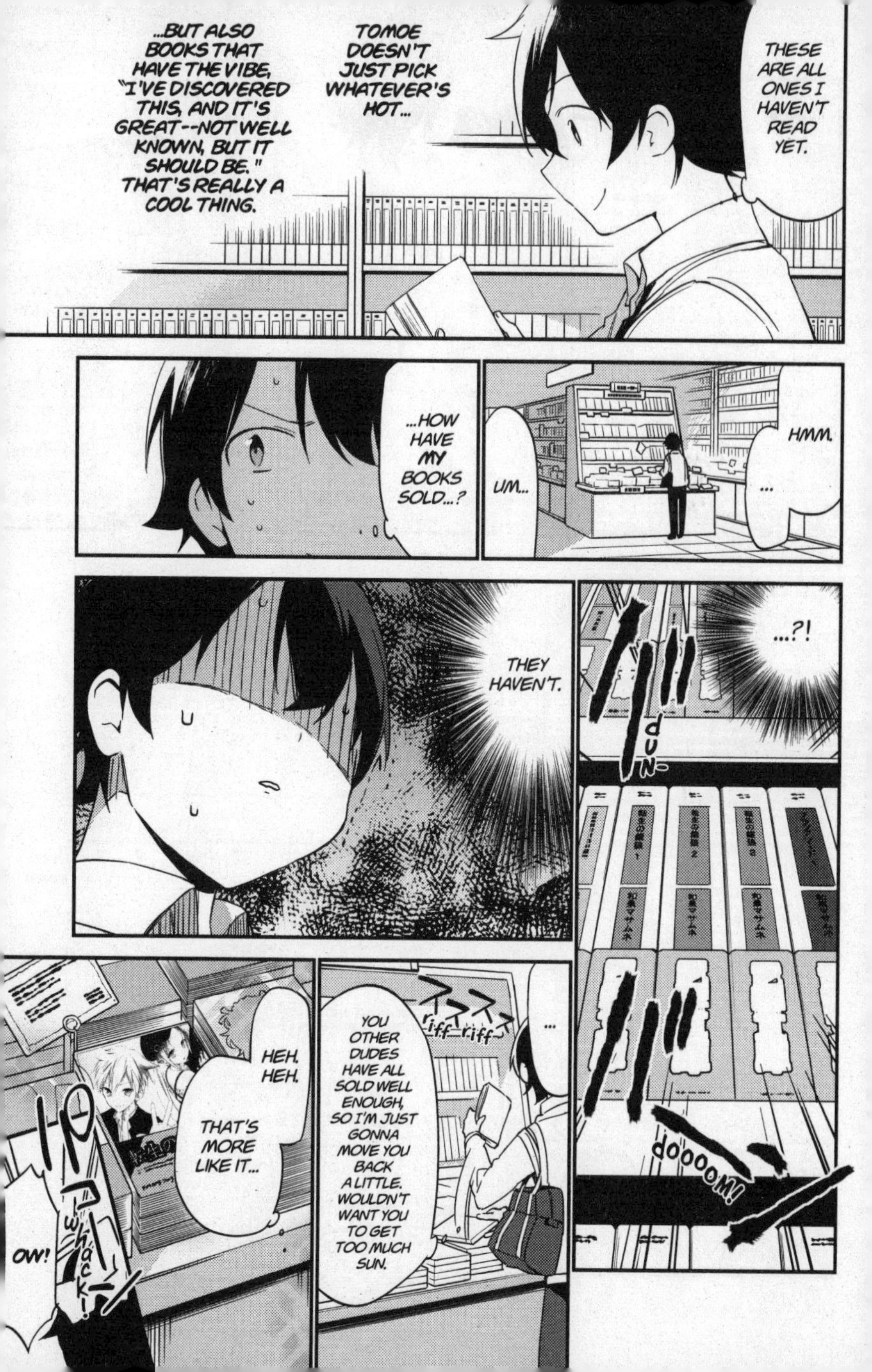
THESE ARE ALL ONES I HAVEN'T READ YET.
TOMOE DOESN'T JUST PICK WHATEVER'S HOT...
...BUT ALSO BOOKS THAT HAVE THE VIBE, "I'VE DISCOVERED THIS, AND IT'S GREAT--NOT WELL KNOWN, BUT IT SHOULD BE." THAT'S REALLY A COOL THING.
HMM.
...
UM...
...HOW HAVE MY BOOKS SOLD...?
...?!
dun-
doooom!
THEY HAVEN'T.
...
riff riff
YOU OTHER DUDES HAVE ALL SOLD WELL ENOUGH, SO I'M JUST GONNA MOVE YOU BACK A LITTLE. WOULDN'T WANT YOU TO GET TOO MUCH SUN.
HEH. HEH.
THAT'S MORE LIKE IT...
whack!
OW!

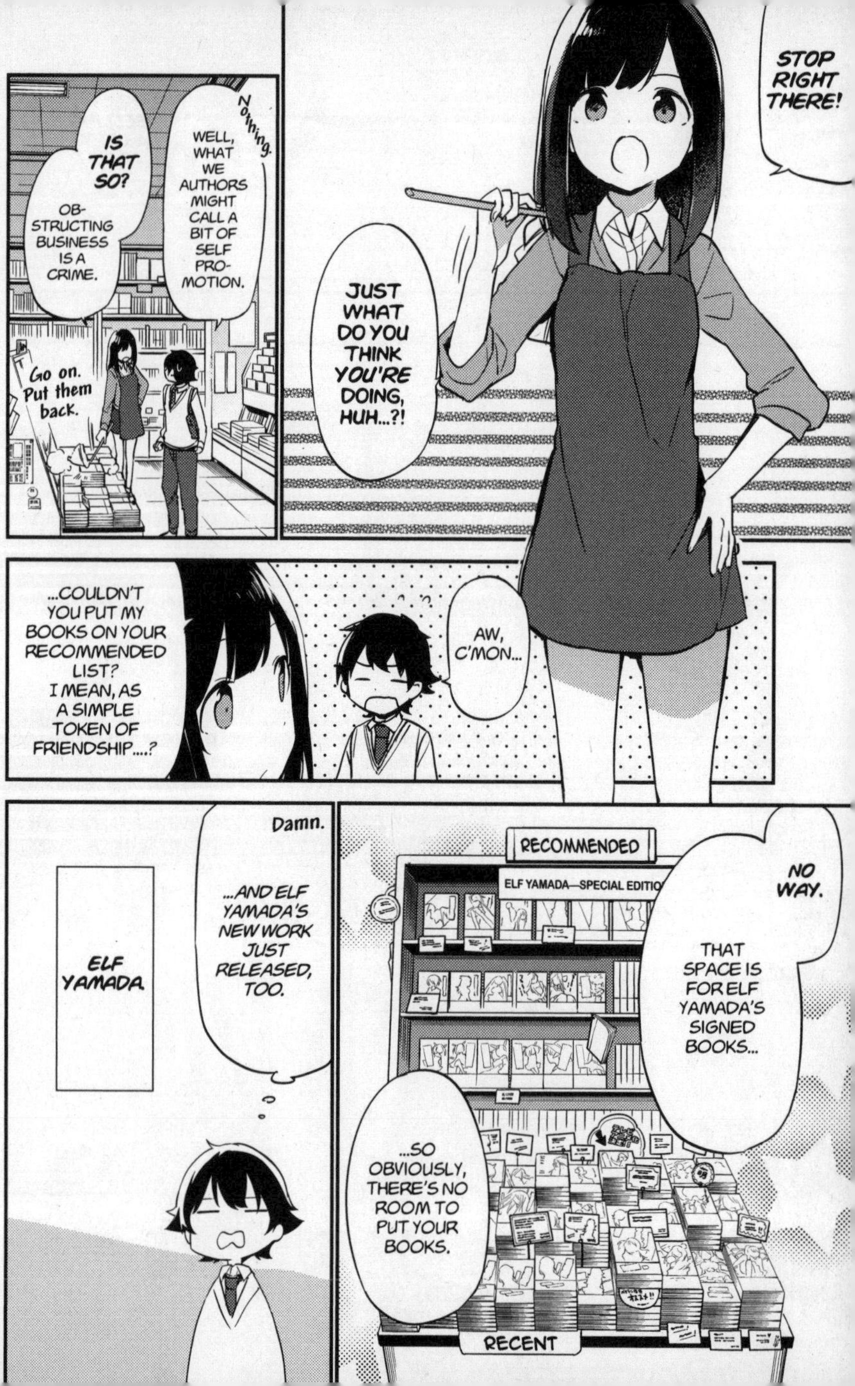
STOP RIGHT THERE!
JUST WHAT DO YOU THINK YOU'RE DOING, HUH...?!
Nothing.
WELL, WHAT WE AUTHORS MIGHT CALL A BIT OF SELF PRO-MOTION.
IS THAT SO?
OB-STRUCTING BUSINESS IS A CRIME.
Go on. Put them back.
AW, C'MON...
...COULDN'T YOU PUT MY BOOKS ON YOUR RECOMMENDED LIST? I MEAN, AS A SIMPLE TOKEN OF FRIENDSHIP....?
RECOMMENDED
ELF YAMADA—SPECIAL EDITIO
NO WAY.
THAT SPACE IS FOR ELF YAMADA'S SIGNED BOOKS...
...SO OBVIOUSLY, THERE'S NO ROOM TO PUT YOUR BOOKS.
RECENT
Damn.
...AND ELF YAMADA'S NEW WORK JUST RELEASED, TOO.
ELF YAMADA

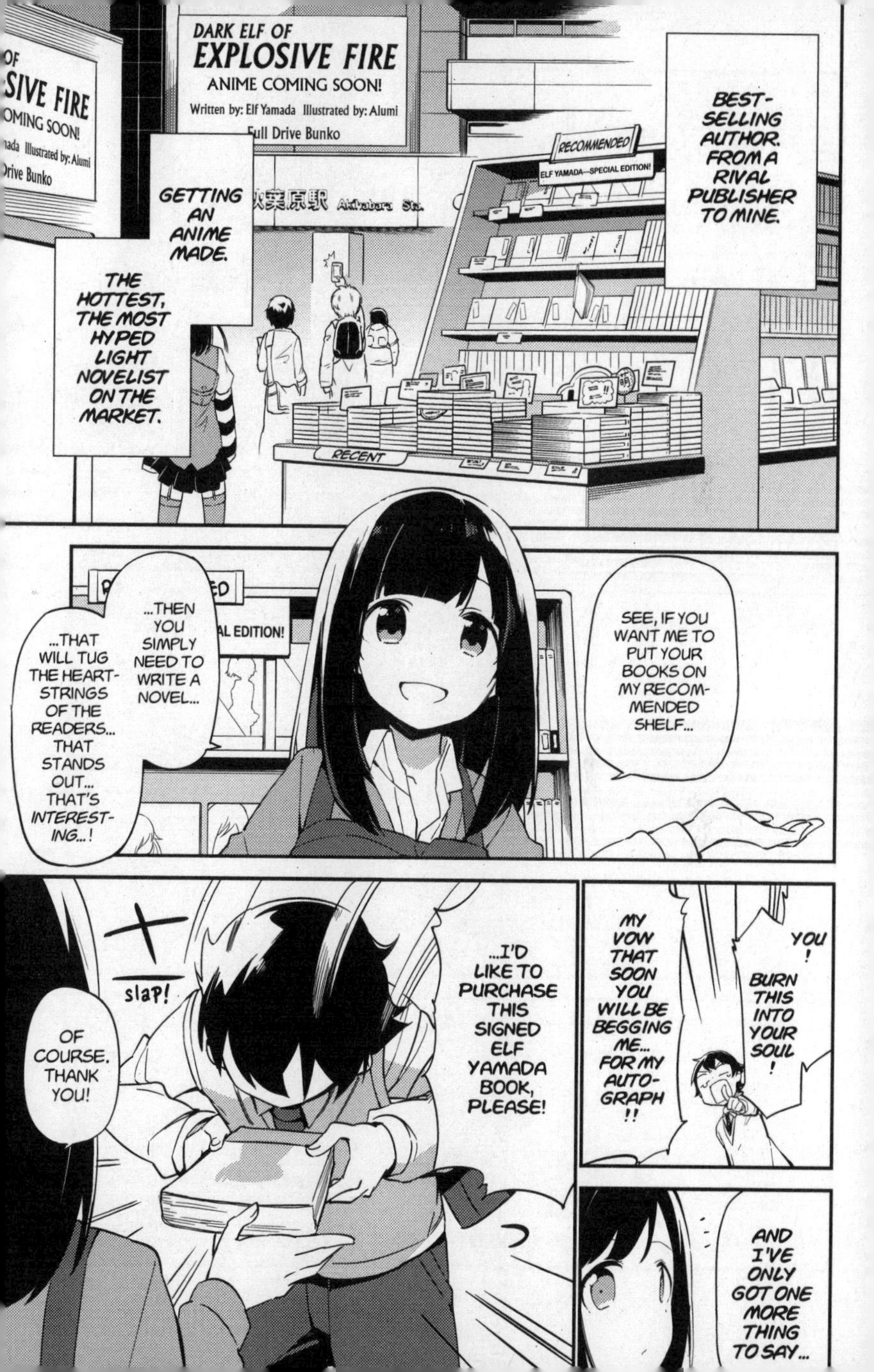
BEST-SELLING AUTHOR. FROM A RIVAL PUBLISHER TO MINE.
DARK ELF OF EXPLOSIVE FIRE
ANIME COMING SOON!
Written by: Elf Yamada Illustrated by: Alumi
Full Drive Bunko
RECOMMENDED
ELF YAMADA—SPECIAL EDITION!
秋葉原駅 Akihabara Sta.
RECENT
GETTING AN ANIME MADE.
THE HOTTEST, THE MOST HYPED LIGHT NOVELIST ON THE MARKET.
SEE, IF YOU WANT ME TO PUT YOUR BOOKS ON MY RECOMMENDED SHELF...
...THEN YOU SIMPLY NEED TO WRITE A NOVEL...
...THAT WILL TUG THE HEART-STRINGS OF THE READERS... THAT STANDS OUT... THAT'S INTERESTING...!
YOU! BURN THIS INTO YOUR SOUL!
MY VOW THAT SOON YOU WILL BE BEGGING ME... FOR MY AUTOGRAPH!!
AND I'VE ONLY GOT ONE MORE THING TO SAY...
...I'D LIKE TO PURCHASE THIS SIGNED ELF YAMADA BOOK, PLEASE!
slap!
OF COURSE. THANK YOU!

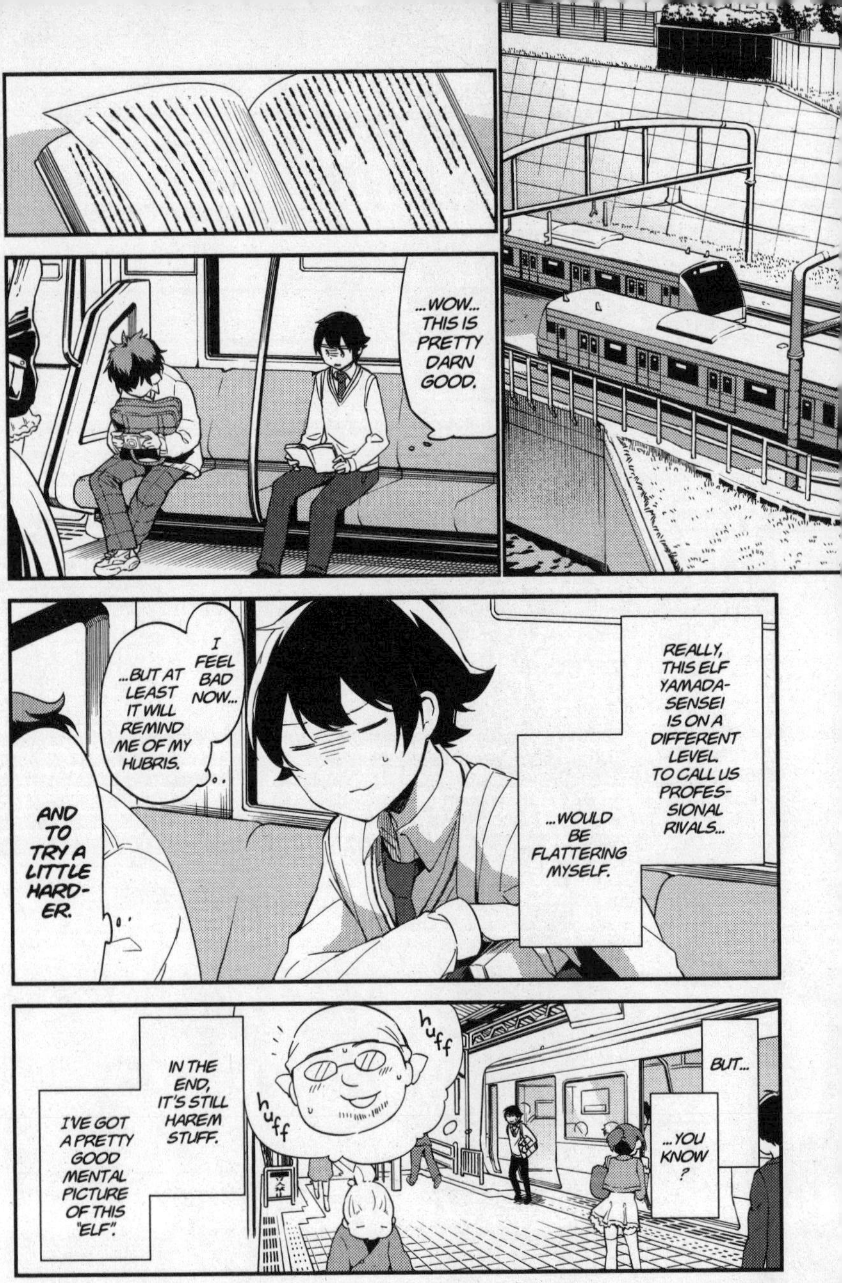
...WOW... THIS IS PRETTY DARN GOOD.
REALLY, THIS ELF YAMADA-SENSEI IS ON A DIFFERENT LEVEL. TO CALL US PROFES-SIONAL RIVALS...
...WOULD BE FLATTERING MYSELF.
I FEEL BAD NOW...
...BUT AT LEAST IT WILL REMIND ME OF MY HUBRIS.
AND TO TRY A LITTLE HARD-ER.
BUT...
...YOU KNOW?
huff
huff
IN THE END, IT'S STILL HAREM STUFF.
I'VE GOT A PRETTY GOOD MENTAL PICTURE OF THIS "ELF".

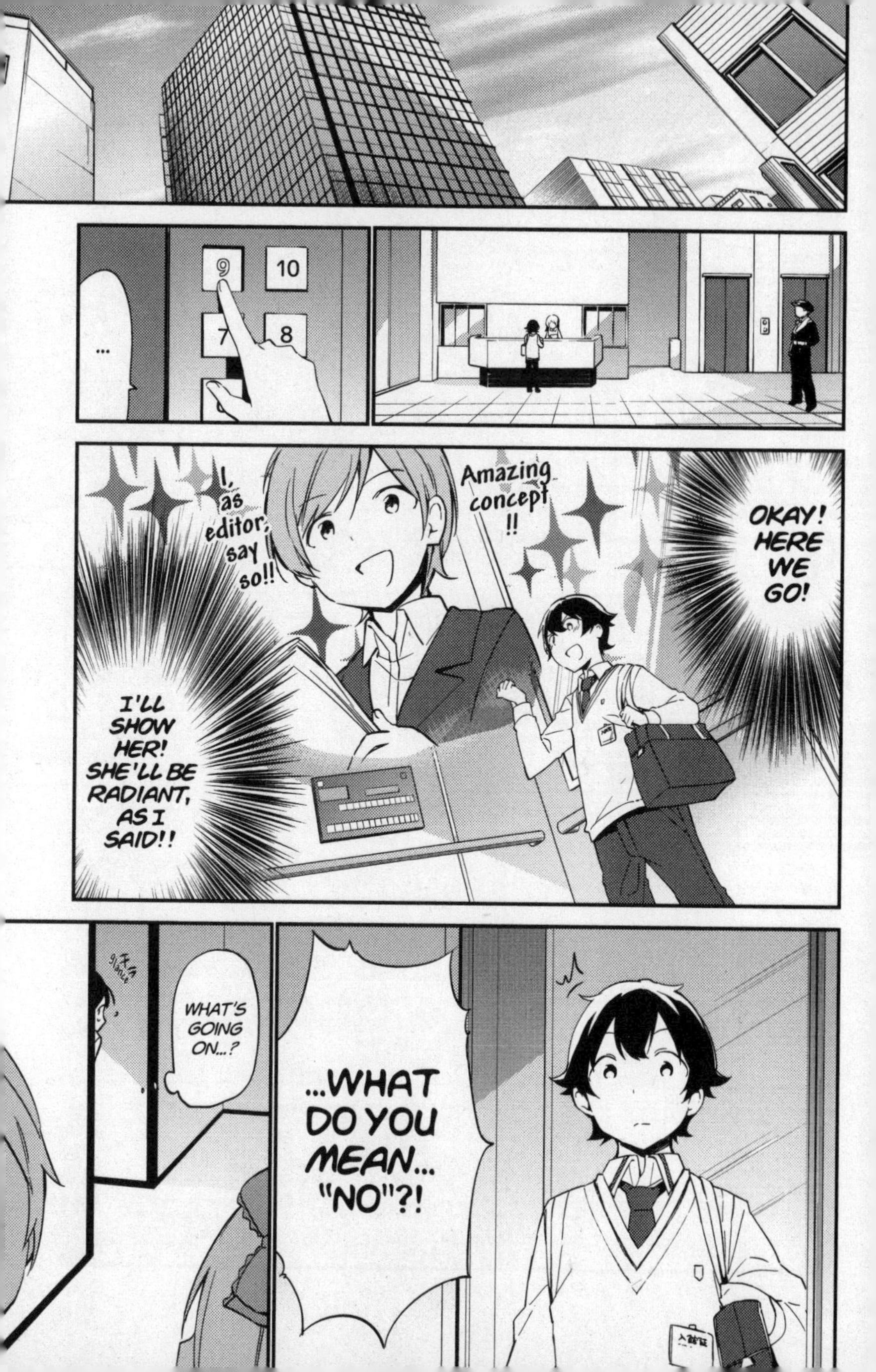
...
OKAY! HERE WE GO!
Amazing concept!!
I, as editor, say so!!
I'LL SHOW HER! SHE'LL BE RADIANT, AS I SAID!!
...WHAT DO YOU MEAN... "NO"?!
glance
WHAT'S GOING ON...?

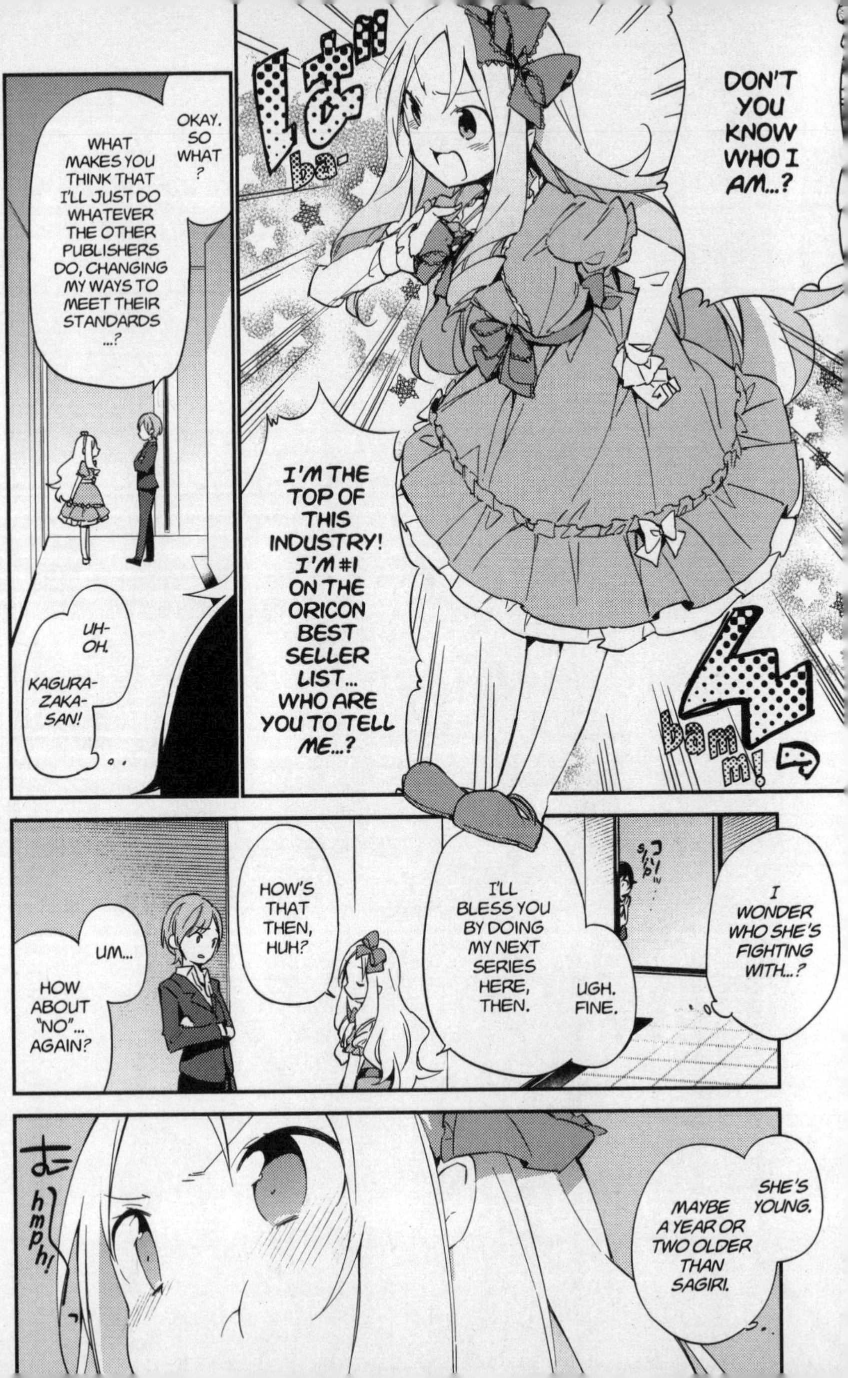
DON'T YOU KNOW WHO I AM...?
ba-
I'M THE TOP OF THIS INDUSTRY! I'M #1 ON THE ORICON BEST SELLER LIST... WHO ARE YOU TO TELL ME...?
bam m!
OKAY. SO WHAT?
WHAT MAKES YOU THINK THAT I'LL JUST DO WHATEVER THE OTHER PUBLISHERS DO, CHANGING MY WAYS TO MEET THEIR STANDARDS...?
UH-OH.
KAGURAZAKA-SAN!
I WONDER WHO SHE'S FIGHTING WITH...?
slip
UGH. FINE.
I'LL BLESS YOU BY DOING MY NEXT SERIES HERE, THEN.
HOW'S THAT THEN, HUH?
UM...
HOW ABOUT "NO"... AGAIN?
SHE'S YOUNG.
MAYBE A YEAR OR TWO OLDER THAN SAGIRI.
hmph!

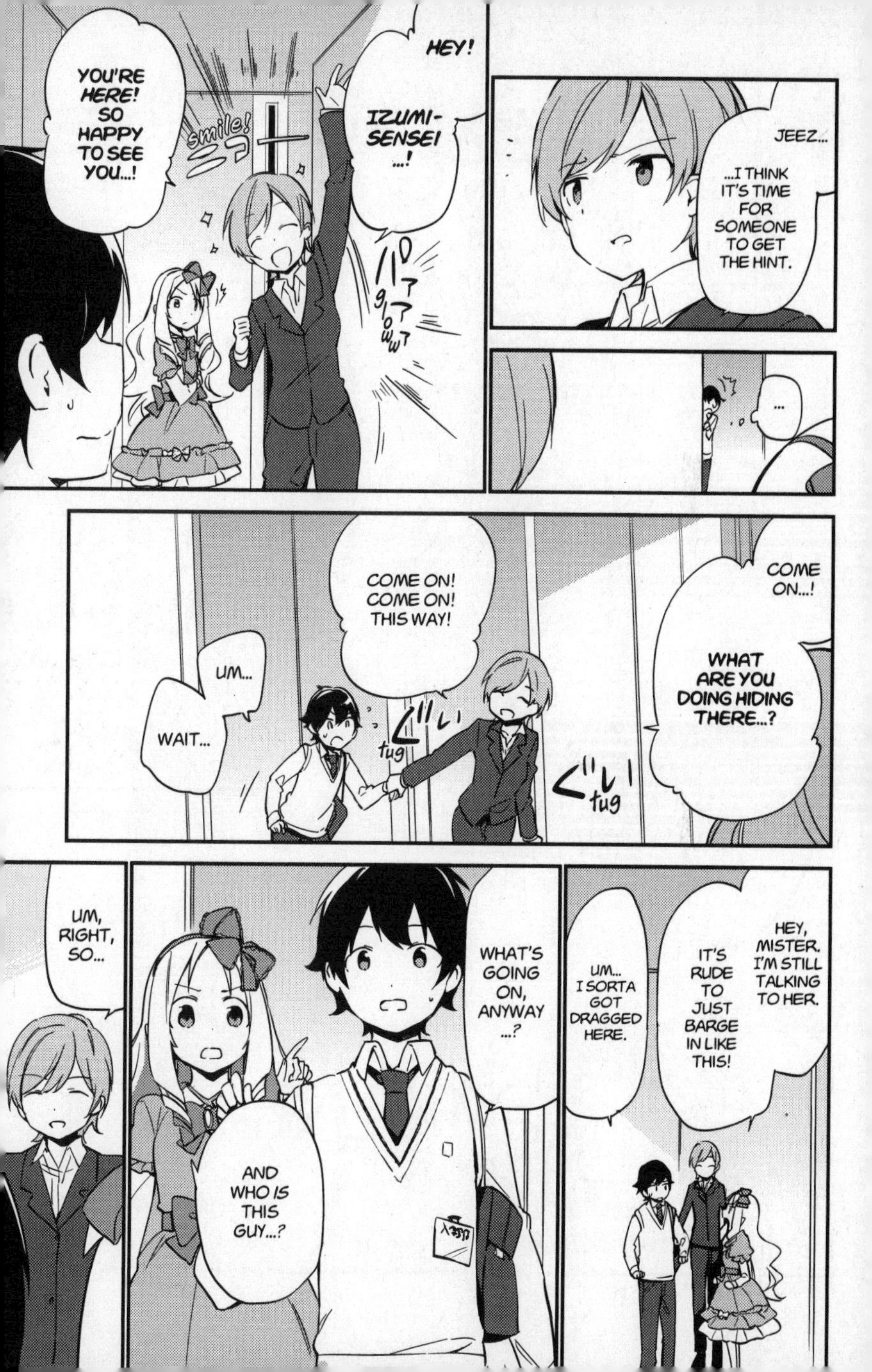
JEEZ...
...I THINK IT'S TIME FOR SOMEONE TO GET THE HINT.
...
HEY!
IZUMI-SENSEI...!
glow
smile!
YOU'RE HERE! SO HAPPY TO SEE YOU...!
COME ON...!
WHAT ARE YOU DOING HIDING THERE...?
tug
COME ON! COME ON! THIS WAY!
tug
UM...
WAIT...
HEY, MISTER. I'M STILL TALKING TO HER.
IT'S RUDE TO JUST BARGE IN LIKE THIS!
UM... I SORTA GOT DRAGGED HERE.
WHAT'S GOING ON, ANYWAY...?
AND WHO IS THIS GUY...?
UM, RIGHT, SO...

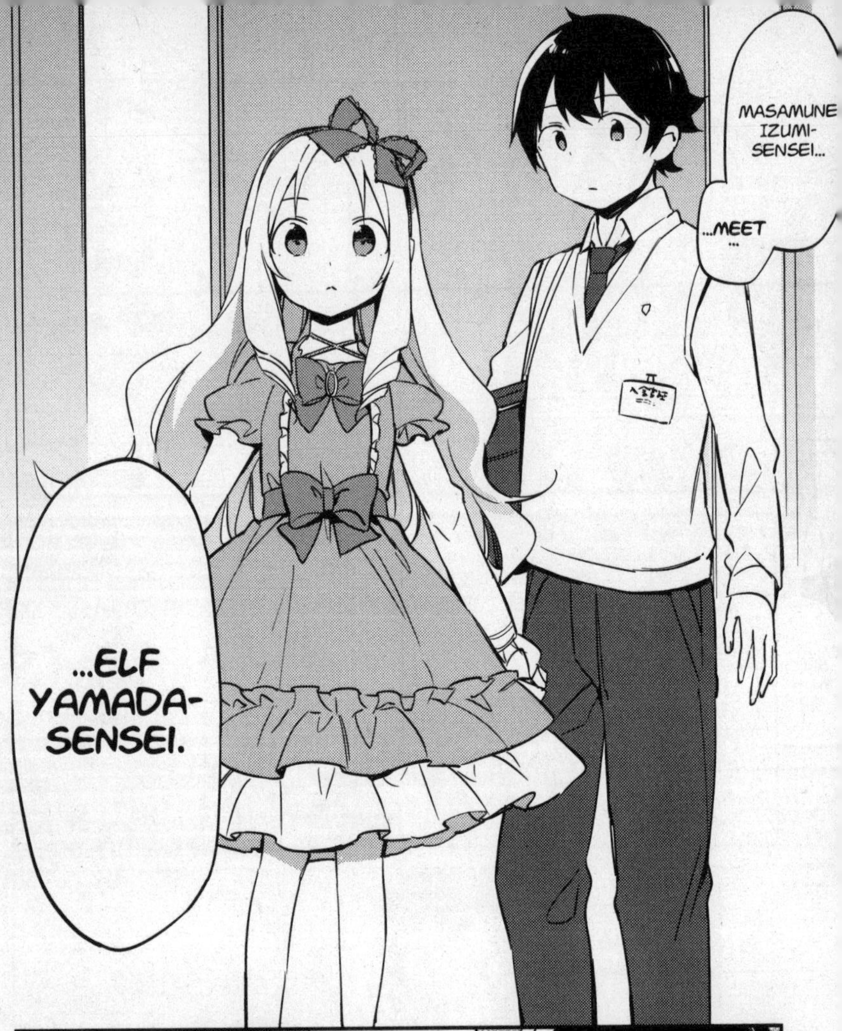
MASAMUNE IZUMI-SENSEI...
...MEET ...
...ELF YAMADA-SENSEI.

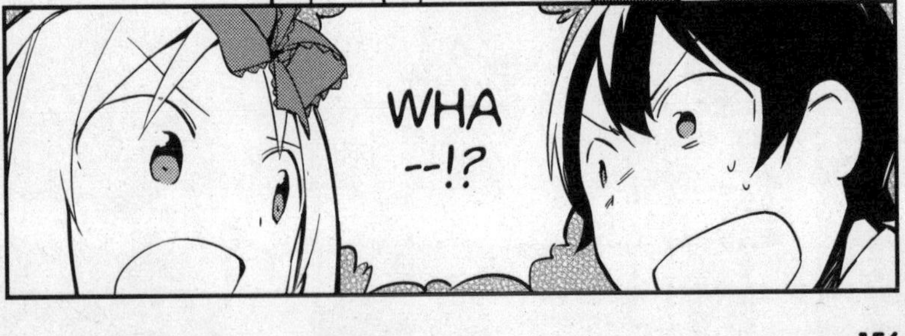
WHA --!?

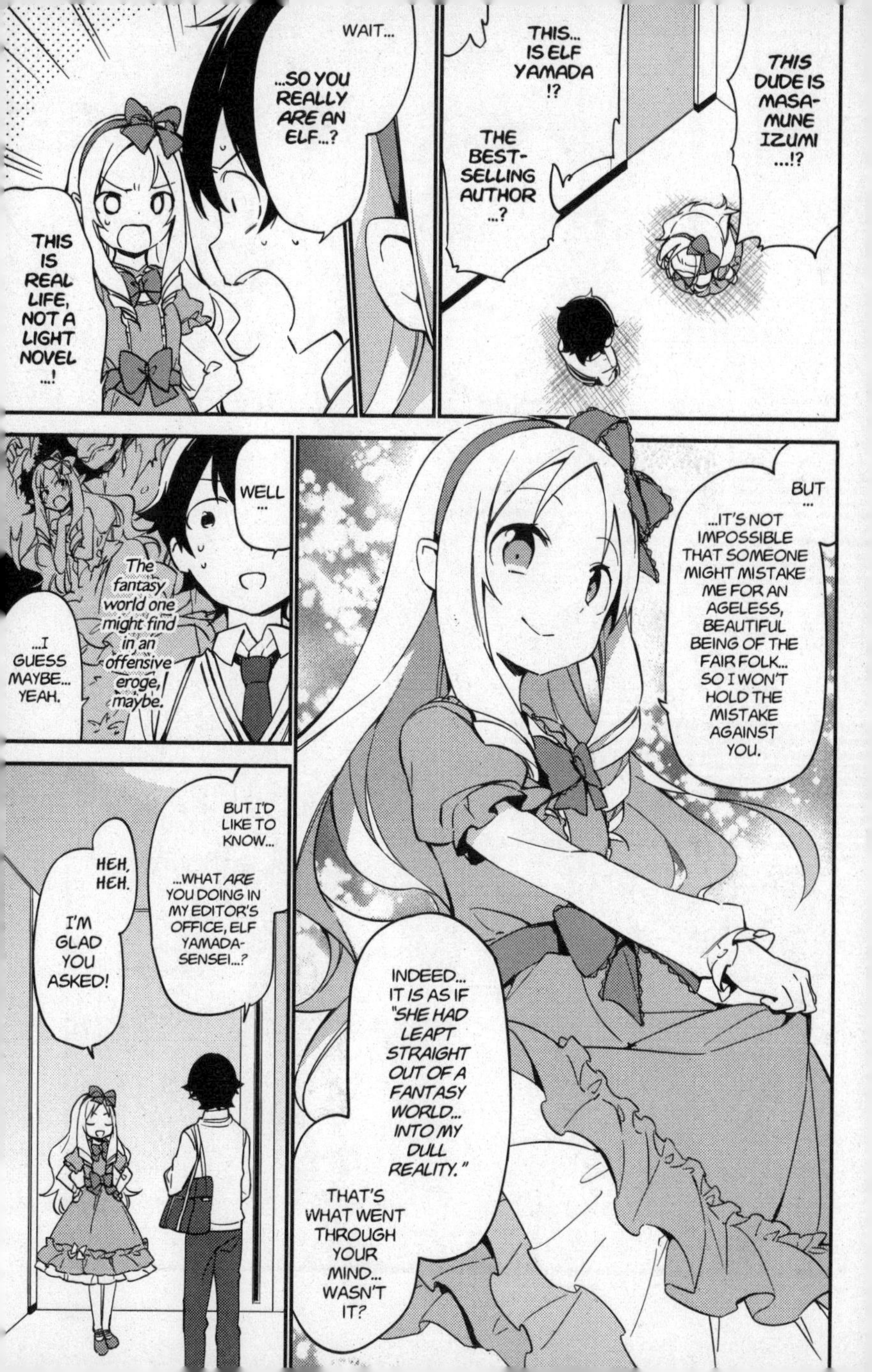
THIS DUDE IS MASA-MUNE IZUMI ...!?
THIS... IS ELF YAMADA !?
THE BEST-SELLING AUTHOR ...?
WAIT...
...SO YOU REALLY ARE AN ELF...?
THIS IS REAL LIFE, NOT A LIGHT NOVEL ...!
BUT ...
...IT'S NOT IMPOSSIBLE THAT SOMEONE MIGHT MISTAKE ME FOR AN AGELESS, BEAUTIFUL BEING OF THE FAIR FOLK... SO I WON'T HOLD THE MISTAKE AGAINST YOU.
INDEED... IT IS AS IF "SHE HAD LEAPT STRAIGHT OUT OF A FANTASY WORLD... INTO MY DULL REALITY."
THAT'S WHAT WENT THROUGH YOUR MIND... WASN'T IT?
WELL ...
The fantasy world one might find in an offensive eroge, maybe.
...I GUESS MAYBE... YEAH.
BUT I'D LIKE TO KNOW...
...WHAT ARE YOU DOING IN MY EDITOR'S OFFICE, ELF YAMADA-SENSEI...?
HEH, HEH.
I'M GLAD YOU ASKED!

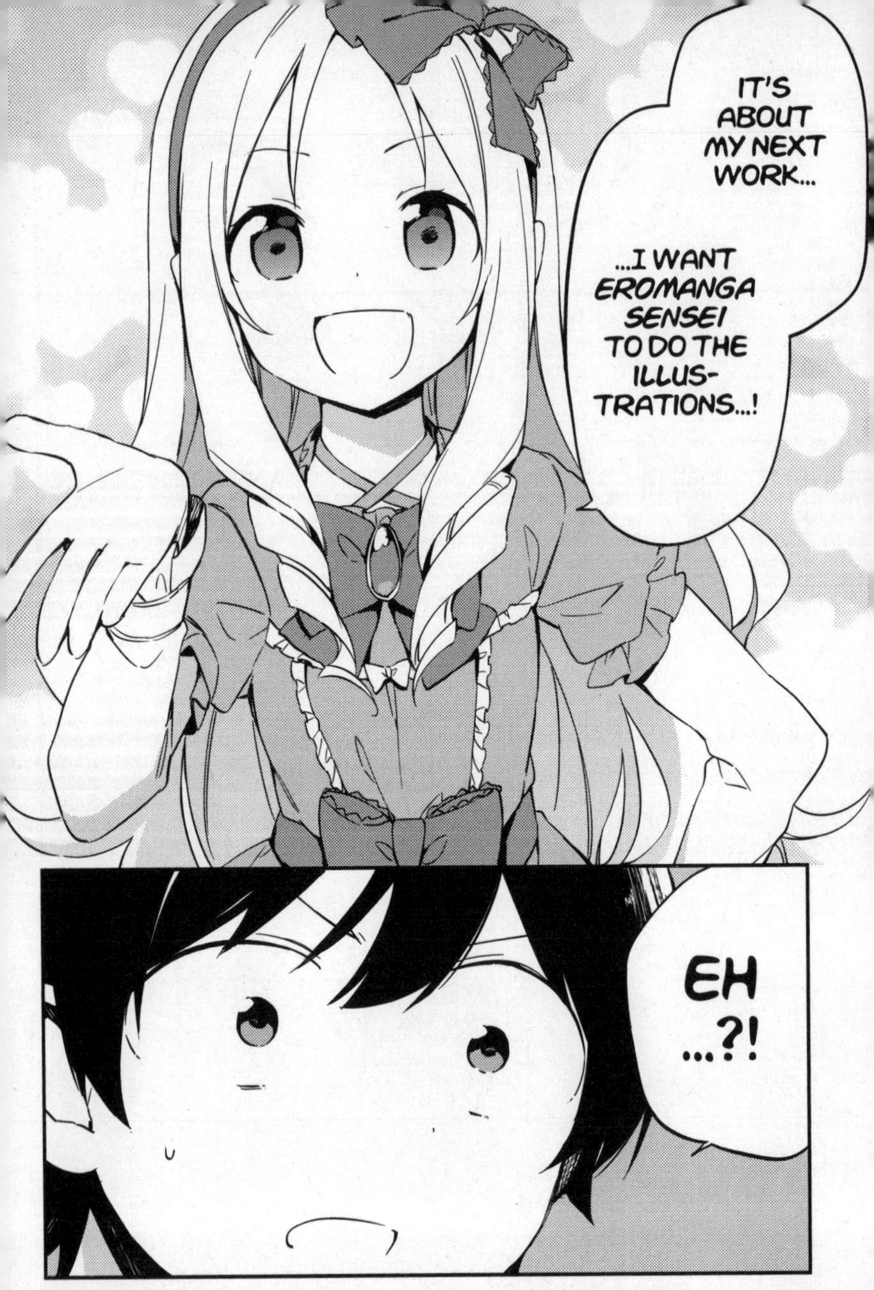
IT'S ABOUT MY NEXT WORK...
...I WANT EROMANGA SENSEI TO DO THE ILLUS-TRATIONS...!
EH ...?!

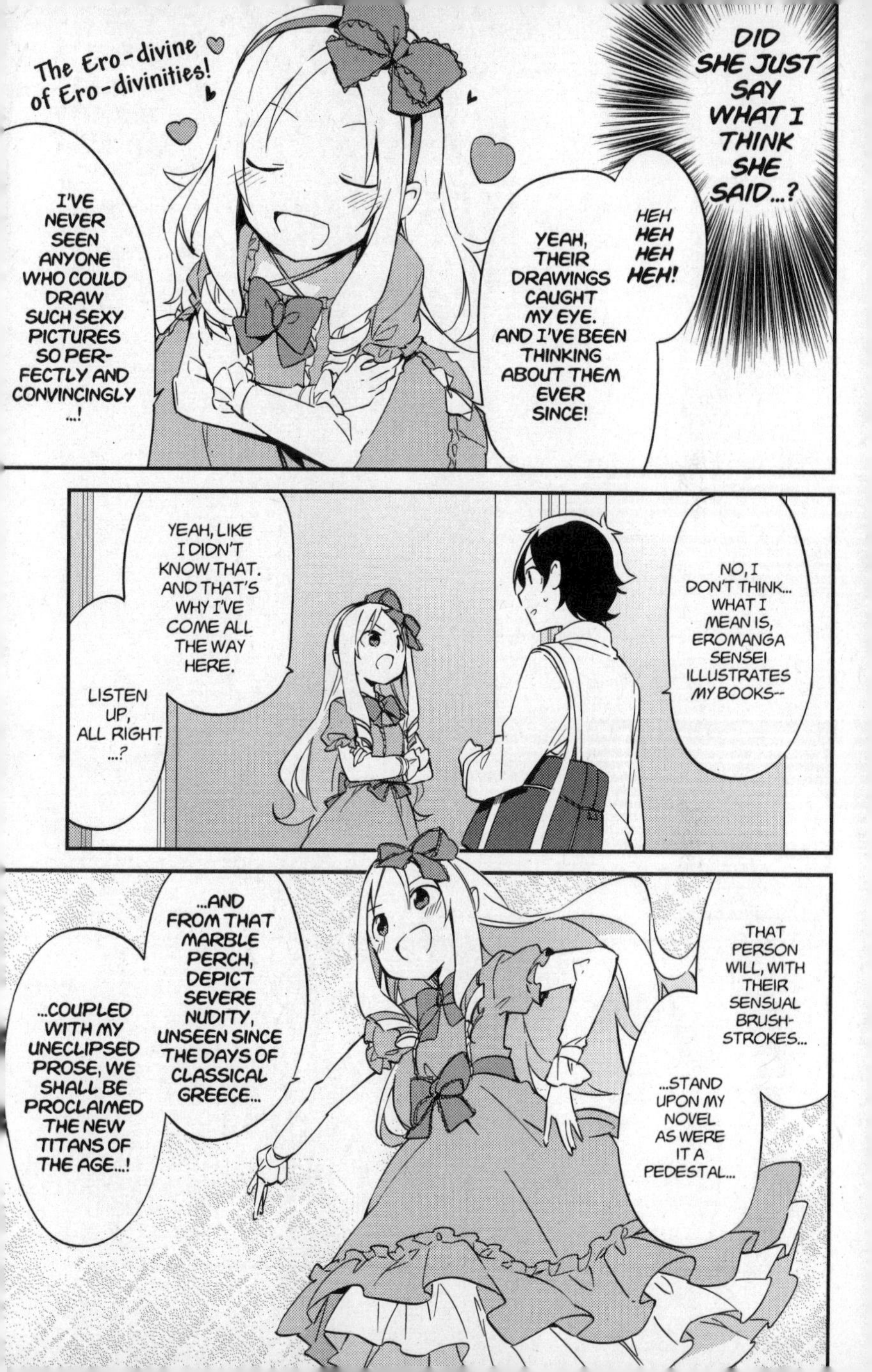
DID SHE JUST SAY WHAT I THINK SHE SAID...?
HEH HEH HEH HEH!
YEAH, THEIR DRAWINGS CAUGHT MY EYE. AND I'VE BEEN THINKING ABOUT THEM EVER SINCE!
The Ero-divine of Ero-divinities!
I'VE NEVER SEEN ANYONE WHO COULD DRAW SUCH SEXY PICTURES SO PER-FECTLY AND CONVINCINGLY ...!
NO, I DON'T THINK... WHAT I MEAN IS, EROMANGA SENSEI ILLUSTRATES MY BOOKS--
YEAH, LIKE I DIDN'T KNOW THAT. AND THAT'S WHY I'VE COME ALL THE WAY HERE.
LISTEN UP, ALL RIGHT ...?
THAT PERSON WILL, WITH THEIR SENSUAL BRUSH-STROKES...
...STAND UPON MY NOVEL AS WERE IT A PEDESTAL...
...AND FROM THAT MARBLE PERCH, DEPICT SEVERE NUDITY, UNSEEN SINCE THE DAYS OF CLASSICAL GREECE...
...COUPLED WITH MY UNECLIPSED PROSE, WE SHALL BE PROCLAIMED THE NEW TITANS OF THE AGE...!

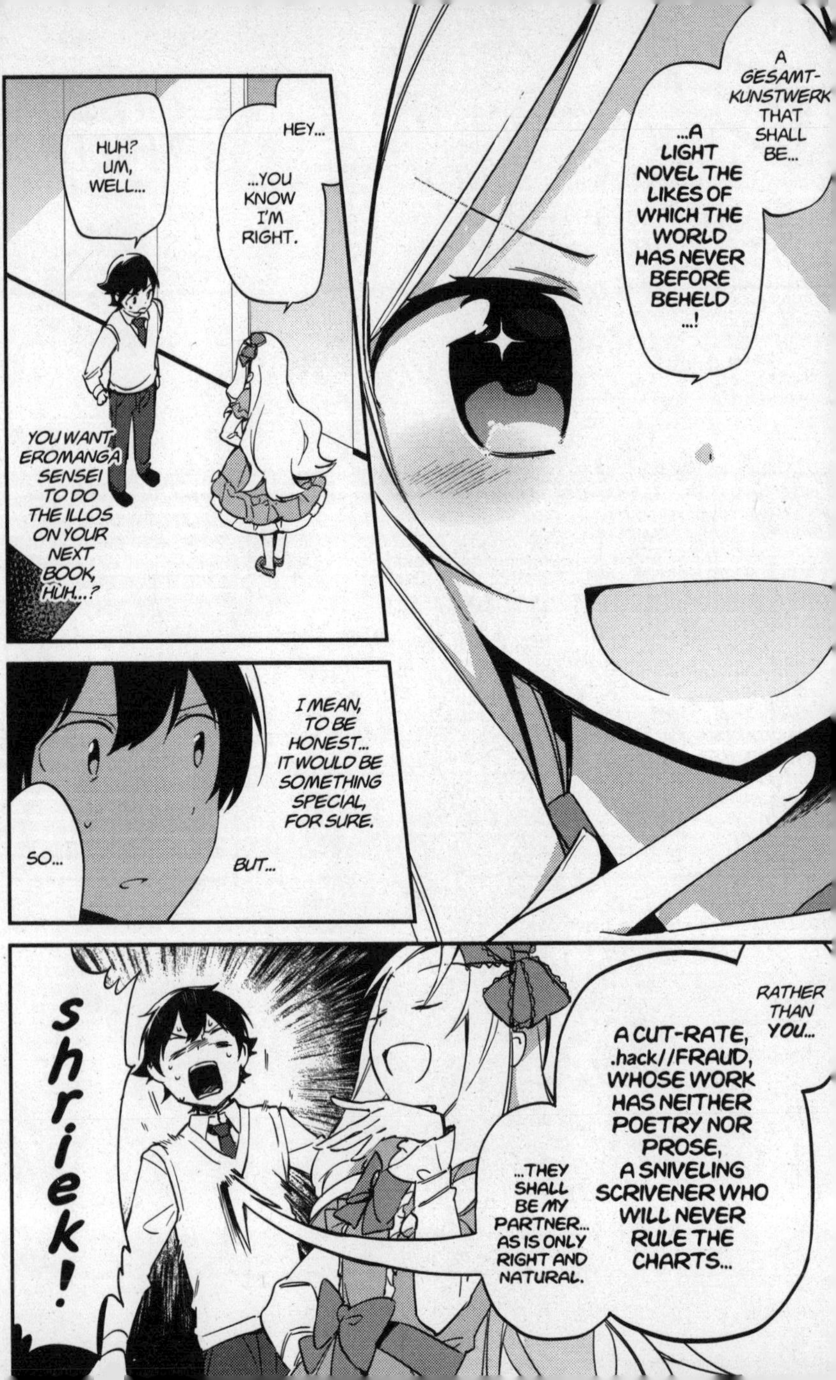
A GESAMT-KUNSTWERK THAT SHALL BE...
...A LIGHT NOVEL THE LIKES OF WHICH THE WORLD HAS NEVER BEFORE BEHELD...!
HEY...
...YOU KNOW I'M RIGHT.
HUH? UM, WELL...
YOU WANT EROMANGA SENSEI TO DO THE ILLOS ON YOUR NEXT BOOK, HUH...?
I MEAN, TO BE HONEST... IT WOULD BE SOMETHING SPECIAL, FOR SURE.
BUT...
SO...
RATHER THAN YOU...
A CUT-RATE, .hack//FRAUD, WHOSE WORK HAS NEITHER POETRY NOR PROSE, A SNIVELING SCRIVENER WHO WILL NEVER RULE THE CHARTS...
...THEY SHALL BE MY PARTNER... AS IS ONLY RIGHT AND NATURAL.
shriek!

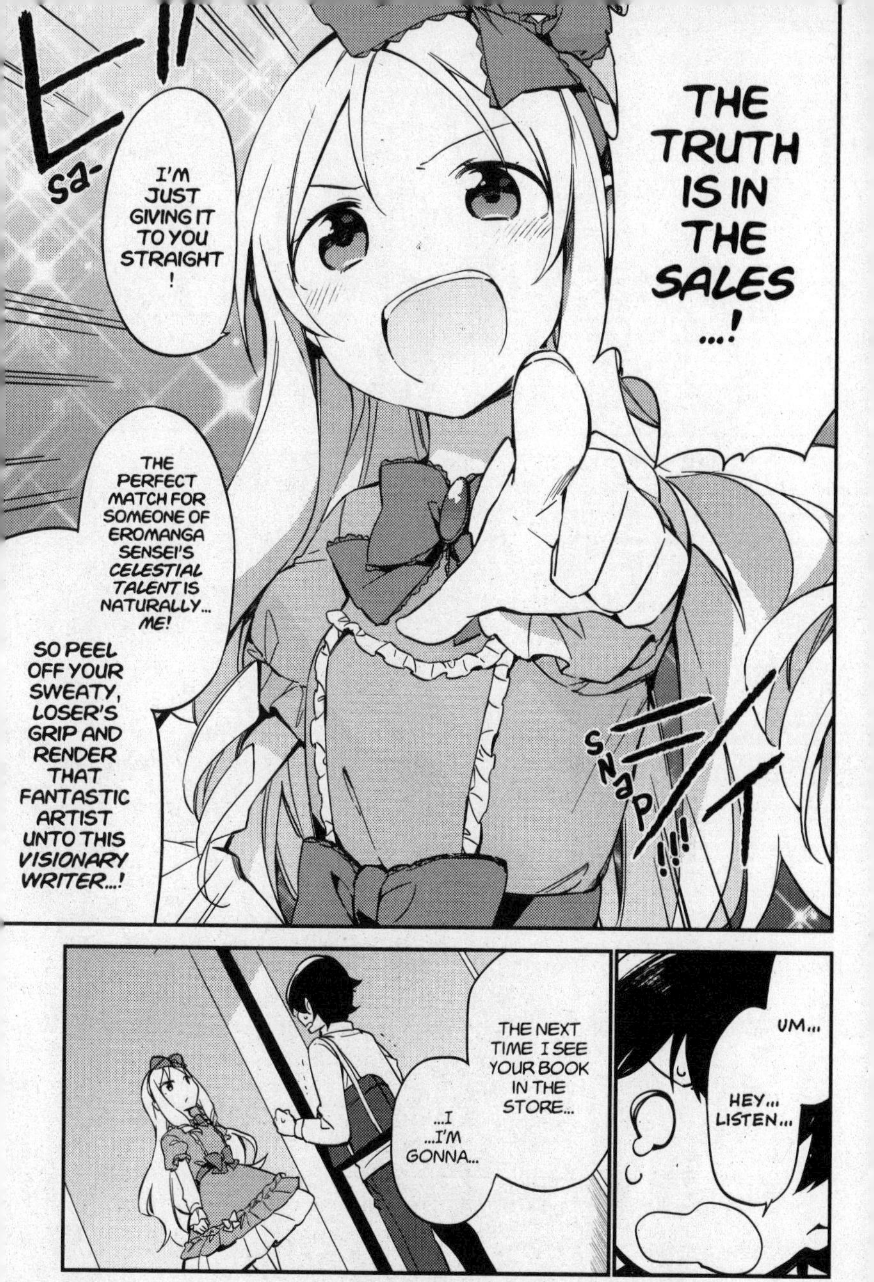
THE TRUTH IS IN THE SALES ...!
I'M JUST GIVING IT TO YOU STRAIGHT!
sa-
SNAP!!!
THE PERFECT MATCH FOR SOMEONE OF EROMANGA SENSEI'S CELESTIAL TALENT IS NATURALLY... ME!
SO PEEL OFF YOUR SWEATY, LOSER'S GRIP AND RENDER THAT FANTASTIC ARTIST UNTO THIS VISIONARY WRITER...!
UM...
HEY... LISTEN...
THE NEXT TIME I SEE YOUR BOOK IN THE STORE...
...I ...I'M GONNA...

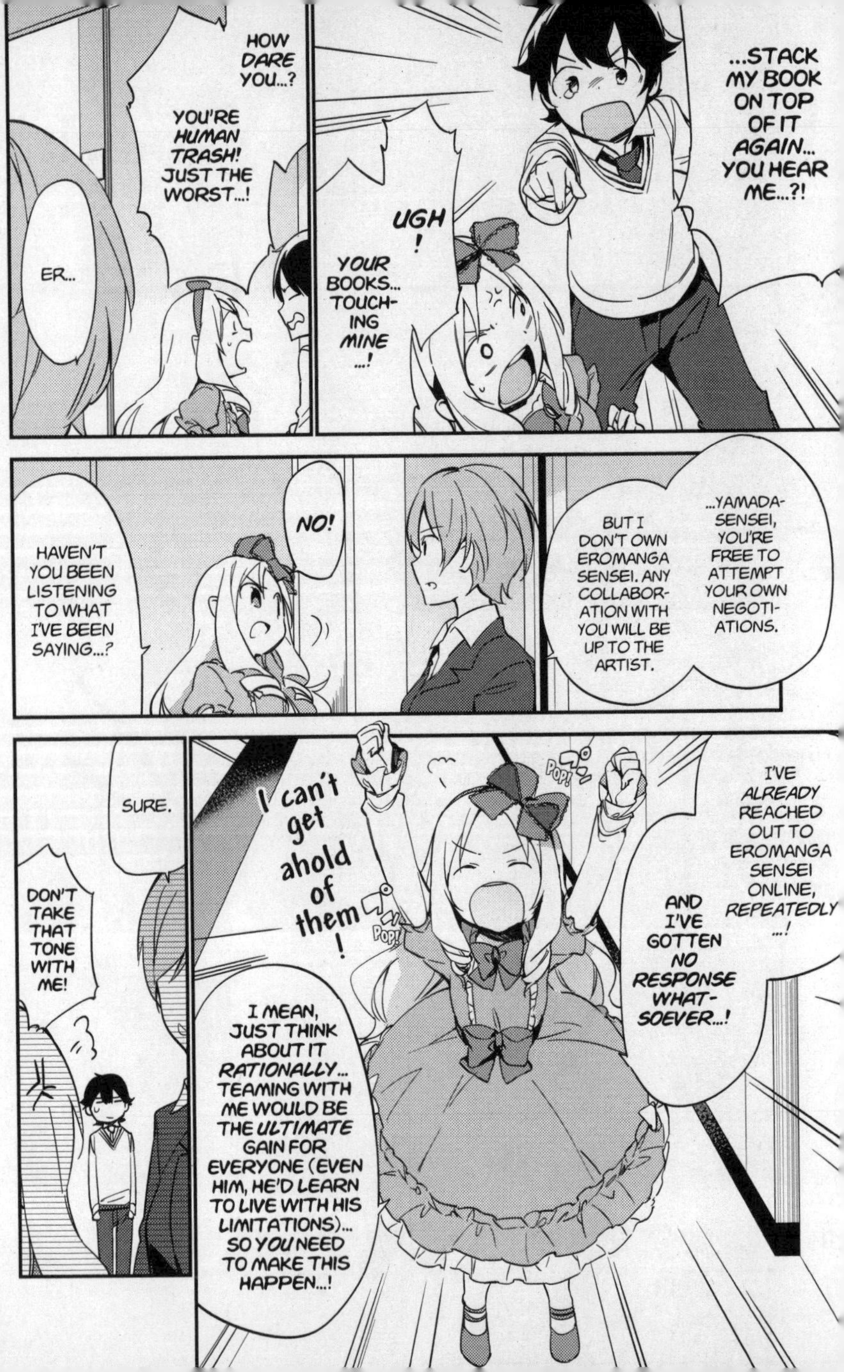
...STACK MY BOOK ON TOP OF IT AGAIN... YOU HEAR ME...?!
UGH!
YOUR BOOKS... TOUCHING MINE...!
HOW DARE YOU...?
YOU'RE HUMAN TRASH! JUST THE WORST...!
ER...
...YAMADA-SENSEI, YOU'RE FREE TO ATTEMPT YOUR OWN NEGOTIATIONS.
BUT I DON'T OWN EROMANGA SENSEI. ANY COLLABORATION WITH YOU WILL BE UP TO THE ARTIST.
NO!
HAVEN'T YOU BEEN LISTENING TO WHAT I'VE BEEN SAYING...?
I'VE ALREADY REACHED OUT TO EROMANGA SENSEI ONLINE, REPEATEDLY...!
AND I'VE GOTTEN NO RESPONSE WHATSOEVER...!
POP!
I can't get ahold of them!
POP!
I MEAN, JUST THINK ABOUT IT RATIONALLY... TEAMING WITH ME WOULD BE THE ULTIMATE GAIN FOR EVERYONE (EVEN HIM, HE'D LEARN TO LIVE WITH HIS LIMITATIONS)... SO YOU NEED TO MAKE THIS HAPPEN...!
SURE.
DON'T TAKE THAT TONE WITH ME!

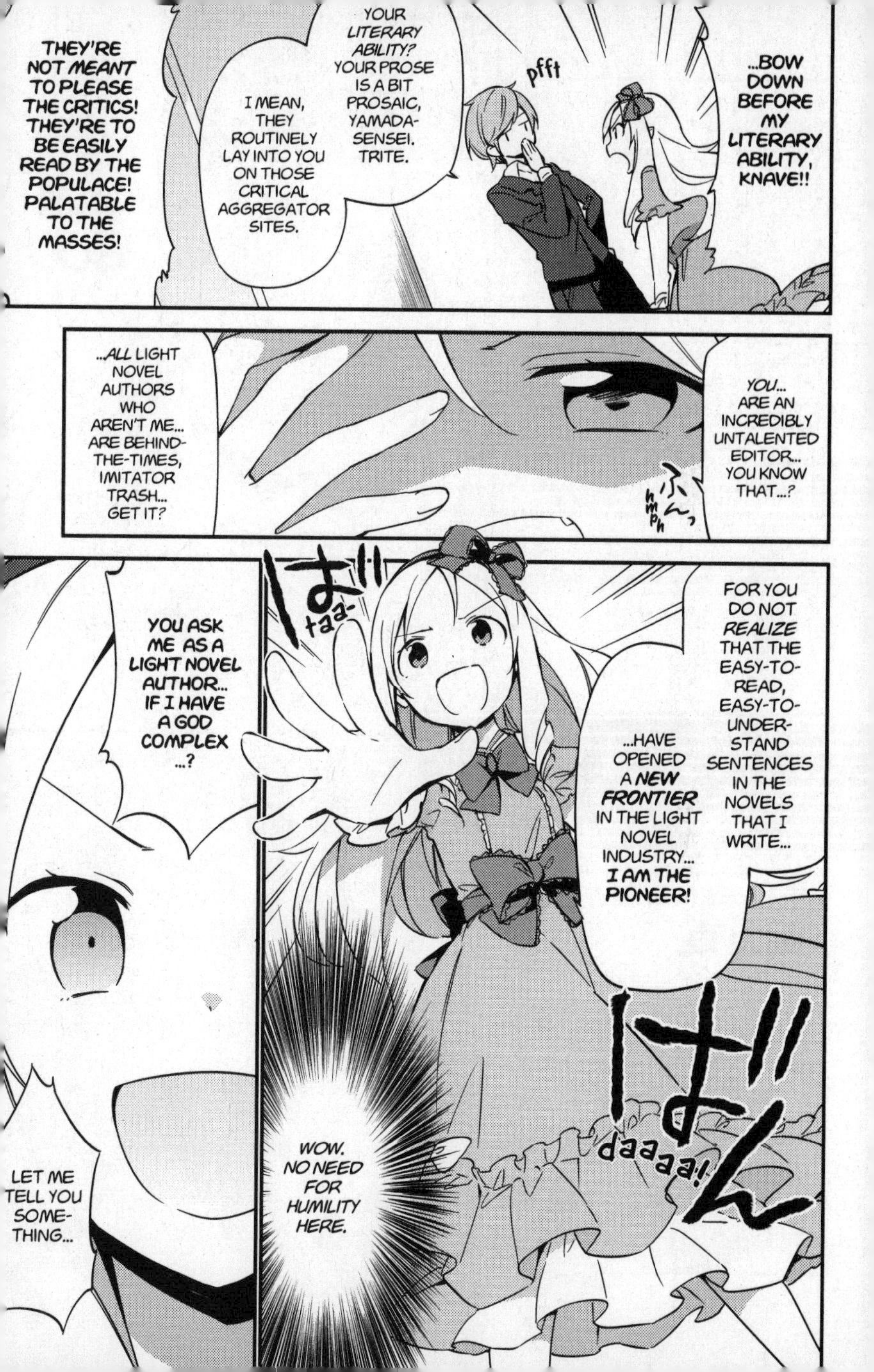
...BOW DOWN BEFORE MY LITERARY ABILITY, KNAVE!!
pfft
YOUR LITERARY ABILITY? YOUR PROSE IS A BIT PROSAIC, YAMADA-SENSEI. TRITE.
I MEAN, THEY ROUTINELY LAY INTO YOU ON THOSE CRITICAL AGGREGATOR SITES.
THEY'RE NOT MEANT TO PLEASE THE CRITICS! THEY'RE TO BE EASILY READ BY THE POPULACE! PALATABLE TO THE MASSES!
YOU... ARE AN INCREDIBLY UNTALENTED EDITOR... YOU KNOW THAT...?
ふんっ
hmph
...ALL LIGHT NOVEL AUTHORS WHO AREN'T ME... ARE BEHIND-THE-TIMES, IMITATOR TRASH... GET IT?
FOR YOU DO NOT REALIZE THAT THE EASY-TO-READ, EASY-TO-UNDERSTAND SENTENCES IN THE NOVELS THAT I WRITE...
...HAVE OPENED A NEW FRONTIER IN THE LIGHT NOVEL INDUSTRY... I AM THE PIONEER!
taa-
daaaaa!
WOW. NO NEED FOR HUMILITY HERE.
YOU ASK ME AS A LIGHT NOVEL AUTHOR... IF I HAVE A GOD COMPLEX ...?
LET ME TELL YOU SOMETHING...

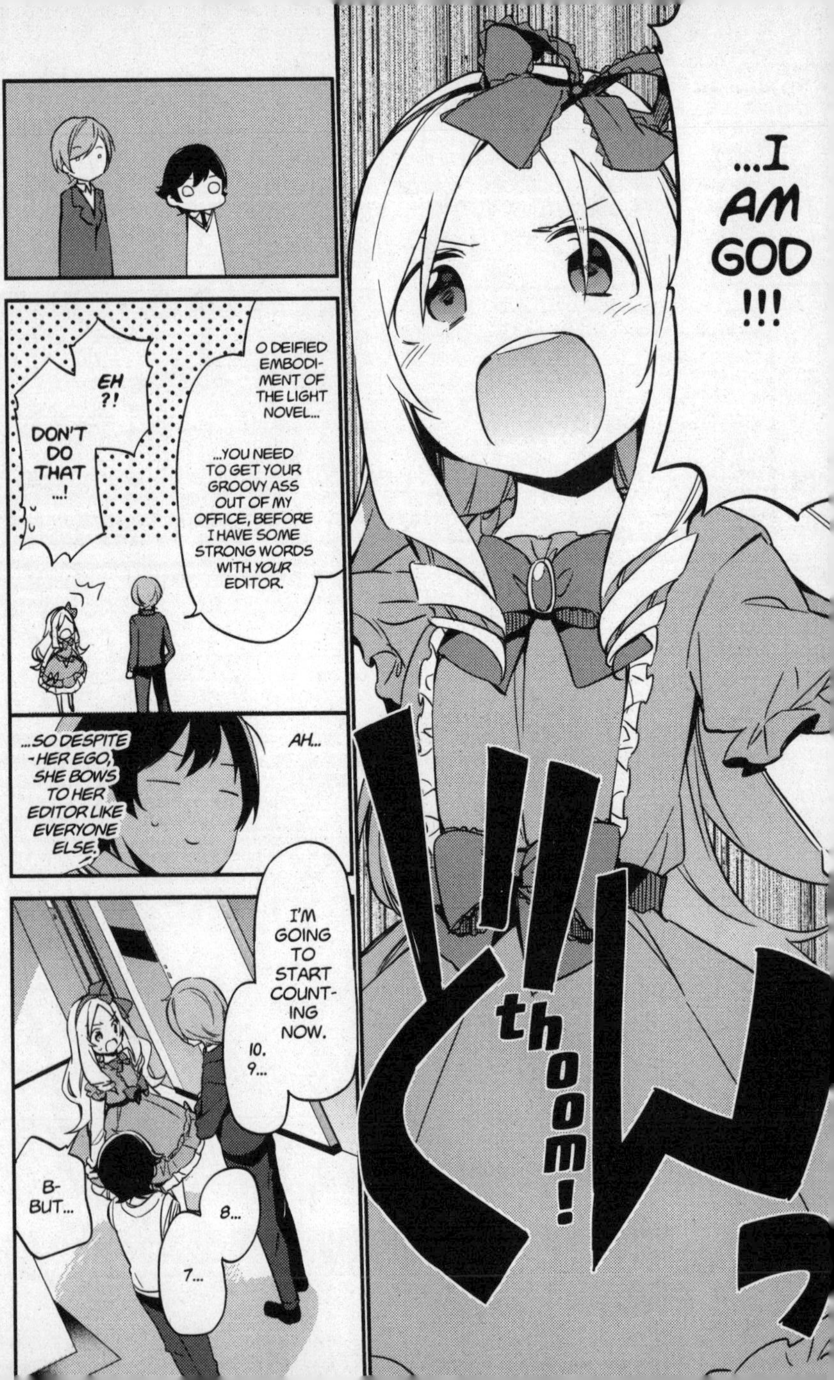
...I AM GOD!!!
thoom!
O DEIFIED EMBODIMENT OF THE LIGHT NOVEL...
...YOU NEED TO GET YOUR GROOVY ASS OUT OF MY OFFICE, BEFORE I HAVE SOME STRONG WORDS WITH *YOUR* EDITOR.
EH?!
DON'T DO THAT ...!
AH...
...SO DESPITE HER EGO, SHE BOWS TO HER EDITOR LIKE EVERYONE ELSE.
I'M GOING TO START COUNTING NOW.
10. 9...
8...
B-BUT...
7...

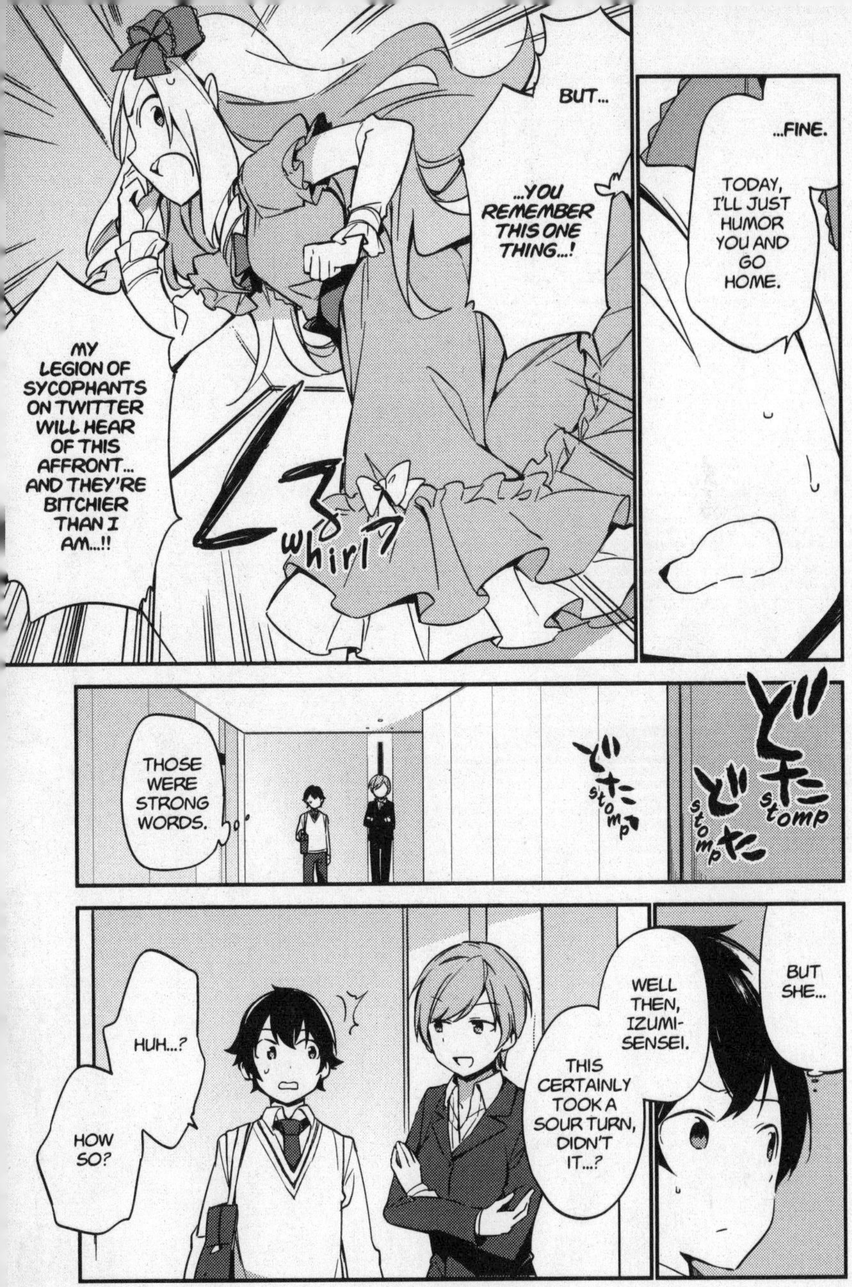
...FINE.
TODAY, I'LL JUST HUMOR YOU AND GO HOME.
BUT...
...YOU REMEMBER THIS ONE THING...!
MY LEGION OF SYCOPHANTS ON TWITTER WILL HEAR OF THIS AFFRONT... AND THEY'RE BITCHIER THAN I AM...!!
whirl
stomp
stomp
stomp
THOSE WERE STRONG WORDS.
BUT SHE...
WELL THEN, IZUMI-SENSEI.
THIS CERTAINLY TOOK A SOUR TURN, DIDN'T IT...?
HUH...?
HOW SO?

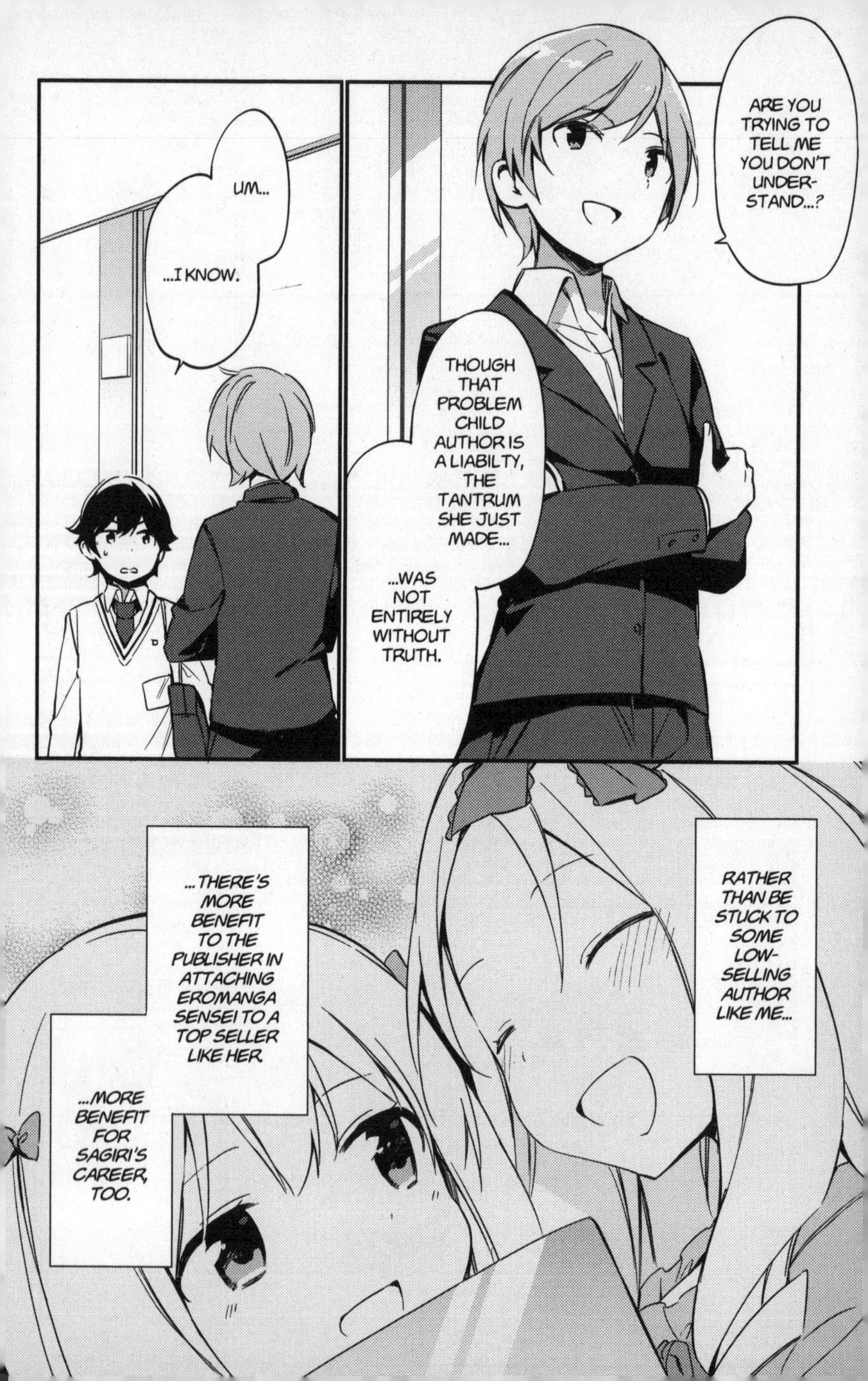
ARE YOU TRYING TO TELL ME YOU DON'T UNDER-STAND...?
THOUGH THAT PROBLEM CHILD AUTHOR IS A LIABILTY, THE TANTRUM SHE JUST MADE...
...WAS NOT ENTIRELY WITHOUT TRUTH.
UM...
...I KNOW.
RATHER THAN BE STUCK TO SOME LOW-SELLING AUTHOR LIKE ME...
...THERE'S MORE BENEFIT TO THE PUBLISHER IN ATTACHING EROMANGA SENSEI TO A TOP SELLER LIKE HER.
...MORE BENEFIT FOR SAGIRI'S CAREER, TOO.

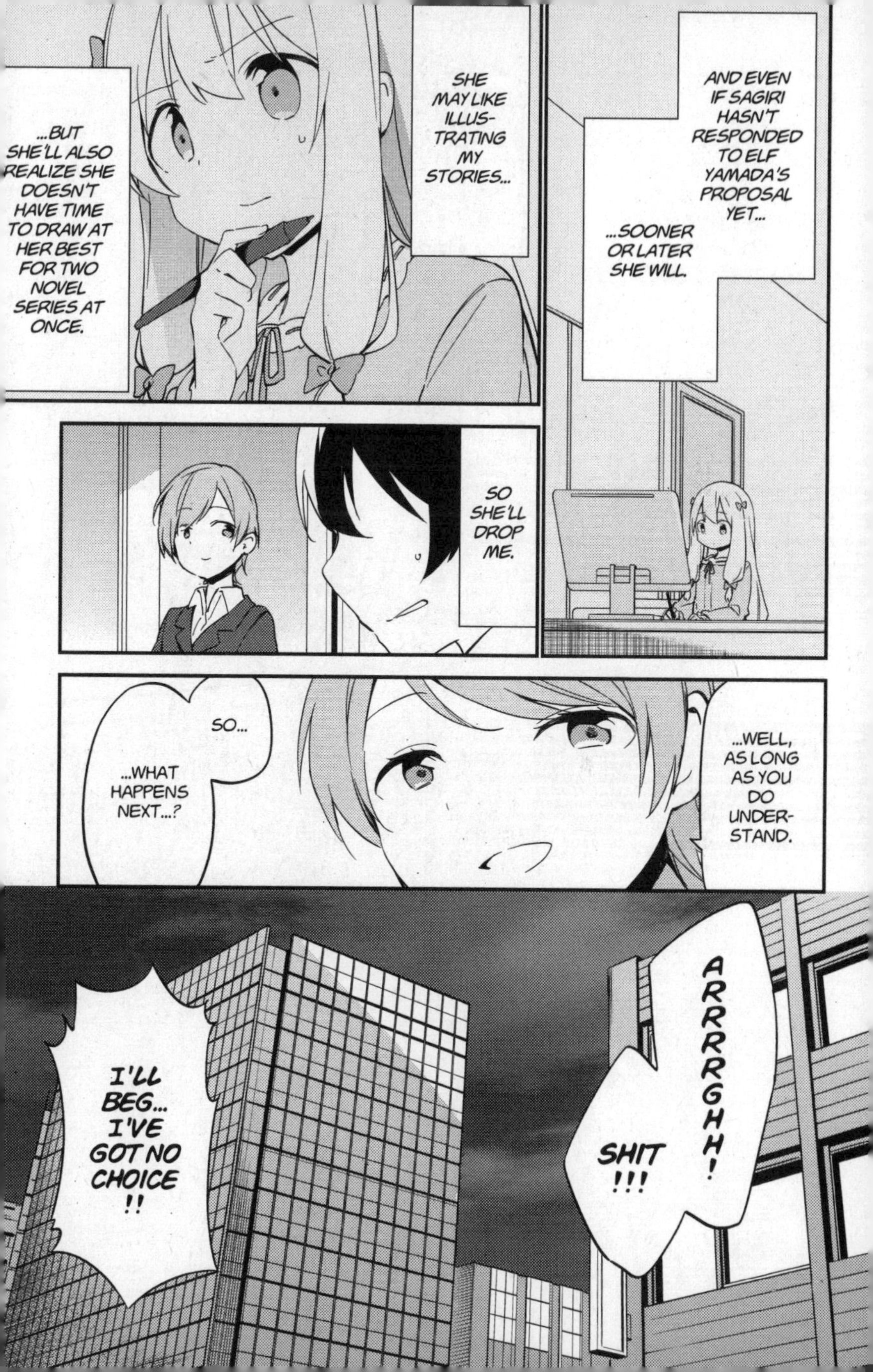
AND EVEN IF SAGIRI HASN'T RESPONDED TO ELF YAMADA'S PROPOSAL YET...
...SOONER OR LATER SHE WILL.
SHE MAY LIKE ILLUS-TRATING MY STORIES...
...BUT SHE'LL ALSO REALIZE SHE DOESN'T HAVE TIME TO DRAW AT HER BEST FOR TWO NOVEL SERIES AT ONCE.
SO SHE'LL DROP ME.
...WELL, AS LONG AS YOU DO UNDER-STAND.
SO...
...WHAT HAPPENS NEXT...?
ARRRRGH!
SHIT!!!
I'LL BEG... I'VE GOT NO CHOICE!!

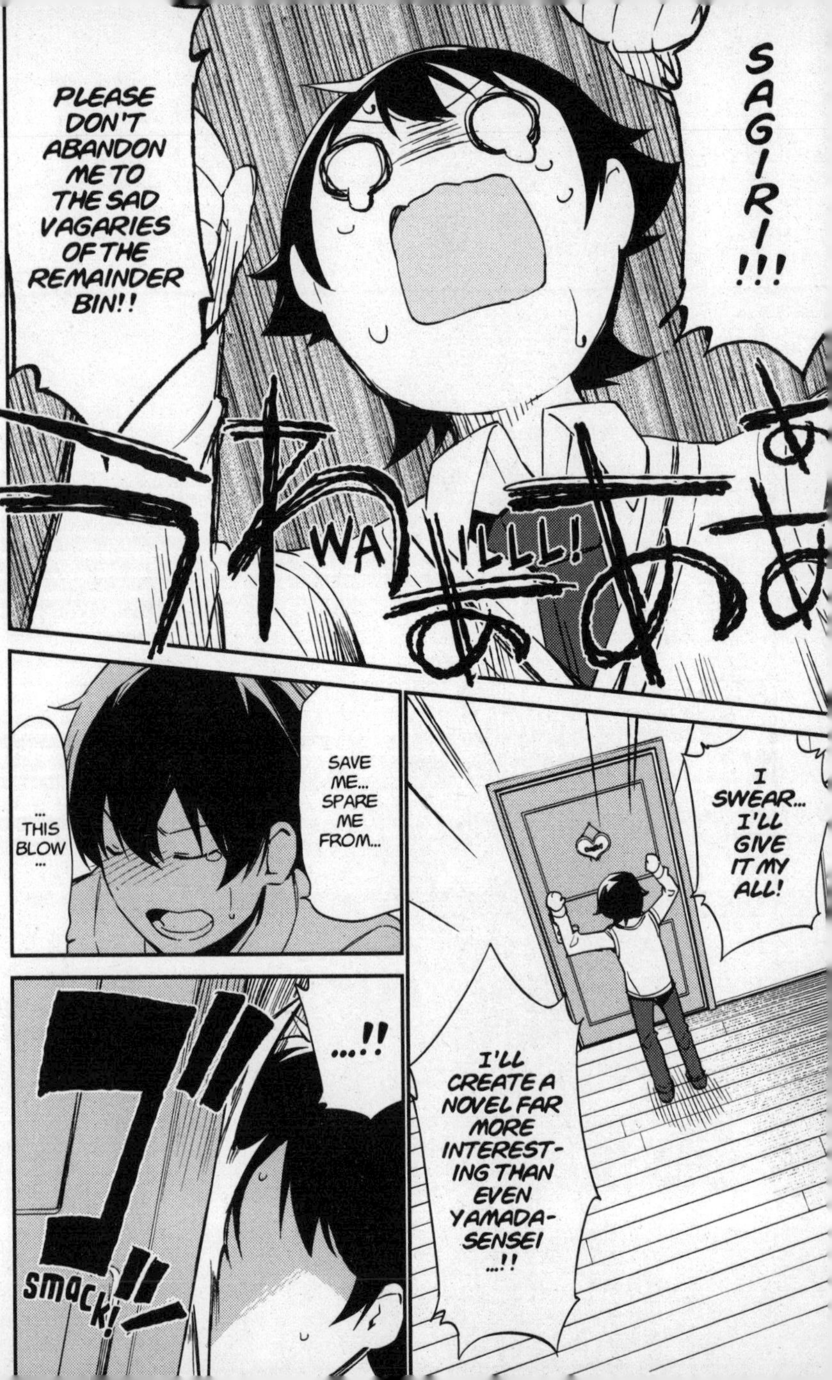
SAGIRI!!!
PLEASE DON'T ABANDON ME TO THE SAD VAGARIES OF THE REMAINDER BIN!!
WAILLL!
I SWEAR... I'LL GIVE IT MY ALL!
I'LL CREATE A NOVEL FAR MORE INTEREST-ING THAN EVEN YAMADA-SENSEI ...!!
SAVE ME... SPARE ME FROM...
...THIS BLOW...
...!!
smack!!

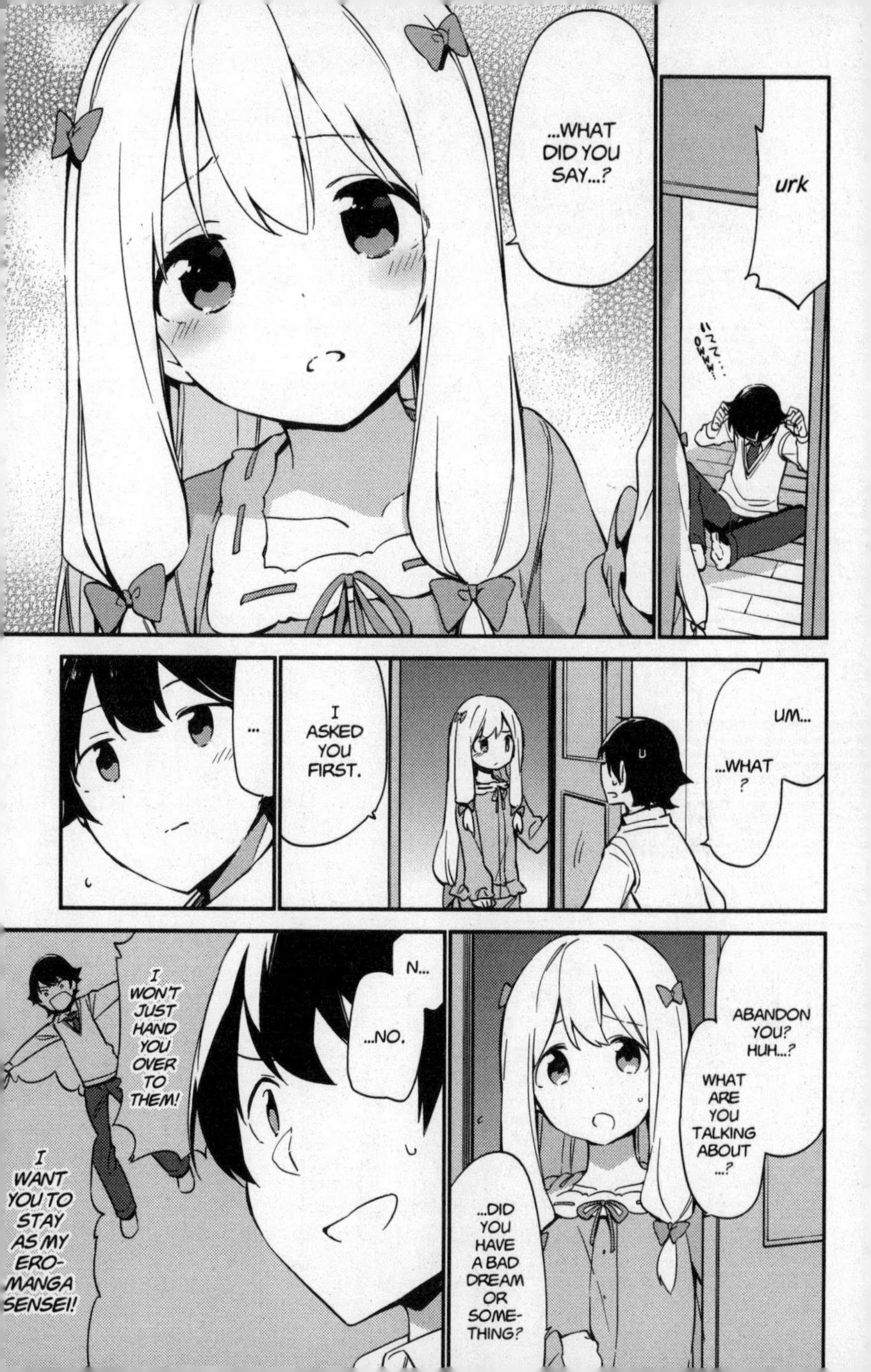
urk
OWWW...
...WHAT DID YOU SAY...?
UM...
...WHAT?
I ASKED YOU FIRST.
...
ABANDON YOU? HUH...?
WHAT ARE YOU TALKING ABOUT...?
...DID YOU HAVE A BAD DREAM OR SOMETHING?
N...
...NO.
I WON'T JUST HAND YOU OVER TO THEM!
I WANT YOU TO STAY AS MY ERO-MANGA SENSEI!

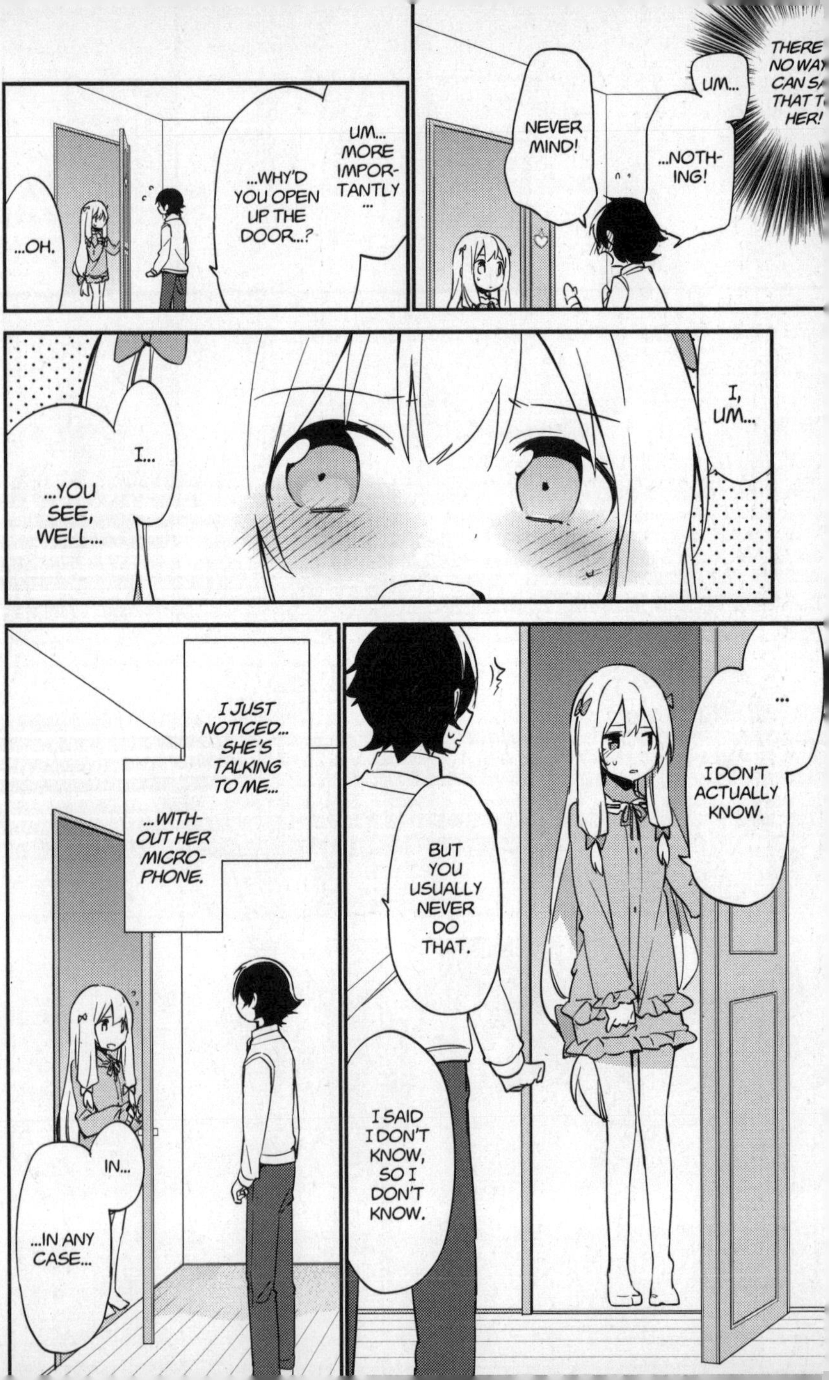
THERE NO WAY CAN SA THAT T HER!
UM...
NEVER MIND!
...NOTHING!
UM... MORE IMPORTANTLY...
...WHY'D YOU OPEN UP THE DOOR...?
...OH.
I, UM...
I...
...YOU SEE, WELL...
...
I DON'T ACTUALLY KNOW.
BUT YOU USUALLY NEVER DO THAT.
I SAID I DON'T KNOW, SO I DON'T KNOW.
I JUST NOTICED... SHE'S TALKING TO ME...
...WITHOUT HER MICROPHONE.
IN...
...IN ANY CASE...

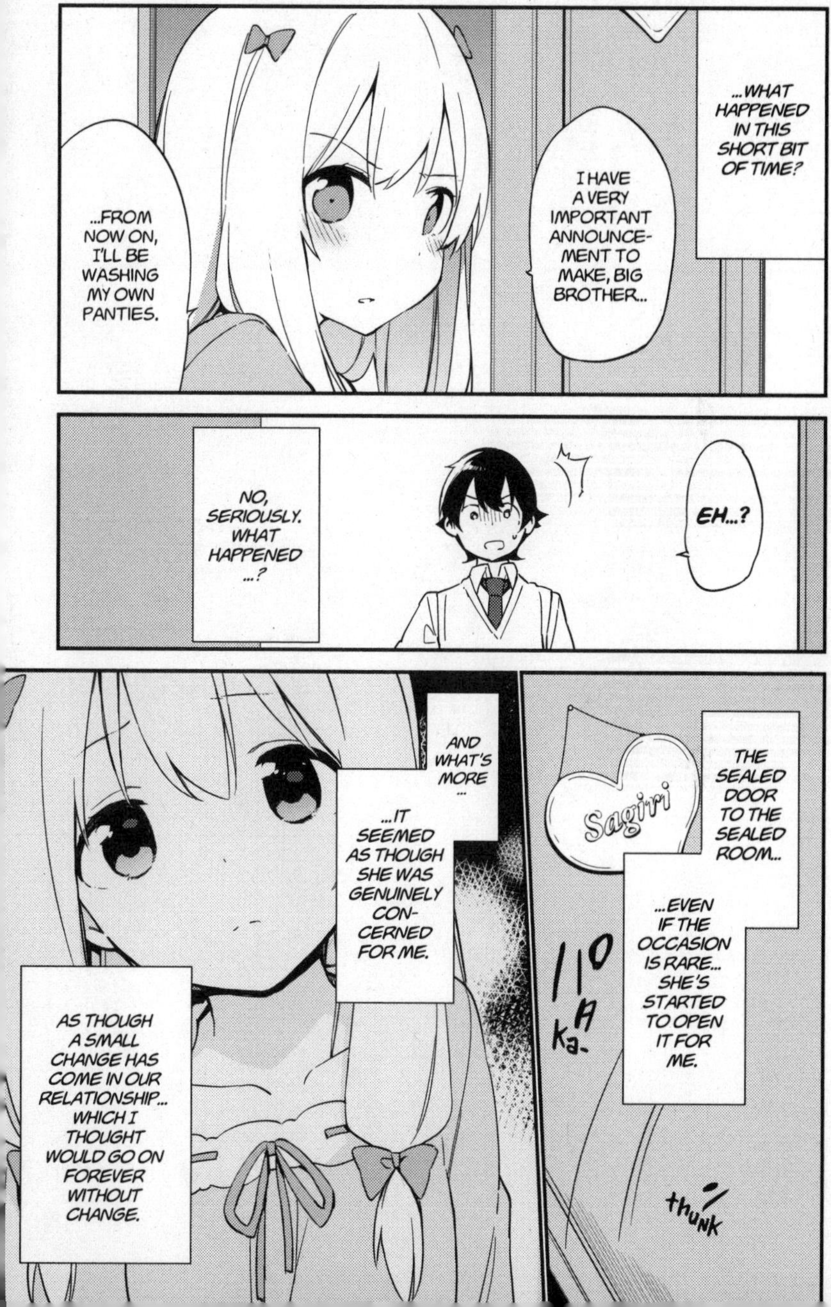
...WHAT HAPPENED IN THIS SHORT BIT OF TIME?
I HAVE A VERY IMPORTANT ANNOUNCEMENT TO MAKE, BIG BROTHER...
...FROM NOW ON, I'LL BE WASHING MY OWN PANTIES.
EH...?
NO, SERIOUSLY. WHAT HAPPENED ...?
THE SEALED DOOR TO THE SEALED ROOM...
Sagiri
...EVEN IF THE OCCASION IS RARE... SHE'S STARTED TO OPEN IT FOR ME.
thunk
Ka-
AND WHAT'S MORE ...
...IT SEEMED AS THOUGH SHE WAS GENUINELY CONCERNED FOR ME.
AS THOUGH A SMALL CHANGE HAS COME IN OUR RELATIONSHIP... WHICH I THOUGHT WOULD GO ON FOREVER WITHOUT CHANGE.

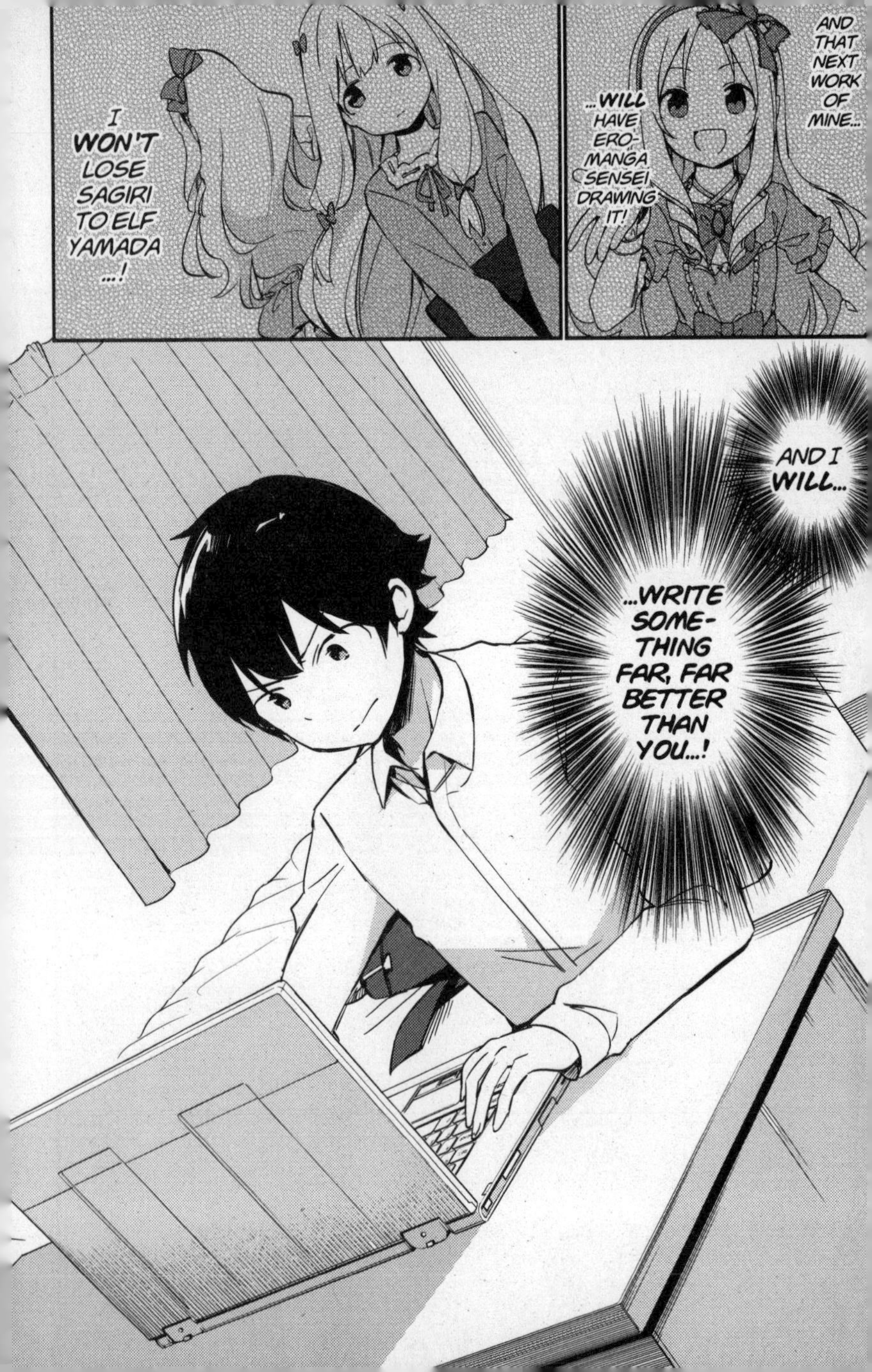
AND THAT NEXT WORK OF MINE...
...WILL HAVE ERO-MANGA SENSEI DRAWING IT!
I WON'T LOSE SAGIRI TO ELF YAMADA ...!
AND I WILL...
...WRITE SOME-THING FAR, FAR BETTER THAN YOU...!

eromanga sensei

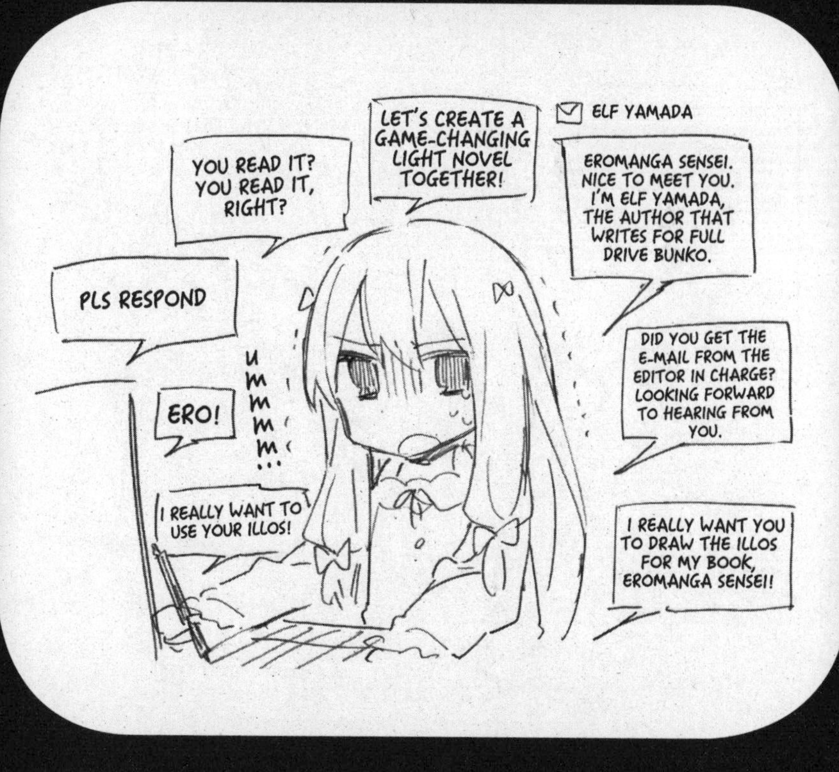
ELF YAMADA
EROMANGA SENSEI. NICE TO MEET YOU. I'M ELF YAMADA, THE AUTHOR THAT WRITES FOR FULL DRIVE BUNKO.
LET'S CREATE A GAME-CHANGING LIGHT NOVEL TOGETHER!
YOU READ IT? YOU READ IT, RIGHT?
DID YOU GET THE E-MAIL FROM THE EDITOR IN CHARGE? LOOKING FORWARD TO HEARING FROM YOU.
PLS RESPOND
I REALLY WANT YOU TO DRAW THE ILLOS FOR MY BOOK, EROMANGA SENSEI!
ERO!
UMMMMM...
I REALLY WANT TO USE YOUR ILLOS!

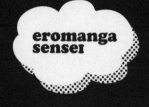

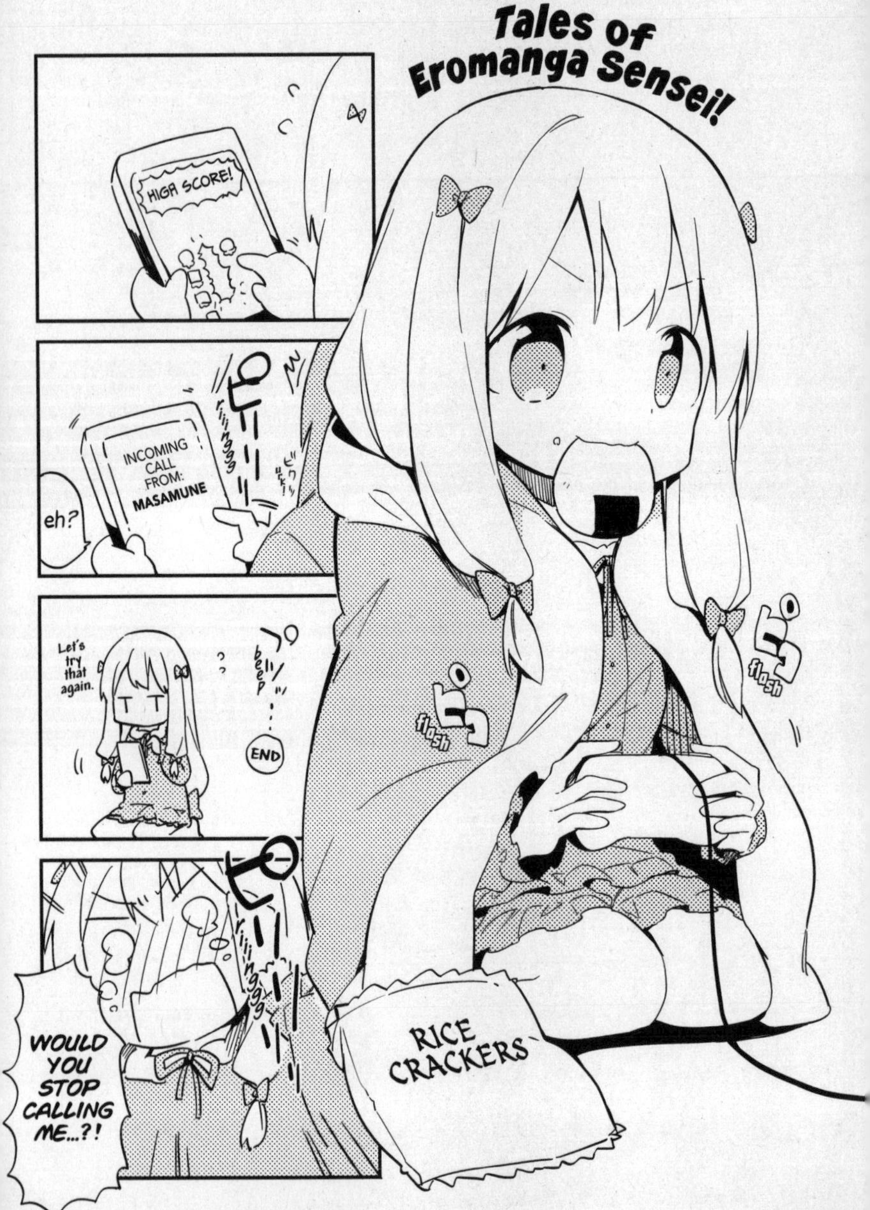
Tales of Eromanga Sensei!
flash
flash
RICE CRACKERS
HIGA SCORE!
riiinggg
INCOMING CALL FROM: MASAMUNE
eh?
beep
Let's try that again.
END
riiinggg
WOULD YOU STOP CALLING ME...?!

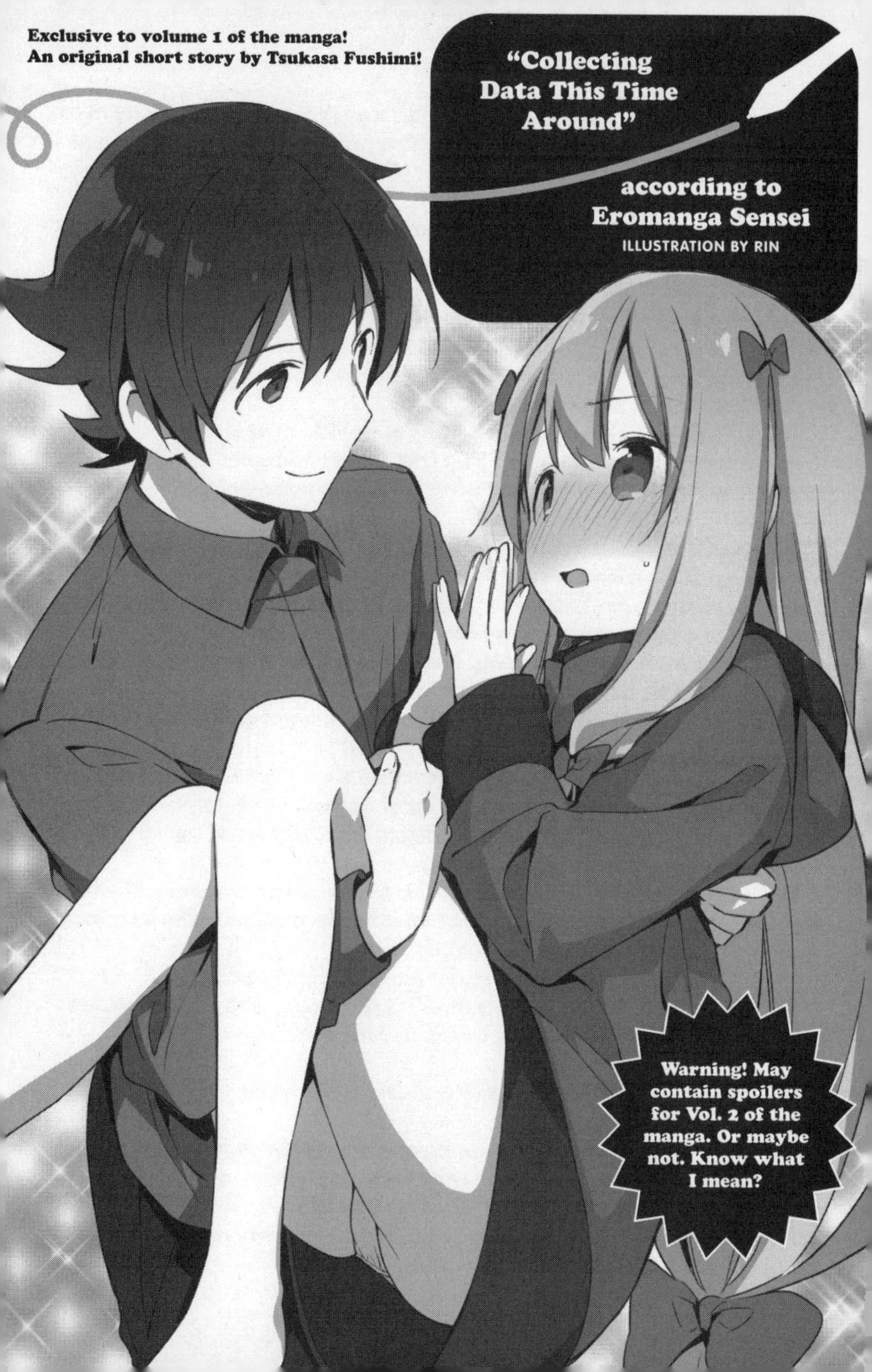
Exclusive to volume 1 of the manga!
An original short story by Tsukasa Fushimi!
"Collecting Data This Time Around"
according to Eromanga Sensei
ILLUSTRATION BY RIN
Warning! May contain spoilers for Vol. 2 of the manga. Or maybe not. Know what I mean?

It was just an ordinary weekday afternoon. I was sitting in my sister's room—also known as "The Sealed Room"—on the floor, and facing her. I had one hand over my face, in what some know as the "pose of torment," while I wailed in despair:

"This is bad. This is really bad. I don't know what to do. I can't—"

"Oh, here we go again," Sagiri said, wearing warm pajamas, while looking at me with cold indifference.

Normally, you can barely make out her voice, but it was amplified by the headset she was wearing, through the speaker in the room.

She continued, "I know that look—that means you have something you need to talk to me about...again. Right?"

"Yeah," I said, and it was true to some degree. The thing is that she rarely, if ever, let me into her room, so I said that I said I had some "work-related matters" to talk to her about, and with that as the passe-partout, I was permitted entry to "The Sealed Room."

Sagiri would not have opened that door to her mere older stepsibling, which is what I am in the context of our personal lives. But in a work context, we are close collaborators, as I happen to be the writer "Masamune Izumi," and she happens to be the illustrator of my novels, "Eromanga Sensei."

So she couldn't just brush this off. She'd at least hear me out. I think.

"I've got a really bad feeling about this, but I'll at least hear you out."

I was right, but this was no time to be smug. A show of gratitude would be wiser. "Thank you...thank you, Eromanga Sensei!"

"Sorry, but I don't know anyone by that embarrassing name." Sagiri was red in the face as she repeated that line, a set of words in heavy rotation for her.

I mean, if it was really that embarrassing to them, why would someone pick that as their pen name in the first place?

But really, though. We'd been through this exchange so many times; in some regards, this had come to replace what for other partners would be a normal greeting, or small talk about the weather.

"Right, so what'd you wanna discuss? Make it quick," said Sagiri.

"Oh, yeah, right, so the thing is that—" I continued, with an unshakable earnestness in my voice and serious expression on my face—

"Please let me pick you up and carry you. Just for a second."

"Um—what?" Sagiri's voice was shaky, and earnest engagement with our collaborative art wasn't foretold in her expression. Disbelief rather was on her face, and her voice was a tremolo that whispered through her lips only to roar out the loudspeaker. "Did you just say you wanted to carry me? Did you say that, big brother? To me?"

"That's right."

"How—why—what in this world could have ever brought you to the point of saying that...?" Her disbelief had deepened into something more profound—a face made up of mingled awe and disgust. It was a new, hybrid genre of a look, somewhere between embarrassment and cosmic horror. I should have really taken notes.

Instead I followed up. "You know, I've been writing that novel recently. The love comedy, right?"

"Right. The love comedy. Yeah, I know. I'm not an amnesiac. I'm the illustrator."

"Oh...yeah. Okay."

This conversational transaction, too, is one that both of us had been through a dozen times.

And so it wasn't surprising how quickly Sagiri regained her composure and said:

"So, you're about to tell me that you need to do it as sort of a 'data collection' to depict a scene more convincingly in the love comedy you're writing, yes?"

Damn, she's smart. Nothing gets by her.

"Right. So, on that note, just let me cradle you up, that's all."

"Big brother, you're really taking liberties these days, aren't you. I run you a millimeter and you ask for a marathon."

Sagiri has big, liquid eyes, so when she drops her lids to the midpoint, to stare at you with judgment and condescension, it's really noticeable. It's like you came down to the pool to take a dip and someone had pulled the cover halfway over it.

When, after a few moments, I had reached her level of discomfort, she piped up:

"So you think that by labeling something 'data collection' or 'research,' you can just get me to do whatever you want, right?"

"Oh, come on. You know that's not what I—" And was cut off.

"That granite we stand upon, big brother, that stone called decency, is worn away little by little through these requests. One day it will become a precipice of perversion into which you will fall, flailing headlong," Sagiri alleged.

"No! This is a total misunderstanding!" I tried to plead.

Misunderstanding? It was a total outrage!

I again tried to plead, and after that, kept trying. "Seriously, I mean it—it's really all just research for my work, for *Let's Make Our Dream Together!*"

"And so, you want me to let you pick me up, your arms under my knees and back?"

"Yeah. That's right." I nodded with utmost seriousness.

"Riiiiiiiight..." Sagiri responded, through pursed lips. Her face was no longer that cosmic mask of shock and repugnance. Rather, it now simply seemed to say, "I smell BS."

She continued: "So, big brother. Let me just postulate a second. If I say 'no,' what happens?"

"Well, in that case, there's not much I can do, is there? I really have no choice. I don't want to put my little sister up to something that would bother her so much."

"Riiiiiiight..." It was her previous response, verbatim.

"What's that supposed to mean? I'm telling the truth."

"I know you are. But..."

Sagiri stopped talking, and immediately stood up. She spun and opened the curtain to the veranda in a very deliberate manner, as if she wanted to make sure someone heard the gesture.

She stared out directly to the house next door—home of the best-selling light novelist, Elf Yamada; more specifically, to the room Elf did her work in. However I tried to interpret it, Sagiri was looking..."there."

"Um, Sagiri. Something going on with Elf?"

"It's just that Elf-chan tends to burst in whenever we have these conversations. But it looks like we're safe. She's sleeping, I think."

"Uh, but it's not even that late in the evening."

So I said, but Elf might very well have turned in early. She could afford to, thanks to her greater sales success. Damn it—some of us light novelists still have to hustle.

Sagiri closed the curtain, turned her back to me and walked a few steps away, uttering the following:

"Big brother, y'know, the other day—when you were collecting data and asked if you could pat my head, and, you know, I turned you down. Well, you went and did exactly that with Elf-chan, didn't you?"

"Do you have to bring that up again?"

It's not like I really wanted to think about it, either.

"You pretended to want to pat her on the head as an excuse. An innocent pretext, to which you then tethered your naughty, perverse whims, and wound up getting lovey-dovey with Elf-chan, didn't you? You're the worst. Just terrible."

"I told you, it wasn't like that at all!"

Sagin, you said the exact same thing to me—those exact same words—the last time you brought it up. Dammit.

"Every time something like this happens, you act like I cheated on you or something. You're my sibling, not my girlfriend, for God's sake."

"Wha—" Sagiri snapped, and she whipped around to face me with a fervor hitherto unseen. Her face was crimson.

And trembling with anger.

"Did—did you just insinuate that cheating is a concept that could exist here? Do you think *you're* my boyfriend or something? How dare you!"

"Dude, give me a break! You started it by saying stuff that made it sound like you were my girlfriend or something! Do you get it now?"

"Wha—wha—are you—I can't even—"

Yeah. Yeah. That's what I thought. Now you realize you're embarrassed at your own words. Get some!

"You're so wrong that you're just—you're not right. Anyway..."

Sagiri seemed to be trying to eke out a calm rebuttal, but switched to simply making fists and pounding them down repeatedly, to the accompaniment of speaker-amplified hollering.

"Big brother, you're sick! Immoral! Depraved! Like I said, you're the worst! No, you know what's worse than your worst? The way you ask Elf-chan to help you when you get into a fix. She's your business rival, you know? Have you no pride—no shame, big brother...?"

"Huh...guess not," I replied, and scratched my cheek casually.

You see, I really did have no problem in asking anyone for help, if it meant I could write a more interesting novel as a result of it.

No problem at all.

This only seemed to further infuriate Sagiri, who puffed out her cheeks in rage.

"Big brother. There's no hope for you. None."

"Yes. Sorry, then."

"Seriously. You're so devoid of self-awareness, numb to the pain of your ignorance. You don't see the magnitude of the problem..."

Sagiri lay on the floor, bereft, and held herself in her own arms, eyes welling up with tears.

"Fine. Fine!"

. . . .

"I—I'll let you do it."

She said it as if the most embarrassing words she could speak had just crawled from her mouth.

"Okay. So, then—"

Okay. So then—wait just a minute. This is a little odd, isn't it? I mean, All I did was ask to let me carry her. From her tone you would have thought that I had requested something so salacious, so lewd, that even the most degenerate perverts would repent their ways at the mere prospect of carrying out the act.

And really! I mean, really! This is the person that calls themselves Eromanga Sensei. And evidently I'm the evil-minded one here.

I put my best effort into the situation, though, and attempted to calmly bring the scene back into the realm of focused sanity.

"Right, so, in other words, I'm okay to pick you up now, right, Sagiri?"

"Uh..."

Sagiri nodded, ever-so-slightly, her consent. Her lips permitted an escape of air. "Just for a bit. Quickly. If you promise it's quick."

"Gotcha."

It took a while to get here, but she said it.

Sagiri's cheeks were once again awash in red, and she continued:

"Just a hug, all right? You'd better not try anything more than that, or anything I might even construe as even slightly depraved, got it?"

Hug? "A carry. Look, don't overthink it."

I mean, I was only doing this in the name of research and data collection for my book. Sagiri, after all, would be the first to accuse me if she judged my writing to be ignorant or uninformed. But the way the whole thing had gone down thus far made me think she had mistaken me for a writer of mature novels, exploring the outer boundaries of Eros, rather than someone who is the literary equivalent of a fast casual restaurant. Not fast food, mind you—I do have my craft.

Hence all this struggle.

Amidst my silent protests, I could see a metaphorical question mark beginning to form above Sagiri's head, and I sensed that we might not have been communicating on quite the same plane.

"What remains the issue here...?"

"It's just that—well, you know—you'll be able to see my panties if I let you do that."

"Wait, what? If I carry you? Do you really know what I'm trying to describe? I can't even imagine what sort of pose you had pictured in your head."

"!"

"I mean, whatever you're picturing, it seems much, much different than what I'm picturing—and what most normal people would picture, too."

"!!!!"

Sagiri wasn't so much upset—no, not so much, more like very upset—as flustered. It was a look that appertained to the idea that she had no concept of what I had actually been asking. Her eyes, which had been squeezed shut, slowly opened, and she attempted to collect herself. She looked up at me and said, as cool as can be:

"Well then, big brother. Tell me. What do you have in mind, exactly?"

"You know, you see it in like, games and whatnot—the brother and sister get along, and they play a game together. And the brother holds the sister protectively from behind..."

"So, you're going to sit behind me, then? Ugh, fine, just don't do anything shocking, then, okay?"

I sighed. "Maybe at this point we'd better start over. Sagiri, what were you imagining throughout this whole thing, then?"

"!!!!!!!"

And boom, like the thunder, Sagiri turned red again. Beet-red. Borscht.

Seeking clarity, I continued. "So what did you think? You didn't think that—"

"Don't say it! Whatever it was! I mean, who cares? It's fine! Just drop it. I have to consider all the possibilities of a gesture; I'm an illustrator, after all!"

Yeah, even without the clarification, it was pretty obvious that whatever she was imagining was far more prurient than my actual request suggested. I mean, what was this stuff about seeing panties? Huh?

But really, she'd always use that excuse: "You have to understand, I'm always thinking like an illustrator." Or words to that effect. It was her perpetual get-out-of-jail-free card; the royal pardon that allowed her to escape without criticism. Really, it was beginning to be an insult to all the other illustrators out there.

"Hm? But, like—well, you know."

It was clear that Sagiri had misinterpreted what I was asking her to do—a simple, loving gesture—as some sort of...well, fan service.

At this moment, I'd now arrived at the inescapable truth via the circuits of her overclocked "illustrator brain."

It must have showed in my face.

"Whaaaa...?!"

Unfortunately the revelation was instantly drowned out by Sagiri's exclamation, which, let us not forget, was on a hot mic.

"What?" she said. "What the...?! What the hell you think do you think you're doing like that, just out of nowhere?!"

"I'm not...doing anything? Seriously, I'm telling you, it's really nothing, so it's really...nothing."

Sagiri moved her face closer to mine, and it was apparent that she was now trying to twist this situation to fit her agenda, her favor.

And indeed she had. Looking slightly relaxed, like she'd thought of a sudden out, a calmness returned to her expression and she exclaimed:

"...Oh, right! I almost forgot. Big brother..."

"Yeah...what?"

"Since you're here, I was wondering if you might help me with a little research of mine?"

And then—

"How'd it wind up like this?"

Just a few minutes later, there I was, "holding" my sister, and sitting with her in front of a full-length mirror. There she was, on my lap, scrutinizing the mirror intently, and sketching us both.

"This is what you want, right, big brother? I mean, the fact that you're 'researching' this to write about means that I will, in all likelihood, end up having to illustrate it."

Oh, so I guess this means that Eromanga Sensei has some policy I was unaware of—of only illustrating that which they have seen with their own eyes. Huh.

Ultimately, however, there was a benefit to both of us to being here, and it would indeed serve as research or data collection for us both.

There was that benefit, but—

"I mean, looking at it, this is pretty embarrassing."

"What?"

Sagiri stared at me hard.

"Well, you were the one who brought this up in the first place, big brother."

"Well, I guess that's true, but..."

I just didn't think that it'd be this embarrassing once we actually did it, though.

And, as expected, any embarrassment was magnified by the mirror, and looking at the mirror.

An older brother who was holding his little sister as she drew.

Once I settled into what was happened, it seemed like it could have been a surrealist painting. Not the melting clock and bowler hat variety; something more uncomfortable. It was downright embarrassing and awkward. So much so that there was a pureness to it; embarrassment straight from concentrate.

"Anyway, here we are, and I'm drawing. So don't ask for anything more, don't distract me, and don't even talk. Just hold still."

"...Okay."

But something was off. This isn't what I meant, anyway, and far from what I had planned.

I mean, sure, this was a pose—but there was just something about sibling skinship and the moment was off. I'd imagined it to be one of those heart-warming scenes that you might glimpse in a manga, but that it wasn't. I mean, in those scenes, you'd never come across the words, "Just shut your trap, or it'll distract me here," uttered in such blunt seriousness.

"Um, right, so—y'know, like..." I offered to the immortal moment.

"Didn't I just say to pipe down? Jeez."

Sagiri inflated her cheeks in that patent-pending squirrel fashion of hers, and pushed out the air like an industrial pump set to "exasperation." And her pen went back to work on her tablet.

"Right, got it again. Now keep still."

Seeing that there was no out from this continued response, I continued to hold my little sister, and watched over her as she resumed her sketching.

Some more time passed.

....

Whoa, she's a little warm. Feverish, maybe?

Maybe it's because there's a little tension caused by this situation?

No, it wasn't that. And if I were to even suggest that, I'd be paraded straight to the corner of the room to wear a large "I'm wrong about my opinions" sign around my neck.

....

Pausing to look, I realized that my sister's hands had put down their work for the moment, and once again, she was red in the face.

"!"

Uh-oh, it's getting hot in here. Or maybe it's just her.

....

She sat there, somehow able to bear all that she was generating—but at last, she finally looked as if she couldn't take it anymore, and Sagiri spoke.

"Big...big brother."

"What is it, Sagiri?"

"Your heart's beating a little loud for me to concentrate. Could you put it on mute?

"Uh, I'd die!"

But, you know...

...I suppose this is all par for the course. Each time, time and again, our research and data collection plays out a little something like this, and goes from the planning stages to the actual creation, in these exciting and confusing ways.

Writing light novels, or illustrating them—it doesn't matter—they're both really hard work, you know.

The End.

eromanga
sensei

eromanga sensei illustration gallery

Of course, in the *Eromanga Sensei* storyline, Sagiri Izumi illustrates the *Silverwolf of Reincarnation* novel series, but the illustrations of the novels' characters featured in this gallery section were actually done by Taishow Tanaka-sensei! We present here for the first time some of the character guides that were used to flesh out the manga story. In the manga, you often can't get a full view of these characters—you might catch just a glimpse, or they might be cut off by the panel arrangement. But here they are in all their glory!

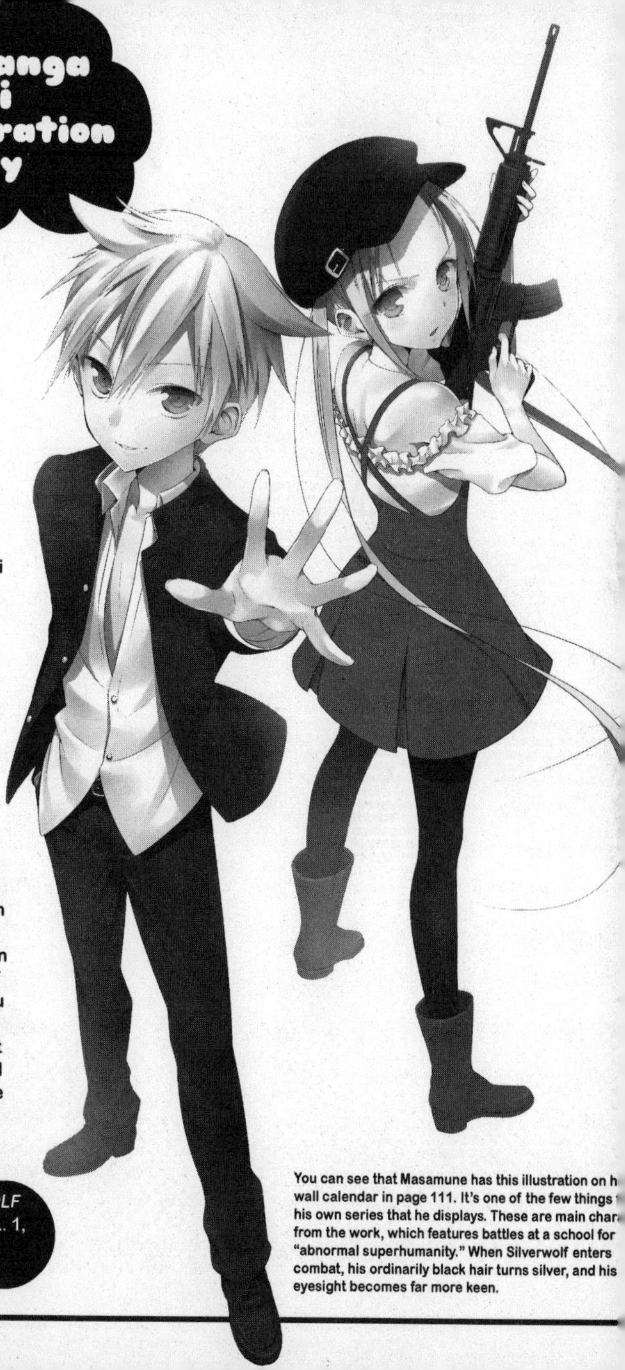

THE COVER OF *SILVERWOLF OF RECINCARNATION* VOL. 1, FEATURING SILVERWOLF AND PENGUIN GIRL.

You can see that Masamune has this illustration on h
wall calendar in page 111. It's one of the few things
his own series that he displays. These are main char
from the work, which features battles at a school for
"abnormal superhumanity." When Silverwolf enters
combat, his ordinarily black hair turns silver, and his
eyesight becomes far more keen.

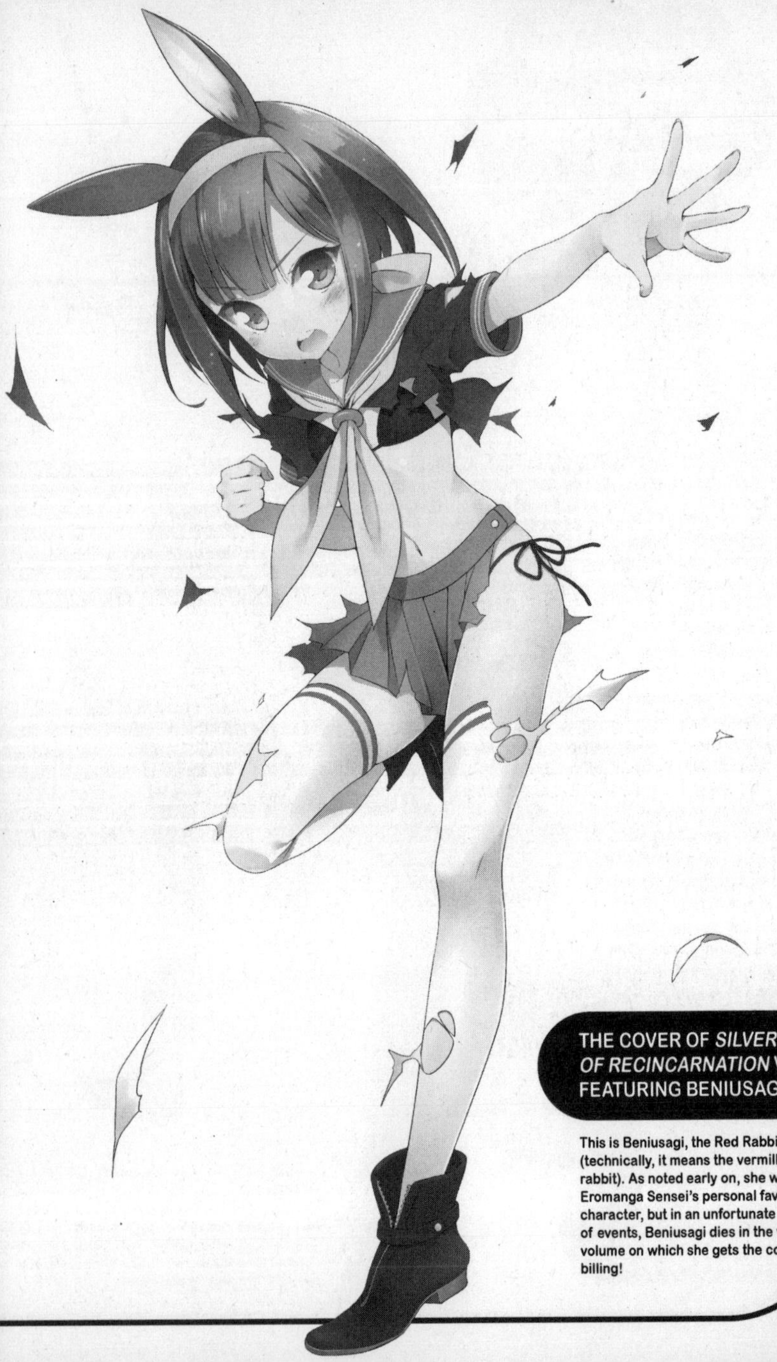

THE COVER OF *SILVERWOLF OF RECINCARNATION* VOL. 3, FEATURING BENIUSAGI.

This is Beniusagi, the Red Rabbit (technically, it means the vermillion rabbit). As noted early on, she was Eromanga Sensei's personal favorite character, but in an unfortunate turn of events, Beniusagi dies in the very volume on which she gets the cover billing!

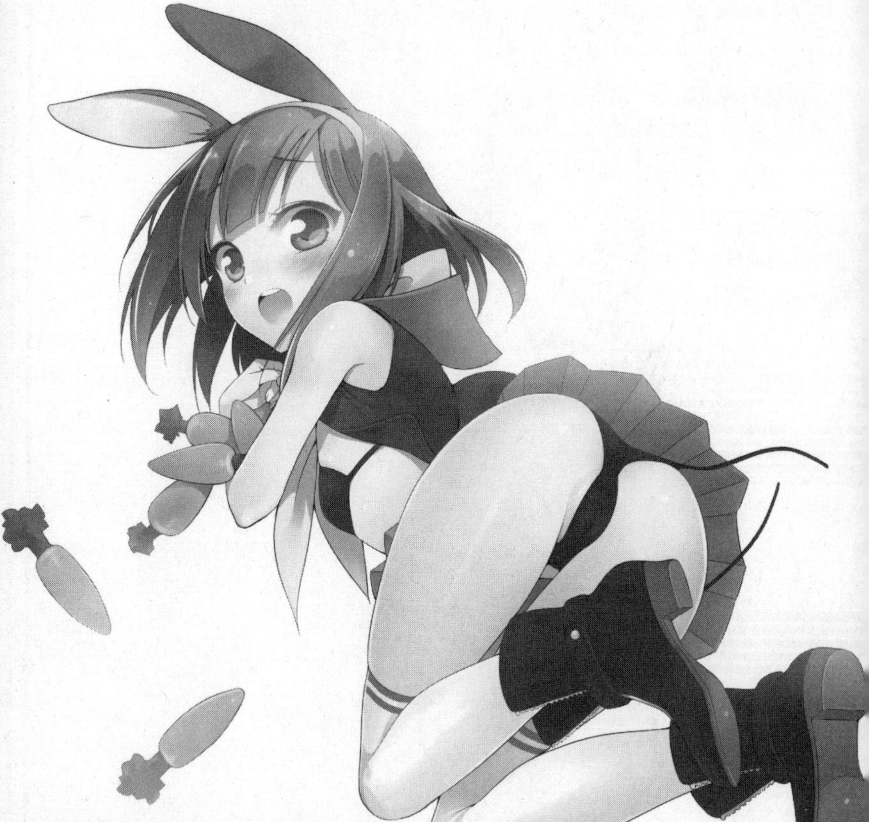

THE ILLUSTRATION OF BENIUSAGI DONE BY EROMANGA SENSEI DURING THE LIVE DRAWING STREAM.

As seen in Chapter 1. The snapped cord on the panties is a special touch, and is known as a trademark flourish of Eromanga Sensei.

THE COMMEMORATIVE *SILVERWOLF OF RECINCARNATION* FULL CAST ILLUSTRATION.

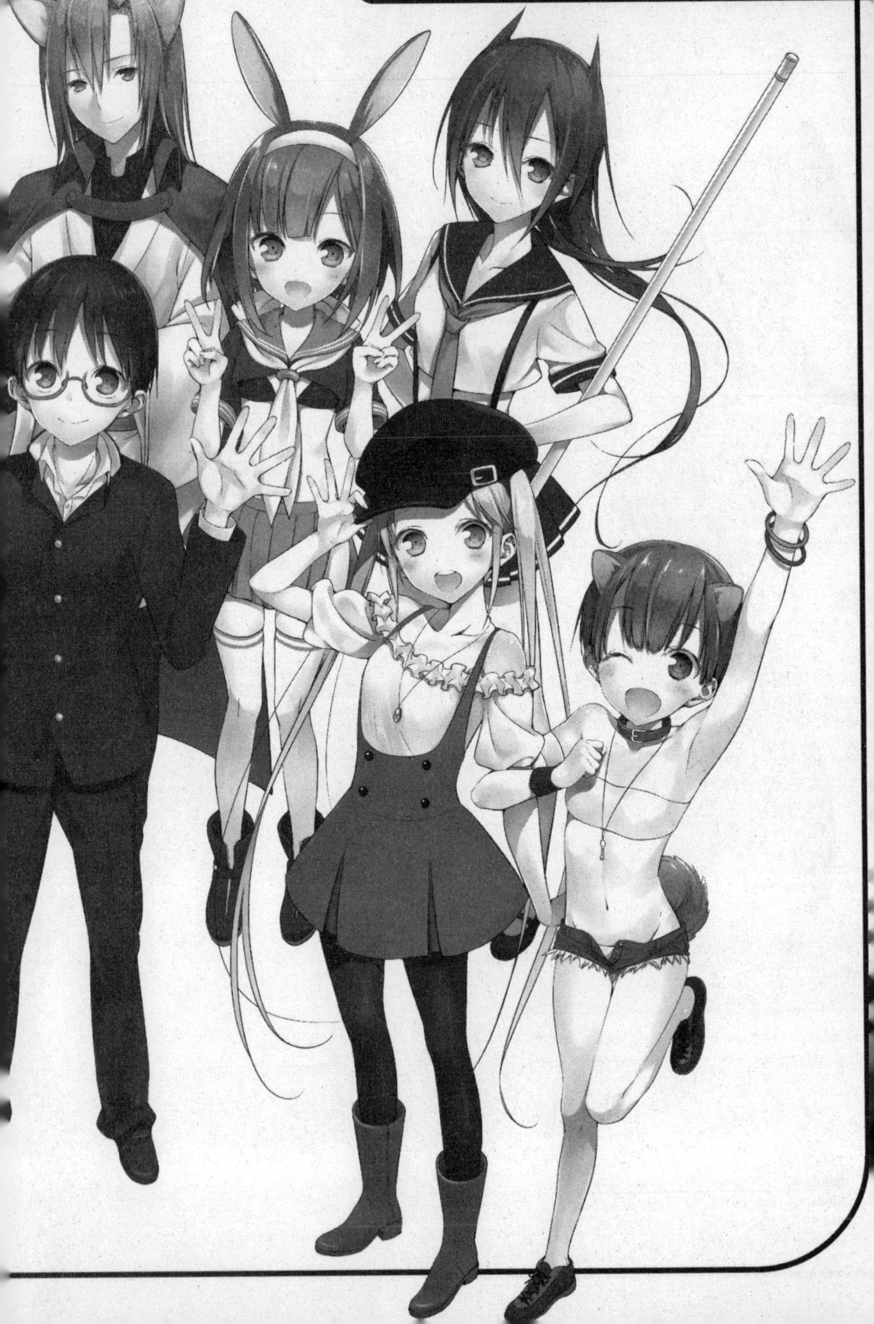

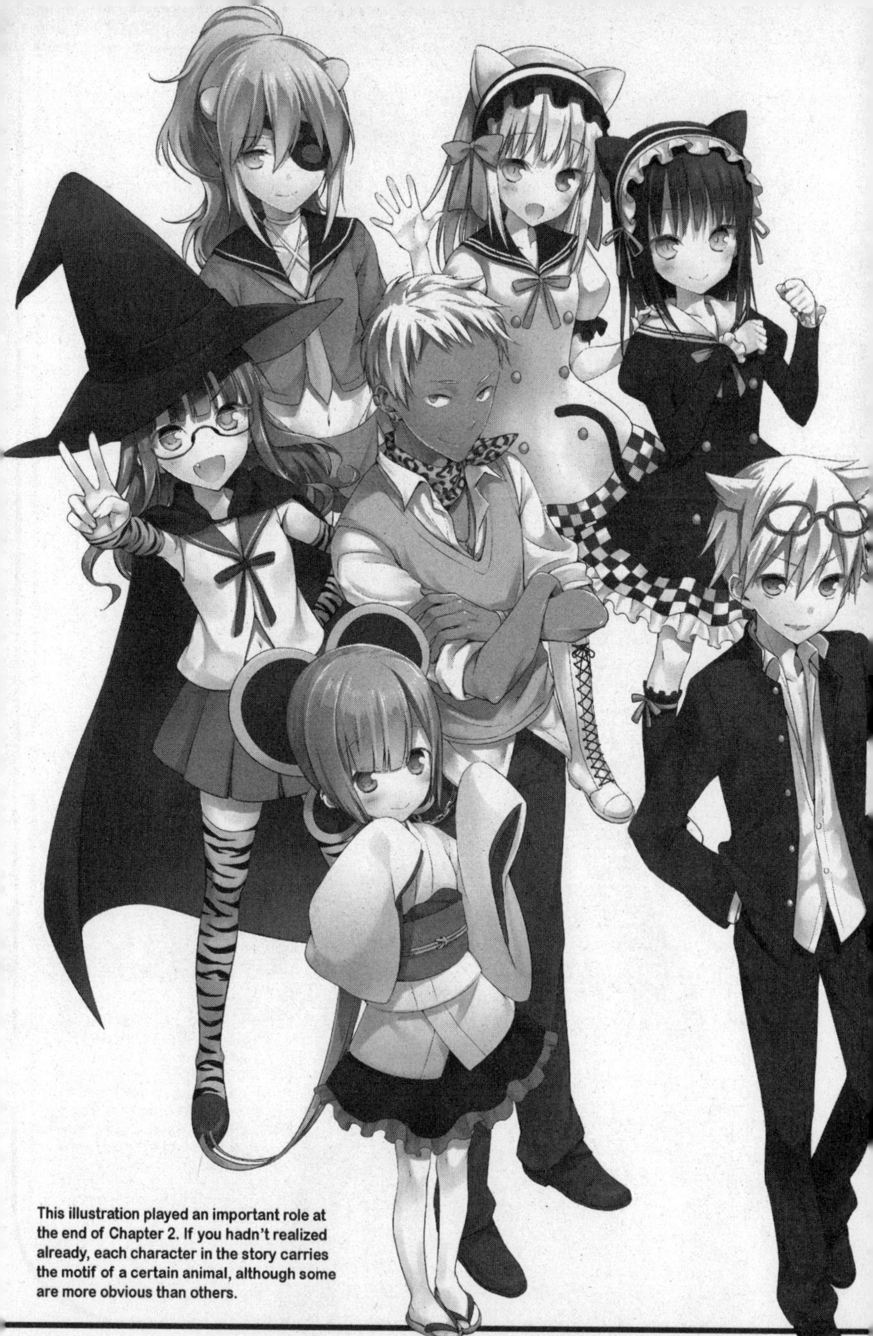

This illustration played an important role at the end of Chapter 2. If you hadn't realized already, each character in the story carries the motif of a certain animal, although some are more obvious than others.

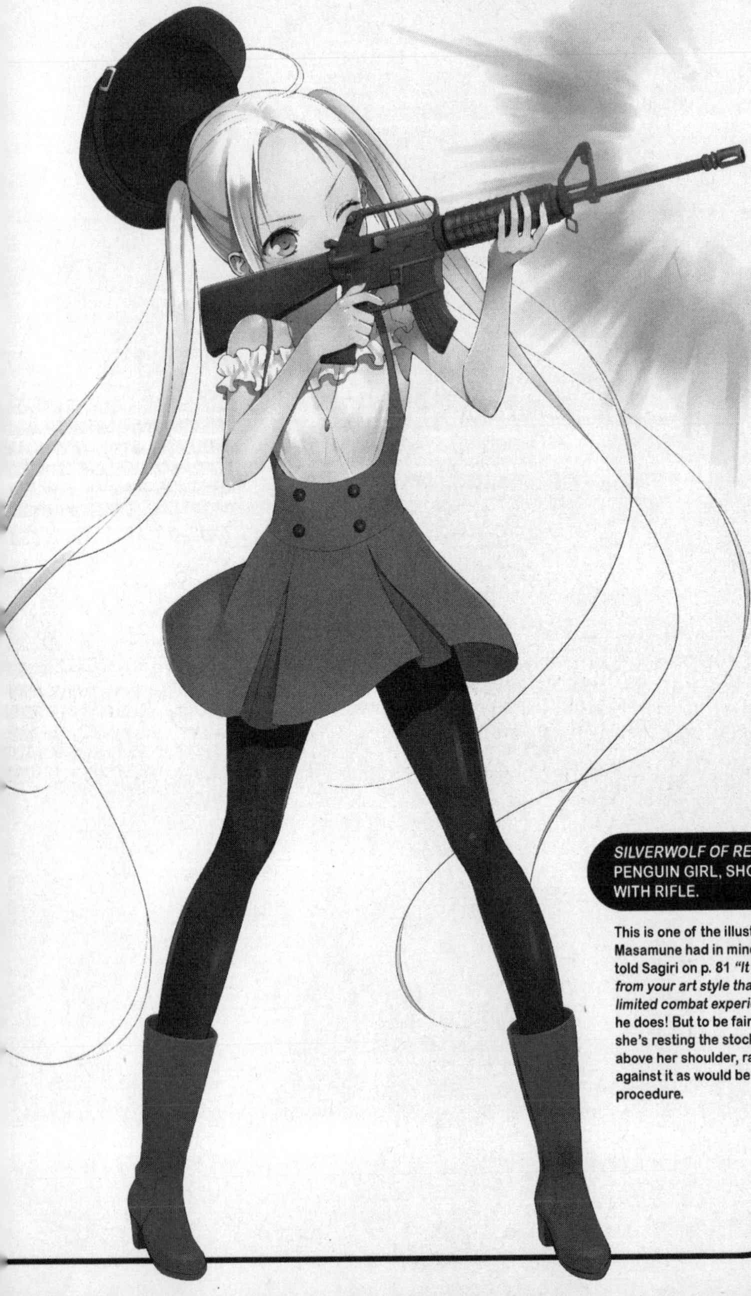

SILVERWOLF OF RECINCARNATION'S **PENGUIN GIRL, SHOWN ARMED WITH RIFLE.**

This is one of the illustrations Masamune had in mind when he told Sagiri on p. 81 *"It's evident from your art style that you have limited combat experience!"* As if he does! But to be fair, it's the fact she's resting the stock of the rifle above her shoulder, rather than against it as would be the normal procedure.

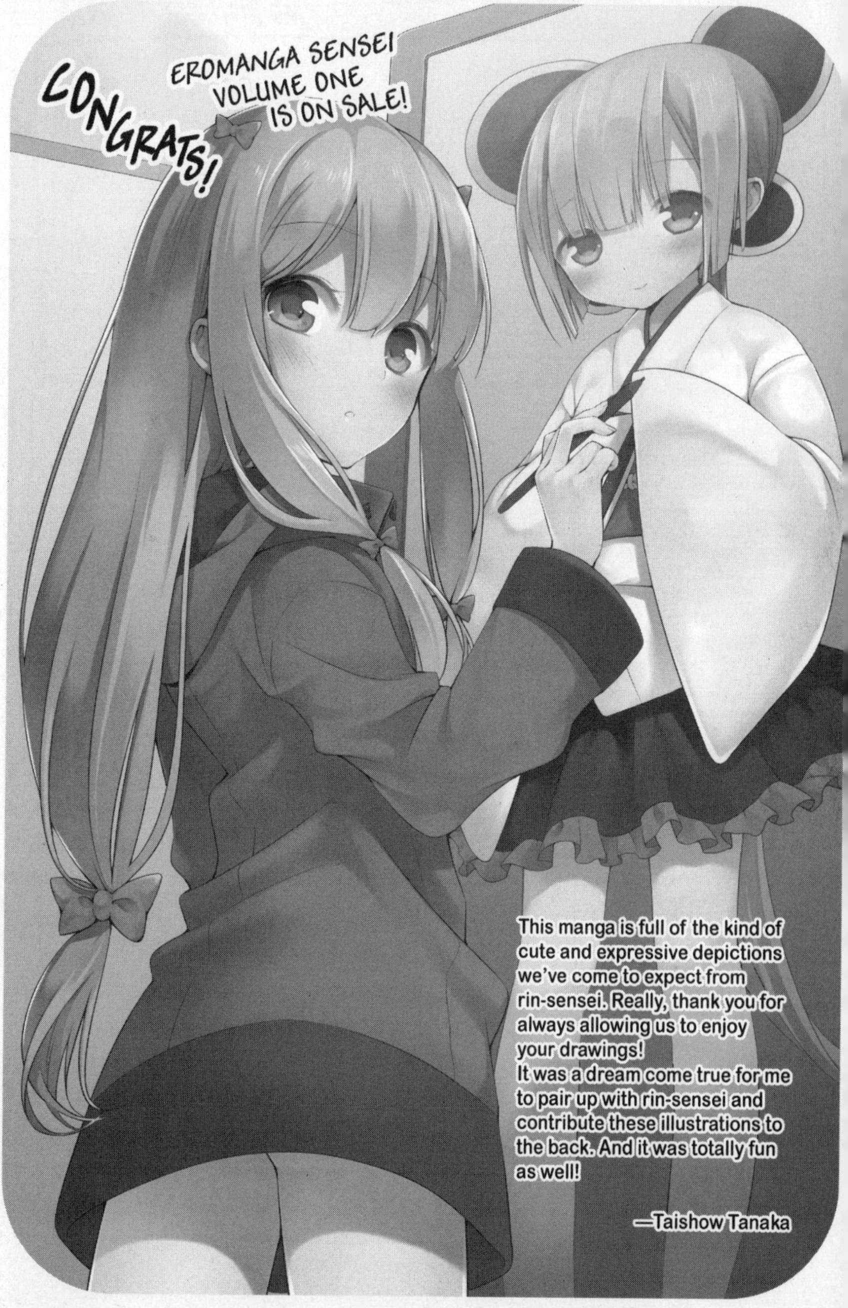
CONGRATS!
EROMANGA SENSEI VOLUME ONE IS ON SALE!
This manga is full of the kind of cute and expressive depictions we've come to expect from rin-sensei. Really, thank you for always allowing us to enjoy your drawings!
It was a dream come true for me to pair up with rin-sensei and contribute these illustrations to the back. And it was totally fun as well!
—Taishow Tanaka

THE AFTERWORD!

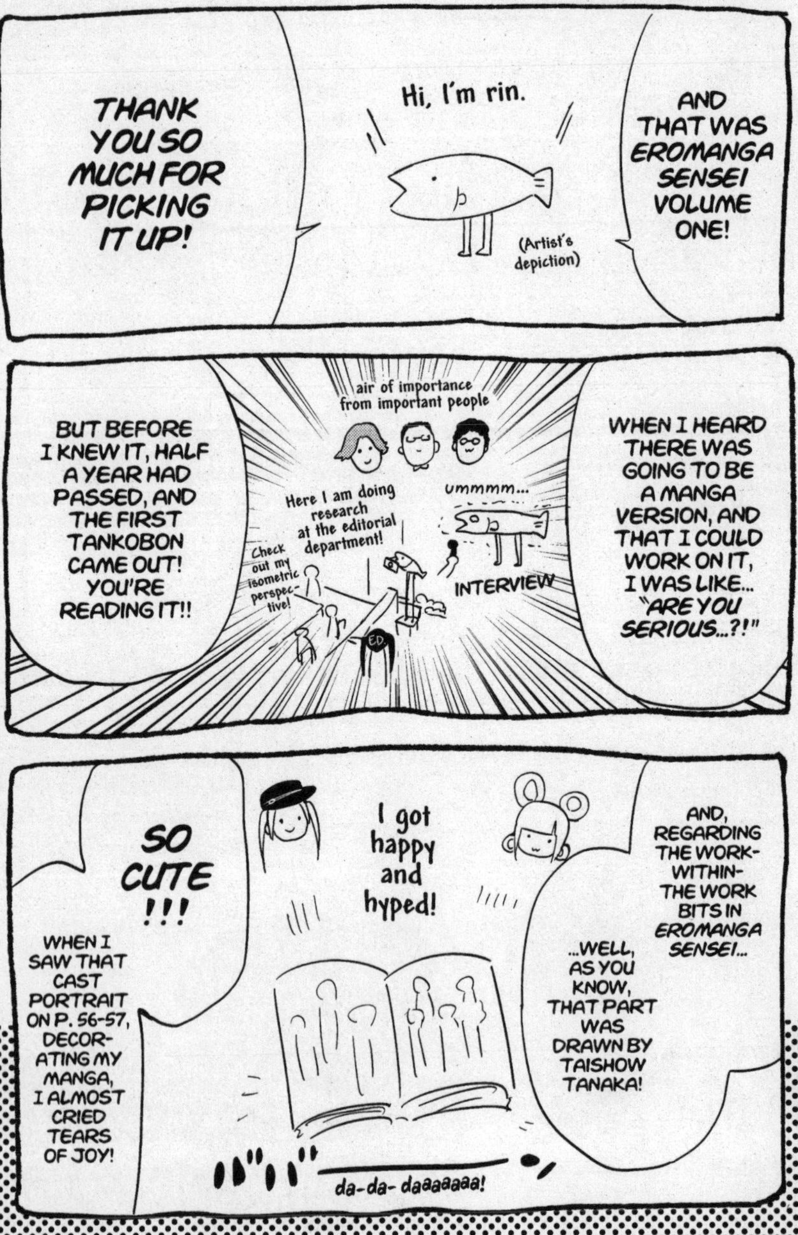
AND THAT WAS EROMANGA SENSEI VOLUME ONE!
Hi, I'm rin.
(Artist's depiction)
THANK YOU SO MUCH FOR PICKING IT UP!
WHEN I HEARD THERE WAS GOING TO BE A MANGA VERSION, AND THAT I COULD WORK ON IT, I WAS LIKE... "ARE YOU SERIOUS...?!"
air of importance from important people
ummmm...
INTERVIEW
Here I am doing research at the editorial department!
Check out my isometric perspective!
ED.
BUT BEFORE I KNEW IT, HALF A YEAR HAD PASSED, AND THE FIRST TANKOBON CAME OUT! YOU'RE READING IT!!
AND, REGARDING THE WORK-WITHIN-THE WORK BITS IN EROMANGA SENSEI...
...WELL, AS YOU KNOW, THAT PART WAS DRAWN BY TAISHOW TANAKA!
I got happy and hyped!
da-da-daaaaaaa!
SO CUTE!!!
WHEN I SAW THAT CAST PORTRAIT ON P. 56-57, DECORATING MY MANGA, I ALMOST CRIED TEARS OF JOY!

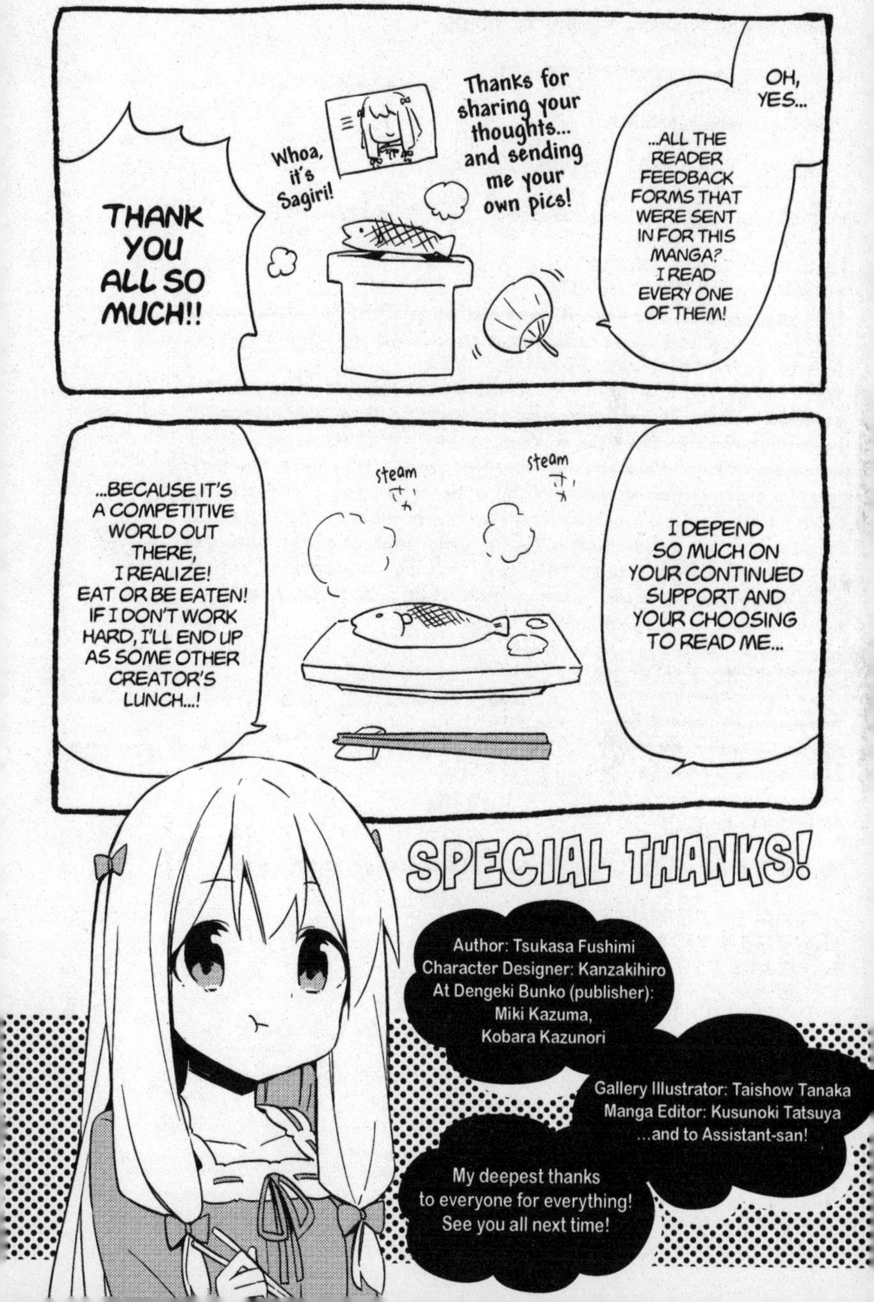
OH, YES...
...ALL THE READER FEEDBACK FORMS THAT WERE SENT IN FOR THIS MANGA? I READ EVERY ONE OF THEM!
Thanks for sharing your thoughts... and sending me your own pics!
Whoa, it's Sagiri!
THANK YOU ALL SO MUCH!!
I DEPEND SO MUCH ON YOUR CONTINUED SUPPORT AND YOUR CHOOSING TO READ ME...
steam
steam
...BECAUSE IT'S A COMPETITIVE WORLD OUT THERE, I REALIZE! EAT OR BE EATEN! IF I DON'T WORK HARD, I'LL END UP AS SOME OTHER CREATOR'S LUNCH...!
SPECIAL THANKS!
Author: Tsukasa Fushimi
Character Designer: Kanzakihiro
At Dengeki Bunko (publisher):
Miki Kazuma,
Kobara Kazunori
Gallery Illustrator: Taishow Tanaka
Manga Editor: Kusunoki Tatsuya
...and to Assistant-san!
My deepest thanks
to everyone for everything!
See you all next time!

President and Publisher / MIKE RICHARDSON

Assistant Editor / JEMIAH JEFFERSON

Designer / ANITA MAGAÑA

Digital Art Technician / SAMANTHA HUMMER

English-language version produced by Dark Horse Comics

EROMANGA SENSEI VOLUME 1
© TSUKASA FUSHIMI / rin 2014
First published in Japan in 2014 by KADOKAWA CORPORATION, Tokyo.
English translation rights arranged with KADOKAWA CORPORATION,
Tokyo through TOHAN CORPORATION, Tokyo.

Published by
Dark Horse Manga
A division of Dark Horse Comics, Inc.
10956 SE Main Street
Milwaukie, OR 97222

DarkHorse.com

To find a comics shop in your area visit comicshoplocator.com

First edition: September 2018
ISBN 978-1-50670-984-0
10 9 8 7 6 5 4 3 2 1

OREIMO

ORDINARY TEENAGE GUY

Kyousuke doesn't get along with his ill-tempered little sister Kirino, but when he discovers Kirino's secrets—she's not only a fashion model and a great student, but she's really into silly anime and X-rated video games!—he finds himself charged with protecting and defending her right to just be the person she is.

This hilarious, charming hit series is filled with surprises and outrageous laughs. Who says girls can't be *otaku*, too?

Ore no imouto ga konnani kawaii wake ga nai—

"I can't believe my little sister is this cute!"

Volume One
ISBN 978-1-59582-956-6

Volume Two
ISBN 978-1-61655-055-4

Volume Three
ISBN 978-1-61655-181-0

Volume Four
ISBN 978-1-61655-221-3

$10.99 each

Available at your local comics shop or bookstore! • To find a comics shop in your area visit comicshoplocator.com.
For more information or to order direct: • On the web: DarkHorse.com • E-mail: mailorder@darkhorse.com
Phone: 1-800-862-0052 Mon.–Fri. 9 AM to 5 PM Pacific Time.

Oreno Imouto ga Konnani Kawaii wakeganai © FUSHIMI / SAKURA IKEDA. Originally published in Japan by ASCII MEDIA WORKS Inc., Tokyo. Dark Horse Manga™ is a trademark of Dark Horse Comics, Inc. All rights reserved. (BL 7100)

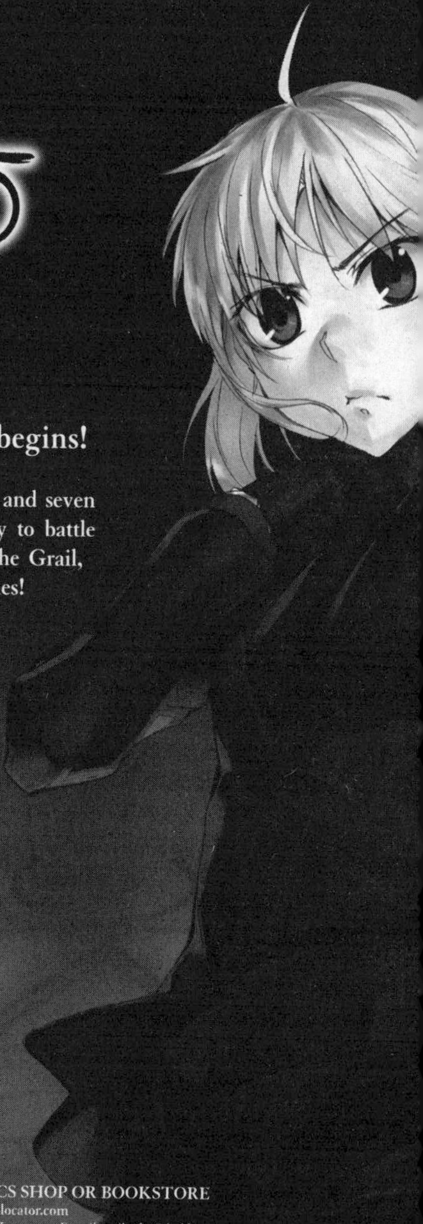

The battle for the Holy Grail begins!

The Fourth Holy Grail War has begun, and seven magi must summon heroes from history to battle to the death. Only one pair can claim the Grail, though—and it will grant them their wishes!

Check out the manga adaptation of Gen Urobuchi and Type-Moon's hit anime and novel series!

VOLUME 1 | 978-1-61655-919-9 | $11.99

VOLUME 2 | 978-1-61655-954-0 | $11.99

VOLUME 3 | 978-1-50670-021-2 | $11.99

VOLUME 4 | 978-1-50670-139-4 | $11.99

VOLUME 5 | 978-1-50670-175-2 | $11.99

VOLUME 6 | 978-1-50670-768-6 | $11.99

VOLUME 7 | 978-1-50670-769-3 | $11.99

not that way!

Most readers will know this already, but *Eromanga Sensei*, like most manga, is made in the traditional Japanese reading order, right to left; therefore, this is the last page of the book, and please turn this book around to begin reading. By the way, if *Eromanga Sensei* is your first manga, then welcome to manga.

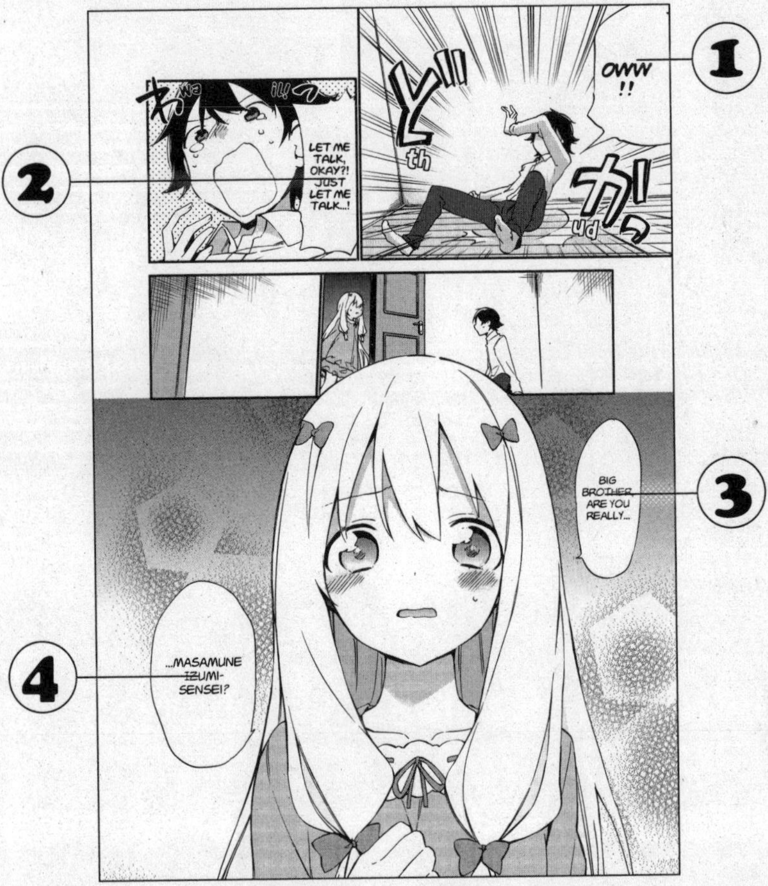
1
OWW !!
th
ud
wa
2
LET ME TALK, OKAY?! JUST LET ME TALK...!
3
BIG BROTHER, ARE YOU REALLY...
4
...MASAMUNE IZUMI-SENSEI?